This book is to be returned on or before
the last date stamped below.

ONE WEEK LOAN

THE LUDDITES
and
Other Essays

THE LUDDITES
and
Other Essays

Edited by LIONEL M. MUNBY,
with an Introduction by
ERIC J. HOBSBAWM

LONDON
MICHAEL KATANKA (BOOKS) LTD
1971

Published by
MICHAEL KATANKA (BOOKS) LTD
160 Edgwarebury Lane, Edgware, Middx.

First Published 1971

© Michael Katanka (Books) Ltd
SBN 902291 01 7
Printed in Great Britain by Flarepath Printers Limited, Colney Street, St. Albans, Herts.

Contents

Introduction

This book reprints a number of studies which first appeared in *Our History*, the periodical of the History Group of the Communist Party. This modest publication first appeared as the *Local History Bulletin* in October 1950, a two-page duplicated sheet. It took its present name in October 1953 and the form of a duplicated pamphlet on a single historical topic in 1956. Since 1969 it has appeared in photo-litho. Over fifty issues have been published containing work by communist and non-communist authors. They have been available only to a few hundred subscribers and purchasers and in a handful of libraries. It seemed worth while bringing a selection of this work to the notice of a wider public.

Though the essays reprinted here have been written by historians, all of whom would probably claim to be marxists, they are not primarily concerned with the discussion of the marxist method in history or with the reinterpretation of problems by means of this method. They are journeys of discovery into the past of the British labour movement, attempts to help the movement to recover its history and its sense of unity with the men and women who fought for their rights and for a better society in the past, as we do today. There is no need to justify this. The political radicalisation of the 1960s has brought into the socialist movement an entire generation for whom all history before the recent Labour government, or at most before Suez, lies beyond personal experience. This does not mean that it is irrelevant. On the contrary, anyone who is professionally concerned with the history of the labour movement knows that there is today a passionate interest in the past of the common people, the working class and its struggles. Learned conferences on Chartism, 'History workshops' on the nineteenth century, have packed audiences. When *Our History* began, it was much more difficult for non-specialists to establish links with this past than it is now, but the present volume may still contribute some knowledge not readily accessible elsewhere.

Its object is not merely to inform, but also to encourage. Several of the studies are based on local work by local scholars and collectors, sometimes 'amateurs' (in the literal sense of people who simply have a passion for what they are doing). Such work can be done by anybody. What is more, if the history of British labour is to progress, it must be done, for one of its important tasks today—perhaps the most important—is to discover the regional and local reality of the working class, its variations and its specific contributions to the national reality. To study Chartism in the Black Country, the farm labourers in East Anglia, the shop stewards in Sheffield, the General Strike in the North-east need not be local antiquarianism, but can be a significant contribution to our understanding of Britain, and indeed of the world—if it is done with a sense of history. Our country has an unusual wealth of material about its working class and its labour movements. Much of it has been hardly touched yet. Local students have great opportunities.

'Knowledge in this field', wrote Sidney Pollard, in what is still one of the rare local studies of labour, 'can be increased most surely by piecemeal attacks; that is to say by expanding the frontier on one narrow sector after another.' This is where historians of labour, amateur and professional, can fruitfully cooperate. In doing so they will not only help students, but, we hope, keep alive and encourage the traditions of struggle which are so fundamental a part of the consciousness of the British working class.

E.J.Hobsbawm

Acknowledgements

The essays reprinted in this book were originally published over many years. The dates of original publication are as follows:

Thomas Bewick: 1962
Luddism: 1956
Chartist Literature: 1960
Chartism and the Trade Unions: 1963
Chartism in the Black Country: 1965—6
Songs of the Labour Movement: 1963
The Lancashire Cotton Famine: 1961
The Revolt of the Field in East Anglia: 1968
Tom Mann and his Times: 1962
The Lesser Fabians: 1962
Sheffield Shop Stewards: 1960
The General Strike in the North-East: 1961.

Our thanks are due to many people: to Ray Watkinson for the loan of the blocks which illustrate this book. To Central Books Ltd for permission to translate Yuri V. Kovalev's preface to *An Anthology of Chartist Literature*, which they distribute in this country. To Edward Thompson for his editorial assistance in the original publication of *Tom Mann and his Times, 1890-92* and for the transcripts of correspondence between Tom Mann and John Burns. To the Sheffield A.E.U. for permission given in 1952 to use the minute books of No. 12 Branch; to the Labour Research Department and Messrs. Allen and Unwin for permission to quote at length from G.D.H. Cole's *An Introduction to Trade Unionism;* and to Brothers Harbinson, Ibbotson, Parsons, Sweeting and Ward for their personal memories of Sheffield Shop Stewards in the First World War.

Above all we are grateful to the authors of these essays and to the successive editors of *Our History:* Mrs. Betty Grant (1—8), Allen Merson

10

(9—14), Joan Simon (15—28), and Lionel Munby (29—54). No attempt has been made to bring these essays up to date, except for the more important references. Some ephemeral material has been removed; errors and misprints have been corrected where possible; there has been some minor rearranging, e.g. of paragraphing; and *Songs of the Labour Movement* has been enlarged with material which was omitted in the original edition for reasons of space.

Lionel M. Munby.

RAY WATKINSON

Thomas Bewick

1753-1828

Thomas Bewick, son of a small farmer, apprenticed to a provincial engraver, was one of England's greatest artists, and the supreme master of the art of wood-engraving. His work falls into a number of clear categories, and much of it was the coarsest hack engraving: but what is to be remembered in looking at all of it, including the most inventive and expressive of his prints, is that he did nothing without a firm appraisal of his purpose. He valued his own achievement as an artist and knew his unchallenged skill as a craftsman, and never feared, in the most utilitarian of day-to-day jobs, that his integrity or the flow of his creative ideas might suffer because his skill and his imagination were brought to bear constantly on quite humble tasks.

From his hands and from his workshop, between 1770 and 1828, came, among much other work, many thousands of engravings to illustrate and decorate books of all kinds; and it is for this work that he is remembered and admired. One thing, however, must be clearly understood about him; he was not, simply, an illustrator. He did make illustrations, and he carried out many engravings which reproduced the designs of other artists. But it is the engravings which owe nothing to a given text, which are direct visual expressions of his own ideas, using the wealth of his observation and experience, which crown his work, and these, as works of art, are on the highest level.

The fact that these prints are limited to black and white, that few of them are even as big as the palm of a man's hand, must not stand in the way of our sharing Bewick's experience and, once having seen the world with his eyes, recognising the degree to which our own experience is enriched. To this artist, the limitations of his medium were not restrictive, but liberating; I know none who commands a greater range of expression within one medium. ʀis engravings vary from the boldest and simplest cutting, to blocks of the most minute and delicate workmanship. But it is not the display of virtuosity that makes them memorable. It is the completeness of comprehension, the apt selection from material intimately known, the musical play of pattern to draw out meaning, that make these tiny pictures the powerful works of art which they are. At this scale, and only at this scale, will this medium, and these tools, by their very limitations and discipline, transform faithful drawing into compelling communication.

Much of Bewick's day-to-day work has disappeared for ever—that is to say, as being likely to be known again for his. For in addition to the wood-engravings, he did much anonymous work. He engraved clock-faces, which in his youth were not yet enamelled; door-plates, coffin-plates, seals; moulds for bottlemaking and clay-pipe making, for buttons and other trinkets; ornamented silverware with coats of arms, inscriptions, and elegant rococo wreaths and borders: etched ornament on sword-blades, gunlocks, caneheads; cut punches for type-founders, engraved plates for the printing of banknotes, shop-cards, trade-cards, bookplates, billheads; cut wood blocks for similar purposes, and for newspaper advertisements, newspaper headings, illustrations for children's books, diagrams and maps; and he cut letter stamps for bookbinders. In fact, the whole range of work which an engraver's shop could, in his day, be called upon to do, Bewick and his partner and their apprentices did.

Most of this work, of course, was done to the order of tradesmen, printers, publishers, craftsmen, manufacturers, and local businessmen, and carried out during a working day lasting from seven in the morning to seven in the evening. Nor was Bewick's attention given simply to the designing and cutting of plates and blocks. He was running a craftsman's shop, and must receive or wait on customers, travel to make drawings, arrange for printing, order materials, keep accounts, write letters, train apprentices. All this he did with a steady unpretentious pride in his independence, confident in his skill, his intelligence, and his principles. This hardly sounds like the description of one of the greatest artists of the Romantic era; yet this in fact is what he was. I do not, in saying so, describe him as a Romantic artist.

The student of English art expects to know, and in varying degrees admire, the paintings of Reynolds, Gainsborough, Wilson, Romney, Lawrence: he may yet know nothing at all of Bewick but the name. Yet Bewick was an artist of no less power than these, and of greater integrity than any. He was not in his life-time ever thought to compete with them as an artist, much as his work was admired. The fashionable patrons of art who were aware of his existence would think of him as 'the ingenious Mr. Bewick'; but it would not occur to them to question whether he might not be a greater artist than the first President of the Royal Academy. Time will largely invert this relation. The work of many of the most successful artists appears more and more shallow as time goes by, for their function and justification, the work they were paid for was the creation in their patrons' minds of images of self-esteem. Bewick had no patrons: he had customers; and when one of them wished him to create such images by drawing his prize sheep and cattle as bigger and fatter than they were, Bewick refused the job. Such artists as he, as Blake, as Hogarth, as Stubbs, as Wright, will keep their significance and their power to communicate.

Having made clear my conviction that very many of the thousands of engravings which Bewick produced have a special claim as works of art, I must now say that no study of Bewick would be worth anything if it did no more than elaborate that assertion, or rested on the abstraction of a few favourite examples from the mass. The man is a whole man, and his achievement as an artist rests largely on the hand-and-eye skill of the craftsman, on his use of particular techniques; techniques which he developed in a revolutionary way from the work of many unknown precursors, but which did not spring to his hand by magic. Behind this again lies his actual condition of life, the circumstance which impelled him to pursue his particular path. He was not simply an engraver; nor, on the other hand, was he, abstractly, an artist. He was a particular kind of artist; one whose work sprang from the printed book which gave him, on the one hand, bread and butter, and on the other, inspiration. Today he would be described as a graphic designer. It was not the printed book, abstractly, that moved him to his achievements. It was the printed book in a given society, in which it had, as he plainly saw, certain functions, a certain potential, which he grasped eagerly. It was the printed book indeed that gave him his independence from patronage.

It would be easy, in looking at Bewick's world through his engravings, to look at him with romantic hindsight and think of him as looking backward with us. Certainly his view of his world was coloured with regret for much that he saw die: the liberty of the poor peasant, the old houses, the green land. But he was actively concerned in the pursuit of knowledge and the support of new ideas both technical and social. His working life was devoted to developing the best techniques of cutting and printing illustrations and pictures which should spread enlightenment among his fellows.

It would be easy, too, to present Bewick as the untaught instinctive genius, the unlettered country boy with a flair for drawing beasts and birds and charming rustic scenes. This would be as truthful and valuable as the traditional tale of Giotto the inspired shepherd boy, discovered by Cimabue creating masterpieces in chalk on the road side stones. In presenting Bewick as the antithesis of the conventionally successful artist of his day, in giving proper weight to his origin and background—an origin and a background which remained at all times sharply in his own consciousness—I do not mean to offer yet another Noble Savage, or to canvas sympathetically his struggles to raise himself above the disadvantages of circumstance.

He was an intelligent and an educated man, whose country childhood and craftsman's training gave him a far richer source of imagery than the tired puppet-pantheon of contemporary artistic convention could ever have done. At the outset of his career, in the full consciousness of his abilities and of the readiness of friends in the capital to help him to success, he turned his back on London and never, until he was an old man within months of death, set foot there again, though many of his dear friends worked there and he did much work for London publishers. He chose to go back to his native Tyneside, and there to produce, among thousands of now forgotten trades-men's jobs, the most remarkable series of prints; and to train at the bench the most remarkable group of wood-engravers and draughtsmen; perfecting, in the process, a new art-form. Before looking closer at his actual work, we should look at this world to which he returned so confidently.

I

Newcastle is not just another provincial town. It has its own special place in English history. Its name is embedded in our language in a traditional phrase: to carry coals to Newcastle is to do something supremely useless and unnecessary. For the Tyne valley is our oldest coalfield, and from Newcastle, at the eastern end of Hadrian's Wall, coal has been shipped to the rest of England, to France and Holland, and even to the Baltic, for nearly a thousand years. As long ago as the year 852, when Alfred the Great was king, coal went from the pits of Tyneside to the great abbey of Peterborough in the fen country. In the fourteenth century at least, ships from Newcastle traded as far as Windau (Ventspils) in Latvia; and a series of royal charters, and monopolies gave the town and its burgesses privileges and protection almost unique, ensuring a high degree of prosperity until the end of the last century.

The Burgesses of Newcastle had complete control of the mining and transport of coal, without rivals until in the mid-eighteenth century the Lancashire and Yorkshire coalfields were developed. The town was a main centre of the glass industry, from the time when James I gave Sir Robert Mansell the monopoly of production and import of glass: the need to develop pumps and engines for the deepening mines made Tyneside an important centre of engineering, and in 1714, when there were only four steam-engines in the country, two of them were in Newcastle. It was here, too, that the development of railways and the industrial production of alkalis began at the end of the eighteenth century. When, in 1639, Charles I was marching against the Scottish Covenanters, he made Newcastle his head-quarters, and set up, though temporarily, the first printing press in any English provincial town; and in 1710, the Newcastle Gazette was one of the first English provincial newspapers, appearing three times a week.

With its concentration of industry and wealth, the town also had a high concentration of literate and indeed educated artisans and tradesmen, and continually attracted more from the whole of the north. It boasted, indeed, of being the 'London of the North' , and it resembled London in having its chief shopping centre on the old bridge across the river. Among these shops, which hung over the Tyne until a great storm swept the bridge away in 1771, there were, from the beginning of the eighteenth century, many bookshops. No other provincial town had so many booksellers, among whom were Bryson, Akenhead, Charnley, Linn (whose sign was the head of John Locke), Fleming, Harrison, Turnbull, Barber, Chalmers, Reed, and Gooding: this at a time when the whole population of Northumberland was about a quarter of a million, and that of Newcastle well under 20,000. Though there was no theatre until 1781, plays were given in the assembly rooms of the large inns, or in the Moot Hall; and John Gay's *Beggar's Opera* was produced in Newcastle in 1728, while it was still enjoying its astonishing success in London.

A town so situated, with such diversity of activity, and such wealth, was naturally the centre of attraction for painters, musicians and other artists in the North. It was the natural place for the Beilby family, all highly skilled and well-educated, to settle. Children of a Durham silversmith, their chief busi-ness was in engraving and glass-enamelling: Newcastle was the chief centre for silversmithing in the North, and had its own Assay office. To Ralph Beilby, on the 1st of October 1767, Thomas Bewick was apprenticed for seven years.

Thomas Bewick was born on the tenth of August, 1753, eldest son of John Bewick, who farmed eight acres of land about his house of Cherryburn on the south bank of the Tyne, twelve miles or so above Newcastle. In addition to farming, he worked, with a few men, a small colliery at nearby

Mickley Bank. His wife Jane was the daughter of a Cumberland schoolmaster and farmer, Wilson of Ainstable, and knew enough Latin to be able not only to keep house for the Rector of Ovingham, as she did before her marriage, but to help him in the village school. This background of solid yeoman independence, of moderate comfort won by constant hard work, of country skills and earnest education, coloured the whole of Bewick's life and outlook. Of the countryside itself, the wooded valley of the Tyne and the high moors stretching up to Scotland, no later circumstance ever impaired the vivid images in Bewick's mind.

In the year of Bewick's birth, there was founded in London the Society for the Encouragement of Arts, Commerce and Manufactures. Two years later, there began the Seven Years' War: the first modern war: the first, that is to say, fought on an intercontinental scale between nations, not dynasties, and resting plainly upon commercial causes. The enhanced power of England after that war, the vast expansion of her colonies and trading interests, and the development of her manufactures, hastened the profound changes hitherto hidden in agricultural and craft improvements, and set in motion the Industrial Revolution. During Bewick's lifetime, the character of England was radically changed; and he was at all times conscious of the process, and of his part in it. In his boyhood, the tattered and crippled soldiers and sailors from the recent war tramped from town to town, begging, seeking work and homes. In his young manhood, the common lands of the village on which the poor labourers could pasture a cow, a few sheep, a few geese, were gathered by the enclosure acts into large farms and estates, and the peasants (whom he describes so lovingly in his *Memoir*) emigrated, were turned into casual workers in the towns, or became paupers.

Nevertheless, in the process of this transformation, Newcastle, like Manchester, Birmingham, and Liverpool, prospered, and Bewick never lacked for work. Very early, he showed his remarkable talent for drawing, and, though as the eldest son it should have been his place to take over the farm, his parents, helped by the legacy from his grandmother of £20 for an apprentice fee, began to look for a trade in which he could exploit his skill. One fine Sunday in 1767, William and Ralph Beilby rode out to Bywell to visit a friend, who was so full of young Bewick's praises that the two brothers, who were looking for an apprentice, rode on to Cherryburn to see the boy. The outcome of this introduction was that, on the 1st of October, Thomas Bewick was apprenticed to Ralph Beilby, and went to live with the Beilby family in Newcastle. He could hardly have been more fortunate in his master.

The Beilbys were not only remarkably skilled and versatile craftsmen: they were well-read, and had musical and scientific interests. In their father's workshop and in others in Birmingham, they had learned engraving, enamelling, glass-painting, and seal and die-cutting. The eldest brother, Richard, had died some years before: but William, Ralph, Thomas, and their no less skilled sister Mary, all worked together. 'The industry, ingenuity, and united energies of this family,' says Bewick in the *Memoir* 'must soon have enabled them to soar above every obstacle.' The pages of the *Memoir* which describe his life as Ralph's apprentice give a vivid picture of the eighteenth century craftsman's shop, and after describing how Ralph Beilby 'undertook everything', Bewick goes on to say 'I think he was the best master in the world for teaching boys, for he obliged them to put their hands to every variety of work.' This included engraving and die-cutting, the polishing of copper plates, the sharpening and indeed the making of tools, at which Beilby was very ingenious; and, sometimes, the cutting of woodblocks for the local press or for tradesmen's billheads.

It was Beilby's distaste for the last type of work that made him turn it all over to Bewick, who took to it very readily, in the very first days of his apprenticeship. All the work was new and interesting to him, and he became particularly interested in this; so much so, that it was all left to him; and he did it with such spirit that more and more wood cuts began to be asked for, not only by shopkeepers and innkeepers, but by the printers and booksellers.

Bewick has often been credited with the invention of wood engraving, both in the sense of first using the graver on the end-grain of boxwood, and in the sense of first using the 'white-line' technique. He invented neither, nor ever claimed to have done so. What he did was to develop a craft which had been in use for perhaps forty years before he ever picked up a graver, to transform it from a reproductive to a creative medium, and to develop it to levels never before dreamed of. There is ample evidence that true wood-engraving had been practised for many years before Bewick began work, though he himself, like many others does not in writing always make clear the essential distinction between wood-engraving, done with the graver on end-grain box-wood, and wood-cutting, done in plank-grain beech, pear, or cherry-wood, with knife and gouge, as by the Formschneider of Dürer's day — a practice dating back to the fourteenth century and continuing into the late eighteenth; and even, for wallpaper and cotton-printing, into our own time.

English printing of the seventeenth century had been poor though plentiful. No masterpiece of literature ever had a worse dress than Paradise Lost. The last decade of the century saw the first developments of native printing and type-founding, which later flowered in the work of Caslon, Baskerville, and Bell. This was largely due to the energy of the bookseller Jacob Tonson, chief promoter of the Kit-Cat Club, most powerful of the Whig pressure groups. He was also the key figure in publishing, and his demands raised printing and bookbinding standards beyond recognition. In exploiting the expanding market for books, he drew at first on French, and yet more on Dutch type-founders, engravers, and papermakers; but before the century closed he had stimulated the native craftsmen to the production of well-printed, well-bound and finely decorated books. A part of this stimulus was also provided by the influx of first-rate French craftsmen, of Protestant faith, who fled to escape religious persecution, after the revocation of the Edict of Nantes in 1685. In the work of these craftsmen who rose to

Tonson's challenge, we may look for the origins of Bewick's art.

Chief and first of them was Elisha Kirkall, a native of Sheffield, very active in the 1720s and 1730s, whose techniques, both in intaglio and relief engraving, derived from Callot and Claude Mellan, anticipated Bewick's in their purity. Some of the cuts in the *Gentleman's Magazine* (run by the enterprising Edmund Cave, who was a partner in a new silk mill in Derbyshire) as early as 1754, are unquestionable wood-engravings, signed W. Pennock: while twenty years earlier, the *London Magazine* had a heading, almost certainly a wood-engraving, signed T. Davies. Two other craftsmen whose work can be identified in the '60s and '70s are T. Gilbert and T. Lister, the latter working in Oxford.

Nearly all their work is cut in strict whiteline, with the graver. Their prints are not facsimiles of line drawings, but tonal renderings of originals probably carried out in pen or pencil-and-wash. From Kirkall on, the artists who developed the medium understood that the use of black lines and of cross-hatching is alien to its essence. The system adopted by Kirkall, in the '20s, was that of building up tones by parallel cuts of the graver: a system originally perfected by such engravers as Goltzius and Callot.

Thus, by the time Bewick went to London in 1776, there was already a well-established practice of wood-engraving, and workshops which supplied the trade with true wood-engravings as well as copper-plates and wood cuts. It remained for Bewick to develop the hardly-suspected range of the new medium.

II

The first job Bewick was set to, on starting work with the Beilbys, was the cutting, on wood, of the diagrams for a book on Mensuration by Charles Hutton, son of a colliery labourer, who was one of the leading mathematicians of the day. In the 1760s, he kept a small school in Newcastle, was friendly with the Beilbys, and, being a writing-master as well as mathematician, used to design for them the lettered portion of bill-heads, banknotes and other copper-plate work. Hutton, writing in 1822, at a date when, had there been any doubt as to facts, Bewick could and certainly would have corrected him—said that it was he who had introduced Beilby—and therefore Bewick—to the use of boxwood and graver, and had got the first boxwood blocks for the illustrations to his book himself, from London. But Bewick, to whom this work was passed by his master, was not long in making himself a special graver with a double point, to cut the black lines at a single stroke.

The mathematical diagrams would not attract any attention; but a pictorial cut done for a bar-bill for the George and Dragon Inn at Penrith did, and it was this which brought more orders for similar work. It also caught the eye of one of the town's best established printers, Thomas Saint. Saint printed and published many children's books, and he saw how much they could be enhanced by this boy's work. One of the first such books with cuts by Bewick was Saint's *New Lottery Book of Birds and Beasts for Children to learn their Letters by as soon as They can speak*, which appeared in 1771. More books of the same kind, often with texts by Oliver Goldsmith, were illustrated by Bewick during and just after his apprenticeship: they include *A New-invented Hornbook; The Child's Tutor* (1772); *Moral Instructions* (1772); *Youth's Instructive Storyteller* (1774); *Select Fables* (Dodsley's: 1776); *Gay's Fables* (1779), and many other story—and spelling-books.

This work exactly suited Bewick's temperament and outlook, and though in many ways his drawing was still unsure or crude, he was, by the time his apprenticeship ended, producing some very fine work indeed. 'Some of the fable cuts were so well thought of by my master', says the *Memoir*, 'that he, in my name, sent impressions of a few of them to be laid before the Society for the Encouragement of Arts, etc., and I obtained a premium. This I received shortly after I was out of my apprenticeship, and it was left to my choice whether I would have it in a gold medal or money (seven guineas). I preferred the latter, and I never in my life felt greater pleasure than in presenting it to my mother.' Two other engravers (both older than he) were awarded premiums at the same time (February 1775)—William Coleman and Thomas Hodgson. The latter was a Newcastle printer who had been working in London for some time, and, like Bewick, had a passionate enthusiasm for wood engraving.

Bewick, after working for a while as a journeyman with Beilby, returned to his family home at Cherryburn, where he spent eighteen months of great happiness, working on wood engravings for Saint, Angus, and other printers; rambling the countryside, fishing, following the hounds, going about the business of the colliery with his father. But in June 1776, with a few spare clothes, and three guineas stitched into his waistband, he set off to walk through Scotland.

Walking to Haydon Bridge, he spent two days with his friend, Thomas Spence, who was now teaching in the school there; went on to visit his mother's relations in Cumberland, and so through Edinburgh, Glasgow, Dumbarton, where he was disappointed at not being allowed to look over the new cotton print works, up into the Highlands, where the kindness of the poor shepherds and farmers moved him deeply; to Falkirk, visiting the Carron Ironworks, then the most modern in Europe, and so by sea to Newcastle, where he arrived on August 12 1776, having tramped about five hundred miles, still with some shillings in his pocket.

But he had not brought the Cherryburn idyll to an end simply to walk through Scotland. The tour had been the prelude to settling down to work for good. First, however, he wanted some different experience of his trade. He stayed in Newcastle long enough to earn his passage money to London, and then, after three weeks in a collier brig, landed in the capital on October 1st 1776.

He had friends and acquaintances already there, for the coal trade had established a longstanding Newcastle community in London. His school friends Christopher and Philip Gregson were already working there, and through them he found lodgings. Thomas Hodgson had work waiting for him, and through Robert Pollard, a fellow engraver, he was introduced to Isaac Taylor, son of a Worcester silversmith, and the leading illustrator and book decorator of the day. From Hodgson and Taylor; from Carnan and Newbery, who were the chief publishers of the sort of books he had so often illustrated for Saint, he got, as he says in the *Memoir*, plenty of work, and earned good money. But he did not like London's crowded streets and contrasts of extreme wealth with extreme poverty, and determined to return home. This cost him the friendship of Taylor, who saw what success this young man could command, and was eager to help him. But Bewick was as obstinate as clever, and in June 1777 he was back in Newcastle with the promise from Hodgson of as much work as would keep him busy for two years. He fitted up a workshop in his old lodgings and settled down happily.

In addition to the wood engravings for Hodgson, he found that Saint and Angus had work to offer again; what was more, some of the local silversmiths brought him engraving jobs. This quickly produced the offer of partnership from Ralph Beilby. It had been Bewick's plan to work alone; but he joined Beilby, whose two brothers had now left to work elsewhere as drawing masters. Ralph Beilby had taken a new apprentice. It happened that John, Bewick's younger brother, had something of his talent; and he also joined Beilby and Bewick as an apprentice. The shop prospered, and never lacked work. Copper-plate and silver engraving fell mostly to Beilby; Bewick thought him the best ornamental engraver in the country. He continued to concentrate on wood engraving.

During the next ten years, a scheme gradually took shape in his mind, which his partner joined willingly. This was the production of a book on animals. It was partly Bewick's love of animals and intimate knowledge of the countryside that had made his illustrations so successful. Apart from the children's spelling books, he had cut several sets of illustrations to fables. The fabulists' convention, in which animals are endowed with human characteristics or made symbolic of human passions, had given his imagination the most fortunate of opportunities.

Not only this: but there was a continual demand for books on natural history. The increasing scientific interest of the eighteenth century Englishman in agriculture, above all in stockbreeding, the many voyages of exploration, and the growing trade with remote countries, all promoted the demand. One of the most popular and often reprinted books of Bewick's youth was the *Three Hundred Animals*, of whose crude illustrations he had, even as a boy, thought very poorly. Now began, in 1785, the production of the *Natural History of Quadrupeds*, for which Bewick provided the illustrations, and Beilby the text. But though this was a considerable project, involving Bewick in cutting blocks of two hundred animals, apart from many tail-pieces, and Beilby in writing a rather larger number of descriptions, the work had to be done in the evenings; nothing must interrupt the routine work of their shop and office. So it went on slowly, and it was not until 1790 that the book appeared. It was immediately popular, and went quickly through several editions. Characteristically, as each was published, Bewick added new cuts, so that no two editions are alike.

Writing about his work in 1819, Bewick said: 'I date the *Quadrupeds* to be my commencement of Wood Engraving worthy of attention.' The book was critically important to him, as being the first completely independent venture, the realisation of his own conception not only in the detail of individual cuts, in which he had always been able to exercise his imagination, but as a complete project; and there is no doubt that its success encouraged him and his partner to go on with the scheme, which had matured while the *Quadrupeds* was in progress, for a book on *British Birds*.

The first volume of this appeared in 1797—the *Land Birds*, having cuts of 117 birds, and 91 tail-pieces. The second volume was nearly another seven years in preparation, appearing in 1804, with 101 pictures of birds and 136 tail-pieces; and this book continues to be thought of by most people as containing the best, the raciest, the most varied and the most inventive of his work. It is significant that as these three volumes were produced, the proportion of tail-pieces to actual representations of animal or bird increased. Bewick's aim had been to produce books whose faithful pictures and accurate descriptions should be such as to supersede the many indifferent volumes of Natural History on the market, and in the pursuit of this fundamentally utilitarian aim he bought, borrowed and read every authoritative book on birds or beasts he could hear of. Friends collected information and specimens for him: in a letter to his brother John in January 1788, he thanks him for a drawing of a lion (probably done in the Tower of London menagerie) and looks forward to the impending visit to Newcastle of a large menagerie which will enable him to draw from life some animals which he must otherwise have taken from Buffon or some other illustrated, but not always reliable, book. He travelled about to make drawings, and came into touch with naturalists like Pennant and Tunstall—for whom, as a by-product of the work of the *Quadrupeds*, he made his largest and most ambitious engraving, the *Chillingham Bull*. With the *Birds*, since the scheme was confined to British birds, he could consistently work from actual specimens; and with many he was of course minutely familiar, as to appearance and habit.

On the *Birds*, too, he was able to work during shop hours, since it was clear that the whole project was commercially successful; and so to some extent the work could be shared by the apprentices; and though the creative responsibility is wholly Bewick's, the physical labour of production was spread in this way, and this partly accounts for the greater number of tail-pieces, the designing and cutting of which was his greatest pleasure. In them, the whole range of observation, beauty, pathos, irony and humour is displayed with an equal variety of styles and techniques.

Other notable works of the first years of the new century were sets of cuts for Thomson's *The Seasons*, one of the best loved and most significant books of the eighteenth century, a lifelong favourite of Bewick's; for *Burns' Poems*—and the affinities between Burns and Bewick are deep indeed; the *Poems of Goldsmith and Parnell*, a beautifully produced volume from the Shakespeare Press, managed by William Bulmer, who as a printer's apprentice in the 1770s had proved Bewick's earliest cuts: cuts to Bunyan's *Pilgrim's Progress;* all these, of course, among a host of minor work for printers up and down the country, to whom now it was a matter of prestige to have at least one 'cut by Bewick' in their books.

There remained one ambition to fulfil. Croxall's *Aesop* had always been a favourite book, and he had probably learned as much from cutting half a dozen variations on the traditional illustrations as from any other source; but he had for a long time wished to produce an Aesop which should have the best possible cuts. In 1812, as he recovered from a nearly-fatal illness, he began to work on the project, and finally completed it in 1818. He did not cut most of the illustrations himself, but drew them in pencil on the blocks, to be engraved by his apprentices, Temple and Harvey, and his son Robert, who became his partner in the same year. The Aesop cuts have often been criticised as too elaborate and often too finely cut. Beautiful and inventive as these all are, there hangs over them a faint shadow of the decay that overtook wood-engraving within twenty years of Bewick's death—the descent into uncomprehending facsimile.

For the last few years of his life Bewick, though he went to his shop every day, spent less time at the bench, and left the business partly in his son's hands, who, though a timid engraver and draughtsman, overshadowed by his father's strong personality and achievement, was intelligent and capable. In 1823 Bewick took a trip to Edinburgh, there to meet again many old friends, and to visit, among others, Ballantyne the printer, who had recently installed a lithographic press. Bewick was interested in this, and Ballantyne very anxious that he should experiment. So, on the morning before he returned to Newcastle, the old man made his only lithograph—a lively drawing, done with the lightest of touches, of a farmer trotting to market.

Many artists and naturalists sought him out, and one of these was Audubon, whose drawings of American birds Bewick admired. Audubon visited him in 1827, and, for the short time that Bewick still had to live, they were warm friends. In the summer of 1828, Bewick, with his two daughters, paid a second visit to London, where his old and now wealthy friend Bulmer was anxious to show him the newly opened Menagerie at Regent's Park, and had arranged a dinner in his honour to which the leading engravers were to come. Bewick was too old and unwell, and three months later, on November 8th 1828, he died.

Just a week before his death, he had taken to his printer a large block on which he had been working with great pains for some weeks. The block was proved, to Bewick's satisfaction. It was intended as the key block of a set, the rest of which would have been overprinted. Bewick had for years been interested in the increased depth and subtlety to be obtained by using two or three blocks, much as had been done in the chiaroscuro prints of the seventeenth and early eighteenth centuries, but with the additional range provided by the techniques of true engraving.

Unfinished as the print is, in terms of this intention, it is nevertheless a profound masterpiece. Its theme is one which recurs throughout Bewick's whole career. He had projected a definitive print of it for many years, and had long since, in 1785, the year of his father's death, written a descriptive text to accompany it. When he left Cherryburn to be apprenticed to Ralph Beilby (his partnership with whom had ended in 1797) he had in his pocket a little drawing of an old horse of his father's which had recently died from neglect after being lent to a neighbour less careful of animals than the Bewick family. Bewick made one of his first etchings from this drawing, and this gaunt, blind, weary creature appears in variation after variation, from book to book, his life-long symbol of suffering, *Waiting for Death*.

The Bewick workshop continued for many years in Robert's capable but uncreative hands; but it was now simply another craftsman's shop.

III

Newcastle in the eighteenth century was not only important for its coal industry, but as a principal centre for the whole Border country, and a stage on the journey to and from Scotland. Many of the migrants attracted to, or pausing in Newcastle, came from Carlisle, Penrith, Kendal, or Berwick; but since the Act of Union, many more were Scots. The disturbance of the Scottish peasantry, due in part to the two Jacobite revolts and in part to the large-scale enclosures practised by the gentry and nobility, on which Bewick comments bitterly in his *Memoir,* sent many of them south to England.

Early in the century, one of the leading booksellers in Newcastle was the Scot Martin Bryson, to whom Alan Ramsay (The Gentle Shepherd) wrote from Edinburgh addressing his letter:

To Martin Bryson on Tyne Brigg—
An upright, downright, honest Whig.

Ramsay's son was Bryson's apprentice, and a later apprentice in the same shop was William Charnley of Penrith, who, in 1750, became Bryson's partner. Bewick did much work for Charnley, whose son and successor was his close friend. The Charnleys, Bryson, Slack, and others of the bookselling fraternity, were Dissenters—Presbyterian, Baptist, Quaker or Unitarian— libertarian supporters of the American and French Revolutions, rationalist and republican in much of their thought.

The steady influx of skilled tradesmen and artisans, with this sort of background, was an important factor in stimulating the intellectual and political life of Newcastle, which otherwise, secure in its monopolies, might well have sunk into lethargic complacency. Among these men, both young journeymen and apprentices like himself, or older tradesmen, Bewick found friends and continued his education. Among them Gilbert Gray is worth especial mention. Bewick wrote at length and with affection of Gray in the *Memoir,* and clearly he was an important formative influence.

A native of Aberdeen, Gray had been intended for the Church, but early abandoned the faith, though not the ethic, in which he had been brought up. 'Of a trouth, Thomas,' he said to Bewick, 'I did not like their ways.' Moving to Edinburgh, he became shopman to Alan Ramsay, and learned to bind books. He left Ramsay to work for Bryson in Newcastle, and when Bewick, as an apprentice, came to know him, he was working as a book-binder. Then in his mid-sixties, he lived frugally, saving all his money either to help down-and-out fellow artisans, or to print his own tracts and fables, which he sold in the market. His workshop became a sort of club which attracted a group of serious youngsters like Bewick. To them he lent his own books, or gave permission to read others in his hands for binding. Similar privileges were granted Bewick by Gray's son William, also a bookbinder in a good way of trade; later he worked in London where he continued his friendship. Another son, George, became a close friend of the Bewick family; an accomplished painter, chemist, and geologist, he travelled, in the last capacity, into Poland and all over North America.

In the Gray's workshops, as well as in the daily course of his work, Bewick also met William Bulmer, apprenticed to the printer John Thompson. Master and boy were extremely interested in the developing technique of wood-engraving, and the blocks which Bewick engraved for the booksellers and other tradesmen in the town were proved by Bulmer, in later life wealthy and famous as the proprietor of the Shakespeare Printing Office. Here too Bewick met Robert Pollard, a life-long friend who, at first apprenticed as a silversmith, became so interested in engraving that on his master's retirement he went to London and bound himself to Isaac Taylor. It was to Pollard, Bulmer, and Thomas Hodgson that Bewick owed the ready flow of work he found in the capital.

But there were others whom he met in Gray's workshop whose acquaintance was no less important. Of these, one of the most significant, and one of the dearest to Bewick to the end of his days, was Thomas Spence.

'In my frequent visits to the workshops of Gilbert Gray and to that of his son William,' says Bewick (*Memoir*, 1862, p.71), 'I first fell in with Thomas Spence. He was one of the warmest philanthropists in the world. The happiness of mankind seemed with him to absorb every other consideration. He was of a cheerful disposition, warm in his attachment to his friends, and in his patriotism to his country . . . For the purpose chiefly of making converts to his opinion "That property in land is everyone's right", he got a number of young men together, and formed into a debating society, which was held in the evenings in his schoolroom, in the Broad Garth, Newcastle.'

Spence was born in Newcastle on June 1st 1750, son of an Aberdonian net and shoemaker who had been about ten years in the town, and was a leading member of the Sandemanian church, or rather community, there. Thomas started in life as a commercial clerk, but became a schoolmaster. Though on the question of the ownership and control of land Bewick never saw wholly eye to eye with Spence, it is clear that the latter's general philosophical and political ideas influenced him a great deal. When, after the death of Bewick's younger daughter Isabella, the last of his goods were sold (1884) a group of Spence's books and pamphlets was among them. It included two copies of *The Teacher of Common Sense* (Newcastle 1779); *The Restoration of Society* (1801); *Gray's Elegy*—printed in Spence's Reformed Alphabet—*The End of Oppression; The Meridian Sun of Liberty* (1796); *The Rights of Swine* (1796); *The Constitution of a Perfect Commonwealth* (1798); *The Trial of Spence before Lord Kenyon* (1801) and *Humourous Songs*. With these was a collection of Spence's tokens.

Spence, says Bewick, 'was afterwards famous in London as the head of the Spenceans. He was sent to Dorchester (should be Shrewsbury) gaol for (I believe) some of his publications, promulgating his doctrines. He taught a school at the Broad Garth, Newcastle; afterwards, writing and arithmetic in the great school at Haydon Bridge: and lastly, he was master of St. Ann's public school, Sandgate, Newcastle . . . I cut the steel punches for Spence's types, and my master struck them on the matrices for casting his newly invented letters of the alphabet for his *Spelling and Pronouncing Dictionary*. (This would be in 1774-5). He published in London many curious books in his peculiar way of spelling. Most of them, I believe, on his favourite subject of property in land being everyone's right. However mistaken he might be in his notions on this subject, I am clearly of the opinion that his intentions were both sincere and honest.'

From the debating society in Spence's schoolroom, there developed, in 1775, the first Philosophical Society (not to be confused with the later Lit. & Phil.) of Newcastle. It had about twenty members, including Spence, Bewick, and the Rev. James Murray, satirist and Hebrew scholar, for whose book *The Theban Harp* Bewick engraved a copper-plate. This society held its first meeting on March 15th: Spence's membership was ended by expulsion in November. The *Newcastle Chronicle* (Nov. 25) announced that this was on account of his breach of a rule against the publication of any of the lectures. The one which Spence had published was, not surprisingly, on 'Property in Land Everyone's Right', given on November 8th. On that occasion he had expected Bewick's support in debate. It was not forthcoming, and they quarrelled, but only for the moment. The expulsion had not been unanimous; Murray had protested against it.

This society had only a short life; it probably did not long survive the expulsion of its founder. But it had been brought into being with other Societies by the impending General Election of October 1774, and by the deeply disturbing reactions to the imminent American Revolution. First was the Constitutional Club whose Charter called for triennial parliaments, no placemen, more equal representation, and the recognition of Wilkes as member for Middlesex. The second was the Independent Club, with similar aims, whose members were all Freemen and electors of the town. The third was the Society of Patriots. To this belonged some of Bewick's friends, but not, I think, Bewick himself.

It is here that a most interesting and unexpected association is uncovered. From 1770 to 1773, Jean Paul Marat lived in Newcastle, practising as a doctor. There can be no doubt that he was closely connected with the members of these societies. In the *Public Advertiser* of May 3rd, 1774, appeared an advertisement of 'an address to the electors of Great Britain' under the title of 'The Chains of Slavery'. With no author's name given, it was written as by an Englishman; but in fact Marat was the author. At the end of the same month, the *Newcastle Chronicle* (published by Thomas Slack) had a paragraph announcing: 'Yesterday (May 27th) the Company of Bricklayers, the Company of Goldsmiths, and the Lumber Troop in this town, received each, by the fly, two large quarto volumes, from an unknown person in London, entitled "The Chains of Slavery" . . . The work is spirited, and appears through the whole a masterly execution.'

The election which the book was meant to influence took place in October, and the progressive candidates (Arctic explorer Captain Phipps, later Lord Mulgrave, and Thomas Delaval, both of whom had been made Honorary Bricklayers) were defeated by Blackett and Ridley, the two chief magnates of the area.

A year later, this gratuitous distribution was followed by a more normal publication, and the *Chronicle* of October 21st 1775 announced—'Next week will be published, price 10s.6d., and sold by the booksellers in Newcastle, THE CHAINS OF SLAVERY, written by Dr. Mariot.' A week later a full advertisement appeared, and Marat's name was given correctly—with his degree of MD. The Newcastle booksellers handling the book were Slack, Charnley and Humble.

In between these two appearances of his book, Marat returned to England, principally to visit the patriotic clubs of the North. He stayed three weeks in Carlisle, Penrith, and Newcastle, and three of the clubs (probably in those towns) presented him with letters of admission in a golden box. That of Newcastle, says Marat's own account, published a new edition of his work, and was one of those which made him a member. This would be the 1775 edition, and evidently Slack, Charnley and Humble were the active agents in the publication. It seems likely that they were also members of one or other of the clubs, for organising which, according to Lonsdale's 'Worthies of Cumberland', Marat was partly, if not wholly, responsible.

Whether Bewick himself met Marat we are not likely now to know; but it is clear that many of his immediate seniors and associates did; and the engraver's later comments on the French and American Revolutions, and on

social and political institutions generally, show that he had deeply absorbed the ideas Marat propagated

'During the eventful period of the French Revolution,' he says in the *Memoir*, 'and the wide-spreading war which followed in consequence of it, and in which our government became deeply engaged, extending from 1793 to 1814—a time of blood and slaughter—I frequently, by way of unbending the mind after the labours of the day, spent my evenings in the company of a set of staunch advocates for the liberties of mankind, who discussed the passing events mostly with the cool, sensible and deliberate attention which the importance of the subject required . . . The causes of this Revolution, and the horrible war which ended it, will form a most interesting subject for the head and pen of some future historian of a bold and enlightened mind. From the best consideration I have been able to give to the question, I cannot help viewing it in this way. In the year 1789, the French Revolution broke out, first of all from the income of the government not being sufficient to defray its expenditure, or, in other words, from its finances having become deranged for want of money, which the people, having been taxed to the uttermost and brought down to poverty, could no longer supply . . . By exaction, cruelty, and tyranny, the people had long been borne down to the lowest pitch of degradation. They were considered, not as rational human beings, equal in mind and intellect to their oppressors, but as beings made for the purpose only of continually labouring to support them in all their real and imaginary wants . . .

' This kind of treatment, so long shown to the people of France, could be endured no longer. They indeed seemed heartily disposed to settle a rational and just government quietly themselves; but this did not suit the views of the surrounding despots, to whom the very word liberty was offensive; and it was determined, at once, that this attempt of the people to resume their rights should be instantly overwhelmed . . . The French people could not bear their condition any longer. They were driven to madness, and instantly retaliated upon their oppressors, who, they conceived, meant that they and their children's children should continue to be doomed for ages to come. (They) rose as one man, and with unconquerable energy and bravery, like a whirl-wind, swept the advocates and the armies of despotism from off the face of the earth. Thus roused, this confederacy of Legitimates, finding or fearing that they might be baffled in their attempts, looked to England for support; and grieved indeed were the advocates of rational liberty, to find that these enemies of freedom had not looked in vain; for the government of this free country and free people—long veering, indeed, from the line of rectitude—had readily found pretexts for entering into a war in support of despotism; and war was begun, in the year 1793, against the Republican government of France.

' It had long been the settled opinion of many profound politicians, that corruption had spread, and was spreading, its baneful influence among the members of the government of this Kingdom; and that the majority cared nothing about maintaining the constitution in its purity, which to them was become like an old song. In this state of things, with Mr. Pitt at their head, and the resources of the British Isles in their hands, it was calculated upon as a certainty that his weight, added to the already powerful confederacy, would soon put a stop to the march of intellect, and if found necessary, put an extinguisher upon the rights of men. Mr. Pitt . . . became the powerful advocate of an opposite and perverted order of things. Thus situated, nothing could to a certainty serve his purpose so well as corruption; and the House of Commons had long been growing into a state befitting to his purpose; for its members had, in a great degree, ceased to be the representatives of the people, and he had only now to begin an invigorated, new, or more extended system of place and patronage, to have the majority at his nod; and, in aid of this, to add an extension of the peerage.

' Arbitrary laws were enacted, gagging bills were passed, and a system of espionage spread over the kingdom to keep the people down, many of whom seemed to have forgotten the exertions of their forefathers, whose blood had been spilt to purchase a better order of things. I felt particularly hurt at the apathy of the country gentlemen in these (politically considered) worst of times. Their faculties seemed benumbed; but, indeed, most of them fell into the vortex of corruption themselves . . . Although the friends of liberty and the constitution were both numerous and intrepid, yet, for want of what they termed respectable heads, they were widely spread and divided, and their efforts proved in vain.

'It was on (the sea) that the tide of affairs was first turned in favour of Britain, who now, by the valour of her seamen, reigned complete "mistress of the deep", and the commerce of the world seemed to be poured into her lap. Estates rose in value to an extraordinary height, and the price of grain, etc., still more so. The shipping interest wallowed in riches; the gentry whirled about in aristocratic pomposity; they forgot what their demeanour and good, kind behaviour used to be to those in inferior stations in life; and seemed far too often to look upon them like dirt. The character of the richer class of farmers was also changed . . . When these upstart gentlemen had left the market, they were ready to ride over all they met or overtook on the way; but this was as nothing compared to the pride and folly which took possession of their empty or fume-charged heads, when they got dressed in scarlet. They were then fitted for any purpose, and were called "yeoman cavalry". When peace came, it brought with it a sudden fall in the price of corn; but the taxes continuing the same to them, and rents still keeping high, they, with a few exceptions, suddenly experienced a woeful change. I cannot say, after seeing so much of their folly, that I was sorry for them; for they mostly deserved this reverse of fortune. Not so with the industrious labourer. His privations were great, and he was undeservedly doomed to suffer for want of employment, and often to waste away and die of hunger and want.'

Though Bewick went little to any sort of entertainment, he was, throughout his adult life, a member of some sort of club or society. 'About the year 1790', he writes, 'I became a member of Swarley's Club, held in the evenings at the Black Boy Inn . . . This was the most rational society or meeting I ever knew . . . No regular debatings were allowed on any subject but such as might occasionally arise out of the passing conversation . . . '. Bewick must have meant to write 1780, not 1790: for his membership card—engraved by Ralph Beilby, and bearing the motto 'Honi soit qui maly pense', and the title 'The Newcastle House of Lords'—was issued on October 17 1778. He seldom missed at least a weekly visit to the club, which took its name from Richard Swarley, the landlord, though pressure of work on the *Birds* kept him away at times, and early in 1792 he was writing of being 'but seldome at Swarley's or in public company—I cannot rise clear-headed in the morning when I spend my evenings out of the company of my wife and bairns.'

He was also a member of another club—the Brotherly Society, which met at Whitfield's Golden Lion Inn. As he himself engraved the floral border for the membership card, and his admission number (December 18 1782) was 32, he was presumably a member from its inception; but of this club he has nothing to say. In February, 1793, the Newcastle Literary and Philosophical Society was founded, promoted chiefly by his friend the Rev. William Turner, a Unitarian minister who was its first Secretary. Though friendly with many of its members, Bewick did not join this club.

His account of Swarley's Club closes thus: 'This happy society was at length broken up, at a time when war on behalf of despotism was raging, and the spy system was set afloat. Some spies, and others of the same stamp, contrived to get themselves introduced, and to broach political questions, for the purpose of exciting debates and feeling the pulse of the members, who before had very seldom touched upon subjects of that kind.'

This must have been in the mid-nineties. On October 4th 1794, Bewick wrote to a now unidentified correspondent (George Gray?): 'I received yours of the 17th ult., and thank you for the opinion you have given me of America. Before I get the Birds done, I have no doubt of matters being brought to such a crisis as will enable me to see clearly what course to steer. My fears are not at what you think will happen in America: it is my own much-loved country that I fear will be involved in the anarchy you speak of; for I think there is not virtue enough left in the country gentlemen to prevent it. I cannot hope for anything good from the violent on either side; that can only be expected from (I hope) the great majority of moderate men stepping manfully forward to check the despotism of one party and the licentiousness of the other. A reform of abuses, in my opinion, is wanted, and I wish that it could be done with justice and moderation; but it is because I do not hope or expect that it will take place in the way I wish it that makes me bend my mind towards America.' This letter is quoted in the appendix to the *Memoir*, and in two or three places in the body of the book, Bewick makes clear his admiration for the American Revolution, the success of the colonials in setting up their republic, and his view that in it lay the hope of mankind.

Though Swarley's Club was dispersed by the reaction of the war years, in the last decade of his life, when the reaction was hardly less black, Bewick spent his evenings at yet another club. Robinson (*Thomas Bewick: 1887*) describes this. ' Mr. Robert Wilson, merchant tailor, now in his 89th year, who, while I was an apprentice, lived in Richmond Court, Pilgrim Street, told me that he well remembered going down in an evening when the business of the day was over, to the Blue Bell Inn, at the Head of the Side, then kept by William Cant, an admirable performer on the Northumbrian small pipes. Here Mr. Bewick was accustomed to repair to regale himself with a pint of good porter. His dog Cheviot invariably accompanied him, and lay down at his feet on entering the room. Bewick was the acknowledged chief and president of a harmless gathering of substantial Newcastle tradesmen who met here to discuss the politics of the day.' Dovaston also draws the same picture. Calling on Bewick in 1823, he was directed to the Blue Bell, where he 'found him seated in an elbow chair by the fire, his dog at his feet'.

Clearly Bewick was not only a Radical, but a convinced one, and a leader of progressive thought in his home town. Like Cobbett, of whose *Political Register* he was a faithful reader, he had a deep vein of nostalgia for a peasant past; he was suspicious, too, of the idea of universal suffrage, though he pays warm tribute to Major Cartwright. Yet he would have rejoiced at the Reform Bill, which was passed four years after his death; and no less over the Catholic Emancipation. He himself, though a regular attender at St. John's church, was essentially a Deist; and an advocate of complete religious tolerance.

'Were our own government', he says (*Memoir*, 282), 'inclined to make this improvement in religion and politics, they would assuredly see the happiest results from it; it would soon be found that there would then be no need to keep Ireland in subjection, like a conquered country, by an expensive military force. The Irish, naturally acute, lively, generous and brave, would soon feel themselves, under our excellent constitution, as happy and loyal a people as any in the world, and as much attached to their country, which, for its healthy climate and fertile soil, may match with any other on this globe . . . Ireland ought instantly to be put on a par, in every respect, with their fellow subjects of the British Isles. To withold Catholic Emancipation from Ireland appears to me invidious and unjust; and if emancipated, it would be found at no very distant period that they would, under the forgoing tuition, individually become enlightened, think for themselves, adopt rational religious belief, and throw off the bigotry and superstition taught them with such sedulous care from their infancy, and by which they have so long been led blindfold.'

Bewick's love and sympathy for the Scots had its origin in the friendship with the Grays. His 'ardent wish for the perfect happiness' of Ireland also had its origin in a personal acquaintance. One of the portraits of Bewick is a miniature, painted by Dennis Brownell Murphy, who also painted William Charnley and, when in London, Wordsworth and John Crome. Murphy was for a quarter of a century an exhibitor at the Royal Academy. He had been a member of the United Irishmen, a friend of Wolfe Tone, Lord Edward Fitzgerald, and Napper Tandy. His wife was English, and after or during the troubles of 1798, he escaped from Ireland, first to Whitehaven in Cumberland, and then to Newcastle, to which town he no doubt came because there was a better chance of pursuing his profession. He was living over Richard Miller's bookshop in 1802, and in 1803 moved to London, carrying with him a letter from Bewick to his old friend Christopher Gregson in Blackfriars, commending him as 'a man of worth, and a first rate artist in the miniature line'.

One final connection with the world of politics lies in Bewick's connection with the Losh family. Bewick engraved book-plates for Thomas, George and William Losh. He also engraved banknotes for the Carlisle and Cumberland Bank, of which George was a director. It was George who first interested Bewick in schemes for unforgeable banknotes. The family was interested in the production of alkalis on an industrial scale, and helped to found the British chemical industry. William, the father, had in the 1780s entered into partnership in this enterprise with Thomas Doubledale and Lord Dundonald, and in 1791 was living in France, from which country he returned to set up plant using Leblanc's technique for the production of soda.

During the following year, a number of young Englishmen of revolutionary sympathies were also in Paris—among them James Watt, son of the inventor, with his friend Thomas Cooper of Manchester. These two were in France as delegates from the Constitutional Club of Manchester to the Club des Jacobins. Whether there on a similar errand on behalf of one of the Newcastle clubs or not, young James Losh, who later became Recorder of Newcastle, was also living in Paris for some months in 1792. 'His love of liberty', says Lonsdale (*Worthies of Cumberland*,) 'not less than a desire to improve his educational status, induced him to visit France during the throes of the great Revolution in 1792 . . . He attended the meetings of the Convention, heard Vergniaud, Danton, the Girondistes; and, being a handsome and conspicuous figure, and elegantly dressed, was an object of suspicion to people in the streets, one of whom he heard say—"Aristocrate! Quelle belle tête pour la lanterne!" '

Watt and Cooper, in the end, were denounced as spies by Robespierre, and fled home through Italy. Losh evidently fell, or feared to fall, under the same suspicion: but the 'patriots' of Newcastle seem not to have lost their belief in the French Revolution for all that, if Bewick's testimony is worth anything. His, at all events, remained quite unshaken after thirty years.

The Luddites in the Period
1779-1830

Strictly, the word *Luddite* applies only to a very short campaign in a very limited area for a very specific purpose—the campaign in 1811—12 of the stocking-makers and lace-makers of Nottinghamshire and district, with the object of preventing the 'frames' from being used for purposes which were detrimental to the trade and to their jobs and wages. But machinery was broken in other areas, before and after the campaign of the Luddites in Nottinghamshire. Sometimes the destruction was part of a wage dispute—'direct action'—in a period when trade unionism was weak or else actually illegal. Sometimes the destruction accompanied a strike, in order to prevent blacklegging: pitmen of the North-east would burn the pithead gear, or Welsh iron-workers would damage the furnaces, to ensure a complete stoppage.

Destruction of a new type of machinery, which endangered the jobs or reduced the standard of life of sections of the working class, is the best-known form of Luddism, using this word now in a broader sense to describe all machine-breaking. But this particular reaction to new machinery should not be dissociated from other reactions. The long period of the Industrial Revolution, when new inventions were applied piecemeal first to this industry, then to that, causing unemployment, dislocation and confusion in the older forms of industry aroused a great deal of discussion. There was a 'battle of ideas' going on: in books, pamphlets and newspapers, which we can still read; *and* in the pubs and trade clubs where workers voiced opinions which are lost to us because they were never put into print. This essay, then, will have to take into account not only the activities of machine-breakers of all kinds, but also the arguments that were being brought forward in the Industrial Revolution, for and against 'unrestricted Machinery'.

The valuable article by Eric Hobsbawm on 'The Machine Breakers' (*Past and Present* No.1, Feb. 1952) analysed the various types of machine-breaking. This analysis provided the background for this essay.

I

It is important to begin by establishing the traditional nature of machine-breaking in the course of industrial disputes. The examples of 'collective bargaining by riot', as it has been called, come mainly from the cloth-making industry, England's basic industry right into the Industrial Revolution.

The article by Eric Hobsbawm gives examples from the early part of the eighteenth century:

> 'Clothiers complained to Parliament in 1718 and 1724 that weavers "threatened to pull down their houses and burn their work unless they would agree with their terms". The disputes of 1726–7 were fought, in Somerset, Wiltshire and Gloucestershire, as well as in Devon, by weavers "breaking into the houses" (of masters and blacklegs) "spoiling of wool, and cutting and destroying the pieces in the looms and the utensils of the trade". They ended in something like a collective contract.'

> 'The great textile workers' riot at Melksham in 1738 began with workers "cutting all the chains in the looms belonging to Mr. Coulthurst. . . on account of his lowering of the Prices." '

This direct method of negotiation continued throughout the century. There are also examples from the coal industry. To these must be added other examples of direct action, for non-industrial purposes, such as the very extensive food riots of 1757, 1766 and 1795, all years of poor harvests and profiteering. These so-called riots prove, on a closer view, to have been well-organised demonstrations in force against millers, merchants and dealers who were hoarding corn or selling it in the markets at exorbitant prices. Destruction of machinery is not a feature of these movements, except that mills were sometimes damaged. Although a few arrests were always made and heavy punishments handed out, there was actually a good deal of public sympathy for the direct action that often succeeded in reducing food prices.

With this background it is not surprising that, as the Industrial Revolution developed and new machinery began to throw men out of work, direct action was resorted to.

At the beginning of October 1779 'a great mob appeared at Arkwright's spinning-house near Chorley'. This is actually mis-spelt 'Ashwright' in the *London Chronicle,* so little was he then known to London. 'The people defended the place with fire-arms. One was killed on the spot, and about fifty wounded; four of five are since dead.'

'On Monday several thousands returned there, armed with guns, scythes, etc., attacked and set fire to the building—it was burning on Monday at 12 o'clock at night . . .' 'The rioters, in flying parties, have destroyed a mill at Bolton, by the bridge; have been at Bury and Ratcliff, and are now going to Toddington, to destroy a mill there . . .'

Then there is news of military steps taken to quell this outburst. Troops were brought across from Yorkshire. The millowners armed their employees and former militia-men. In Stockport 'The Castle cotton works once more became a place of arms, and the embrasures filled with Sir George Warren's cannon, which commanded Manchester Hill, Stockport Bridge, and the ford of the Mersey.' After a week this revolt against machinery was subdued.

There are several points to notice about this episode. In the early part of the eighteenth century the cotton industry in Lancashire had a certain equilibrium: one weaver needed five spinners to keep him busy. Weaving was a man's job, a definite trade. But spinning, on the spinning-wheel, was for women and children; it was also a sideline in rural areas—dairy-maids and domestic servants would be set to spinning at slack times. Then the new flying-shuttle, applied to most handlooms by 1760, speeded up weaving and upset the equilibrium. In 1768 two new inventions began to be used. But they had very different effects. The spinning-jenny was a frame on which eight threads could be spun at a time; the number was later increased to as many as eighty. It was operated by hand, and was small enough for a cottage. It was no threat to the workers, but merely increased their output. It was therefore not opposed, but welcomed. But Arkwright's water-frame (a spinning-frame worked by water power) was essentially an invention for a factory worked by a mill-wheel. By 1776 Arkwright had three cotton mills working in Derbyshire. Then he came to Lancashire and built a new factory at Chorley, large enough to employ 500 men; and he was quickly imitated by others. It was this development that aroused the direct action of 1779.

The cotton workers of Lancashire were correct in seeing spinning-mills as a threat to their domestic industry. But in this case the result was not so serious as they had expected. The spinning-mills had been opened at a time of depression due to the War of American Independence, so the effect was immediately felt. But later, the foreign market expanded enormously and mechanised spinning increased the demand for weavers so that for a time Lancashire workers were kept busy. The spinning-mills did kill the rural spinning industry; but these scattered workers could not protest.

The next action against new machinery was in the woollen district of Wiltshire in 1802, when several factories were burnt down. This was merely a part of a campaign through the whole of the West of England and the West Riding against the introduction of gig-mills—machinery for raising the nap of woven cloth, replacing the teazle. Gig-mills had been in use on a small scale for many years, but the threatened extension of their use in 1802 was resisted by the shearmen, i.e. the men who completed the finishing of cloth by shearing the nap after it had been raised. The shearmen were also threatened more directly by the mechanical shearing-frame, carrying several pairs of shears, which could do their job in one-fifth of the time.

The shearmen refused to 'work after machinery'. In spite of the Combination Acts which made trade union activity illegal, the Wiltshire shearmen kept close contact with those in Yorkshire; and other trades all over the country supported them financially. The shearmen in Wiltshire put pressure on the factory-workers not to work with machinery; and some factories were burnt down. When some of the employers met a deputation of shearmen, and offered to refrain from using the machinery so long as shearmen were out of work in that district, the leader of the men 'declared he would rather be hanged than recommend the shearmen to accept Mr. Jones's offer, or to work after machinery'. Local sympathy was with the men. The Home Office was informed that 'there is good reason to think they are supported and encouraged by contributions from many of the innkeepers and other inhabitants of the place'. (A. Aspinall's *Early English Trade Unions* p.41)

A letter from a demobbed soldier to the local M.P. (quoted by the Hammonds in *The Skilled Labourer*) shows that the campaign was closely connected with the problem of unemployment. The War had temporarily ended, by the Treaty of Amiens. 'Now the contending nations are at peace with each other we are sent home to starve.'

'The burning of factorys or setting fire to the property of people we know is not right, but Starvation forces Nature to do that which he would not, nor would it reach his thoughts had he sufficient employ. We have tried every effort to live by pawning our cloaths and chattles, so we are now on the brink for the last struggle.'

The employers, in close contact as always with the Home Office, asked for help in breaking the combination. The shearmen's committee was arrested and several members imprisoned. A man was hanged for burning a factory. The large crowd at his funeral showed the public feeling against machinery that put men out of work.

II

The Yorkshire shearmen (or croppers) got gig-mills abolished in Huddersfield, and in other places in the West Riding employers were afraid to use them. When the employers in the West of England tried in 1803 to get Parliament to repeal various ancient restrictions on the trade—including a statute against gig-mills upon which the shearmen were relying—the shearmen counter-petitioned, calling on weavers and small manufacturers as witnesses on their side. In 1805 the shearmen, backed by weavers and small masters (39,000 signed a petition in Yorkshire) got a Bill introduced making gig-mills illegal, as well as restricting apprenticeship and limiting the number of looms to be used in any one house. The Bill was withdrawn pending the Parliamentary Inquiry of 1806, but when at last a new Act was passed in 1809 the Government had come down on the side of the employers. All this time gig-mills were gradually coming into use; and the ending of the War in

1815 and consequent increase in unemployment were taken advantage of by the employers in the West of England to speed up the mechanisation of the finishing jobs.

[In the West Riding gig-mills were in general use by 1811. Then shearing-frames were introduced on a large scale. The woollen trade was already in a state of slump owing to the blockade imposed against European ports by the Orders in Council.] In February 1812, while the Nottinghamshire Luddite movement (for quite different purposes) was coming to a close, the York-shire Shearmen started a similar campaign of destruction. Armed with large hammers, called 'Great Enoch' after the smith who made them, they entered finishing establishments and mills and broke up the shearing-frames.

The campaign was proceeding successfully. But in April a large-scale night attack on Rawfolds Mill, a finishing mill entirely converted to machinery, met with strong resistance from the mill-owner Cartwright, who had installed soldiers to protect the machinery. This is the incident described in Charlotte Bronte's *Shirley*. [Two men were left mortally wounded, and Cartwright's callous behaviour towards them (he was alleged to have left them without water or medical attention in the hope of forcing a confession about their accomplices) was, according to the Hammonds, largely responsible for 'the passionate desire for vengeance which diverted the movement from attacks on machinery to attacks on men'. Both men died game; the funeral of Sam Hartley was attended by thousands; the authorities took alarm and had John Booth buried secretly.]

A week later Cartwright gave evidence against one of his soldier-guards who had refused to fire on the crowd, and the soldier was sentenced to public flogging. As Cartwright rode home, he was shot at by two men—it was said that twelve men had drawn lots for the honour. The shots missed him. But ten days later another equally unpopular manufacturer, Horsfall, who had mechanised his factory and was an active enemy of the Luddites, was shot dead by four men. [Although this was a planned murder, so great was public sympathy for the shearmen that no informers could be found for many months.]

The campaign next took the form of raids on houses for weapons. The magistrates were afraid to act; the soldiers were impotent. The Government appointed a special body of soldiers to act as spies and make arrests and examinations, as though in enemy territory, but this yielded no results. Then a Mr. Lloyd, operating for the Home Office, developed a special method of his own which consisted in kidnapping possible witnesses until they gave him information. [At last, six months after the murder of Horsfall, Lloyd got on the track of an accomplice who turned King's evidence.] At the next Assizes a large number of men were put on trial for raiding for arms, destruction of shearing-frames, attacking Rawfolds Mill, and the murder of Horsfall. Seventeen men were hanged, and seven transported.

The above account is a mere skeleton of the extraordinary story which is told in detail in Frank Peel's *Risings of the Luddites* and re-told, with additional facts from Home Office papers, by the Hammonds in their *Skilled Labourer* (chap.xi). The disastrous twist given at Rawfolds Mill to what began as a campaign against machinery has tended to discredit the campaign of these Yorkshire Luddites. But the whole episode should be seen in the context of the abject poverty caused in the woollen trade by the later stages of the Napoleonic War, and the Government's intense efforts to repress the democratic political movement and all working-class activities.

The Nottinghamshire Luddites, the only genuine followers of the imaginary 'Ned Ludd', operated in 1811—12, their campaign coming to an end just at the time when the Yorkshire campaign began. There was no organisational link, for the purposes were quite different, though the methods had some similarity. As in the woollen industry, there was a tradition of machine-breaking in the course of industrial disputes. In 1778—9 the framework knitters of cotton hosiery tried to get a minimum wage established by Parliament. When their efforts were frustrated by the opposition of the employers (hosiers), stockingers from the villages swarmed into Nottingham and destroyed several hundreds of the hosiers' frames. The hosiers then agreed to a new price list. As the Hammonds comment: 'Rioting in fact had proved more successful than applications to Parliament.'

After a fairly prosperous period, when the whims of fashion favoured all kinds of fancy stockings, the trade passed into a state of depression in the later stages of the Napoleonic War—partly due to changes in fashion, and partly because foreign markets were closed by blockade. So the Luddism of the framework knitters, breaking out in 1811, was connected with the problems of low wages and unemployment, like all other nineteenth century examples of machine-breaking.

But the Nottinghamshire campaign was for a very special purpose. It was *not* directed against new machinery—there was no new machinery in the trade. This needs emphasising, since this particular misconception has existed since the first mis-statement was made in the House of Lords in the discussion on the 'Framebreakers' Bill'. Even Marx seems to have been misled about this. The sympathetic editor of the *Nottingham Review* made a very clear statement on Dec. 6th, 1811, about the purpose of the frame-breaking campaign. Owing to the depression in the hosiery trade, certain wide frames had been used by unscrupulous employers 'in making pieces which are cut up into gloves, socks, sandals or stockings'. The raw edges were stitched 'in the same manner as a tailor stitches a garment'. But, having no selvedge, the edges unravelled, and the whole hosiery trade had come into disrepute because of these 'cut-ups'. In the lace trade, too, a similar thing had happened. A poor quality lace, 'made up with STARCH', had been imposed on the customer with 'the gloss of the vendor's tongue'. In both cases, better-class employers were being undercut by 'adventurers' who were ruining the trade.

With these facts, the action of the framework knitters, both of hosiery and lace, becomes understandable. They were directly affected because, on

top of the general depression and high food prices, their own wages were
being cut down and one-fifth were unemployed. It seemed likely that the
lowering of the quality of the product would end by destroying the trade.
The workers saw themselves as protectors of the trade. A Luddite song,
quoted by the Hammonds, promises that Ludd will not 'sheath his conquer-
ing sword'.

> 'Till full fashioned work at the old fashioned price
> Is established by Custom and Law.
> Then the Trade when this ardorous context is o'er
> Shall raise in full splendour its head,
> And colting and cutting and squaring no more
> Shall deprive honest workmen of bread.'
> ('colting' = employing unapprenticed men)

Destruction of frames only began after negotiations and appeal to Parliament had failed. In fact, it began only after certain hosiers had practically
invited some such thing. For in the spring of 1811, at a conference between
some hosiers and stockingers, the hosiers agreed 'to give the men unabated
wages, provided they would join in bringing up the under-paying masters to
the same standard, and to put down cut-up work'. This significant statement,
quoted in *The Skilled Labourer*, comes originally from Gravener Henson,
who led negotiations on the men's behalf.

Soon after this, a very discriminating campaign of frame-breaking began.
Only the offending wide frames used for 'cut-ups', and lace-frames used for
the inferior kind of lace, were broken. In the whole main period of Luddism
(i.e. during March 1811, and again from November 1811 to February 1812) a
thousand frames, out of a total of about 25,000, were destroyed. One of
many accounts of the raids on houses, for the industry was entirely a
domestic one, is typical of the method:

> 'At Basford' (on Sunday evening) 'while three soldiers were in the
> house of one William Barns, to protect three frames, a party of Luddites
> entered the house and immediately confined the soldiers; and while two
> of the party stood sentry at the door with the soldiers' muskets, others
> demolished the frames; and when the mischief was done, the muskets
> were discharged and the soldiers liberated, the depredators wishing them a
> good night.' (*The Times*, 31/1/1812).

During the frame-breaking campaign, negotiations for higher wages were
conducted by an organisation which, in spite of the Combination Acts, was
practically a trade union committee. On December 28th, 1811, an agreed
price-list was published for the hosiery trade. In the meantime various hosiers
had increased wages to save their own frames from destruction. What was the
relationship between the frame-breaking campaign and these negotiations?

Gravener Henson denied any connection.

The Luddites were a comparatively small number of men, acting in a disciplined manner as guerrillas. They sometimes went armed, but the only casualty in the whole campaign was a Luddite, shot dead by a frame-owner. Like guerrillas in enemy-occupied territory, for the whole district was patrolled by troops, they were admired and cherished by the rest of the population. The Hammonds quote a clergyman who wrote to the Home Office:

> 'There is scarcely a stockinger who will not give half his victuals or his money to those "friends of the poor man" as they are styled.'

There were no betrayals, and the main argument used by those M.P.s and peers who opposed the 'Framebreakers' Bill' in February 1812, which imposed the death penalty, was that if the Government had failed to secure any convictions when the penalty was only fourteen years transportation, they were even less likely to succeed now that a man's life was at stake.

As for the efficacy of this method of direct action, the wage increases speak for themselves. The 'cut-up' trade was checked, and in February 1812, *before* the death penalty was imposed, the Luddites ceased their work. It was generally believed by this time that Parliament was now ready to listen to their complaints. An advertisement for a delegate meeting of framework knitters to formulate their statement ready for the expected Parliamentary inquiry begins:

> 'The troubled state to which the above places are reduced by the pressure of the times and the operations of the frame-breakers, having at length excited the attention of the Legislature. . .'

But all they got from Parliament was the death penalty. In the discussion on this Bill, Mr. Lamb, later Lord Melbourne, said:

> 'As to the disputes between the masters and the manufacturers' (hand-workers) 'I do not think it right to inquire into them as causes of the riots—such inquiry only tends to inflame the minds of the working-men, who generally conclude that they have rights which are infringed upon by the masters, and that they are justifiable in retaliating violence on them for the infringement of those supposed rights.'

The struggle for a living wage continued in Nottinghamshire, by trade union organisation (although still illegal), by negotiation, and by spasmodic frame-breaking. As in the case of the Yorkshire shearmen, the Luddite campaign was later marred by a violent incident with tragic consequences, which, by confusion with the earlier period, has discredited the true Luddite campaign of 1811—12.

The circumstances of this incident were altogether different. A certain Heathcote had built a factory for making bobbin-net by machine. Several other manufacturers pirated his invention and began to undersell him. He then reduced his wages which were, for the district, exceptionally good, by one-third. To prevent his underselling his rivals and so forcing them to reduce their wages also, some workers decided to break his machines. On June 28th, 1816, a night attack was made by seventeen men, and the machines were all destroyed. Unfortunately, a watchman who threatened to shoot was himself wounded, though not fatally. One man was identified, and was hanged. The crowds at his funeral show that the daring methods of the old Luddites still held their respect. Some time later, one of the other raiders gave away his companions, and six more men were hanged and three transported for life. It was this disastrous incident of 1816 which roused Cobbett to write his 'Letter to the Luddites'—an argument in favour of machinery, which is obviously written in complete misunderstanding of the issues involved. He admitted he did not know 'very clearly' what the dispute was about.

III

In 1816, in the depth of the post-war depression, there were other examples of machine-breaking, in this case of threshing-machines. But these occurred as part of a campaign of direct action against starvation, a series of 'riots' that began in late May and continued into July. What is noticeable is that on the whole these were successful in their limited objectives.[1]

In Suffolk, where there had been individual cases of rick-burning and breaking of threshing-machines, a crowd of people marched into the market town of Brandon demanding a reduction in prices of bread and meat. After some disturbances and violence, the leading inhabitants 'guaranteed the price of flour at 2/6 per stone, with an advance of wages of 2/- per head' until the millers would reduce their prices.

At Bideford in Devon, a crowd tried to prevent the export of potatoes from this little port. At Frome, crowds in the market prevented an increase in the price of potatoes. At Norwich, flour was taken from the new mills and thrown into the river. Pitmen in Durham went on strike against the high price of corn; but the magistrates, accompanied by two troops of soldiers, 'induced' them to return to work.

Into Downham Market, in Norfolk, came a demonstration of 1500 people, who entered all the shops of millers, bakers and butchers, and carried away their goods. Magistrates called in the cavalry and read the Riot Act, and the crowd dispersed. Next day the townsmen went out with the cavalry 'to meet the rioters, who armed themselves with guns, pitchforks, clubs and other weapons ready for a general attack'. But battle was avoided by the 'gentlemen' present making an agreement to advance wages and to release prisoners already taken; which victory 'induced them to return peaceably to their homes'.

At Ely 'an immense body of armed Fen-men' attacked a magistrate's house, and went round demanding money. Troops were called in to deal with this 'desperate insurrection', and in a pitched battle at Littleport the Fen-men were routed and many prisoners taken.

These actions did not involve machinery. But at Freshingfield, in Essex, 200 men 'armed with implements of agriculture as their weapons' destroyed the threshing-machine at one farm and at another 'a plough of a new construction that did not please them', and proceeded to a third farm to destroy another machine. At Hockham in Norfolk a threshing-machine was destroyed by a crowd of 100. While at Bury in Suffolk a hostile crowd demonstrated outside the premises of a hosier who had installed a spinning-jenny.

These riotous proceedings were reported, as they happened, by William Cobbett in his weekly *Political Register*. When they began he wrote:

'Some weeks back I observed that it was impossible for things long to go on quietly as they were then going on. I said that millions of people could not starve; that it was impossible for things to go on till the highways were strewed with dead bodies. . .

'It may be proper to call the offending persons "insurgents, savages, villains, monsters, etc." as the *Courier* newspaper does. But then, there are great numbers of Englishmen who are insurgents, savages, villains, mon-sters. There is no getting out of this dilemma. The fact is, they are people in *want*. They are people who have nothing to lose, except their lives; and of these they think little, seeing that they have so little enjoyment of them.'

Destruction of threshing-machines has a special significance, because it became for a time, together with rick-burning, the recognised method of struggle of the farm labourers. Threshing by flail was the main winter occupation when the weather was unfit for other jobs; without it, life in the villages became practically impossible for landless labourers. The threshing-machine was invented in Scotland about 1786 and came into use during the Napoleonic War when farmers could afford new machinery. Its obvious effect in the post-war depression was to drive people from the land, and in this way the threshing-machine added to the troubles of the handloom weavers in the towns. In 1810 Thomas Smith, sent from Glasgow by a committee of mechanics and weavers to give evidence to a Parliamentary Committee on the cotton trade, said that the number of cotton workers had been inflated by redundant farm-workers:

'I remember well enough two men were necessary for one plough, one man does that business now. I remember likewise when it took perhaps four men to thrash the corn, that is all done by machinery.'

In 1830 J.W. Greaves wrote in 'A Reply to Mr. Geary's Appeal to the

Weavers of Norwich' (i.e. an appeal to accept a wage-cut) that

'in consequence of machinery superseding the use of manual labour in agricultural pursuits, the country inhabitants have flocked into the city to weaving, and caused a redundancy of hands for the work'.

Norwich was a good place to observe the effect of machinery on agriculture. The handloom weavers, struggling against low wages and unemployment in their ancient trade which was hit, not by machinery directly, for their own organisation was strong enough to prevent this, but by the competition of the West Riding, could sympathise with the farm-labourers. When a number of these were brought into Norwich in 1822, after their campaign against threshing-machines, to be lodged in the Castle for the Assizes, a crowd turned out to greet them, and as the Suffolk Cavalry came out of the Castle again 'they were received with a shower of stones and brickbats, and were stoned completely through the city'.

These labourers came from the villages between Attleborough and Diss. For about ten days they had marched around, destroying every threshing—machine they could find. Magistrates and other mounted gentry dispersed them wherever they could, but the crowd would reappear in another parish, re-assembled by the sound of a horn. In the end they were overtaken in the village of Buckenham 'by a party of gentlemen, farmers and others. . . accompanied by the Eye (Suffolk) Yeomanry Cavalry. . . The insurgents scrambled over the hedges, and some into ditches; the pursuit was most actively carried on, and they succeeded in securing about thirty.' (*Norwich Mercury*, March 9th, 1822).

Destruction of machinery was not, of course, the only way of showing opposition to it. Attempts were made from time to time to get Parliament to pass restrictive legislation. None of these were successful. In fact, the aristocratic Parliament of the pre-1832 days was quite as determined as later Parliaments not to interfere in industrial matters.

In 1817 the Petition of the cloth-dressers of the West Riding against the use of gig-mills and shearing-machines was ignored. Mr. (later Lord) Brougham of the Opposition, said that 'to check the use of machinery' would be 'as unpolitic as it would be impracticable'. No one disagreed with him. In 1820 a Petition from the cotton weavers for a tax on 'a machine called a power loom' and for a fund to provide land for unemployed weavers, was turned down. David Ricardo, the economist, said the duty of the government was 'to give the greatest possible development to industry . . .'. The weavers' proposal would 'violate the sacredness of property, which constituted the great security of society'. In 1821 the ropemakers of London sent in a Petition with 700 signatures to say that machinery had put two-thirds of them out of work. They complained particularly of a machine called 'The Devil' which, employing only half a dozen men, could do the work of 97 men. But 'the work so done was extremely imperfect, and would of course

injure the character of that manufacture in foreign countries'. They therefore asked for a tax on the machine. All that happened was that Mr. Curwen
reminded the House that on a previous occasion they had decided that 'the
discouragement of machinery would be highly injurious to the country'.

In April 1823 the Manchester cotton weavers complained of their distress
caused by machinery. Mr. G. Philips 'denied that the weavers were injured by
the use of machinery', and Peel assured the House that after making inquiries
he was sure 'that the weavers could afford to live in comparative comfort'. A
month later the Stockport weavers sent a similar Petition. The local M.P. who
presented it declined to support it. Mr. Philips, who seemed incapable of
distinguishing between handloom weavers and factory workers, said that
'where machinery was used the wages were the highest. . .they were paid
more for managing machinery than for the mere labour of their own hands'.
Another M.P. referred with approval to Cobbett's 'very useful publication on
the subject of Machinery', i.e. his 'Letter to the Luddites' of 1816. But
Ricardo rebuked him by pointing out that in fact machinery, by 'throwing a
large portion of labour into the market' without creating a corresponding
demand for labour elsewhere did 'operate prejudicially to the working
classes'. All the same he 'would not tolerate any law to prevent the use of
machinery'. It is not surprising that the unresponsive attitude of Parliament
drove the working class at times to direct action.

IV

The next example of direct action against new machinery was the 'Power-
loom Riot' in Lancashire in 1826. The trouble began on April 18th in
Accrington, with the stoning of some manufacturers and the breaking of
windows at Sykes's power-loom factory. Large-scale attacks on power-loom
mills in the whole area then developed, and continued for a fortnight. The
first warning of trouble was an assembly of some thousands of handloom
weavers on a hill at Henfield, not far from Blackburn. People who saw them
march into Blackburn said: 'They came in good order and quietly into the
town; about 500 were armed with pikes, several with fire-arms (and these
were called captains); some with large hammers, and the remainder with
various weapons.'

During the whole campaign, which was executed in a disciplined fashion,
it was estimated that 20,000 men and youths, with some women, were
marching from place to place, dividing up at times to deal with several mills at
once. They would demand admittance, then storm the doors and make for the
weaving shop. Only power-looms were destroyed; spinning machines (no
longer a threat, since hand-spinning had already died out) were left alone.
Sometimes cloth woven on power-looms was also destroyed. But nothing
was stolen; on one occasion a man seen removing a strap from the gear was

firmly told by his 'captain' to put it back, 'for we have not come here to plunder'.

After the first shock of surprise, the magistrates and manufacturers took action. Urgent messages set troops of cavalry in motion, fetched from this place to that place, and then on to somewhere else; sometimes actually meeting and passing through enormous crowds of weavers en route. With Peterloo in their minds, the people stoned the soldiers when they tried to prevent entry into the mills. Only rarely were the soldiers able to save the power-looms from destruction, for with a planlessness that may not have been altogether unintentional, they usually arrived just too late, and the weavers would escape through windows on the far side of the building. However, this was not just a 'phoney war'. The soldiers did shoot on several occasions, and at Chadderton seven people were killed, including a woman who 'bled to death', and a large number of people were wounded. The magistrates, more enthusiastic than the soldiers, arrested many weavers, and in the Assizes that followed ten were sentenced to death, but sentence was commuted to transportation for life.

One magistrate, more kindly than the rest, tried to remonstrate with the men on their way to Chadderton. The gentlemen of the county had met, he said, and 'we are going to send people round to inquire into your situations, to inspect your habitations, and to see what you stand in need of'. The men answered: 'We are starving now, and our children are famishing at home. We have nothing to eat and nothing to do. Speaking will fill no bellies. We will break looms whatever may be the consequences, and if one half of us are shot, the other half will break the looms. Away! Away, lads!', and down the hill they rushed to the mill.

The revolt spread to Manchester, where meetings of 15,000 or more in St. George's Fields argued about the best course of action. A certain Jonathan Hodgkins, a journeyman spinner, who advised yet another petition to Parliament, was heckled with cries of 'We've petitioned long enough', and one man called out 'Will you let me eat at your table till the answer comes?' A majority decided for direct action against the power-looms, and several factories were attacked and one set on fire. Then the movement seems to have got out of hand. Individual weavers went round to shops demanding money or food; and numbers of common thieves and criminal elements started looting and robbing, so that for several days the city was in a state of chaos. But eye-witnesses distinguished sharply between the original action of the weavers and this later development.

Meanwhile the campaign in the cotton towns, having achieved its immediate object, was petering out. But before looking at the results of the campaign, the circumstances should be noted. 1826 was a year of depression, particularly in the cotton trade. Handloom weavers were already driven very low, partly by the direct competition of factory power-looms, and partly because their numbers were inflated by immigration from the countryside and from Ireland. There was a large pool of unemployed weavers, and those still at work were paid very low wages. The slump of 1826 meant that factory owners, to keep their machines running, employed still fewer handloom weavers.

Before the destruction of the power-looms began, Blackburn was known to be completely destitute. On April 5th the Vicar had appealed in the local paper on behalf of 'the afflicted poor at this time of unparalleled distress'. The Home Office had been informed on April 18th that 14,000 people, out of a population of 26,000, were only kept from actual starvation by the charity of others. Food prices were rising however. On April 18th a Mr. Whitmore moved in the House of Commons for a 'revision of the Corn Laws'. This motion was defeated by 215 votes to 81. So 250,000 quarters of imported wheat continued to lie in bonded warehouses, while the people starved.

In these circumstances, the campaign against the power-looms takes on the character of an unemployed demonstration backed by force. It was in fact seen in somewhat this light at the time. *The Times* on April 22nd called the riots 'one of the most usual and fearful consequences of famine', and while insisting that 'Property must be protected', *The Times* continued to comment on the day-to-day events with some sympathy. It noted with approval that 'a part of the master manufacturers have entered into resolutions to pay higher wages'. It criticised the Government:

'What has Government done? They have sent soldiers to quell the riot. Have they sent nothing else? It is hard to give men who ask for bread, bullets and bayonets, and only bayonets and bullets.'

Being an Opposition paper, *The Times* was pleased to report that 'the circumstance which appears to have driven the poor weavers at length to desperation is the extinction of all hope of an alteration in the Corn Laws. We have been informed by several manufacturers that they have heard a number of their weavers say they have been waiting to see what would be done as regards the corn laws. . .' When, after a fortnight of power-loom destruction, the Government reversed its own decision and released some of the bonded corn, *The Times* commented:

'This is the first indication of fear, or of feeling, on account of the distresses which have driven the manufacturers' (in this context the word means hand-weavers) 'into their present unhappy state of riot.'

Sympathy for the 'distressed poor' of the manufacturing districts was very general. The City of London, at a meeting presided over by the Lord Mayor and addressed by the Home Secretary and the Archbishop of Canterbury, raised £12,000 for 'relief to the working classes now suffering distress through want of employment'. In Liverpool a Town's Meeting was requisitioned to raise money for the unemployed weavers of Lancashire. At Yeovil in Somerset, then a wool-weaving town, money was collected specifically for the weavers of Blackburn, the centre of the riots. It seems, then, that far from being a failure, the campaign of direct action did draw attention to the needs of the unemployed weavers.

Sympathy was shown in other ways too. As hinted above, the soldiers called out to protect the power-looms and break up the crowds showed no keenness for the job. Most reporters noticed that the cavalry only struck with the sides of their swords, that the soldiers took 'every opportunity of expostulating with the mob', and that they refrained from shooting, even when stoned, or shot over the heads of the crowd. At Chadderton, where the fighting was most serious and the seven deaths occurred, the mill-owner, Mr. Aitkin, tried to stop the soldiers, while his wife had hysterics, and both of them 'have since said that they would rather have had their property destroyed than that the life of one human being should have been sacrificed'. In other words, while no doubt the real ruling class were more concerned with imposing the usual 'Law and Order', the weavers did succeed in winning a considerable amount of public sympathy.

These things should be taken into account in assessing the effect of the Power-loom Riot of 1826. The handloom weavers had little choice as to method. They had never had regular trade unions, and the new trade unionism that was now growing up in Lancashire was amongst the factory workers. In any case, with most of the handloom weavers out of work, the problem was really one of organising the unemployed. That such a degree of solidarity was achieved in 1826 is something worthy of respect. As for the actual object of the campaign, it was said that not a single power-loom remained in Blackburn or for six miles around. Total damage was estimated at a thousand looms, valued at £30,000. This is a reminder that the power-loom, although invented many years before, was only just beginning to take a hold on the industry. The destruction allowed a breathing space for the handloom weavers in the depths of a slump. It slowed down mechanisation for a short while, for apart from the expense of replacement the mill-owners proceeded with a little caution.

V

The campaign also brought to the fore the discussion about unrestricted mechanisation. Just as the campaign was subsiding, the *Bolton Chronicle* wrote:

> 'Machinery may be extended too far. And we think it incumbent on Government to lay a heavy tax upon it. It consumes neither food nor clothing; but the shopkeepers, publicans and others in the manufacturing

districts obtain the greater part of their livelihood by the money which the working people lay out with them from their wages.'

The proposal to tax the new machinery was popular with many manufacturers who could not afford mechanisation or saw no need for it. The new machinery was also opposed by ratepayers in general, who bore the burden of Poor Relief necessitated by the displacement of handloom weaving. The social upheaval caused by this displacement, with its possible dangers for established authority, was also in the minds of some.

These three trends came together at a meeting held in Rossendale, then still a woollen district, in November 1822, when the 'merchants and woollen manufacturers' condemned the application of steam or water power to weaving as 'unnecessary as it is uncalled for'. They deplored the 'evil consequences' to the numerous hand-working population, if machinery were not restricted. They viewed with 'painful apprehension' the increase of 'unnecessary machinery (which is calculated to rob the poor of their domestic employment, and thereby endanger the peace of the country)'. They strongly recommended legislation 'for the protection of manual labour', and thought that the best method would be 'an assessment upon power looms for the relief of the poor', the assessment to be laid by the Vestry upon the 'extra profit derived' by the use of power.

The resolutions passed at this meeting were later published in a pamphlet, the writer of which, probably the chairman of the meeting, enlarges on some of the arguments. Naively telling us that he himself is far from having 'radical principles', and that 'domestic employment and good morals are, in my opinion, the best cure for sedition and disloyalty', he goes on to distinguish between those 'mechanical improvements' which increase the employment of the 'labouring poor', and those which have the opposite effect. If power-loom weaving is adopted, what substitute is to be provided for handloom weaving? Until this question is answered practically, he says, 'the peace of the country may be endangered and a lawless rabble will make it a pretext for committing all the mischief in their power'. He then produces an economic argument:

'The pecuniary advantage which speculative adventurers may derive from the first introduction of power looms will be but temporary; and it will eventually recoil upon themselves, by overstocking every market, producing ruinous competition, and ultimately that want of employment which was so seriously experienced throughout the manufacturing districts not three years ago.'

This fear of a glut on the market—plenty in the midst of poverty—appears in other pamphlets. In 1832 G.C. Burrows wrote 'A Word to the Electors' (of Norwich) 'on the Unrestricted Use of Modern Machinery', in which he asked

'How is it that starvation stalks among us while plenty stares us in the face? . . . Machinery is the hydra of the present day, starvation is her offspring, and as long as the land is cursed with unrestricted machinery, machinery vying with itself, the inhabitants of the whole earth cannot consume the produce. Every market must be glutted, the industry of the human race be of no avail . . .'

He points out that 'nations compete with nations, machinery with machinery; to get this gold, mankind are slaves to things inanimate . . . their sustenance, to make cheap goods to meet this competition, reduced to just starvation point'. He blames Machinery for having reduced wages and caused unemployment, and he warns that human subsistence can be driven very low indeed. Already in Scotland 'cabbages and barley form the principal article of diet; in the North of England, rye, oats and vegetables; in Ireland, potatoes; to the same fare the people here (Norwich) are fast approaching.'

However, his gloomy picture is relieved by a vision of an alternative:

'Societies of men can form communities of common stock, have all things in common, and use machinery, no one aggrieved, all equally receiving the benefit of its use—all equally enjoying the leisure by it produced—all will find time to cultivate the arts, the sciences, philanthropy, philosophy . . .'

So far it might seem that the ratepayers, non-mechanised employers, and mere on-lookers were more vocal than the distressed handloom weaver himself, who was more likely to take to direct action than to reasoned argument. But this impression is mainly due to the fact that the middle classes had easier access to the printing press. Discussions of working men in this period were not normally recorded. We get a little nearer to their point of view when they themselves are associated with other sections in their protests. In 1827, for example, the 'manufacturers, workmen and others' of Frome, a centre of woollen weaving in Somerset, sent petitions to King and Parliament on the distress caused by new machinery in their trade. They begged for the prohibition of

'gigs, shearing frames, and the whole mechanical apparatus for dressing of cloth, power and single handed spring broad looms, and a newly invented machine called the mule . . . because they are of no real advantage, either to the manufacturers or the purchasers of woollen cloth, while they operate most fatally on the labouring classes, and have already deprived upwards of sixty thousand honest and industrious men and their families of their customary employment.'

In a pamphlet they make a clever appeal to many interests. Smaller manufacturers find the market glutted by the machine-made goods and have to sell at a loss. Craftsmen like dyers, carpenters and smiths, are put out of their trade because the 'great manufacturer' employs his own finishers and maintenance men. Shopkeepers lose by the general depression. Farmers and landowners are hit by the heavy Poor Rate. At last we come to the 'minor and subordinate classes of the people', otherwise known as 'the labouring poor'. This pamphlet, for its own polemical purposes, gives a somewhat idealised picture of a Past that has been destroyed by Machinery, a Past in which every weaver 'had boiled or roast meat almost every day, a firkin or two of fat ale in the pantry, and a brawny chined grunter in the sty'—a state of prosperity, one should add, that was only attained because 'every man, woman and child in the woollen trade had their hands full of employment'.

But now, says this pamphlet, not only are the weavers, their families and journeymen, out of work, but because of this they are not able to pay the rents of their houses with weaving shop attached. Four hundred of these houses lie empty, while in others two or more families of weavers have crowded together in their poverty. In an outburst that rings true, the writer of this pamphlet attacks the school of thought that preaches the 'march of the intellect';

> 'With the haggard and woebegone skeletons of our once happy neigh-
> bours every where around us, this heartless and inhuman cant about "the
> march of intellect and mechanical ingenuity" is as disgusting as it is
> wicked.'

It becomes obvious that opposition to the new machinery was based on the observed results of Capitalism: unemployment and under-employment, the ruin of the home market in the interests of profit, the squeezing out of small capitalists by their big brothers. For lack of economic and political theory, the blame was laid on machinery as such—or, more accurately, on the *unrestricted use* of machinery. Yet technical progress itself was accepted, provided it was adapted for use by the hand workers themselves, e.g. the flying shuttle on the loom, or that the dislocation caused by it was temporary and soon overcome, e.g. the spinning inventions which increased total production of cloth and provided more employment in the towns—though, it is true, at the expense of the rural industry.

The power-loom was in a different category because it not only competed with the handloom weaver but made his product uneconomic. However many more hours the weaver and his family toiled, they still could not compete with two looms run by power and watched over by a mere girl. Yet the handloom weavers still hoped for some mechanical invention that would put them on equal terms with the power-loom, as the following story shows. Somewhere about 1828 John Harvey Sadler, an inventor and engineer, came from London to Manchester to demonstrate his power-looms on which he had patented certain improvements. But the factory he was visiting had no steam-engine yet, so he fixed the looms temporarily to work by hand. A rumour quickly went round the mill, and very soon round the whole city, that he had invented a pair of looms that could be worked by one man. A deputation of handloom weavers came to see the new looms.

'But never shall I forget how their countenance fell at the first sight of them; they saw they were steam looms, and they found new enemies where they had hoped to find friends. The deputation remained with me nearly three hours, during which I heard a full recital of all their grievances . . . '

From that moment Sadler became 'a decided adversary to power weaving' and he promised the weavers that he would try 'to contrive machinery to give them all those advantages they so much needed'. The deputation told Sadler of attempts already made to adapt their looms by 'fixing one warp above the other in the same loom, so as to weave two webs in one loom; but it was found on trial that a man required to have double strength to weave double work that way.' One of the men said that 'he with others had bought power looms, hoping that with the aid of a fly wheel they should be able to contend against their masters with their own weapons; but the action of turning a fly wheel with only two looms attached was found too laborious for any one man to stick to the whole day through, and so that attempt failed, as indeed did many others which at that time were thought of and tried.'

Sadler kept his word. In 1830, after 'many a sleepless night', he patented a pair of looms that could be worked by one man by means of a pendulum mechanism. A weaver who had tried it wrote in the *Star* newspaper that it required only a knack which could be easily learned; he was confident that now the handloom weaver would be able to compete with steam-power. The only advantage at that time of steam-power in the factories was that a girl could watch two looms; the looms themselves did not, it seems, operate more quickly than the handlooms.

Sadler next demonstrated the looms in Huddersfield, where they caused a great stir amongst the handloom weavers, who foresaw the extension of power-weaving into the woollen trade. They were sure that Sadler would be induced to sell his looms to the factory-owners. To relieve their minds Sadler called a delegate meeting of woollen workers in the West Riding. Amongst others on the platform was Richard Oastler, champion of the factory children. Here Sadler pledged his support for the handloom weavers in their struggle against machine-made cloth. With his looms, he believed, with the inventor's usual optimism, that 'every hand weaver's cottage in England' could have an income of 12/- per week. He intended also 'to bring back to cottage labour' everything connected with spinning, and he held up a model spinning machine worked by 'a rotary motion produced by the backward and forward stroke of a pendulum'. To an enthusiastic audience he expressed his belief that 'a fair division of the benefits of all this grand machinery hitherto invented for, and operating to, the injury of man (Hear! Hear!) will now, I feel certain, be brought to be conducive to his wants'. (Cheers).

He believed, he said, that he had shown 'the men of ingenuity in Britain' that there was 'another road for them to exercise their abilities on . . . The old road leads to the people's destruction, but the new one to their comfort and happiness . . .' He hoped to live to see 'every weaver and every spinner in the kingdom, and all others connected with them, happily employed in their cottages, with their families around them in comfort and peace'.

This, then, was the ideal in the minds of the hand workers of the early 19th century—an ideal that, at the theoretical level, can be classed as backward-looking, Utopian, and fundamentally anti-socialist. But if we approach it from the earlier period, without our own acquired knowledge of later developments, we can sympathise with the aspirations of these hard-pressed human beings, for whom the sun of Socialism based on mechanised industry had not yet risen. Clearly, the handworkers had no hatred of machinery and inventions if only they could be harnessed to the simple needs of the working people.

The end of this story is pathetic. The poverty-stricken handloom weavers could not afford to buy new looms. Sadler tried to float a company with a capital of £282,350 to supply one million looms at 1/6 per week rent. But who could be expected to invest money in an invention that could be outdated by the simple expedient of improving the power-looms themselves?

There was an ugly side to Mr. Sadler's abortive invention. At the time when weavers were still optimistic about it, i.e. in 1831, Thomas Worsley of Stockport wrote a testimonial for Sadler which included the following passage:

'The Saxon weavers . . . will find themselves eclipsed. France . . . will be an importing country. The extensive manufactures at Syria, Armenia, and Persia, and even the Chinese will be equally paralized, as are the calico weavers now in Hindostan; and the Pacha of Egypt, with his power-looms, will have the world to begin again.'

Increased production under Capitalism, whether by power or by hand, would be at the expense of other peoples of the world, and particularly of the defenceless colonial people. At the very time when Thomas Worsley was gloating over this prospect, the 'calico weavers of Hindostan' were dying of starvation. In 1834-5 the Governor-General of India reported: 'The misery hardly finds a parallel in the history of commerce. The bones of the cotton weavers are bleaching the plains of India.' (quoted by Marx, *Capital* vol. I, chap. 13.)

Worsley was perhaps an unimaginative man, easily impressed by national-istic arguments. But his attitude was not typical of the hand workers of the period. It is to the credit of the victims of 'unrestricted machinery' that, in spite of incessant propaganda from the capitalists, they refused to see foreign workers as their enemy. Against the argument that machinery *must* be introduced into British industry in order to do the foreigners down, they put the ideal of a fully developed home market based on the well-being of the workers themselves. Continually they gave the warning that the uncontrolled introduction of machinery at the expense of the hand workers was simply ruining the home market. An anonymous pamphlet published in York in 1826 answers the criticism 'What! Would you stop the progress of science and let foreigners have the advantage of us?' by saying:

'I call it a meagre sort of science, or at any rate a gross misapplication of science, if it is to be directed towards the starvation of a deserving and once-flourishing population . . .' (and as to the advantage to be gained by foreigners) 'The advantage would not be gained over *us*, it would be gained over the mercenary views of a few capitalists.'

This shrewd distinction between 'us' and 'a few capitalists' seems to be characteristic of the 1820's. The pamphlet published in 1827 on behalf of the 'manufacturers, workmen and others' of Frome (referred to above) draws a clear line between themselves and 'our great manufacturers' who alone could afford to instal new machinery in new factories. A pamphlet of 1825 called *Manual Labour versus Brass and Iron*, written by a Lancashire weaver after reading an advertisement of a 'Self-acting Mule' asks the question: 'What ADVANTAGE is to be expected from this invention?' and answers it by saying that 'The Capitalists, after having accumulated princely fortunes from the united industry of the working classes' now hope to be able to dispense with their labour altogether.

VI

In 1830 arguments on paper gave way again to direct action against machinery. In a mass campaign beginning in Kent in the early autumn and spreading through the whole of the southern counties and South Midlands, agricultural labourers destroyed threshing machines, burnt corn-stacks, and forced farmers to raise their wages.

The bare facts cannot do justice to this extraordinary episode in English history, when the down-trodden villagers of a dozen counties, without any previous organisation, rose up and forced a living wage out of the gentlemen-farmers. Neither can the mere statement that as a result 9 men were hanged, 457 transported to Australia and 400 imprisoned in this country, convey much idea of the magnitude of the movement. [2]

Every observer seemed agreed about the desperate poverty of the farm-labourers. When the campaign was still confined to Kent, *The Times* quoted with approval a leading article in the *Kent Herald*:

'The fact is that the labouring classes have been long borne down, oppressed in every way by their superiors, and by the political system upheld by their superiors. They have been gradually thrust down and trampled on, despised, driven to starvation, misery and despair . . .' (and while the farmer has become a gentleman, so that 'an insuperable barrier has been raised between the "parlour" and the "kitchen" ' the labourer has become merely 'a labouring animal on the estate').

(Oct. 30th)

As late as Dec. 6th *The Times* wrote: 'Let the rich be taught that Providence will not suffer them to oppress their fellow creatures with impunity.' But by December 18th the Government had already put the first batch of 300 of its fellow creatures on trial at Winchester.

During the autumn it had become obvious that on the whole the farm labourers had the sympathy of all classes in these counties—except for the most rabid believers in poverty as the natural state of the poor. Landowners like Lord Winchilsea spoke for them in the House of Lords, while locally the landed class mostly acted as mediators between the labourers and their employers, the farmers. The small farmers showed their opinion by refusing to act as special constables to prevent the riots. Even the farmers who were forced to sign agreements to pay higher wages were not unwilling to coop-erate with the men in inducing the vicar to reduce his tithes. It was also noticed that in many cases the farmers had offered no real resistance to having their threshing-machines broken, and in fact had often put them out ready.

This was mainly a campaign to get wages raised to 2/6 per day, or 2/- in the poorer counties, by what can only be called mass deputations. In Sussex, particularly, whole villages, including the better-off craftsmen, turned out and demanded the attendance of all the farmers, who were then asked to sign a new wages agreement. In some places the unpopular Overseer of the Poor was run out of the parish in a dung-cart. Although in some counties money was demanded at the farms when threshing-machines were destroyed (the 'charge' was normally £2 for their trouble!) absence of personal violence was a feature of the whole campaign, the only casualty being a labourer.

In some places there was destruction of other property. In Wiltshire where the domestic woollen industry was a dying trade, a woollen mill containing machinery was damaged, the leader of the attack saying 'he was going to break the machinery to make more work for the poor people'. A cloth factory was also destroyed. In Hampshire a factory making threshing-machines was destroyed, and two workhouses were sacked, the sick inmates being guarded from harm. In Buckinghamshire, papermills at Aylesbury employing machinery were attacked by unemployed men. The reason for the destruction of the threshing-machines was—as in 1816—because they took away the main winter employment. The men believed that if all the machines in the area could be got rid of, no farmer would suffer from competition from the quicker method, and threshing by flail could continue; the farmers seem often to have agreed. So the remarks of Mr. Baron Vaughan, one of the judges at the Winchester trials, were particularly asinine:

'The same argument which justifies or recommends the destruction of the threshing-machine could also apply to the abandonment of the use of the flail, the spade, the hoe, the axe . . .'

This ridiculous assumption that the working people were so stupid as to hate machinery as such is found in pamphlets of the time. Even Cobbett, the champion of the working people, had been guilty of this mistake in his 'Letter to the Luddites' of 1816—which explains why the Society for the Diffusion of Useful Knowledge had his pamphlet re-published in 1831. This Society, whose main job was the diffusion of the kind of knowledge that it was useful for the ruling class that the working class should have, also published in 1831 a 200-page booklet explaining to the ignorant working men how civilisation had gradually been built up by the invention of more and more tools, and how, if they now destroyed all tools and machines, the country would be reduced to a state of savagery! And in the meantime, if the foolish mob continued to destroy machinery, 'capital would make itself wings and fly away to other countries, where men still acted as reasonable beings'.

Why was 1830 the last occasion of machine-breaking on any considerable scale? Why was there no machine-breaking after 1826 in the basic cotton industry? The cruel sentences imposed on the farm labourers might help to account for their acquiescence in poverty after 1830, though six men of Tolpuddle were not intimidated. But this explanation does not hold good for the industrial North. Neither does the theory that the handloom weavers lost heart, and gave up the struggle for survival, fit the facts—unless Chartism is also, like Luddism, to be dismissed as a movement of despair! The eventual triumph of mechanised industry, and the assimilation of the handloom weavers into other jobs, does not account for the transitional period of the 1830's and 1840's.

The explanation may be as follows: Machine-breaking, whether seen as part of an industrial struggle or as an unemployed campaign against the machine itself, was merely one form of the struggle against poverty. But there were many other possibilities opening out for the working class by the 1830's. In the first place, trade unionism was legalised in 1824, and quickly became the normal method of struggle of the new factory workers. This could not fail to influence the methods of the older type of hand workers also, and in the 1830's we find Committees established in hand-weaving districts for the specific purpose of campaigning for legislation to regulate wages, as in Kilmarnock, or to protect the handloom industry, as in Bradford. Committees representing handloom weavers were not a completely new thing, for they had been formed from time to time before the passing of the Combination Acts to get petitions signed and sent to Parliament, or to negotiate with the employers; in Norwich the Weavers' Committee was a power even during the period of illegality.

In the second place, the method of 'direct action' could be diverted to other aims. The 457 exiled farm-labourers had scarcely left the shores of

England before mass demonstrations, leading later to destruction of property, began in industrial centres—for the Reform Bill. A few years later, the industrial North was destroying workhouses, provided under the New Poor Law of 1834 very largely to drive the victims of the Industrial Revolution into the factories.

In the third place, apart from these examples of direct action, there were the mass campaigns that developed in the 1830's with the object of obtaining certain specific legislation—the Short-time campaign to reduce factory hours for children to ten per day; the campaign for the repeal of the New Poor Law; and later, the development of the Chartist movement for political rights. Handloom weavers took part in these campaigns, and in these different ways they were helping themselves.

If these campaigns were a valuable political experience for the working class, and a step forward in the class struggle, the earlier phenomenon of Luddism in all its forms had helped to provide the pattern of solidarity and mass action.

REFERENCES

(1)   Since this essay was written A.J. Peacock's *Bread or Blood* has described the events of 1816, in East Anglia, at length

(2)   The story has been written with great sympathy by the Hammonds in their *Village Labourer*, where they comment that 'Most of the agricultural population . . . had made itself liable to the death penalty, if the authorities cared to draw the noose.' Since this essay was written a fuller and more up to date account has been written—*Captain Swing* by E.J. Hobsbawm and George Rudé

YURI V. KOVALEV

Chartist Literature

This essay is a translation by Joan Simon of the Preface to *An Anthology of Chartist Literature (Moscow 1956)*, edited by Yuri V. Kovalev, a lecturer in English and American literature at Leningrad University.

At the close of the 1830's there arose in England a powerful workers' movement—Chartism, which V.I. Lenin characterised as 'the first broad, truly mass and politically organised proletarian revolutionary movement'.[1] Those taking part in this movement called themselves 'Chartists', since they were fighting for the adoption in law of the Charter, a document drawn up by the originators of the movement. The Charter consisted of six points, the chief of which was the demand for universal suffrage.

The introduction of universal suffrage would not, of course, have brought complete emancipation for the English proletariat, as the Chartists hoped, but it might have prepared the ground for social revolution. Marx and Engels particularly underlined the significance of the basic point of the Charter at this time: 'The introduction of universal suffrage would be, for England, a victory embodying much more socialist spirit than any measure to which this honourable title is applied on the continent.'

By the mid-nineteenth century England had outstripped other countries in economic development. Large-scale capitalist industry was already in existence. The concentration of production, and correspondingly the concentration of the proletariat, had reached important dimensions. 'There exists in England', wrote Marx and Engels, 'the most numerous, concentrated and classic proletariat.'[2]

The English working class had acquired solid experience of economic and political struggle before the close of the 1830's. Participation in the fight for the electoral reform of 1832, and above all its outcome, had brought home that the interests of the working class were incompatible with those of the bourgeoisie. Hence arose the striving for an independent class organisation which, under the influence of deepening contradictions between labour and capital, took the form of Chartism.

The Chartist movement lasted for about a decade and a half. It had its high points and periods of decline. The times of stormy upsurge (1839, 1842, 1848) alternated with periods of falling away. There were moments when a fearful English government called out the army and 'honourable' bourgeois organised 'volunteer police detachments' which marched through the London streets 'just in case'. Then mass legal proceedings were instituted against the Chartists, accompanied by severe sentences.

There were dissensions within the Chartist movement owing to its heterogenous composition (particularly in the early stages of development), and the lack of a clear scientific understanding of the whole struggle and its methods. The Chartist movement was a typical struggle of the proletariat at a time 'when the workers' movement and socialism existed separately from each other and went their particular ways—and in every country such lack of contact led to the weakening of socialism and the workers' movement'.[3]

During this first noteworthy emergence of a workers' movement the English proletariat threw up many talented political leaders, orators, journalists, poets and prose writers, whose productions were printed in Chartist newspapers and periodicals. Their creative legacy, which reflects all the specific features of Chartist ideology, constitutes an independent literary trend.

Chartist literature has a firm place in the literary history of the nineteenth century. It rested on the tradition of the democratic literature of the close of the eighteenth century, in particular the works of Godwin and Paine. In origin it was connected with the poetry of the great progressive romantics such as Byron and Shelley, the work of the best radical poets of the '30's and '40's, with popular workers' poetry and the Methodist hymns widely known among the people. As Chartist literature developed these links did not weaken but rather grew stronger.

The Chartist movement and its writings enriched English literature with new themes, extended its scope, drew the attention of writers to aspects of the life of the people which had hitherto remained relatively obscure. Indeed, the very broad scope of the proletarian movement and its reflection in literature compelled writers to see life from a new angle. This helps to explain the inspired insight of such literary masters as Dickens, Thackeray and Elizabeth Gaskell; those 'eloquent and graphic portrayals of the world' which have 'revealed more political and social truths than all the politicians, publicists and moralists put together'.[4]

The work of the Chartist writers belongs to the progressive sector of mid-nineteenth century English literature which conducts an energetic struggle against the material and spiritual oppression of man by capitalist society. There were many divergences and disagreements between the critical realists, 'New Poets'[5], Chartists and other groups in this sector, and controversies were not infrequent. Caustic remarks aimed at Dickens or

Thackeray are to be found in Chartist newspapers, while the work of Charlotte Bronte and Mrs. Gaskell was often simply ignored. But much more significant is the fact that all were drawn to a humanist defence of human dignity. Each in his own way rebelled against social injustice and strove for human happiness. The sharing of this high aim enables us to unite them in one democratic camp despite important divergences in ideology, on political questions and artistic method.

The tradition of Chartist culture, revived by the socialist movement of the 1880's and carefully preserved by the English proletariat, is alive to this day. Prominent progressive writers in England revert to it. In his recently published book on Meredith, Jack Lindsay, appraising the progressive English poetry of the mid-nineteenth century, rightly notes that its lifegiving fire was kindled by Chartist torches.[6]

It is regrettable that there has not been any major study of Chartist literature as a whole. But this is not surprising in view of the known difficulties, the main one being the lack of a systematised collection of the relevant materials. During the century which has elapsed since the time of the Chartist movement not a single attempt has been made to assemble the work of Chartist poets and prose writers. Only in the last few years have progressive English historians shown some activity in this direction.[7] Thus the present anthology constitutes a first attempt to collect in one volume those writings of Chartist authors which are most characteristic and have the greatest literary significance.

The study of Chartist literature is still further complicated by the fact that there are comparatively few named professional poets, such as Ernest Jones, William Linton, Gerald Massey and some others. The kernel of this body of literature consists of the productions of worker-poets who either sign their work with pseudonyms, or initials, or not at all. An enormous number of such anonymous works was published in the central organ of the Chartists, *Northern Star,* and in *Northern Liberator, Friend of the People, Chartist Circular, Red Republican* and other Chartist periodicals.

During recent years some of the pseudonyms and initials have been deciphered. It is now known, for instance, that 'Spartacus', 'Bandiera', 'Terrigenus' were the pseudonyms respectively of Linton, Massey and O'Connor, and that the initials J.W. and S. cloaked John Watkins and Samuel Kydd. But the majority have not yet been deciphered and the writers of unsigned pieces also remain unknown.

I

The rise of Chartist literature must be assigned to the years 1838-9, that is to a period when the relatively wide dissemination of Chartist ideas had begun and the first published organs of the movement had appeared. Early Chartist literature was primarily journalistic. It comprised exhortations to the people by Chartist leaders, descriptions of the position of the workers, articles, reports of lectures, speaking tours and meetings. Chartist poetry and literary prose developed somewhat later. Though early Chartist publications had 'Poet's Corners', or poetry sections, these usually featured the work of the revolutionary romantics (above all, Shelley and Byron) and popular workers' songs which were often reprinted from the democratic publication of the 1830's, *Poor Man's Guardian.*

Of the greatest interest among early journalistic departures are the fiery messages of George Julian Harney in the London *Democrat.* In 1839 Harney led the London Democratic Association which Engels called 'the radical fraction of the English party of the movement in 1838-9'.[8] 'This radical fraction', wrote Engels, 'consisted of Chartists, proletarians . . . who clearly saw the aim of the Chartist movement and strove to speed its realisation. While the majority of Chartists were still thinking only of the transfer of state power into the hands of the working class, and only a few had yet managed to think about the use of this power, the members of this Association, which played a major part in the ferment of that time, were unanimous on this question. They were for the most part republicans who proclaimed the constitution of '93 as the symbol of their faith and rejected any union with the bourgeoisie including the petty bourgeoisie, who upheld the view that the oppressed are entitled to use against the oppressor all means which the latter employs against them.'

In the very first number of the London *Democrat,* organ of the London Democratic Association, Harney made a call to the people which he entitled 'The Friend of the People to the Enslaved, Oppressed, and Suffering Classes of Great Britain and Ireland'. Harney was unconditionally on the side of revolutionary coercion, that is, in Chartist terms, he belonged to 'the physical force party'. Though he thought of the winning of the Charter only by revolutionary means, his conception of struggle itself was conditioned by the state and level of the Chartist movement in its early stages. He saw revolution in the guise of a march by an army of a million 'people of the North' supported by the most revolutionary section of the London proletariat. He clearly underestimated the role of proletarian revolutionary organisation.

To give Harney his due as a writer, he was a magnificent publicist and a master of the stylistic resources of the language. He could grip the reader with the revolutionary elan of his appeals: in this he was probably without equal among the Chartists. Many of his articles and writings, which may now seem somewhat naive and pompous, at the time carried away thousands of people. His work undoubtedly deserves close attention as an example of Chartist journalism. Among other publicists of this period Rider and Combe deserve mention.

In succeeding years Chartist journalism expanded so greatly, and made such deep inroads into other genres, that it is not easy to define its limits. The range of subject matter extended considerably. In Chartist publications articles-can be found on almost any subject, from the inhuman exploitation of child labour in the factories to socialist utopias. But whatever Chartist authors wrote about, their point of departure was invariably the Chartist movement and its concrete problems. All Chartist publications, without exception, printed political surveys, open letters to politicians and the editors of bourgeois newspapers, sociological articles, literary sketches and essays, historical sketches and the speeches of Chartist orators.

Chartist journalism gradually attained maturity of thought and disclosed the phenomena of social and political life more profoundly and fully. Marx and Engels contributed to the journals edited by Harney and Jones; their influence is apparent in many articles by Jones himself and by certain other journalists.

The literary characteristics of Chartist journalism were determined to a considerable degree by the nature of the audience authors were addressing. As a rule this consisted of tens of thousands of workers, gathered at Chartist meetings. Chartist journalism grew, as it were, out of public speaking. If early journalistic articles were often reports of speeches at meetings, later ones retained much of the oratorial style, energetic expression, emotional appeal, characteristic of public speaking. Simplicity, clarity of thought and expression, concreteness and vivid imagery in language, these were the stylistic characteristics of Chartist journalism.

II

In 1838-9 poems by members of the Chartist movement, as yet few in number, began to appear in the pages of *Northern Star*. These were the first swallows heralding the luxuriant flowering of a poetry of the masses. From a literary point of view Chartist poetry is a complex and specific phenomenon. It consists for the most part of poems and songs written by those who had little literary experience. But, though the general artistic level of Chartist mass poetry is comparatively low, Chartism gave rise to some poets of natural talent whose work has aesthetic significance.

A characteristic feature of Chartist poetry was its unusually topical quality, an ability to respond instantly to any events in English political and social life, whether an act of parliament or a sentence on Chartist leaders. The Chartist poets themselves saw poetry above all as a means to struggle. This determined to a considerable degree the content and genre of their poetry, which consisted in the main of songs and hymns intended for collective performance at Chartist meetings.

For the first few years Chartist poetry was predominantly imitative in character. The models taken were usually popular workers' songs, more rarely hymns, and certain works of Shelley, Byron, and other democratic poets of the early nineteenth century. But with the development of the movement themes connected with particular events multiplied. One such was the Chartist uprising in Newport (Wales) in 1839 which was rigorously suppressed by the government. The tragic fate of the leaders of this rising—Frost, Williams and W. Jones received the death sentence, 'graciously' commuted to penal servitude for life—and the death of others who took part, for long figured in the works of Chartist authors. By every post editors of Chartist newspapers received a pile of letters, acrostics, sonnets, epitaphs, odes, dedicated to the participants in and leaders of the Newport rising. Many of these never saw the light; even so, those which were printed would fill a book. By no means all were of equal literary merit. The best examples—Watkins' tragedy of John Frost and a cycle of sonnets by an unknown author who used the pseudonym 'Iota'—are printed, in part, in this anthology. The 1839 rising demonstrated to Chartist poets and prose writers what limitless material the movement provided for creative artists.

A satirical genre in poetry began to develop comparatively early. Chartist journals and newspapers printed witty and caustic epigrams, couplets, verses, satirising reactionary politicians, corrupt bourgeois judges, the avarice of the ruling classes, the absurd philanthropic pretensions of sensitive gentlemen and so on. In these verses the edge of satire was not infrequently turned against the Chartists themselves; the poet Sankey, for instance, accused them with bitter sarcasm of passivity and vacillation and demanded action. In the course of the revolutionary struggles of 1848-9 Chartist poet-satirists stood as one man against European reaction and the English government which had taken up 'a position of non-intervention'.

In the process of development themes were enriched and ideas ripened. Already in the mid-1840's there is a rapid broadening of subject matter. A feeling of responsibility for the fate of the country and its people enters Chartist literature and international motifs find a greater place.

Among the poems of this time are many testifying to a lively interest in democratic movements in other countries. The Polish rising of 1830-1, the rising of 1846 in Cracow, American abolitionism, the revolutionary ferment in Ireland, the tragic death of the Cuban revolutionary and poet Placido—such events found the most lively response in Chartist poetry, prose and literary criticism. No less interest was shown in the democratic literature of Russia, Germany, France, Poland, the U.S.A. and other countries. The revolutionary events of 1848-9 in Europe gave a particularly strong impetus to internationalist tendencies in Chartist literature, as indeed the movement as a whole. These tendencies, resting as they did on the activity of the society, the Fraternal Democrats with its not very clear programme, were still far from proletarian internationalism, but they undoubtedly constituted a step on the way.

In the final years of Chartism poetry gradually lost its mass character. The periodicals of this time published the work of comparatively few authors, the names of Ernest Jones, Linton and Massey occurring most frequently. In effect, the very character of Chartist poetry changed. Short poems, songs, couplets, hymns, gave place to lengthy poetic cycles and monumental epics. In conditions of a general decline of the movement there was evidently a demand, not for the previous 'topical' poetry, but for examination of the road that had been travelled, for an artistic generalisation of the experience of long social struggle; this compelled poets to master a more 'capacious' genre. These years saw the writing of 'New World' and the cycle of poetry from prison by Jones, Linton's 'The Dirge of the Nations' and the cycle 'Rhymes and Reasons against Landlordism', and the best work of Massey—i.e. those works among the legacy of Chartist poetry, which are the most mature on the plane of ideas and have the most literary merit.

III

The history of Chartist literature covers not only efforts to find new themes but also a complex quest for a new artistic method. The vital material newly entering literature, the new view of the world and its processes, insistently demanded from Chartist authors new ways of depicting reality in artistic form. The process of working out a literary method was very difficult, contradictory and essentially remained incomplete. We now have the necessary historical perspective to determine the direction and fruitfulness of the search by Chartist writers for new methods.

Early Chartist poetry leaned heavily for its method on the revolutionary romantics. The Chartists knew perfectly, and valued highly, the poetry of Byron and Shelley, particularly the latter. 'Shelley, the genius, the prophet', wrote Engels, 'Shelley and Byron with his glowing sensuality and bitter satire upon our existing society, find most of their readers in the proletariat.'[9] The works of the two poets were continually printed in popular Chartist newspapers and lines from their revolutionary songs were inscribed on banners and placards carried at mass demonstrations and meetings. Naturally, the works of these great revolutionary poets were the most frequently imitated in Chartist poetry. Among early Chartist poems more than a dozen recall to a surprising extent the 'Song to the Men of England', various passages from 'The Mask of Anarchy', 'An Ode to the Framers of the Bill against Frame-breakers' (1812), 'Song for the Luddites' and other poems by Byron and Shelley. As an illustration the 'Ode' of the Chartist poet Sankey, included in this anthology, may be compared with Shelley's 'Song to the Men of England'.

Chartist poets were attracted by the angry élan of Byron's rejection of the bourgeois world, his fiery preaching of revolutionary 'war to the knife', and by the great historical optimism of Shelley's poetry. To survey the whole output of early Chartist literature is to recognise the predominance of a typically romantic view and portrayal of the world. This is natural enough:

the very character of the Chartist movement and ideology in 1838-9, when Chartist literature was born, disposed towards an artistic perception of this kind. The same applies to literary prose, the first examples of which appeared somewhat later. Early Chartist novels, including 'Confessions of a King' and 'Novel about the People' by Jones, are still far from a consistently realist conception and depiction of actuality.

The sharpening of the struggle and the development of the movement reinforced the realist tendency in Chartist literature. But it only became predominant after 1848 when the historic experience of the revolutionary movements in Europe gave Chartist writers a deeper understanding of social reality and the laws governing the class struggle. It was precisely on this foundation that Chartist literature achieved new realist conquests, expressed in the selection and characterisation of phenomena, in a new approach to depicting man and reality.

The character of realism in mature Chartist literature is one of the most complex problems for the student of the Chartist legacy. It must be remembered that Chartist authors were searching for methods at the period of the highest development of English critical realism. The fame of Dickens, author of *Pickwick Papers, Oliver Twist, Nicholas Nickleby,* and *Martin Chuzzlewit,* had spread far outside England, and all England was reading Thackeray's 'Snobs' published in *Punch.* The struggle the great realists conducted against the Victorian survivals of romanticism reached its highest point in 1847-8. It was in these years that the best works of the 'brilliant pleiad' saw the light: Dickens' *Dombey and Son,* Thackeray's *Vanity Fair,* Charlotte Bronte's *Jane Eyre,* and Mrs. Gaskell's *Mary Barton.* Appearing within such a short interval of time, these novels delivered a concentrated blow against anti-realist and anti-democratic art. During these years critical realism became the dominant trend in English literature.

The powerful and rapid advance of realism could not fail to influence Chartist authors. The Chartists were attracted by the force of Thackeray's satirical exposures and by the inspired mastery and vast humanity of Dickens. Passages from the works of these two writers were often reprinted in Chartist newspapers and journals and some Chartist authors attempted to imitate them. But the Chartist attitude was not confined to admiring the talent of these two authors and approving their realism; it was considerably more complex than this.

The artistic approach of the critical realists simultaneously attracted and repelled the Chartists. They keenly appreciated the democratic outlook of Dickens, accounted him a writer of 'their' camp and eagerly popularised his works. They recognised Dickens as a people's writer and on this plane put him on a level with Burns, the highest honour Chartist critics could confer. 'The cause of the people is a sacred cause', wrote *Northern Star,* 'and . . . Dickens upholds this cause against the cruel, hypocritical, ungodly and unnatural theories and actions of the ruling classes in society.' The same newspaper wrote elsewhere: 'Dickens is the poet of the poor. Prouder position, greater glory for now and for all time no man could hope to acquire'. (10) Chartist newspapers urged readers 'to get and read without fail' one or other of Dickens' works. At the same time the Chartists were undoubtedly disillusioned by Dickens' attempts to reduce all social conflict to a clashing of abstract concepts of good and evil. The fears expressed by Dickens and Thackeray of the revolutionary workers' movement were alien to them. They were put off by the conciliatory note in the work of the great realists.

Aware of the necessity for a realist art the Chartists attempted to work out their own realist method. They did not produce any kind of literary manifesto, and there is hardly any work specifically concerned with literary theory. The critical sections of Chartist publications were usually filled with articles popularising the creative heritage of the great democratic poets and writers of the past; less frequently they included reviews of new books. But articles of this type often posed questions of creative method, the connection between literature and the class struggle, democracy and humanism in literature.

IV

At the beginning of the 1840's *Chartist Circular*, organ of the Scottish Chartists, published a very interesting series of articles under the general title 'The Politics of Poets'; among these are to be found, as well as essays on literary history, not a few fiery phillipics against bourgeois critics with an affirmation of the Chartists' attitude to the role of poetry and the poet in the social and political life of country and people. A good example is the first article in the series, included in the present anthology. But only towards the close of the '40's did questions about the content and purpose of art, the tasks of poetry and the poet's role in the social struggle, popular literature and the civic duty of the writer, become a subject of the liveliest interest and general appraisement in the pages of Chartist periodicals and newspapers. Jones wrote on these matters in his articles in *The Labourer*, Linton's poetic works were concerned with them ('The Poet's Mission', 'The Dirge of the Nations'), as later was Massey who published a whole series of articles of literary criticism in *Red Republican* and *Friend of the People*.

To bring together and analyse the statements of Chartist critics, scattered throughout book reviews, critical articles, notices etc., is to form a good idea of the demands the Chartists made on literature. Briefly formulated these were: literature must truthfully depict the conditions of the people and their struggle for emancipation; literature is one of the most powerful weapons in the people's struggle and in turn is nourished by the ideas which arise in the course of this struggle; the true popular writer is one able to express in his works the thoughts and feelings of the people and the 'spirit of the age'.

Clearly these demands guided Chartist literature along the path of realism; whether the Chartists wished it or no, a realist method was established in their literature under the strong influence of the novelists of the 'brilliant pleiad', and this was very fruitful. While this influence enriched Chartist literature it did not become overwhelming. The Chartists strove for a realism of a new type. They strove to retain the best features inherited from the revolutionary romantics, particularly their fighting, offensive spirit and looking to the future.

In the quest for methods, however, the creative achievements of the Chartists tended to lag behind their aesthetic theory. Though in theory they understood the need for a new realist art, writers of prose and poetry were unable fully to work out concrete forms. The Chartists, therefore, only succeeded in making the first steps towards a new literary method. Chartist literature, like the movement itself, was in existence for too short a time to succeed in this direction. But the fact that these first steps were taken is of immeasurable significance in literary history. The Chartists were the first to . set out on the long and difficult road travelled by greater and lesser writers, for different lengths of the way at different times. Some, having started along it, have almost immediately retreated. Others have followed this road, throughout their creative career. This was the road taken by the writers of the socialist movement of the 1880's (William Morris and others), by Bernard Shaw and Ralph Fox. Some, with a scientific view of the world, have gone directly ahead. Others have wandered and turned aside, but the general movement continues. Today many progressive writers of contemporary England, inspired with the ideas of socialist realism, are taking this road.

Unfortunately Chartist literature attained a relative maturity of method only at a time when the movement itself was beginning to decline, and Chartist poetry was losing its mass character. The later literature consists essentially of the work of a few poets and writers, the most important of whom are Ernest Jones, William Linton and Gerald Massey.

V

Of these three poets only one, Linton, went the whole way with the Chartist movement, though he was less actively engaged than Jones and Massey. His poems, signed with the pseudonym 'Spartacus', appeared from time to time in different Chartist publications, from 1839 onwards, but his full talent developed later, in the period of crisis preceding the revolutionary upheavals of 1848-9. Some of the works he wrote at this time are correctly evaluated by historians of Chartist literature as the best examples of Chartist poetry and belong to the golden treasury of this literature. Such, for instance, is the well known poem 'Labour and Profit', included in the present anthology.

The revolutionary struggles of 1848 greatly stimulated Linton's creative activity as poet and publicist. With other Chartist poets he believed that the force of revolutionary example could inspire the Chartist masses, and therefore did his best in every possible way to draw attention to the events in France, Italy, Hungary, etc. An enormous number of articles and poems by Linton, dealing with the revolutionary events in Europe, was published in *Northern Star*, and the journals *Democratic Review* and *Republican* in 1848-9. The questions covered are far-reaching and many-sided. The hunger riots in Ireland, the heroic defence of Rome, the bloody reprisals of the French bourgeoisie against the Parisian proletariat, the theories and social practice of the French Utopian socialists, the position and tasks of Chartism in England—such is a far from complete list of the questions touched upon in Linton's work during these years.

In 1849 Linton's great poem 'The Dirge of Nations' appeared in the journal *Republican*. The theme—the poet and the social struggle—is common enough among Chartist poets but here it was treated in a specific way. Linton posed the question confronting the Chartist poet in 1849: what is the poet's role in a period of defeat of the revolution? At the centre of this poem, which in structure closely resembles Shelley's 'Prometheus Unbound', stands the figure of a poet-Titan, chained to a rock and witnessing with anguish the general triumph of reaction.

Before his eyes pass, in funeral procession, whole peoples, bearing to the grave the heroes who fell in the revolutionary battles of 1848; he remembers the bloody 'feats' of Metternich, Cavaignac and Nicholas I; he sees the Austrian army tearing to pieces freedom-loving Italy, and bourgeois England taking up the cowardly and shameful position of 'non-intervention'. Everywhere there is gloom and desolation. Everything is dead. Was the struggle worth while?—asks the poet. And, above all, what is to be done next? The conclusion the poet reaches is important not only for himself but also for many of the leaders and participants in the Chartist movement, confused in face of the harsh measures of reaction; the struggle continues, it is the poet's task to seek out, rally, the living fighters and with them prepare a new assault on the tyrants' strongholds.

The events of 1848 compelled Linton to re-examine many of his former views. Particularly important for him, as poet and Chartist, was the fact that the experiences of 1848 completely destroyed illusory hopes about universal suffrage, which the Chartists had thought to be the single necessary condition for the social emancipation of the proletariat. The bankruptcy of the idea of 'legal revolution' became obvious in these years. Linton began to understand that they should envisage the sweeping away of the bourgeois system as such, instead of attempting to establish justice within the framework of this system.

This new outlook found expression in his practical political activity and in his creative work. Many aspects of reality which he had earlier conceived of in isolation—as separate social vices, more or less accidental 'class abuses'— now appeared to the poet as elements in a whole system; they were linked by profound internal ties. It is in the light of this new understanding of reality that he constructed his long poetic cycle 'Rhymes and Reasons against Landlordism', written in 1850-1 and published in part in *Red Republican* (later called *Friend of the People*) and in part in *English Republic* which he edited himself from 1851.

This cycle includes poems which, in title, have nothing to do with landlordism; 'Emigration', 'Free Trade', 'The Workhouse' and so on. In fact Linton's conception of 'landlordism' had a specific content, which may be defined as follows: the system of social relations in the epoch of industrial capitalism. It is with the concrete manifestation of these social relations that the different poems are concerned.

Almost all have some lines referring directly or indirectly to the growth of revolutionary activity among the masses. In addition, the class struggle is the central theme of a whole series of poems. The poet depicts the spontaneous and organised class struggle as a phenomenon brought into being by capitalist relations, the poverty and exploitation of the masses. In some poems Linton attemps to forecast the outcome of this struggle, drawing pictures of a bright future, of free labour as the symbol of the greatest happiness man can attain.

But, though he recognised the need to destroy the bourgeois system, Linton could not show his readers the way to achieve this aim. The limitations and immaturity of Chartist ideology, as also the peculiarities of his own world outlook formed under the influence of the ideas of the bourgeois enlightenment and of utopian socialism, helped to draw Linton towards petty-bourgeois republicanism; further than this he did not go, though he understood to a certain extent the inadequacy of its programme.

In literary ability, Linton was inferior to Jones and Massey. He lacked the robust poetic imagination of the former and the eminently graphic thought of the latter. His poems, somewhat dry and very rational, reflect a lack of emotional range. Certainly 'feeling' has an important place in Linton's poetry, the more so in that his basic genre was the political lyric, but for him feeling is more an 'emotion of the brain' than an 'emotion of the heart'. Only in his later works did Linton overcome the dryness and rationality of his poetic manner. In this connection 'The Dirge of the Nations' marks a great achievement, as also do some verses of the cycle 'Rhymes and Reasons against Landlordism' in which thought and feeling are organically fused in artistic form.

VI

The most important Chartist poet was Ernest Jones. He had unusual energy and an inexhaustible fund of creative power. When it is remembered what an enormous amount of his time was taken up with speaking tours, addressing meetings, editing and publishing, the extent of his literary production is astonishing. Within two years (1846-48) he wrote and published several dozen poems, two long poetic works, two novels, some ten articles of literary criticism, and historical research on popular uprisings in Europe, not to mention innumerable articles in *Northern Star*.

As a young man Jones was passionate, sincere and easily swept off his feet. These qualities often led him to uphold impossible enterprises; thus he was carried away by the idea of organising a world republic by bringing together peoples of different races—so realising the slogan of the Fraternal Democrats, 'All men are brothers'—and later he popularised O'Connor's land scheme. But in the midst of these enthusiasms he always retained a rational kernel which progressively came to the fore. Thus, his first enthusiasm led to the practical activity of organising international proletarian connections which inevitably brought him into the ranks of the Communist League, his second led on to agitation for nationalisation of the land.

Despite the fact that many of his ideas were contradictory and Utopian, and many of his early works imitative, the writings of Jones bear the stamp of a great talent and, at times, an inspired insight into life. Hardly any other Chartist writer could transmit so forcefully the people's resentment and anger, their passionate desire for emancipation. The highly emotional quality of Jones's poetry was conditioned by his deep understanding of the thought, feelings and aspirations of the people. But this emotional quality never degenerated into empty pretentiousness, since he himself took part in leading the people's struggle and his poetic thought reflected the ideas and feelings engendered by the ebb and flow of the Chartist movement. His towering collective hero—the people, who create colossal wealth but struggle in the grip of want, who suffer and fight on—is one of the clearest embodiments of the new spirit of proletarian self-consciousness and class solidarity brought to birth by Chartism.

In 1846-7 Jones wrote a series of poems dealing with the winning of the Charter by force, the international solidarity of the workers, the national liberation movement in Poland and Ireland, O'Connor's land plan and so on. The year 1848 was a turning point for him, as it was for Linton. The experience of the revolutions on the continent and of the Chartist movement in England brought home that the social emancipation of the proletariat within the framework of Chartism was impossible. The necessity for social revolution became obvious to him.

Jones's change of outlook is illustrated in his great poem 'The New World', written in the prison to which he had been consigned as one of 'the most dangerous Chartists'. The poem is allegorical. The action takes place in Hindustan, but it is not difficult for the reader to realise that it is about England, the fate of the English people. In content this is specifically a poetical history of the class struggle in England and its chief hero is the people. After describing 'past ages', Jones looks to the future and depicts a people driven to desperation overthrowing the rule of the bourgeoisie. The final episodes of the poem, which paint a utopian picture of a free society, indicate that the poet has not yet fully overcome the limitations of the Chartist movement. Only later (1851-54), under the direct influence of Marx and Engels, did Jones approach a marxist understanding of the laws of social development. During the period of mass strikes and the fight to call a Labour Parliament he produced work noteworthy for its maturity and artistic depth.

In addition to many poetic works—such as 'The Prisoner to the Slaves', 'The Song of the Future'—Jones wrote several novels and stories: 'Women's Wrongs', 'De Brassier: A History of the Democratic Movement', and others. All these provide evidence of a deepening of the realist tendency in his work and the influence of the 'brilliant pleiad' of English realists, which in his case proved very fruitful.

In the poems he wrote in these years are to be found surprisingly 'plastic' images of people, sometimes whole peoples. In the lines of his verses people 'live' in the full sense of the word, live the complex, wide-ranging, emotionally tensed lives of participants in, and makers of, history. Jones had a magnificent feeling for, and mastery of, language. He succeeded in developing a style which conveyed a feeling of the epic grandeur of events, the titanic power of a people in revolt. No other Chartist poet attained such a wealth of rhythm, such variety and perfection in rhyme, so exact and acute a use of words. The literary significance of Jones's work far transcends the limitations of Chartist poetry. He was an outstanding English poet of the nineteenth century, worthy of a place among the most talented pupils and heirs of Byron, Shelley and Keats.

Jones was not only poet, novelist and publicist. From his pen came also a considerable number of articles of literary criticism, written for the most part in 1847-8, in which he formulates certain principles of Chartist aesthetics. These articles were mainly concerned with questions of the cultural heritage, the popular roots of literature, its progressive direction, that is those qualities which, in his eyes, were indispensable to artistic creation. Most of these articles were either literary surveys of a period or special treatments of eminent foreign writers (Russian, German and Polish). An article about Pushkin, in this anthology, is of particular interest. Though there are some factual errors, in general it gives a correct appraisement of the great poet, whose work Jones greatly valued for its popular roots, progressive tendency, hatred of the oppressors of the Russian people and ability to express 'the spirit of the age'. It is interesting to note that, by contrast with all Pushkin's biographers at this time, Jones blamed the Russian autocracy for the poet's death.

As a literary critic and theorist Jones had wide horizons and great erudition. His critical articles often contain an element of research and are directed to clarifying the path of literary development. At the same time they have a frankly propagandist quality and touch in passing on innumerable topical questions of a social and political nature.

VII

The last great poet of Chartism was Gerald Massey. He came from a working class environment and had himself suffered all the horrors of factory work; in this sense his experience of life was richer than that of Linton or Jones and his hatred of the exploiters was of a more emotional, less rational, character. A theoretical interpretation of his own sympathies and antipathies, an understanding of their social character, came later when Massey became an adherent of Chartism.

Massey developed as a Chartist poet when the movement was in its final phase. He strove, with Harney and Jones, to revive Chartism and his works during the period 1850-54 were devoted to this end. He had great poetic talent. His works are marked by strength of emotion, expressiveness and richness of language. He was one of the popular poets of his time and such works as 'The Men of '48' are not inferior in literary merit to the best poems of Jones and Linton. It can only be regretted that Massey's talent did not develop to the full, did not find full expression in his work. He might have become a poet of great stature had his convictions been more stable, his outlook more independent. By contrast with Jones and Linton he lacked the roots of long practical experience in the English workers' movement. In addition he had no systematic theoretical education. Hence the element of superficiality and vacillation in his outlook.

The years 1850-54 were the most fruitful period in Massey's creative life. Swept along by the revolutionary fervour of 1848 he joined the Chartist left and became one of the most active contributors to Harney's journals *Red Republican* and *Friend of the People*. In these were published a number of poems which testify to his talent, the most important of which are included in this anthology.

Massey's verses are full of symbolical terms and allegorical images, for which he usually drew on biblical tradition. This is to be explained by the fact that he highly valued the literary heritage of the English bourgeois revolution of the 17th century. Indeed to Massey the greatest poet of all time and all nations was Milton, to whom he specially dedicated verses and poems. In this respect Massey was no exception, for the revolutionary tradition of the 17th century was widely diffused among the Chartists and the tendency to express revolutionary ideas in symbolic biblical form is to be found in much Chartist literature. But Massey's tendency towards complex symbolism and allegory often went beyond the framework of tradition. The cause of this clearly lies in the poet's unstable world outlook, in the lack of clarity among the English proletariat of the mid-19th century as to the character of the class struggle. Only in this light is it possible to explain the unnatural parallels drawn in his articles and poems; when, for instance, he compares the contemporary Chartist proletariat with the Israelites emerging from slavery in the land of Egypt, or draws parallels between the activity of Christ and Ernest Jones.

Considerable interest attaches to Massey's articles of literary criticism, published in Harney's journals and usually signed with the pseudonyms 'Bandiera' and 'The Spirit of Freedom'. In his literary assessments Massey took as his point of departure the principles formulated by Jones in the late '40's. His articles were concerned with the creative work of the leading democratic poets, but he did not confine himself to English literature. For instance, he wrote articles about Petőfi, then almost unknown in England, Dupont, Freiligrath and others; attempting to show the revolutionary significance of their work, underlining its positive social features and extolling their devotion to the popular cause. But even in this case Massey did not for long uphold the Chartist position. He gradually moved away from the revolutionary democratic programme to preach the incompatibility of art and politics.

In the mid-1850's Massey became transformed into a prosperous and acknowledged bourgeois poet and broke entirely with the workers' movement. But his best works have not been forgotten. They are known and loved in democratic England to-day; the progressive writer Jack Lindsay used one of Massey's poems as an epigraph for his novel 'The Men of '48'.

VIII

The prose of Chartist authors is greatly inferior to their poetry. Prose writings, though regularly printed in Chartist publications, fell well below the literary level of the poems. As in the case of poetry, so also Chartist prose reflects the struggle between basic trends in Chartism. Thomas Cooper came forward with stories upholding Christian morality, O'Connor wrote stories about the land plan which set out to prove the superiority of a small-farm economy, Watkins published in the *London Chartist Monthly* a whole series of stories on the theme of the oppression of the workers and peasants by the ruling classes.

Beside these comparatively insignificant authors stood two important Chartist prose writers, Thomas Wheeler and Ernest Jones, whose works portrayed the awakening social consciousness and political activity of the people. The Chartists' prose advanced in a questing way, as did their poetry, but perhaps to an even greater degree. The achievements of English critical realism were gradually mastered but the works of Chartist writers have a central figure quite other than the hero of a Dickens or a Thackeray. This new hero is the revolutionary fighter who joins battle with the enemy for social justice.

Chartist prose writers usually attempted to portray great popular movements. They saw the revolutionary struggle as 'the most moral theme of the age' and firmly upheld belief in it as the fundamental way to gain social happiness for the people. Since they did not neglect criticism of the contemporary social structure, they combined a critical portrayal of bourgeois-aristocratic society with the idea of the revolutionary class struggle; and in this they had an unquestionable advantage over the representatives of English critical realism.

Many prose writers, Jones in particular, portrayed revolutionary movements of the past, and sometimes imaginary social clashes, with the aim of warning the Chartists against possible mistakes. This coincided with the general aim of Chartist literature, to prepare the people for struggle and show them the way forward. Examples are 'Novel about the People' in which Jones recounts the struggle of the Poles for national independence and social justice, or his series of sketches 'A History of Popular Movements'. On this plane Chartist literary prose is closely analagous to the innumerable sketches, articles, notes about revolutionaries of the past—by Paine, Milton, Cromwell, Robespierre, the Decembrists and so on.

Chartist prose writers saw it as their main aim to disseminate the experience and clarify the tasks of revolutionary struggle. But many did not succeed in presenting these ideas in artistic form and there resulted a mechanical conjunction of political tract and sentimental story. The lack of organic unity between the form, the subject and the idea of a work necessarily detracts from its literary value. There are many 'Works' of this kind and only comparatively few of the novels and stories written by Chartists have literary merit.

Such, in very general outline, was the literature of one of the greatest proletarian movements of the nineteenth century. It is naturally impossible, in a brief article, to examine all aspects of this literature, but the reader may judge of its complexity and variety from the material in the anthology.

REFERENCES

(1) *Lenin on Britain* (1959 ed.), 395
(2) *Collected Works, vi,* 246
(3) Lenin, *Collected Works, vi,* 343
(4) Marx & Engels, *Literature and Art* (New York, 1947), 133
(5) Horne, the young Browning, Bailey, Smith, Dobell and others
(6) J. Lindsay, *George Meredith* (London, 1955)
(7) See *Ernest Jones: Chartist,* Selections from the writings and speeches of Ernest Jones, with an introduction and notes, edited J. Saville (London, 1952)
(8) *Collected Works, vi,* 30-31
(9) *The Condition of the Working Class in England in 1844,* trans. F.K. Wischnewetsky (1950 ed.), p.240
(10) *Northern Star,* December 21st, 1844

ALFRED JENKIN

Chartism and the

Trade Unions

Thomas Cooper, a journalist who had begun his working life as a shoemaker, once went to report a Chartist meeting in Leicester. Walking home with a group of Chartists after the meeting he was struck by the noise of stocking-frames which were still working although it was very late at night. He asked: 'And what may be the average earning of a stocking weaver?' and was told: 'About four and sixpence.' Cooper tells us: 'That was the exact answer; but I had no right conception of its meaning. I remembered that my own earnings at a handicraft had been low, because I was not allowed to work for the best shops.' Cooper replied: 'The wages are not too bad when you are in work', but the Chartists said: 'What are you talking about? You mean four and sixpence a day: but we mean four and sixpence a week.' The anecdote is illuminating since it shows that besides the 'two nations' into which England was divided according to Disraeli's *Sybil* each of these was itself subdivided into groups which knew little of one another. The weavers came to look upon themselves as a class of doomed men, who had been abandoned even by their fellows who had gone to work in the factories. At the same time the wages of the power-loom weavers were depressed by the existence of a vast army of domestic workers, since they knew only too well that if they asked for too much there were others to take their place.

There were of course groups of skilled workers in London and elsewhere whose standards were still relatively good, but they were a small minority of the working class and their position was very precarious. An apologist of the manufacturers was obliged to admit that male workers in the cotton mills reached their maximum earnings between the ages of 31 and 36 and female workers between 36 and 41, and few mule spinners were to be found at work after the age of forty.[1]

These random examples are given in order to illustrate the point that the working-class during the industrial revolution was far from homogenous. The economic and social conditions of different groups of workers differed widely. It is important to understand this if the different attitudes to trade unionism and to Chartism of workers in different trades and industries at different times is to be properly understood.

Trade Unionism had ceased to be illegal in 1824. 'From that day Labour became a power in England.'[2] Lord Melbourne, Home Secretary and afterwards Prime Minister in the Whig Government of the Reform Bill, wrote on 26 September 1831 to Sir Herbert Taylor, Private Secretary to King William IV: 'When we first came into office in November last, the Unions of Trades in the North of England and in other parts of the country for the purpose of raising wages etc., and the General Union for the same purpose, were pointed out to me by Sir Robert Peel in a conversation I had with him upon the then state of the country, as the most formidable difficulty and danger with which we had to contend; and it struck me as well as the rest of His Majesty's servants in the same light.'

The Trade Union Movement of 1830-4 was not a mere flash in the pan, but was the culmination of a series of struggles which had gone on since 1825, and had been preceded by earlier movements during the period of illegality. It is true that the General Consolidated Trades Union had been joined by many thousands of workers who joined such an organisation for the first and last time in their lives, but there was also a core of experienced trade unionists. The collapse of the Grand National Consolidated Trades Union gave rise to all kinds of defeatist moods. More deep reflection, however, showed that the real reason for the defeats of 1834 was the failure of the workers to gain political power, a lesson driven home by the savage sentences on the Tolpuddle Martyrs and the New Poor Law of the same year. This was not something which had been immediately grasped, for the rules of most unions forbade the discussion of political and religious topics. These rules had partly been designed to safeguard the unions at a time when even economic activities were illegal, but they were also a survival from the epoch when it was considered foolish and dangerous for poor men to concern themselves with politics. Only gradually was this prejudice broken down, largely as the result of the activity of such pioneers as William Lovett the cabinetmaker and Robert Hartwell, a compositor who survived to take a leading part in the agitation for the second Reform Bill of 1867. These leaders and others came together in the London Working Men's Association of 1836, which established contact with similar bodies throughout the country and drafted the document known as the People's Charter.

The ensuing twelve months were the scene of an ever-growing agitation, culminating in the meeting of the Chartist Convention in London and the presentation of the National Petition to Parliament. The petition was, however, rejected and the Convention was driven to consideration of the question of what was to be done next. The Chartist leaders had no precedents for their guidance, since there had never been an independent movement of the working class anywhere in the world. It is true that the previous ten years had seen two successful agitations, for Catholic Emancipation and for the Reform Bill, but the classes which had led them were now opposed to the

Chartists. A section of the Chartists, principally in Wales, were ready to resort to arms, but this was hardly the attitude of the majority. The most effective policy seemed to be that of a general strike or 'Sacred Month' such as had already taken place at Glasgow in 1820 and which had been actively propagated by William Benbow of Manchester since 1832. The Convention was greatly heartened by a letter from Newcastle dated July 12th, 1839:—

'TO THE SECRETARY OF THE CONVENTION—SIR,—I am instructed by the council of the Newcastle Political Union, to inform you that nearly all the colliers in the North are laid in with a stern determination on the part of the men not to commence work again until they have gained their rights. We have done all in our power to try to get them to wait for the commands of the Convention. The answer is, that they have waited long enough for aught they have to expect from their tyrants. They add, "We are prepared to commence." In fact, they have done so, for no sooner did the news of Dr. Taylor's arrest arrive, followed by that of Messrs. Collins and Lovett, than the strike commenced, and it has gone on increasingly until now. There are more than 25,000 pitmen alone on strike, besides the town trades, who are in expectation of your orders daily. It is earnestly requested that the time of strike be not delayed, but that it be put in force on Monday next, or the consequences in this district will be dreadful to contemplate; and if the Convention wish to retain the confidence of the people here, they must speedily act. In expectation of a speedy answer, I am, in haste, etc.

P.S. Since writing the above, I hear that ten more of the collieries have struck, with the aggregate amount of men—namely 7,000.'[3]

Encouraged by this message, the Convention voted on July 15th to recommend a general strike *to begin on August 12th and asked the trade unions to co-operate.*

It was, however, soon obvious that this could not be carried out. Northumberland was exceptional in its militancy, and the 'united trades' were not ready to take action. Nor was the Convention itself of one mind, since the strike resolution had only been carried by thirteen votes to six out of thirty members present, and not all the thirteen were from industrial areas. Under the circumstances the Convention thought it best on July 22 to rescind the call for a 'Sacred Month' and to call for token strikes 'of two or three days, in order to devote the whole of that time to solemn processions and meetings'. The actual response was very varied. At Manchester a great meeting in the Carpenters' Hall addressed by the Owenite leader Lloyd Jones voted against the strike, but in Bolton there was a general turn-out and a demonstration on the Market Square which was dispersed by the police. In Northumberland and Durham several thousand miners struck but they were rounded up by the police and sentenced by the Justices of the Peace for breach of contract. On the whole the attempt at a general strike was a failure; it was followed by the abortive Newport rising and severe repression.

Out of the arguments which followed the events of 1839 there emerged a general agreement among Chartists that the old form of organisation handed down from previous movements was no longer adequate. Instead of a Convention, composed of delegates nominated by local Working Men's Associations and endorsed by mass meetings which might or might not be representative, a more centralised organisation was required, and this was provided by the National Charter Association set up at a delegate conference in Manchester in July 1840. This was the first labour party anywhere in the world, and in many respects set an example to future generations.

The organisation grew steadily, and an address of the Executive Council in February 1842 showed that 40,000 membership cards had been issued. A large proportion of these were members of trade unions, though of course there were many trade unionists who were not Chartists and some Chartists who were not trade unionists. An account by one member says that 'the tact which the Chartists have displayed in conducting their affairs was acquired in the same schools in which they learned their political and economic creed— the trade unions', but that 'there is a rule in most Chartist Associations that those belonging to them shall join in no agitation but for the Charter'.[4]

A new feature was that besides the ordinary 'localities' or residential branches there were also 'Chartist clubs' of workers in particular trades. Thus Spitalfields had its 'silk weavers' locality' and Manchester the 'Carpenters' Hall locality' composed of workers in the building trades. The most active organiser of this activity was Peter Murray M'Douall, a native of Newton Stewart in Wigtownshire who practised medicine at Ramsbottom near Bury. 'The Doctor', says the Chartist historian Gammage, 'was of an ardent fiery temperament, and though naturally possessing strong reflective powers, was impulsive to the last degree, and by no means deficient in courage.' More than any of the Chartist leaders he had an intimate knowledge of the life and problems of the industrial workers, and of the need to combine trade unionism with the political struggle. This was the theme of his propaganda among the unions, both in his speeches and in the columns of *M'Douall's Chartist Circular and Trades' Advocate*. His prestige is shown by the fact that he headed the poll for members of the Executive in 1841 and was again returned by an increased majority in the following year.

The harvest of 1841 had not been good and trade was now rapidly growing worse. There had been crises before, but no one could remember such a crisis as now developed. On March 25th, 1842, the number of paupers was officially returned as 1,427,187, and if the New Poor Law had been enforced literally the workhouses would not have been large enough to hold them. Colonel Thompson, a prominent member of the Anti-Corn-Law League, published an article on 'the Siege of Bolton', prompted by a visit to the market place where minute quantities of meat were being offered for a penny. At Stockport so many workers had been evicted for inability to pay rent that one could see chalked on the walls 'Stockport to Let', and similar scenes could be seen in other towns. What was significant was that the crisis had involved the skilled workers. Of 800 mule spinners employed in Stockport in 1835 only 140 were left in 1843, and outside the cotton

industry matters were even worse. H. Ashworth, a prominent member of the
League, estimated that 60% of the millworkers at Bolton were unemployed
but the percentages for carpenters, bricklayers and stonemasons were 84, 87
and 66% respectively.[5] It is not surprising that the Chief Constable of
Manchester reported, early in 1842, that many 'tradesmen' were now in
favour of the Charter, whereas few had been in 1839.

In July 1842 the Anti-Corn-Law League held a Conference in London, at
which speeches were made which might have landed a Chartist in prison. Not
only did the mayors of large towns of the North rise in turn to state that if
riots broke out they would not allow the military to fire on the crowd, but a
speaker who called for the formation in London of a Committee of Public
Safety to rouse the metropolis from its apathy informed the audience that a
friend of his, a 'gentleman' had informed him that he was prepared, if the
order was given, to assassinate Sir Robert Peel. Though the speaker could not
approve of the suggestion of murder, he could not refrain from observing
that on the day of Peel's funeral very few tears would be shed.[6] It was
generally believed that millowners were prepared to close their factories with
a view to diverting the anger of the workers against the Government, and it
seems that both the League and the Chartists were trying to find out one
another's intentions.

I

By this time the initiative had been taken by the workers themselves, in the
form of strikes of the miners in Lanarkshire and South Staffordshire, which
were the culmination of a long period of agitation and organisation. On
August 13 the *Northern Star* published a letter from John M'Lay, secretary
to the miners' union in the Glasgow district: 'The average wages of the miners
of coal and iron vary from 1/7½d to 2/5½d for putting out one-third or more
labour than they did, one year ago, receive 4s. a day for; and at the same time
could, in many cases, get their money when earned, while now we go to our
masters' store and take our labour in goods; or if the employer has not a
store, he, according to his laws, makes us pay one penny for each shilling
lifted before pay day.' The *Northern Star* commented: 'We are glad the
miners, like other trades, have hoisted the banner of the Charter. In the
principles of that invaluable document must centre all their hopes.'

The decisive events, however, took place in the textile areas. At the end of
July there had been some improvement in trade, but at this juncture three
firms in Ashton and Staleybridge announced a further reduction in wages. In
the words of Richard Pilling, leader of the Ashton weavers: 'A room that
would hold a thousand people was crammed to suffocation, and the whole
voice of the meeting was that it was of no use trying to get up a subscription
for others, but to give up. And that was just the way the strike began; it rose

in a minute from one end of the room to the other: Whigs, Tories, Chartists, sham Radicals, and others.'[7]

Deputations from the weavers persuaded two of the firms to take back the reductions but the third, Messrs Bailey and Co., told their workers 'if this did not please them, they had better go and play a bit'. This proved the last straw and on Friday, August 5th, the workers at Bailey's struck work and marched through the streets, cheering O'Connor, the *Northern Star* and the Charter. They were joined by the operatives from other factories and by the week-end the whole of Ashton was idle. Great meetings were held which were attended by shopkeepers and others as well as by weavers and a demonstration at Mottram Moor called for a general strike 'until the Charter becomes the law of the land'.

On Tuesday, August 9th, a great procession of several thousand weavers and miners marched to Manchester, where they met with a reception which was unprecedented, and perhaps not quite what they had expected. 'The crowd was met on the way in Pollard Street by a group which included Mr. Maude, the stipendiary magistrate, and Colonel Wemyss, the commander of the military, supported by a troop of cavalry, a company of the 60th Rifles in reserve and the whole of the C division of police. This halted them for half an hour, and there was a parley between Mr. Maude and the leaders of the crowd, who told him that no violence was intended and that, if allowed to proceed, the crowd would follow a prescribed route. These assurances were accepted, the cavalry were withdrawn to allow the crowd to get away, and Mr. Maude started to lead the crowd on the way it should go. What followed might perhaps have been foreseen. The crowd broke up into small groups, and though soldiers and police denied to them certain obvious places of meeting, they managed to reassemble in an open spot near Granby Row. Here they were harangued by Chartists before they set about going round Manchester, turning out the workpeople. Their leaders had told them not to pillage, and they did not do so, though they demanded bread from the shops. In one or two places there were tussles, and at one mill, that of Messrs. Birley, something like a regular siege took place. By Thursday it was calculated that nearly 130 cotton mills and perhaps as many dyeworks, machine shops, and foundries in Manchester were idle, affecting about 50,000 hands. The 'Trades' in Manchester supported the strike and the Chartists, and the authorities told the mill owners that they could not be protected if they tried to restart their mills. Messrs. Birley continued to work with about a third of their people, but they were blamed for doing so, and indeed were rebuked by a magistrate, Mr. John Brooks, for causing a disturbance. It was subsequently noted that Mr. Brooks was an eminent member of the Anti-Corn-Law League and Messrs. Birley were not members at all'.[8]

On the whole, the shopkeepers and middle classes adopted a friendly or neutral attitude and opinion both at home and abroad was impressed by the fact that although one of the wealthiest commercial centres of England was in the hands of the workers for more than a week, there was no pillaging and hardly any disturbance.

Much of the success of the strike was due to the support of the skilled workers and above all of the engineers, a fact which has often been misrepresented by later writers. Prominent in the movement were Robert Robinson, Secretary to the Steam Engine Makers, and Alexander Hutchinson, Secretary to the Friendly United Smiths of Great Britain and Ireland. On the 11th a great crowd assembled outside Nasmyth's engineering works in Patricroft. In Gammage's words: 'They gathered into a mass, and held a meeting, which was addressed by a person named Morrison. It was proposed that a deputation should visit the various works and request the hands to turn out; but an amendment was carried that the meeting should proceed in a body for that purpose. They accordingly proceeded to the works of Mr. Nasmyth, but found that the men had gone to breakfast; when they returned, a meeting took place between the two bodies. Those on strike requested the others to turn out. Morrison told them that although they might think they were well off, the distress would ultimately reach them, and that if they did not turn out quietly, they would bring such a force as would compel them. "We are come" said one, "We are come, like a clock, to give you warning before we strike; and you may consider that you have warning." They were told by the foreman of the works that the men should cease working.' On the same day the strike spread to Bolton, where the magistrates who were members of the Anti-Corn-Law League made no resistance, and to Stockport where there was a riot caused by an attempt by the strikers to demolish the workhouse.

Everyone therefore was in favour of the strike but there was considerable difference of opinion as to its object. One section wished to see a strike for the Charter while another would have been satisfied with 'a fair day's wage for a fair day's work', or more specifically 'the wages of 1840'. The matter was considered by the 'five iron trades', in other words the United Trades Association, which had been set up at the instance of Alexander Hutchinson in 1840 to comprise the 'Five Trades of Mechanism, viz., Mechanics, Smiths, Moulders, Engineers, and Millwrights' and which was the best organised group of workers in Manchester. They forthwith established contact with the other unions and on August 11th and 12th a conference of eighty delegates met in the Carpenters' Hall. The Conference decided to put forward the Charter as the aim of the strike but to seek endorsement from a wider area. They accordingly issued a manifesto which was printed in large red type and placarded on the walls of Manchester:

'Justice, Peace, Law and Order!

'We, the delegates of the various trades, having been duly and legally elected by our various trades, have again met in solemn conference, empowered by our constituents to watch over and to guard the interests of the people, do most earnestly implore you not to be led astray by the machinations of your enemies, but remain firm in your purpose to uphold your just rights, as set forth in the Carpenters' Hall on the 11th and 12th inst. We call upon you to be prompt in the election of your delegates to the great

Delegate Conference which will be held on Monday, August 15.

'We most solemnly pledge ourselves to persevere in our exertions until we achieve the complete emancipation of the working classes from the thraldom of monopoly and class legislation by the legal establishment of the People's Charter. The trades of Great Britain carried the Reform Bill. The trades of Great Britain shall carry the Charter.'

The conference assembled punctually on the morning of Monday the 15th and sat for two days, with Alexander Hutchinson as President and a certain Charles Stuart as Secretary. Thousands of workers lined the streets outside the hall and as the delegates from each town arrived they were greeted with resounding cheers. Credentials were carefully examined and the delegates proceeded to business. Many of them spoke at considerable length but it was evident that the partisans of a purely economic strike were very much in the minority. A telling speech was made by the delegate from Patricroft, who said that his constituents would not have been interested in an economic strike since they were amongst the highest paid workers in the country, but a contest for political liberty was an entirely different matter. On Tuesday morning the vote was taken, the most reliable account being that of the Northern Star of August 20th: 'Of the eighty-five delegates, fifty-eight declared for the Charter; seven for making it a trades' contest; nineteen to abide the decision of the meeting; and one, the representative of the stonemasons of Manchester, stated that his constituents were individually for the Charter, but that he had no instruction from them as a body, and could not therefore pledge them to any precise course of action.' The resolution adopted was: 'That this meeting recommend the people of all trades and callings to forthwith cease work, until the above document becomes the law of the land.'

In the meantime the strike had spread far beyond Lancashire. For fifty miles around Manchester not a stroke of work was done except flour-milling and the gathering of the harvest, although in some places the strike committees allowed work in hand to be finished before closing the factories. There was very little violence but the strikers generally raked out the fires from under the boilers and removed the plugs to prevent them from re-starting, whence the movement was sometimes nicknamed the 'Plug Plot'. The scenes which took place were however unparalleled until the General Strike of 1926 and the 'more looms' struggle of 1932. Columns of men and women marched from town to town, sometimes carrying heavy sticks and often singing hymns. The strikers from Burnley marched to Bacup and Todmorden and then crossed the Pennines into the West Riding where a general stoppage took place. On August 14th a great demonstration took place on Bradford Moor, and on the next day thousands of men and women, many of them badly clad and barefoot, marched to Halifax. Outside the town they were met by a party of troops. The Riot Act was read and the crowd was called upon to disperse. The soldiers called upon the women to 'Go home', to which they replied: 'We have no home! Shoot if you dare!' and struck up the 'Union Hymn'. Many arrests were made, but a further demonstration of 15,000 workers took place the following day, at which the women took a leading part and called upon the men to storm the prison.[9] By this time the strike had spread from Aberdeen to South Wales and the mines were stopped throughout the country.

The Government was now thoroughly alarmed. They had of course plenty of experience in dealing with home-made plots and attempts at armed insurrection, but general strikes were without precedent, and they were greatly disquieted both by the spread of the strike and by the failure of the Manchester magistrates to cope with it. On Saturday, August 13th, the Prime Minister wrote to Queen Victoria: 'Sir Robert Peel presents his humble duty to your Majesty, and is sorry to be under the necessity of troubling your Majesty so suddenly, but he is sure your Majesty will excuse him for making any proposal to your Majesty which the public service may render requisite.

'The accounts received this morning from Manchester with regard to the state of the country in the neighbourhood are very unsatisfactory, and they are confirmed by the personal testimony of magistrates who have arrived in London for the purpose of making representations to your Majesty's servants on the subject.

'A Cabinet has just been held, and it is proposed to send a battalion of Guards by the railway this evening. The 16th of August (Tuesday next) is the anniversary of a conflict which took place in Manchester in the year 1819 between the Yeomanry Cavalry and the populace, and it is feared that there may be a great assemblage of persons riotously disposed on that day.

'Under these circumstances it appears desirable to your Majesty's confidential advisers that a proclamation should be immediately issued, warning all persons against attendance on tumultuous meetings and against all acts calculated to disturb the public peace. It is necessary that a Council should be held for the issue of this proclamation, and important that it should arrive in Manchester on Monday.' [10]

Parliament having been prorogued on August 12 the Cabinet could proceed without being troubled by fear of too much criticism.

The dreadful bogey conjured up by the Tory back-benchers of a coalition between the Chartists and the Anti-Corn-Law League obviously affected their minds, for they issued a warrant to the Home Office to open the letters of two M.Ps, Duncombe and Cobden, between August 18th and 20th. As regards Duncombe they probably did not find anything which they did not know before, but they must have been greatly heartened by reading a letter from Richard Cobden written on August 16th to his brother Frederick, who was then in business in Manchester and whom he suspected of being a weakling: 'Depend upon it, nothing can be got by fraternizing with trades unions. They are founded upon principles of brutal tyranny and monopoly. I would rather live under a Bey of Algiers than a Trades Committee.'[11]

Encouraged by the Government from the rear the Lancashire magistrates were now emboldened to act. The initiative was taken at Preston, where the employers had long been known for their consistent opposition to trade unionism. Ever since 1810 the cotton Spinners' unions had tried in vain to organise the town and as late as 1860 it was said: 'applications for an increase in wages are sometimes granted elsewhere, in Preston never.' It is not surprising, then, that it was at Preston that the Mayor called upon the troops to fire on a procession of strikers, four of whom were killed. The Blackburn magistrates followed the example of Preston; and immediately after the Manchester trade union conference had passed the Chartist resolution the police forced their way into the hall and gave the delegates ten minutes to disperse. On the 15th the troops had fired on the strikers at Hanley, where violent disturbances took place.

Despite the fact that the rank and file of the strikers on their own initiative had raised the slogan of the Charter neither the full-time Executive of the National Charter Association which sat in Manchester nor the editorship of the *Northern Star* in Leeds had shown marked initiative in the matter, and Campbell, the Secretary to the N.C.A., had gone to London for some purpose which is not clear. For some time past, the N.C.A. had been making arrangements for a national conference in Manchester on August 16th, the anniversary of Peterloo, to unveil a memorial to Henry Hunt and also to discuss questions of organisation, and everything had been going on quietly, according to plan. What happened is told by Thomas Cooper, the famous Midlands leader, who had left Hanley to avoid arrest and had walked to Crewe to catch the train to Manchester. He found a carriage occupied by Campbell and other delegates, and when the train drew into Manchester they were surprised by the absence of the customary cloud of smoke over the city, a phenomenon which was not seen again until 1926. 'Not a single mill at work' said Campbell, 'something must come of this and something mighty serious too.' On arriving in the city they found it flooded with troops, and the problem of finding a meeting place was serious. The only help came from a minister of the Bible Christian church (an offshoot of the Swedenborgians), the Rev. James Scholefield, and the conference assembled on the night of the 17th in the Round Chapel at Ancoats, about forty delegates being present.

All thought of the original agenda was left aside and only one thought was uppermost in the minds of those assembled. After the reports from various places had been given, M'Douall, on behalf of the Executive, moved a resolution pledging the conference to support and extend the strike. This was seconded by Cooper, full of excitement after this experiences in Hanley, in a fiery speech. He declared that a peaceful general strike was an impossibility and called on the conference to mobilise the people for revolt against the Government. The opposition to this came from Hill, editor of the *Northern Star*, who declared that the whole movement had been fomented by the Anti-Corn-Law League and that the Chartists should not fall into the trap. He only received six votes, but one of them was that of Harney, who had always been looked upon as a revolutionary of the extreme Left. The view of the majority of delegates was probably represented best by O'Connor, who supported M'Douall but did not endorse Cooper's arguments, on the ground that: 'We are not here to talk about fighting. We are met to consider and approve the resolution of the trades.' The conference passed the resolution and instructed the Executive to issue a manifesto which was drawn up by M'Douall and is worth quoting at some length:

'Brother Chartists - The great political truths which have been agitated during the late half century have at length aroused the degraded and insulted white slaves of England to a sense of their duty to themselves, their children, and their country. Tens of thousands have flung down their implements of labour. Your taskmasters tremble at your energy, and expecting masses eagerly watching this great crisis of our cause . . .

'Nature, God, and reason, have condemned the inequality, and in the thunders of a people's voice it must perish for ever. He knows that labour, the real property of society, the sole origin of the accumulated property, the first cause of all national wealth, and the only supporter, defender, and contributor to the greatness of our country, is not possessed of the same legal protection which is given to those lifeless effects, the houses, ships, and machinery which labour have alone created. He knows that if labour has no protection, wages cannot be upheld, nor in the slightest degree regulated until every workman of twenty-one years of age and of sane mind is on the same political level as the employer. He knows that the Charter would remove, by universal will expressed in universal suffrage, the heavy load of taxes which now crush the existence of the labourer, and cripple the efforts of commerce; that it would give cheap government as well as cheap food, high wages as well as low taxes, bring happiness to the hearthstone, plenty to the table, protection to the old, education to the young, permanent prosperity to the country, long-continued protective political power to labour, and peace, blessed peace to exhausted humanity and approving nations; therefore it is that we have solemnly sworn, and one and all declared, that the golden opportunity now within our grasp shall not pass away fruitless, that the chance of centuries afforded to us by a wise and all-seeing God, shall not be lost; but that we do now universally resolve never to resume labour until labour's grievances are destroyed, and protection assured to ourselves, our suffering wives, and helpless children, by the enactment of the People's Charter.

'Englishmen, the blood of your brethren reddens the streets of Preston and Blackburn, and the murderers thirst for more. Be firm—be courageous—be men. Peace, law, and order, have prevailed on our side; let them be revered, until your brethren in Scotland, Wales and Ireland, are informed of your resolution; and when a universal holiday prevails—which will be the case in eight days—then of what use will bayonets be against a public opinion? What tyrant can then live above the terrible tide of thought and energy which is now flowing fast under the guidance of man's intellect—which is now destined by the Creator to elevate His people above the reach of want, the rancour of despotism, and the penalties of bondage. The trades—a noble, patriotic band—have taken the lead in declaring for the Charter. Follow their example. Lend no whip to rulers wherewith to scourge you. Intelligence has reached us of the wide spreading of the strike, and now within fifty miles of Manchester every engine is at rest, and all is still, save the miller's useful wheels, and the friendly sickle in the fields.

'Countrymen and brothers—Centuries may roll on, as they have fleeted past, before such universal action may again be displayed. We have made the cast for liberty, and we must stand like men the hazard of the die. Let none despond; let all be cool and watchful, and, like the bridesmaids in the parable, keep your lamps burning; and let your continued resolution be like a beacon, to guide those who are hastening far and wide to follow your memorable example. Brethren, we rely on your firmness. Cowardice, treachery, womanly fear, would cast our cause back for half a century. Let no man, woman, or child, break the solemn pledge; and if they do, may the curse of the poor and starving pursue them. They deserve slavery who madly court it. Our machinery is all arranged, and your cause will in three days be impelled onward by all the intellect that we can summon to its aid. Therefore whilst you are peaceful, be firm; whilst you are orderly, make all be so likewise; and whilst you look to the law, remember that you had no voice in making it, and are therefore slaves to the will, the law, and the price of your masters. All officers of the Association are called on to aid and assist in the peaceful extension of the movement, and to forward all monies for the use of the delegates who may be expressed all over the country. Strengthen our hands at this crisis; support your leaders, rally round our sacred cause; and leave the decision to the God of justice and of battle.'

Very little however was done to carry this resolution into effect. The Executive and the conference dispersed and O'Connor (who was not a member of the Executive) went to London where on the 18th he and Duncombe addressed a meeting in Lincoln's Inn Fields. The Chartists had in fact thrown the responsibility back on to the trade unions, which had no central body and had made no arrangements for organising the strike. Many workers had believed that the Anti-Corn-Law League was really on their side, and the fraternisation of the first two weeks had not prepared them for the repression which followed. The divisions among the Chartist leaders increased the confusion. Harney's attitude was bewildering to those who had idolised him, and many could only explain it by the supposition that he had been bribed by the Government, of which there is not the slightest proof. The real truth seems to be that his revolutionary ideas had been derived partly from reading of the French Revolution and partly from his contact with the unorganised silk-weavers and miners, but that he had no real grasp of industrial conditions. When speaking at Sheffield he was questioned on his attitude to the strike and said: 'O'Connor is in favour of the strike and I am against it.' Six unions in Sheffield voted for a strike and seven against, and as a consequence there was no strike. Nor does the subsequent career of Cooper suggest that he was a responsible revolutionary. The only Chartist leader who seems to have had a thorough grasp of the issues at stake was M'Douall, who by himself was unable to bring about a fundamental change.

By this time the inherent weakness of the strike was evident. The unions had entered the struggle without any funds, the Ashton weavers having only had 20/- in their treasury, and their credit was soon exhausted. Nor had the strike been effective all over the country. It was true that the fact that the small workshops in London, Birmingham and Sheffield had not been closed made very little difference, but a much more serious weakness was the failure to stop the railways, which were manned by a small group of hand-picked workers and where trade unionism was completely banned. This was of decisive importance, since the railway companies put their facilities at the disposal of the Government for the transport of troops.[12] This placed a tremendous weapon in the hands of the Government since the lines between the main cities had now been completed, which they had not been in 1839. In some places the strikers tried to tear up the railway lines and one electric telegraph was demolished, but the communications were too well guarded to be exposed to serious damage. The attempt to win over the troops which had been made by William Rider in 1839 was not repeated and they remained impervious to propaganda. It is true that many of the soldiers were Irish and had grievances of their own but O'Connell was able to boast that he had kept the Irish people aloof from the Chartist agitation.

The workers were thus forced to admit defeat and on August 20 the police allowed another trade union conference, which recommended a return to work, to take place. It has been claimed that this was all due to O'Connor: 'Suddenly, a week later, when trades as far north as Aberdeen were considering joining the strike, he swung round. He denounced the strike in the Star, and declared he would stop it. It had failed in Manchester; it was bound to be defeated; it was an Anti-Corn-Law plot. The effect of this was to shatter a movement that was already weakening at the centre. The strike ended as soon as the *Northern Star* was put on sale.'[13] This ignores the fact that the *Northern Star* merely endorsed the decision of the conference on August 20, and it also ignores a letter from M'Douall which was published in the same issue. M'Douall said that the occasion was not ripe for a revolution, because the middle classes were opposed to it and the workers themselves were divided. On the other hand the Chartists were bound to have supported the strike, since to have opposed it would have benefited the landlords while to have stood aside would have played into the hands of the League.

Nor is it true that the strikes came to an end automatically on August 27. It was not until September 26 that a correspondent from Manchester was able to report to the *North of England Magazine* that: 'The turn-outs, with the exception of the Bolton spinners, have resumed their occupations without any advance of wages, in some instances, indeed, under a trifling reduction.' This, however, was not wholly true, as a perusal of the *Northern Stars*, and *Times* will show. Thus in October it is reported that about half the employers in Ashton had taken back reductions in wages while the factories belonging to others were still stopped. In the Lothians many miners had secured the rate of wages paid before the reductions and were paying a levy to help those still on strike. Other miners in Scotland were still on strike in the spring of 1843, one of those who was victimised for his activities being Alexander Macdonald, who became one of the first labour M.Ps in 1874.

From the short-term point of view, however, the exhaustion of the workers led to a heavy defeat. On the whole the employers refrained from using their advantage to the extent that they did in 1926 and the spokesmen of the Anti-Corn-Law League claimed that there was very little victimisation. Repression by the Government was, however, very severe, over 1500 Chartists being arrested, including O'Connor, the Rev. Scholefield, Richard Pilling, Thomas Cooper and many others. It is, however, significant that the first arrest of a prominent Chartist, that of O'Connor, only took place when the strikers had gone back.

With the consent of the other members of the Executive M'Douall, who was regarded as most seriously compromised, went into hiding and after many hair-breadth escapes succeeded in reaching France. On one occasion, says Gammage, 'he was going into Manchester, and called at a house on the way, where he saw the *Northern Star* portrait of himself hanging against the wall; he was dressed in a short dirty working jacket, and a cap, and his graceful locks were turned up out of sight. He asked his hostess how she dared have the portrait of such a man in her house. Her reply was encouraging. Pulling off his cap, his hair fell down, and the woman recognised him at once. In order with greater security to continue the journey, he prevailed upon the woman, who was in her working dress, to accompany him; he could not, however, on this occasion escape the eye of one of the police whom they met on the road. The woman looking back after passing him the policeman beckoned her to him, and advised her to get her companion out of the way as soon as she could, for the next policeman they met might not be so friendly.'

When the trial of the arrested Chartist leaders took place, O'Connor conducted his own defence. His object was to establish that the strike had not been prepared beforehand, that it had been of a peaceful nature and that it had been condoned by the Anti-Corn-Law League. On the whole the witnesses whom he called bore out his case whereas those for the Crown cut a poor figure, and some of the evidence elicited did not much tend to the credit of the League. When Richard Pilling gave his description of the sufferings of the operatives many persons burst into tears and the Attorney-General went out of the court in some embarrassment. The case against seven of the defendants was abandoned during the course of the trial and twenty-one were acquitted by the middle-class jury after a trial of eight days. The jury acquitted another sixteen defendants on charges of sedition and conspiracy but found them guilty on the fourth count: 'That they tumultuously and unlawfully assembled together, and forced certain peaceable subjects to leave their occupations, with intent thereby to cause terror and alarm, and by means of such terror and alarm unlawfully to cause certain great changes to be made in the constitution of this realm.'

Feargus O'Connor and fourteen others were found guilty on the fifth count: 'that the defendants did endeavour to excite her Majesty's liege subjects to confederate, and to leave their several employments, and to produce a cessation of labour throughout a large portion of this realm.' On this point however the learned judge expressed some doubt as to whether by law it was an offence and said that this was a point which must be decided by the Court of the Queen's Bench. In actual fact O'Connor and the other defendants were never called to appear in the Court of Queen's Bench and no judge was found to pronounce on the illegality of general strikes until Mr. Justice Astbury in 1926.

II

The failure of the general strike caused a large section of the workers to lose faith in the Chartists and in political action generally. Thus on September 2nd 1842 a vote of censure was moved by the Manchester No. 1 branch of the Steam Engine Makers on Robert Robinson for his 'impropriety of conduct during the Late Excitement' and four days later the rule was laid down that no member could claim donation benefit for being out of work due to 'any Political or Popular Movement' though the Society did issue a circular asking for voluntary subscriptions to help those who were imprisoned or unemployed.[14]

But this type of reaction was by no means universal and the continuing Trade Union support for Chartism has been greatly underestimated, as has the degree of understanding of the trade unions shown by O'Connor. When trade revived and with it the trade union movement, the first initiative was taken by the miners. Although they had gained very little out of the general strike of 1842 it had been the first time in history when the miners throughout the country had taken part in a national struggle, an experience which was not repeated until 1893, and they had acquired a new confidence in their own strength. The date of the foundation of the Miners' Association of Great Britain and Ireland, the first national organisation of its kind, is November 7th 1842 (not 1841 as claimed by the Webbs). [15] O'Connor displayed great interest in the union from its beginning and it was on his advice that the Association appointed the famous Chartist solicitor William Prowting Roberts as its legal advisor.

On November 23, 1844, O'Connor announced the removal of the *Northern Star* from Leeds to London and the change of its title to the *Northern Star and the National Trades Journal*. 'In London' he wrote, 'The Star will be the means of rallying the proper machinery for conducting the Registration Movement—the Land Movement—the National Trades' Movement—The Labour Movement—and the Charter Movement.' From now on the paper was intimately linked with the trade unions and became the official organ of many of them. O'Connor wrote: 'I invite you to keep your eye steadily fixed upon the great Trades' Movement now manifesting itself throughout the country, and I would implore you to act by all other trades as you have acted by the Colliers. Attend their meetings, swell their numbers, and give them your sympathy; but upon no account interpose the Charter as an obstacle to their proceedings. All labour and labourers must unite; and they will speedily discover that the Charter is the only standard under which they can successfully rally: but don't interpose it to the interruption of their proceedings.'(16)

At the same time he warned against the dangers of a narrow craft policy which would isolate certain sections of the working class. By this time a group of unions had come into being which were successfully pursuing a craft policy and were drawing away from politics and even from other trade unions. It must however be remembered that this tendency though growing was not yet dominant in the unions. The Webbs gave great attention to the unions, which they have cited, precisely because they built stable organisations, which survived, and they did not give so much attention to the struggling societies whose proceedings are to be found in newspapers rather than in minute books. O'Connor was quite alive to the problem. 'By union, and by union alone, can the "poor oppressed" contend against the injustice of the "rich oppressor". And let not the printers, if well paid, suppose that any injustice against the tailors, if badly paid, will not sooner or later come home to their own doors! Let not the spinners, if better paid than the handloom weavers, lose sight of the fact that a "surplus" of handloom weavers will constitute a reservoir for the masters to fall back upon, as a means of reducing the wages of the spinners. Let not the bricklayers imagine that a reduction in the wages of their labourers will not be followed by a reduction in their own wages. A blow successfully struck at one order of labour will as successfully wound all others.' These sentiments were appreciated by the lower-paid workers and we read that when in 1843 O'Connor visited Aberdeen he was received by the United Bakers in their full lodge attire, consisting of 'rich pink muslin suits with splendid turbans'.

Two examples, from later years, may illustrate the continued trade union support for the Charter. On April 10th, 1848, the day on which the Charter was once again presented to the Commons, John Bright also presented a petition from a delegate conference representing 6,000 Manchester workers which called for the Six Points of the Charter, a reduction in the hours of work, local boards for the regulation of wages and the abolition of primogeniture and entail.

Among the delegates to the last conference in 1858 which buried the National Charter Association were representatives of the London building trades, then preparing for the great Nine Hours' struggle, and of the West End Bootmakers. A historian tells us that: 'The list of those who took part in the discussions did not include any prominent middle-class radicals but it contained many who worked in and with the Trade Union Manhood Suffrage and Vote by Ballot Association (formed in the summer of 1862) and the Reform League of 1865. Representatives from several London trade societies were present, including, in their private capacity, William Allan and William Newton of the Engineers.'(17)

REFERENCES

(1) Baines, *History of the Cotton Manufacture,* p.437
(2) Frederick Engels, 'Trades Unions' in *The Labour Standard,* 28th May 1881
(3) *Charter,* July 21 1839
(4) *Leeds Times,* January 1842
(5) 'Statistics of the present depression of trade in Bolton', in *Journal of the Statistical Society,* (1842) 74
(6) *Morning Chronicle,* July 5, 1842: *Morning Herald,* July 15, 1842: *Anti-Bread Tax Circular,* August 11, 1842
(7) *State Trials,* New Series, Vol. 4, 1839-43
(8) G. Kitson Clark, 'Hunger and Politics in 1842' in *The Journal of Modern History,* Vol.XXV, No.4. December 1953
(9) H. Schlüter, *Die Chartistenbewegung,* New York 1916, p.306
(10 *Letters of Queen Victoria,* Vol.1, pp.528-9
(11) Morley's *Life of Cobden,* 1903 edition, p.299
(12) F.C. Mather 'The Railways, the Electric Telegraph and Public Order during the Chartist Period, 1837-8' in *History,* February 1953
(13) G.D.H. Cole and Raymond Postgate, *The Common People 1746—1838,* p.285
(14) James B. Jeffery's *The Story of the Engineers 1800-1945,* p.22
(15) Statement by John Hall, the miners' secretary, *Report by the Commissioner to inquire into the state of the population in the Mining Districts, 1847,* p.14
(16) *Northern Star,* 16 November 1844
(17) John Saville's *Ernest Jones: Chartist,* p.68

GEORGE BARNSBY

Chartism in the Black Country 1850-1860

From Chartist days to the present time there has been no lack of commentators ready to set a date to the end of Chartist activity and influence. It is widely suggested that the movement collapsed amid derisory laughter after the 'fiasco' of the Kennington meeting in April 1848. Others claim that the upsurge of 1848 was a flash in the pan and that Chartism had effectively disappeared after the presentation of the second petition in 1842. As far as the Midlands are concerned, it is even held that Chartism was a spent force after the defection from the Chartist Convention of Attwood and the middle class Birmingham leaders early in 1839. A study of Chartism in the Black Country gives little support to the above views.

Chartist origins in this area can be traced to the disillusionment with the Reform Bill of 1832. After this time the leadership of the Political Unions, through which the Reform Bill had been achieved, was seized by the working class, and in most Black Country towns the transition to Chartism came directly through the Political Unions. Black Country Chartism achieved its greatest mass influence in the middle of 1842 and at this time it is probably true that the Bilston Association was the strongest in the country. From 1842 to 1848 Chartism remained organised throughout the Black Country. This long period of six years played an important part in the development of the mass influence which the Chartist leaders, notably Joseph Linney of Bilston, Samuel Cook of Dudley and John Chance of Stourbridge were to enjoy until the end of organised Chartist activity in 1860. Two basic activities of this period 1842—48, absorbing a great deal of Chartist energies, were the building of Trade Unions and the organisation of the Chartist Land Company to which many hundreds of Black Country workers contributed, fifteen of whom were actually settled on the land.

The study which follows deals entirely with organised Chartist activity in the decade 1850—60.* In the original study two other chapters deal with

---

*A fuller exposition of the argument in this essay is in 'The Working Class Movement in the Black Country 1815—67' by G. Barnsby (Birmingham University M.A. thesis 1965).

Chartist participation in what would today be known as mass organisations. From this it emerges that whenever discontent took an organised form, it was to the Chartists that the working class looked for leadership. The story of the building of stable trade unions in the two basic industries of the area, coal and iron, has still to be written, but enough is known to demonstrate that Chartists played a leading part. From 1844, the energies of John Jones, the Bilston Chartist barber were channelled into trade union activity. Throughout the 1850s Joseph Linney was the leading figure, whether paid or unpaid is not known, in organising the miners. Chartists often took part in negotiations with masters even where their actual relations with the trade unions are obscure, and at mass demonstrations it was invariably a Chartist who was called to the chair.

In other spheres, Chartists were equally active. In the agitation against church rates Chartists took a leading part, especially Samuel Cook the Dudley draper and Benjamin Danks the Wednesbury tube manufacturer. In the fight to improve social conditions, Chartists also took the lead. During the 1850s Linney was an Inspector of Nuisances under the Bilston Improvement Act. He dealt with such matters as the sale of bad meat with a vigour which was obviously unusual at that time. In August 1851 when a public enquiry opened into the sanitary state of Dudley, where the death rate of 28 per 1,000 was the worst in the country, there were only twelve to fourteen people present, but among them was Samuel Cook who never let the Health Inspector out of his sight during the time he was in Dudley. Also in Dudley, where the impact of Chartist activity on the affairs of the town was very deep, a long battle was fought from 1848 for a working class Mechanics Institute. This reached its peak in 1859 when the Chartists opened a rival Working Men's Institute.

Finally, two instances of agitation against the high price of food can be cited as evidence of Chartist leadership of the working class in this last decade of organised Chartism. The first occurred in 1855 in the middle of the Crimean War. At this time mass meetings attracting crowds of up to 35,000 people were claimed. This agitation led on to the very real revival of Chartism which took place during the war and to the publication of the *Democrat and Labour Advocate*, the only local Chartist newspaper ever to be published in the Black Country. The other agitation, against the high price of meat, occurred in the summer of 1860 only a few months before national Chartist organisation disappeared. Both in Dudley and in Oldbury, Chartism was very virile at that time.

Later Chartist activity must be seen against the economic situation of the time. This is much more complex than the usual generalisation, that after the 1840s 'conditions improved', would leave one to believe. The first half of the century had been gashed by the long Depressions of the period, 1815 to 1823, 1826 to 1833 and 1838 to 1843. From 1844 employment conditions improved and remained good until the slump of 1847—8. Economic expansion was resumed until the winter of 1855—6 when there was another slump.

Large scale unemployment again returned to the Black Country in 1858—9. The 1850s were therefore a 'good' decade compared with what had gone before. They were also better than what followed, for the 1860s were a period of almost chronic depression in the Black Country. This led to a revival of the open class-warfare which had characterised the early forties.* By this time organised Chartism was dead, but the great advance of that decade—the Reform Bill of 1867—was a large instalment of the Chartist programme and, in the Black Country, Chartist leaders played a leading role in that agitation.

Organised Black Country Chartism, which existed continuously throughout the decade 1850—60 exhibited two distinct phases. For the years 1850—56 Bilston was the strongest branch and took the initiative in organising the area. In the latter years of the decade, this position was taken over by the Dudley branch which performed the same function. At times, the Bilston and Dudley branches were not only the strongest in the area, but ranked among the three or four most important branches in the country.

I

At the beginning of 1850, Black Country Chartism was beginning to stir again, stimulated by the Chartist Delegate Conference held in London in December 1849. In the first week in January a meeting of Bilston Chartists was held at the house of John Jones of Wolverhampton Street. There it had been 'unanimously agreed to join the National Charter Association established by the late Conference in London'. The meeting was adjourned until the next week at John White's, Hall Street. [1] In February the National Land Company was under discussion. It must be remembered that the Land Company was not dissolved for many years and that Chartist functions continued to be held at O'Connorsville; in addition the local branches were still in existence, presumably with some connection with the national body. This meeting of the Bilston Land Company took place at John White's with T. Davis in the chair. The meeting was very critical of the behaviour of the directors of the Company and 'condemned the crafty petition presented by Mr. Henly'. It also believed it was high time that the directors reduced their salaries. [2] Organisation at Dudley is testified to by the acknowledgement by Mr. William Rankin of sums of money received by the *Northern Star*. These included 2/- 'per William Dunn from the Chartists who meet in Campbell Street', 2/- from William Moir, shilling donations from six people, six 6d donations, including one from Samuel Cook, 2/6 per William Besley from 'Democrats of Kates Hill', 2/6 from William Insull, bookseller of

*See the Centenary Booklet, *Origins of the Wolverhampton Trades Council* (The Secretary, Wolverhampton Trades Council, 48 Dickinson Avenue, Wolverhampton, Staffordshire), 2s.

Stone Street and other donations totalling the not inconsiderable amount of 24/-. [3]

In April, the Dudley branch of the National Land Company met and decided to wind itself up. A special, numerously attended meeting of shareholders took place at the meeting room in Campbell Street. A resolution was passed totally opposing the winding up of the Land Company by the government or the House of Commons. It agreed to wind up the Dudley branch by forming a Redemption League for the purpose of buying up the shares of all dissatisfied shareholders, 'and presenting them to Feargus O'Connor to be used by him for furtherance of the glorious Land Plan'. A short address to accompany the resolution was moved by Simon Watts which said 'Let us rally to the rescue of the future and save it from the poisonous fangs of the blood sucking capitalists. Shall the Land Plan be lost when our co-operation can save it?' The report was signed by John Davies, chairman and William Rankin, secretary. The sum of £2 was paid in to commence with [4].

In June 1850 there was a pleasure trip to the Land Company's estate at Great Dodford. 'The estate was visited by large numbers of friends from Birmingham and Dudley who were delighted with the improved appearance since their visit last year.' [5] The Bilston branch of the Land Company took steps in July. A preliminary meeting of members was held at Linney's public house, the White Horse Inn, and a resolution was passed that the members 'assist Feargus O'Connor to wind up the affairs of the Land Company'. Linney was elected secretary in order to further this work. [6] In October there was news of the Brierley Hill Chartists. They had met at William Dodd's Spread Eagle Inn, New Chapel Street to pass a resolution applauding the brave conduct of the men of Barclay and Perkins Brewery in London towards the inhuman monster Marshal Haynau. [7]

Activity in 1851 was at a lower level. In January Linney was in Mansfield on Land Company business transmitting 10/6 for the national Winding Up Fund. Donations to this fund also came from the Black Country. [8] At the end of March there was a conference of the National Charter Association. Birmingham, Wolverhampton and Coventry were entitled to two delegates, but in fact of the twenty or so delegates who assembled, none was from the Midlands. This is likely to have been due more to differences of opinion among Chartists than the inability to support a delegate. This Conference rejected an alliance with the middle class and was a defeat for O'Connor and a victory for Ernest Jones. [9] That Jones' view was not unanimously held in the Black Country was indicated by a meeting in Walsall in August which was addressed by Jones. In his weekly report to the N.C.A. executive Jones stated that he had lectured in Walsall in a large room which was crowded, with a number of people outside beneath the open window equal to the numbers inside. At least 100 people stepped forward to be enrolled on the chairman's invitation, when some members of the Chartist body would not allow the enrolment to take place nor would they take any cards for the future. Jones continued: 'When I asked why, they stated that they were in touch with leading members of the middle class and hoped to win them over and with a good deal more about Unitarians and Baptists etc. which was perfectly unintelligible to me. This miserable, pusillanimous spirit must be put an end to. No wonder the Chartists have been low at Walsall.' He went on to say that by truckling to the middle classes no movement had ever made headway. There could have been an Association of fifty members last Friday and soon there would have been 500, for he had never seen a better spirit than at Walsall. This is the case for believing that the Midlands were not represented at the March Chartist Conference because of differences of opinion. However, in the same report, Jones gave the following estimate of the position in Birmingham which might have had some application to the Black Country: 'Nothing can exceed the apathy and inertness of this large town. I was told that this was the best political meeting for some time. If so, all I can say is that bad is best. Trade is too brisk. Yet the temper of the meeting was excellent. Eighteen people joined, a fair proportion of the audience.'[10] In November, however, there was the huge Birmingham demonstration to welcome Kossuth in which, 'The neighbouring towns of Wolverhampton had poured forth their thousands.'[11] It is not easy, therefore, to estimate the position of the movement during 1851.

Of 1852 little can be said, partly due to the failing of sources. The *Northern Star* was at last coming to an end. In the first two months of the year there are industrial reports from the Black Country and also acknowledgement of subscriptions to the National Charter Association: 1/- from John Chance of Stourbridge and 1/- from William Muir of Dudley. [12] On 20th March the paper became the *Star and National Trades Journal* and in April it passed to Julian Harney who renamed it *Star of Freedom*. From April until November when this great working class newspaper finally stopped publication there were reports from Birmingham, but none from the Black Country.

Light dawns in 1853 with the *People's Paper* of Ernest Jones. This paper took over the best features of the *Northern Star* including its punctilious reportage of the activities of Chartist branches. It is from this, one of the neglected newspapers of the working class, that most of our subsequent knowledge of Chartism is drawn. By January 1853 activities were in full swing. The Dudley Mutual Improvement Society was in operation. The *People's Paper* could be bought at E. Hutchings, 5 High Street, Dudley; B. Allen, of Rolfe Street, Smethwick; James Mill, The Square, Walsall and Mrs. Plant, The Market Place, Willenhall. Contributions to the fund of the paper were being sent from Brownhills, near Walsall, Willenhall, Dudley, Walsall and West Bromwich. [13] No important public activities seem to have taken place during the year and one is tempted to conclude that this was one of the years when Chartism was at its weakest. Yet in a year which brought the vast Chartist meetings at Blackstone Edge and Halifax with crowds of 200,000 it would be dangerous to conclude that the influence of Black Country Chartism was negligible.

1854 was a year of uncertainty. In March, Jones called the Labour Parliament, the idea for which had arisen from the united support given to the weavers in the famous Preston Lock-out. This was one of Jones' less useful ideas. [14] The Parliament met in Manchester and the only Midland's delegate was John Oxford from Birmingham, [15] although Walsall contributed 6/- for expenses. Also in March, the Crimean War broke out and the paper was quite carried away with its own patriotism and Ernest Jones was drawing large audiences speaking on the war. [16] It was not until 1855 that jingoism faded out and the Chartist movement saw a solid growth in its influence throughout the country. Routine organisational work and some public activity, however, did go on in the Black Country during 1854. In February, Ernest Jones, notwithstanding his previous experience, again spoke in Walsall. It was a numerous meeting, despite a more than ordinary charge for admission. Mr. Shenton was in the chair and great applause was given. [17] Also in February Ernest Jones sent a parcel of handbills for the *People's Paper* to R. Rudler at Dudley. [18] John Jones, the Bilston Barber, reappeared in the Correspondence Columns seeking advice to prevent tenants being evicted. [19] During 1854 Ernest Jones launched a £200 fund to reduce the price of the paper; in May it was enlarged to twelve pages and had a pictorial supplement with some very fine engravings of such things as scenes from the Crimea. This made it the largest working class newspaper ever produced, and at that time both technically and journalistically it was undoubtedly a magnificent achievement. Readers responded enthusiastically to the call to reduce the price of the paper and, although the supplements had to be discontinued because of rising costs, the paper was reduced in price in December from 5d to 3½d. Black Country Chartists contributed to this with donations from Bilston, Bradley, Cradley and Darlaston. [20]

The revival began early in 1855. In January, Wednesbury Chartists were enquiring through the columns of the *People's Paper* whether there were any Bilston Chartists and whether they were prepared to unite with the men from Wednesbury. Back came the prompt reply that there were Chartists in Bilston and they would be pleased to co-operate. [21] The next communication from Wednesbury stated that they had met at the Three Horseshoes and had resolved to hold a locality meeting there on Sunday February 10th. The men of Darlaston, Tipton, Princes End, Bradley and Bilston were invited to attend. [22] The notice was signed by Richard Hill of Kings Mill. The next week an article appeared in the *People's Paper* and it was announced that this was by a talented writer who had promised to contribute regularly to the columns of the paper. The article was signed 'H.V.M. Bilston'. The first article was on education. It stated that it was the duty of parents to see that their children were educated. The writer would have a national system of education since the voluntary system had failed. There should be secular education in all state schools and schoolmasters should be trained. [23] Bilston had received an injection of new blood. John Jones was still helping with other people's problems and writing to the *People's Paper* when he needed assistance, receiving such intriguing replies as the following: 'He might sue you for withholding the balance. His not giving a receipt for that paid is no exoneration from paying the whole.'[24]

In February, Birmingham Chartists proposed to ballot for some magnificent, large, framed pictures of democrats and donate the proceeds to the *People's Paper* fund.[25] Richard Hill of Wednesbury appeared in the Answers to Correspondents Column in March. He wished to procure Chartist tracts. The editor recommended Dr. M'Douall's *What is a Chartist?* and R.G. Gammage, *The Chartists—What do they Want?* but he had no idea where these tracts could be obtained and asked if readers could inform him. Two weeks later there was a reply from a Rochdale Chartist, stating that he had 1,000 copies of Gammage's pamphlet.[26]

Articles continued to appear from H.V.M of Bilston. One called on Chartists to organise themselves.[27] Another, an open letter to the Miners, Forge and Furnacemen of South Staffs stated that a strike at the moment would be suicidal as they had nothing to sustain the conflict with. The answer was to cast off their present political apathy and work for the Charter. The national Birmingham ballot ran into the same trouble that the Bilston one had experienced in previous years. There were appeals for the branches to take tickets. Eventually 800 tickets were sold and £42 raised of which £33 was given to the *People's Paper* fund. The Bilston branch sold most tickets followed by the Ripponden branch.[28]

Chartism was now growing so rapidly that area organisation was essential. A start was made when Bilston democrats meeting at the Three Horseshoes appointed deputations to meet Walsall and Dudley friends.[29] As a result of this, a delegate meeting was arranged at E.S. Scholey's Temperance Coffee House. Dudley Street, Walsall for June 3rd, 'to take into consideration the best means of spreading the principles of the People's Charter'.[30] When the meeting took place there were delegates from Birmingham (Oxford, Alger and Scrimshire), Bilston (Mears, Davis, Smith and Hall), Dudley (Cook, Watts and Muir) and Walsall (Hartley, Smith, Hodgkins and Osborne). The first matter considered was the Chartist attitude to the middle class Administrative Reform Association. A resolution was passed stating that Chartists had no confidence in them. They were not sincere, they repudiated them in toto and advised all localities to bring the People's Charter before the public at any meeting convened by the A.R.A. A second resolution was passed that each locality should bring up the question of the Black Country preparing its own tract on Chartism. A third resolution concerned a district lecturer and requested that Mr. Robinson should give lectures in the district when his present engagements were concluded. Finally, Mears was elected district secretary and Smith district treasurer.[31]

As soon as regional organisation was established, however, Black Country Chartists were embroiled in a dispute with Ernest Jones, largely as a result of their connection with Birmingham. John Oxford of Birmingham had criticised Jones' use of money in connection with the *People's Paper*.

Jones had been very short with Oxford in the paper, partly as a result of Jones' domestic problems at the time—his wife was seriously ill[32]—and partly because all Chartists knew that Jones was spending his whole fortune on the Chartist movement and charges of the improper use of monies were ludicrous. In Bilston there was a discussion on the paper and a resolution in support was only passed by two votes. The report stated that the secretary was instructed to ask why the *People's Paper* could not pay its way, yet local papers with only half its circulation and facilities of production and distribution were profitable. Jones gave a very short answer—advertisements.[33] The next month, the same matter was taken up at a delegate meeting. Present were Parker, Hall and Smith from Bilston, Scholey and Hartley from Walsall, Cook and Goodwin from Dudley, and Oxford and Scrimshire from Birmingham 'as friends'. The report of this meeting was printed in the paper interspersed with Ernest Jones' own comments. Jones was still very touchy and his remarks scathing. The report began by stating that a large number of letters from Ernest Jones to John Oxford were read and it was resolved that the Birmingham committee of the *People's Paper* were justified in asking for a balance sheet. (First intervention by Jones—This is a poor trick. He knows how often I have myself urged an audit. The offence is not there, but in the infamous accusation of dishonesty against me. Where is Mr. Oxford's balance sheet?). The letters from Mr. Oxford were couched in sufficiently respectful language not to call for the stringent and severe remarks of Mr. Jones. (The persons who voted for that under the friendly auspices of Mr. Oxford are as destitute of any notion of honour as any scamp in Birmingham. We cannot be civil to people who are insolent). Mr. Cook abstained from voting deeming it foreign to the business of the meeting. He expressed full confidence in Mr. Oxford and urged the advisability of starting a South Staffs Chartist and Complete Suffrage Association operated from Bilston and showed the necessity of co-operation among reformers. Mr. Oxford concurred generally with Mr. Cook's suggestion (What! Start a new movement. Split the old one when united strength is vital? Oh, oh, Mr. Oxford!). The meeting dispersed with a resolution that having heard Mr. Cook's proposal, it should be made known among the localities and there should be another meeting in a fortnight.[34]

In August 1855 the Bilston branch voted for the three man Chartist executive. The votes are interesting. They gave thirteen to Abraham Robinson, the comparatively obscure Chartist whom they wished to have as their district lecturer. This was equal to the votes given to Ernest Jones. Finlen received eight votes and then George White, the local man from Birmingham, six. Shaw received three and Williams two.[35]

On August 30th 1855, Feargus O'Connor died. A meeting in Bilston recognised the invaluable services rendered to the Chartist movement by O'Connor and pledged support for any memorial fund. Monies were collected both for O'Connor's funeral and for the Memorial Fund.[36] Unfortunately Chartists were again divided and at least two memorials were eventually raised to O'Connor.[37] The Bilston Chartists again rubbed Ernest Jones up the wrong way by passing a resolution that they would collect, but until the Committees could agree on a memorial they would withhold the money. The editor commented: 'There could not be a more unwise resolve. The Committee at Friar Street Literary Institute is competent in every way.'[38]

The year ended with the Dear Bread mass agitation indicating that, at this time, the Chartists were influential enough to assume the leadership of any political or trade union question that roused the working people.[39] Walsall Chartists held a public meeting in that month. The report from the *Walsall Courier* spoke of a 'vast assemblage' chiefly of working men at the Assembly Rooms to hear James Finlen with Mr. Scholey in the chair. All passed off quietly.[40] Such events gave solid grounds for hope that the long-awaited renaissance was at hand, but at this moment, Black Country Chartists began to quarrel with each other. The first matter of dispute concerned George White.

At the end of 1855 George White, the Birmingham Chartist started a newspaper called the *Democrat and Labour Advocate*. It was published by John Newhouse and printed by Edward Taylor at 100 Steelhouse Lane, Birmingham. At least ten numbers of this paper were printed, although there are only five in the British Museum. So, for the first time, a local Chartist journal was circulating in the Black Country. The Dear Bread agitation, led by George White in the Black Country, was cause or effect of this paper. The first indication that all was not well was an announcement in the issue of 8th December stating that by authority of the democrats assembled at Moxley, Lye Waste, Bilston and Wednesbury the printing of the paper had been transferred to Samuel Russell, 24 Old Meeting Street, Birmingham, for the proprietor, Francis Hazeldine, Cock Inn, Lichfield Street, Bilston. The same issue carried a copy of a letter from White which had been sent to the Birmingham Journal, rebutting charges by Taylor, the previous printer, that White had not paid his bills. This was the last number of the Democrat to be found in the British Museum and for the continuation of the controversy one has to turn to the *People's Paper*. Apparently, White had discussed the position of the paper with the Bilston branch and had persuaded Hazeldine to take over its ownership and the Bilston branch had passed a resolution supporting White's conduct.[41] Early in January 1856 the Dudley branch heard a statement by George White on the paper and unanimously resolved in consequence of the breach of contract by Mr. Russell the Birmingham printer to advise Mr. Hazeldine of Bilston to enter into an action against Mr. Russell to recover the amounts charged. Nothing further is heard until April 1856 when the *People's Paper* took up correspondence it had received from the Shelton locality. It stated that this branch had written exposing the infamous behaviour of George White. The locality lent him the use of types, press and a house, made him an elector and subscribed more than £20 to his paper. His drunken and scandalous behaviour and base ingratitude exceeded belief. The locality had sent a long statement, but the editor asked to be excused from printing it as the exposure of even so insignificant a person is hurtful to our cause. The locality wish all other localities to be on their guard. A secret correspondence was being carried on between the little clique at Soho and Mr. Aulton in Walsall and George White. The members had resolved that the name of George White be erased from the membership book on account of his drunken and disorderly conduct.[42] This brought a sharp retort from D. Arthur Aulton of Bradford House, Walsall who stated that the paper had been misinformed in coupling his name with that of George White. He had been the first to suffer from White's hands during his campaign in the 'black country'. He had been among the first to expose him and had the Birmingham and Bilston brethren listened to him they would not have suffered so deeply in pecuniary matters, which threw the defrauds of the Shelton brethren in the shade.[43] It is difficult to pronounce on this controversy at this distance. That White's conduct was bad, can be believed; that it was exaggerated by his opponents is likely. Hazeldine of Bilston, who was likely to have been the greatest sufferer did not enter into the controversy, although it is perhaps significant that he never again played a leading role in the movement and may have withdrawn in disgust at White's behaviour. On the other hand, White had been a Chartist from the beginning and remained a militant. It might well be that his conduct was condemned most by those whose political views differed from his. Aulton was certainly one such person, and if we consider other differences of opinion in the movement, some light may be shed on the White affair.

The basic cause of the dispute—which made minor disagreements more likely—was the perennial middle class question. In the spring of 1855 the middle-class Administrative Reform Association had been formed. Ernest Jones had taken his first steps towards middle class co-operation by suggesting that consideration might be given to the programme of the A.R.A. In opposition, the State Reform Association had been formed in July and although it was Chartist dominated, there was almost as much disagreement as to the dissipating effort in this new Association as there was with regard to co-operation with the A.R.A.[44] This was the background to disagreements with the Walsall branch dating back to Jones' meeting there in 1851 and Samuel Cook's proposal for a Chartist and Complete Suffrage Association. In March 1856 disagreement became more open. Aulton of Walsall sent a report of a delegate meeting held at Bilston to the *People's Press*. Ernest Jones printed his comments rather than publishing his report. He said that he had received a report from Aulton which would have filled half a column. As the paper was pressed with matter, as a glance at the columns would show (this was not entirely true—G.B.), the report could not be given in full, but the main point was that it was proposed to build a new Association for the Midlands called the Central League of National Chartist Brotherhood. Jones felt convinced from bitter experience that all such sectional and isolated movements were fatal to the Charter. He did not feel justified in excluding bona fide Chartist matter to make room for a programme in direct contravention to a united movement. He trusted that the friends, for whose kind sentiments expressed in the resolution he felt thankful, would see the justice of this course and abandon isolated action.[45] Aulton's actions were repudiated by the Walsall Chartists. They discountenanced the conduct of Aulton in sending the report. They did not know how he had brought the matter before the Bilston friends, but they were sure it did not have the sanction of Walsall Chartists. Aulton had been appointed financial secretary and had no right to send the report. The Dudley branch also met and stated that they were disposed to support the organisation and policy proposed by Jones.[46] Aulton's differences with the Black Country Chartists and Ernest Jones continued, for he signed the letter in which his name was coupled with George White: 'I remain, an admirer of your literary production, but an opposer of your present political course.'[47] It appears that the League of Brotherhood was set up in the Midlands, for there is a report of a tract published by that organisation,[48] and D. Aulton proposed to set up a new organisation with a new newspaper. He was answered by James Capewell of Walsall who wrote: 'Are we few men to divide and re-divide our efforts until we become but ropes of sand? The wisest course would be to concentrate all our efforts on the association already in existence, namely the National Charter Association which was inaugurated and sustained by the health, wealth, liberty and life of the people's friend, beloved O'Connor and others.'[49]

Meanwhile the work went forward through 1856. Early in the year, Jones, in his period of depression, proposed the one man executive which the N.C.A. eventually became:

'If you so confide the movement to our hands, you must expect no explanations ... If we say "organise", you must organise—"assemble" and you must assemble ... A thousand times give me the worst dictatorship, than the blabbing squabbles of contending fractions in our ranks.'[50]

At a meeting in Walsall, this proposal of Jones was approved.[51] In February, the monthly delegate meeting took place at Samuel Cook's at Dudley,[52] and in March at Jesse Fletcher's, Court No. 2. Temple Street, Bilston.[53] In Cradley Heath ten Chartists contributed 2/6d to the Charter Fund, the money being transmitted by the secretary of the branch S. Stringer.[54] The Dudley branch functioned regularly with W. Hyde as secretary.[55]

In July 1856 John Frost, at the age of 70, returned from exile. This was an emotional occasion. Black Country Chartists had been unremitting in their efforts to procure the return of the three 'martyrs' of Newport and now their work had been crowned with success. Attempts were made to get Frost to a Black Country demonstration. A delegate meeting took place at Mr. Parker's

Noah's Ark Inn, Wolverhampton Street, Bilston,[56] and a further meeting in Bilston agreed on getting out collecting sheets for a Frost demonstration. In September there was a London demonstration for Frost when nearly one million people turned out,[57] but Frost was old and not as militant as he had been in 1839 and presumably refused the invitation of the Black Country Chartists, for no more is heard of the project.

Ernest Jones' circumstances and temper improved in 1866 and this was reflected throughout the movement. In the autumn he began his famous political soirées 'Evenings with the People'.[58] These were published as 1d pamphlets and they filled the need for working class literature, which the Wednesbury Chartists had first spotlighted, in a remarkable way. At a Dudley meeting it was recorded: 'We read your speech which was loudly cheered.' and twenty five copies were ordered. A Birmingham Chartist, Noble, wrote: 'Your address is calculated to move the most apathetic. I cannot express what my feelings were when I read it. A copy should be in the home of every working man in the kingdom.'[59]

II

From 1857, the Dudley branch took the limelight and not only assumed leadership of the Black Country, but attained a national importance as well. The first part of the year was taken up with preparations for the election in which Jones stood for Nottingham. Collections were taken, particularly in Dudley, while Wednesbury contributed £1 0. 6d.[60]

In March, Samuel Cook wrote to the *People's Paper*. He stated that he had seen extracts from the *Era* and also the *Leader* recommending a conference of all reformers and he was pleased to see that Jones had also recommended such a conference at Smithfield, where there had been an immense demonstration in January addressed by Jones.[61] Cook asked what Jones would do should such a general conference of reformers be called. Jones' answer was: advocate the Charter; support nothing less.[62] Such advice was easy to give, but the problem was vastly complicated and the Dudley Chartists returned to this matter in connection with a meeting in London at which Chartists and middle-class reformers had met. At their weekly meeting they passed a resolution that it would have been advisable to have held a private conference before the meeting to have agreed to a resolution to be put and that it was unwise of the Committee to insist that all should pledge themselves to be Chartists before the Committee would assist them in their agitation for reform. A note by Jones begged to correct a slight misunderstanding among his friends. The object of the meeting had been to show the willingness of Chartists to co-operate with the middle-class without giving up their own agitation.[63] This was acknowledged by the Dudley branch the next week who expressed sincere approval of the conciliatory tone of Jones to the middle-class reformers and hoped that a united organisation would be effected to secure a real, honest and satisfactory Reform Bill.[64] The above is a typical example of an increasingly outspoken attitude the Dudley Chartists were prepared to take and which Jones printed in the *People's Paper*. It is clear that from early 1856 the strongest Black Country Chartist branch was prepared to co-operate with the middle-class and prepared to accept less than manhood suffrage. It is possible that Jones' thinking was affected by the Dudley Chartists, for it was the next week that Jones made his proposal for a conference of reformers.[65] This conference proved to be the last great landmark of organised Chartism. It took nearly a year to prepare and by that time a large number of localities had been re-formed and were represented at the Conference. In the Black Country, the Dudley Chartists performed almost superhuman feats in resurrecting branches such as Wolverhampton, and Black Country Chartism was brought to another peak which it was never again to achieve.

Jones' idea was for the Chartists to convene a meeting to which leading reformers of other viewpoints would be invited. 'If the Middle-class will not take the initiative, we must. We will not let the Russells and Palmerstons produce any bill they think fit,' Jones wrote. The Dudley Chartists approved the idea of such a conference and proposed:[66]

1. That a delegate be sent from Dudley, and an endeavour be made to solicit the whole of the surrounding areas.
2. That the next meeting discuss the amount of reform it would be best to agree to demand.[67]

They lost no time in convening a delegate meeting. An interesting report indicates the difficulty of deciphering in London the hand-writing of working class correspondents, for delegates were requested from, among other towns, Burley Hill, Brodeley and Walesown! The report continued: 'We should have invited Birmingham, but surely that large town is capable of sending two delegates. The government has promised a reform bill next session. If we speak gently the Reform Bill will be gentle and small. If we speak in thunderous tones we may get what we have asked for in vain these twenty-five years—the right of every man to vote.'[68] The delegate meeting was held within a fortnight. Delegates were present from Bilston, Stourbridge, Cradley, Dudley Port, Kate's Hill and Dudley. It will be noted that the last three areas named are all in Dudley. Samuel Cook as the veteran of democracy was called to the chair. It was moved by John Chance and seconded by J. Tompson of Bilston that they approved of a Chartist Conference. It was moved by Messrs. Wallwork and Woodhouse (of Cradley) that the delegates collect the necessary subscriptions.[69] In July another delegate meeting took place with representatives from Bilston, Dudley, Willenhall, Wednesbury, Dudley Port, Stourbridge and Birmingham etc. with John Chance in the chair. It was resolved to send £1 to Ernest Jones towards the cost of the hall, to postpone electing the delegate for a fortnight and to approve Jones' suggestion that John Frost be the chairman of the conference.[70] In August the Dudley Chartists nominated John Chance and Daniel Wallwork as candidates for election at a subsequent district meeting and when this meeting took place with representatives from Dudley, Bilston, Stourbridge and Wednesbury, Wallwork was the delegate finally chosen.[71] But meanwhile, the idea of a Reformers' Conference was snowballing and the date of the event put back to give time to organise wider support. This breathing space was taken full advantage of in the Black Country.

In August, John Pierce, a veteran Chartist in Tettenhall sent a payment of 10/- indicating that the *People's Paper* was read in Tettenhall. He was thanked for his money and told that the paper was always sent on time; lateness was due to deficiences in the postal services.[72] In September Ambrose Thompson lectured at a meeting at the Lancasterian School, Dudley, with Wallwork in the chair. At this meeting Samuel Cook moved the following resolution: 'Any reform short of the People's Charter will not confer on the people their just rights. But seeing the present disposition of Reformers we are prepared to unite and co-operate with them for any measure of reform that will be of substantial benefit to the people.' Cook went on to say that he went further than the Charter and if any constituency was in favour of sending any lady to the House of Lords or House of Commons they should remove the impediments to the exercise of that right. (cheers)[73]

Now it was that the Dudley Chartists went out to revive flagging or non-existent branches. A deputation was appointed 'to wait on the friends of democracy in Walsall at Mr. Scholey's Temperance Hotel', and urged every reader of the *People's Paper* in Wolverhampton to arrange a meeting in that town. The Walsall meeting took place when 'several earnest friends from Walsall and Birmingham were present'. They resolved to form themselves into a locality. Further deputations from Dudley were appointed to wait on Bilston and Wednesbury. Activity in Dudley even seems to have galvanised the Birmingham Chartists and Thomas Noble reported a meeting there. At Walsall the first meeting of the branch was attended by only three people, Scholey, Grainger and S. Hodgkins, together with Dudley friends.[74] Since the delegates to the Conference had already been elected, the Dudley Chartists now suggested that the newly forming localities might like to take the opportunity of instructing the delegate who had been elected. The Dudley report went on: 'We are glad that Walsall, Wednesbury and Bilston have begun to work, but where is Wolverhampton? The Barlows, Whittinghams, Gibsons, Griffiths, Gallimores and Ashtons and others have it in their power to form an organisation such as Wolverhampton has not seen for years.'[75] This public admonition seems to have had the necessary effect for by the end of the month the first Chartist meeting for many years occurred at B.R. Barlow's house in Tower Street with J.P. Ashton in the chair. Resolutions were passed on the Indian revolt and concerning a

Wolverhampton delegate to the Conference. Speakers at this meeting included Barlow jun., Galleymore, Spurr and Whittingham.[76]

By now the *People's Paper* was printing names of middle-class reformers it was proposed to invite to the Conference. These included, Bright, Cobden, Holyoake, Kingsley, William Newton the A.S.E. leader, etc. To this list Dudley added others including Robert Owen, Rev. A. O'Neill, George Edmonds, Clutton Salt and Samuel Cook.[77] In the Midlands, the Wednesbury branch was now meeting at William Taylor, the secretary's house in King Street. Bilston were meeting at the Noah's Ark and Birmingham at Grove's Temperance Hotel, 55 Hill Street.[78] Wolverhampton branch was progressing so well that a Committee of eight had been formed.[79] At the November district meeting at Dudley twenty delegates were present who regretted Frost's letter saying, that he saw no point in a conference.[80] A Walsall member dug up a glazed picture of Feargus O'Connor which the branch proposed to raffle at 6d a ticket.[81] The December delegate meeting was held in Walsall. Represented were Bilston, Dudley, Wednesbury, Walsall, Willenhall, Stourbridge and Birmingham. The question of a second delegate to the Conference was raised, but postponed until the intentions of Wolverhampton and Birmingham were known.[82]

In Dudley, public activity was being prepared. An order for 1,000 copies of the People's Charter with the names of the six Members of Parliament and the six working men who drew it up was sent to the printers. Copies were to be sent to Palmerston, the Archbishop of Canterbury and Lord Brougham demanding that they incorporate this in their Reform Bill. At subsequent meetings, extracts from Blackstone were to be read and perhaps published. At Wednesbury a delegate meeting took place and John Chance was elected as the second delegate to the Conference. Permanent area organisation was set up with Wallwork as District Secretary and Taylor of Wednesbury as Treasurer. A public meeting was arranged for Boxing Day at Spoil Bank, Spon Lane.[84] In January 1858 another branch was formed in Dudley when a meeting was held at Mr. Coffin's, Stafford Street to form another association in that part of the town.[85] At the end of January the last delegate meeting before the Conference met at Mr. Sykes' house in Bilston. The representatives voted that their delegates at the Conference should not accept less than Manhood Suffrage and No Property Qualifications. The delegates were to be allowed £3 5. 0d. expenses each and the question of the Chartist executive was to be left to the discretion of the delegates.[86]

The long-awaited Chartist Conference met in March 1858. Forty delegates assembled and the Conference was in two parts. The first few days were taken up with the question of Chartist organisation and the terms on which Chartists would co-operate with middle-class reformers. The second part of the Conference consisted of meetings with some middle-class reformers and the setting up of the Political Reform League to be launched with a £100 fund.[87] The Dudley Chartists played their part in the proceedings. Before the Conference opened Samuel Cook had made a suggestion in the *People's Paper*. The reply he received from Jones was that his suggestion would best be brought forward at the Conference which it was hoped that he would attend.[88] Despite the earlier suggestion that Cook should be one of the honoured guests, there is no record that he attended the Conference. Wallwork, however, was vocal on the proposal that the Chartist executive should consist of one man. This proposal was eventually adopted and Ernest Jones, of course, became the single executive member. Wallwork defended this proposal arguing that if there was an executive of more than one there would always be a split. Answering the charges of dictation, Wallwork said that Jones always submitted his plans to the localities. It would therefore be the localities that dictated and Ernest Jones would execute (applause).[89] The final resolution before meeting the other reformers was that they would unite with the middle-class on Manhood Suffrage and No Property Qualifications, as the middle-class were in favour of the Ballot, Equal Electoral Districts and Shorter Parliaments. They pledged themselves, however, not to abandon the agitation for the Charter.[90]

The Black Country branches met to hear reports back from the conference, but these discussions merged with a financial crisis for the *People's Paper* which was to lead to its being taken over in time by Baxter Langley, a middle-class reformer, and to the paper's extinction in September. Such a disappointing outcome of the Conference led to the disintegration of the newly formed branches, including those in the Black Country, until the Dudley branch stood alone, virtually throughout the country. In Dudley the branch assembled to hear a report from the delegates. They expressed their indignation at the want of veracity in Reynolds' report.[91] The next week a district delegates' meeting assembled at Wallwork's house in Flood Street to hear a long report from the delegates. They approved the conduct of their delegates and pledged themselves to raise £1 of the £100 fund.[92] The next week Thomas Whittall of 36 Merridale Street sent 4/11d in postage stamps to the £100 fund in the name of the Wolverhampton Reform Committee.

But more urgent matters intervened. Jones announced that he needed to raise £80 immediately if the paper was to be continued. The Chartists responded nobly and £40 was contributed within a fortnight. Dudley at once raised £1. 0. 4d to pay off the debts of the paper. They also discussed the £100 fund. There was confusion in the branch, since it was not clear whether this fund was to be used for Chartist purposes or for the new organisation. It was finally agreed in Dudley to raise money for Chartist purposes and only then raise money for the Political Reform League.[93] The next week the Dudley branch sent another 10/- to Jones' £80 fund, but they were critical of his proposal to start a new 1d paper called the *London News*. The Dudley Chartists were in favour of cutting down the size of the *People's Paper* and instead of charging the existing price of 5d that the price be cut to 2½d or 1d. Jones argued that this could not be done because four pages of the *People's Paper* were donated at £4-£5 less than they cost. But since the only person who 'donated' to the paper was Jones himself, this does not seem a very valid objection.[94] The Dudley branch accepted Jones' decision loyally, however, and it was agreed to send for handbills for the new 1d paper and do all they could to give it a good circulation.[95]

Jones' next proposal was for a National Parliament of the Unenfranchised and at this the Dudley Chartists jibbed. They considered it was impractical considering the apathy of the people. At this time the branch became utterly absorbed in the subject of 'Poverty, Prostitution and Celibacy, their cause and cure'. Wallwork led the discussion 'fortifying his arguments from the Political Economist and the writings of Malthus'. Two hours animated discussion followed.[96] The next meeting was a full one with Mr. Massey in the chair. Regret was expressed that Jones was not able to come to the provinces as the £100 fund and the union of the middle and working classes were topics hardly heard of in the last few weeks. Other remarks were made 'indicating that there was not perfect satisfaction with things in connection with the paper'. The address of the Political Reform League was then read and approved. A letter was also sent to the member for the Borough, H.B. Sheridan expressing surprise at his absence at the division on the Repeal of Property Qualification Bill. Finally the meeting resumed its discussion on Poverty, Prostitution and Celibacy. 'After 2-3 hours earnest discussion it was again adjourned. The subject has so many bearings that it has excited more discussion than any other.'[97]

The letter to Sheridan mentioned above was of some importance to Chartists, since the Bill referred to achieved the first of the six points of the Charter. Jones, in his 'Current Notes' in the paper, observed that they would now be able to concentrate the more on the remaining five points. He also brought up the question of the Political Reform League saying that the middle-class were alleging that the Chartists were doing nothing about it. Chartists replied that it was they who had brought it into existence. Jones, however, exhorted Chartists to do more and also proposed that of the £100 fund half should go to the League. Jones' 'Current Notes' were always read at each branch meeting and the next Dudley meeting agreed with Jones' points calling for more effort for the Political Reform League. They then resumed their discussion on Poverty, Prostitution and Chastity, making the following comment: 'This subject has now been discussed for five successive Sundays. As Ricardo, Mill, Martineau, Rossi and others have observed, food and population affects everything—morals, politics and national and domestic economy. We recommend every Chartist locality to discuss this question.'[98]

In June Baxter Langley took over the *People's Paper* with the proviso that as long as the paper continued to come out, Jones would be allotted two columns for reporting Chartist news. The next week at the Dudley branch meeting these changes were approved, some people thinking that it would give Ernest Jones more time to travel and relieve him of his financial worries. There was unanimous agreement, however, that the *People's Paper* and Jones' still independent 1d *London News* should be merged and brought out at 2d. A letter was then read from Benjamin Lucraft, who had been one of the chairmen at the Charter Conference, that having brought about a union of the middle and working classes, Chartists were doing nothing about it. 'The letter was so excellent that it was the unanimous desire of the meeting that it be published in the *People's Paper*.' But this was not to the liking of Jones who commented in his truncated space that the letter was a libel on the Chartist movement. The conference which had brought the union into existence had cost not less than £1,000. That was to begin with. He trusted that they would raise the promised £50 and they would then see what the middle-class could do.[99]

In Dudley, a larger meeting room was procured and about this time Jones put out a list of the localities which he thought were strong enough to stand Chartist Parliamentary candidates. In the Midlands this included Dudley, Coventry and Worcester but not Birmingham. [100] In August quarterly elections took place in Dudley. Daniel Wallwork had to give up the secretaryship and John Wadely was elected in his place. Simon Watts was re-elected treasurer. Bills were authorised to be issued announcing public lectures on Sunday evenings, and a tea party was to be arranged by a joint committee of the Miners and Mutual Improvement Society.[101] The next week there was a long letter in the paper announcing that Jones had quarrelled with Langley and a fortnight later a letter saying that Langley had offered the *People's Paper* back to Jones for £100, but Jones could not recommend the localities to consider it. So the *People's Paper* came to an end.

Within a few weeks Jones had established another newspaper. This was the *Cabinet Newspaper* of eight smallish pages costing 2d unstamped and 3d stamped. The Dudley Chartists immediately resumed reports of their meetings. On November 21st, with Mr. Silk in the chair, a motion had been passed stating that nothing but manhood suffrage, short parliaments, the ballot and a just equalisation of electoral districts would meet the needs of the people and a public meeting would be called in December to take opinions on this subject.[102] The next week Jones announced 'a perfect torrent of congratulations, votes of approval and confidence and condemnation of our unscrupulous opponents (i.e. Reynolds—G.B.) have come to hand again this week'. Among these was a letter from W. Smith of Willenhall. In Dudley at the Miners' and Working Men's Society Room, New Mill Street with Samuel Cook in the chair, it had been resolved to form themselves into a society called the Manhood Suffrage Association.[103]

By 1859 the Chartist movement, despite its previous intention to uphold its independent agitation, was taking the initiative in setting up, and beginning to merge itself with, wider organisations of reform. In Wednesbury at a meeting at the British Queen with Benjamin Danks in the chair it was resolved to set up the Wednesbury Parliamentary Reform Association.[104] In Dudley meetings were being held in the meeting room of the Mutual Improvement and Miners' Protection Society[105] and at Walsall the M.P. was being quizzed as to his intentions with regard to the £6 ratal clause of

Lord John Russell's Reform Bill.[106]

The failure of Lord John Russell's phoney Reform Bill of 1859 really marked the end of Chartism. The *Cabinet Newspaper* ended in February 1860. It was replaced by a *Penny Times and Weekly Telegraph* which quickly disappeared. Ernest Jones had by this time, not unnaturally, become thoroughly worn out with his role of sole leader of the Chartist movement. Moreover, he had begun to move towards a position of collaboration with the middle-class which indeed, in the short run, was to bring the Reform Bill of 1867, but which, in the long run, was a blind alley for the working-class, as the experience of the next twenty years was to show. That the Chartist movement was not entirely played out was demonstrated by the subscriptions to the fund which enabled Jones to sue Reynolds when his scurrility, which played its part in the demise of the Chartist movement, became intolerable. Nearly £100 was subscribed,[107] including donations from Wednesbury, Dudley and Willenhall. After Jones had won his action and had claimed only an apology from Reynolds a testimonial fund was opened for him. In the Black Country a district subscription was opened at Parker's Noah's Ark Inn, Bilston.[108] But Jones' will to survive was gone and he exchanged the . . . 'shabby coat buttoned close up round the throat, (which), seemed to conceal the poverty to which a too faithful adherence to a lost cause had reduced him',[109] for the barrister's silk of the Northern Circuit. Black Country Chartism survived to the very end. It was left high and dry without a national leadership and without a newspaper to organise and agitate. Under these circumstances it did not continue as an organised body.

What can be said of Black Country Chartism at the end? That an organised branch in Dudley and scattered individual Chartists in other towns did not constitute a mass movement is self-evident. But political parties do not necessarily have to have large memberships to survive and exercise influence. None of the first Socialist societies of the 1880s was large, yet their influence was enormous. Chartism in the Black Country had the priceless advantage that whenever a mass agitation occurred workers would turn to it for leadership, and this was to be demonstrated again in the part that Chartists played in the 1867 agitation. It is probably true that the influence of Chartism was largely due to the activity of a number of ageing men—Cook, Linney, Chance, Danks etc. Yet at least in Dudley, new cadres could be brought forward to replace old leaders—Wallwork, Wadeley and Silk. G.D.H. Cole has remarked that until 1867 a working class political party was impossible. Perhaps he is right. If so, Ernest Jones came near to achieving the impossible; the Black Country Chartists came even nearer.

REFERENCES

(1) *Northern Star* 5th January 1850
(2) *Ibid.* 23rd February 1850
(3) *Ibid.* 2nd March 1850
(4) *Ibid.* 20th April 1850
(5) *Ibid.* 29th June 1850. The latter visit was the one of which Joy MacAskill writes: 'It (the Great Dodford Estate) was only used in July 1848 for a meeting of Land Company sympathisers from the Black Country as a gesture of defiance of the "slanders contained in the (Select) Committee Report".' 'Chartist Land Plan' in *Chartist Studies* ed. Briggs p. 327
(6) *Ibid.* 3rd August 1850
(7) *Ibid.* 5th October 1850. Haynau, known as the Hyena, was the Austrian General who had butchered the Hungarians in 1849, and whose visit to London the Government incautiously approved. He was taken to the show brewery of Barclay, Perkins, where Garibaldi was to be rapturously received in 1864, and so assaulted by the workers that he took refuge in a dustbin
(8) *Ibid.* 4th January, 18th January 1851
(9) John Saville—*Ernest Jones, Chartist* pp. 43-45
(10) *Northern Star* 30th August 1851
(11) *Ibid.* 16th November 1851
(12) *Ibid.* 14th February, 21st February, 6th March 1852
(13) *People's Paper* 5th March, 14th May, 4th June, 24th December 1853
(14) Saville op. cit. pp. 54-55
(15) *People's Paper* 11th March 1854
(16) *Ibid.* 12th August 1854
(17) *Ibid.* 11th February 1854
(18) *Ibid.* 25th February 1854
(19) *Ibid.* 13th May 1854
(20) *Ibid.* 6th May, 25th November 1854, 13th January, 20th January 1855
(21) *Ibid.* 27th January 1855
(22) *Ibid.* 3rd February 1855
(23) *Ibid.* 10th February 1855
(24) *Ibid.* 24th February 1855
(25) *Ibid.* 24th February 1855
(26) *Ibid.* 24th March 1855
(27) *Ibid.* 17th March 1855
(28) *Ibid.* 30th June 1855
(29) *Ibid.* 5th May 1855
(30) *Ibid.* 19th May 1855
(31) *Ibid.* 16th June 1855
(32) Saville op. cit. pp. 60-62
(33) *People's Paper* 21st July 1855
(34) *Ibid.* 11th August 1855
(35) *Ibid.* 11th August 1855
(36) *Ibid.* 13th October 1855—6/- from James Vipond, Gospel
(37) D. Read and E. Glasgow—*Feargus O'Connor* (1941) p. 144
(38) *People's Paper* 6th October 1855
(39) 'Working Class Activities 1850-67' in Barnsby thesis, op. cit

(40)   *Walsall Courier* report quoted by *People's Paper* 24th November 1855
(41)   *Democrat and Labour Advocate* 8th December 1855
(42)   *People's Paper* 12th April 1856
(43)   *Ibid.* 26th April 1856
(44)   Saville op. cit. p. 60
(45)   *People's Paper* 22nd March 1856
(46)   *Ibid.* 8th April 1856
(47)   *Ibid.* 26th April 1856
(48)   *Ibid.* 28th June 1856
(49)   *Ibid.* 5th July 1856
(50)   *Ibid.* 26th January 1856 quoted by Saville op. cit. p. 6ln
(51)   *Ibid.* 2nd February 1856
(52)   *Ibid.* 23rd February 1856
(53)   *Ibid.* 8th March 1856
(54)   *Ibid.* 1st March 1856
(55)   *Ibid.* 5th April 1856
(56)   *Ibid.* 16th August 1856
(57)   *Ibid.* 20th September 1856
(58)   Saville op. cit. pp. 61-2
(59)   *People's Paper* 15th November 1856
(60)   *Ibid.* 11th April 1857
(61)   *Ibid.* 24th January 1857
(62)   *Ibid.* 7th March 1857
(63)   *Ibid.* 18th April 1857
(64)   *Ibid.* 25th April 1857
(65)   *Ibid.* 2nd May 1857
(66)   *Ibid.* 2nd May 1857
(67)   *Ibid.* 16th May and 23rd May 1857
(68)   *Ibid.* 30th May 1857
(69)   *Ibid.* 13th June 1857
(70)   *Ibid.* 25th July 1857
(71)   *Ibid.* 8th August and 22nd August 1857
(72)   *Ibid.* 22nd August 1857
(73)   *Ibid.* 19th September 1857
(74)   *Ibid.* 10th October and 17th October 1857
(75)   *Ibid.* 24th October 1857
(76)   *Ibid.* 7th November 1857
(77)   *Ibid.* 7th November 1857
(78)   *Ibid.* 7th November 1857
(79)   *Ibid.* 14th November 1857
(80)   *Ibid.* 21st November 1857
(81)   *Ibid.* 5th December 1857
(82)   *Ibid.* 12th December 1857
(83)   *Ibid.* 19th December and 26th December 1857
(84)   *Ibid.* 26th December 1857
(85)   *Ibid.* 30th January 1858
(86)   *Ibid.* 6th February 1858
(87)   Saville op. cit. pp. 68-9 for a report of the Conference
(88)   *People's Paper* 30th January 1858
(89)   *Ibid.* 13th February 1858

(90) *Ibid.* 13th February 1858
(91) *Ibid.* 20th February 1858. G.W.M. Reynolds was then at daggers drawn with Ernest Jones and slandered him and the Chartist movement in his paper *Reynolds News* to such a degree that Jones was forced to sue him and won the case
(92) *Ibid.* 27th February 1858
(93) *Ibid.* 20th March 1858
(94) *Ibid.* 27th March 1858
(95) *Ibid.* 17th April 1858
(96) *Ibid.* 29th May 1858
(97) *Ibid.* 12th June 1858
(98) *Ibid.* 19th June 1858
(99) *Ibid.* 3rd July 1858
(100) *Ibid.* 24th July and 31st July 1858
(101) *Ibid.* 7th August 1858
(102) *Cabinet Newspaper* No. 1. 27th November 1858
(103) *Ibid.* 4th December 1858
(104) *Ibid.* 25th December 1858
(105) *Ibid.* 15th January and 12th March 1859
(106) *Ibid.* 26th March 1859
(107) *Ibid.* 5th February 1859
(108) *Ibid.* 17th September 1859
(109) W.E. Adams—*Memoirs* Vol. II p. 230 quoted by Saville op. cit

JOHN MILLER

Songs of the Labour
Movement

In March 1961 the Council of Czechoslovak Ethnologists and Folklorists, a section of the Czechoslovak Academy of Science, held an International Symposium for research into 'Workers Songs'. This was the first conference of its kind and covered a wide range of subjects. It revealed that work in this subject is taken very seriously, and that a great deal of research has been done in the Socialist countries, compared with those of the capitalist countries that were represented. This is true particularly of Great Britain, where the subject is not recognised officially, or academically, and no grants are given towards research. The only small exception was, when, as part of the Festival of Britain, A.L. Lloyd was asked to arrange a competition for songs relating to miners and the mining industry, which led subsequently to the publication of his *Come all ye bold miners* by Lawrence & Wishart in 1952. Since then there has been a revival of interest in what might be termed 'industrial' or 'workers' folk-song, including the creation of new songs in the folk—song idiom, which are being enthusiastically sung by young people in the many folk-song clubs that are springing up all over the country, and also in the CND and peace movements.

It is not possible or necessary to give a definition of workers' songs, but it will be agreed that included in the description are not only the 'industrial' folk-songs mentioned above, which are the urban equivalent of 'classical' folk songs collected in the first folk song revival of sixty years ago, but consciously composed songs of workers' conditions and lives, e.g. music hall songs, and the songs of revolt which stimulate and inspire the people in their efforts to improve their lives by struggle against an unjust social system and by striving to bring about a better one. Such songs of revolt on the part of oppressed classes have existed since society was divided into classes and examples are found in all periods and all countries. Our country is no exception, as is proved by the songs and ballads about the legendary Robin Hood, the songs of the Peasants' Revolt of 1381, and the songs of the English Revolution of the seventeenth century.

115

There follows an attempt to give an account of those songs of revolt that have been sung in the British Labour movement since its beginnings at the end of the eighteenth century. This includes all categories of song associated with the Labour movement, whether folk song, art song or hymn, but will exclude 'industrial' folk songs not dealing with the organised workers' struggle; it will, for example, include 'Blackleg Miners', which exhorts the blacklegs to join the union, but not 'Fourpence a day', which describes the terrible conditions of child labour in the mines. It will include songs written by workers and also by members of other classes who have thrown in their lot with the workers. As so little research has been carried out in this subject and not a great deal of material is available, there will be many gaps in the story, and the conclusions may be proved quite wrong by further evidence.

There are certain characteristics common to these songs; with few exceptions most of them had a short life, either because they dealt with local events in a topical fashion and became dated, or because they were not good enough to last. The folk songs may be rougher than the 'classic' folk song because the latter has had longer to be perfected at the hands of many singers. The other songs, at least until the end of the nineteenth century, used tunes borrowed from other sources, such as national airs, popular songs and hymns. On the whole, therefore, their music has no specific quality, such as have the songs that came out of the Russian Revolution.

Although so little study into these songs has been carried out in this country, Soviet historians have shown much interest in them, as they have in all aspects of our Labour movement. This is shown for example in *An Anthology of Chartist Literature* by Y.V. Kovalev, published in 1956, a translation of the foreword to which is printed in Chapter Three, and *Mass Poetry in Britain at the end of the Eighteenth and the beginning of the Nineteenth centuries,* by A.N. Nikolyukin, published in 1961. This essay is written primarily to arouse interest in the subject, in the hope that others will be stimulated to look for more material. Until many more examples are available, it will not be possible to pass from the stage of collection to that of analysis, comparison, and evaluation without the risk of reaching incorrect conclusions. It is proposed, therefore, to give a number of examples from each historical period for which examples are available, with a few introductory remarks on it.

I

RADICAL SONGS

After the end of the English Revolution of the seventeenth century, one of the first signs of political agitation in which the ordinary people were involved was the movement that developed around John Wilkes, under the slogan 'Wilkes and Liberty' in the 1760's. Wilkes was released from King's Bench prison on Wednesday, 18th April, 1770, and a book of songs celebrating this event was published in London called *The Patriots' Jubilee*.

It contained songs with titles such as 'The Enlargement', 'Middlesex', and 'Invocation to Liberty', set to popular tunes like 'Rule Britannia', and others taken from the ballad operas of the day such as the 'Maid of the Mill' by Samuel Arnold. The use of these tunes, which were sung in the pleasure gardens at Vauxhall and Ranelagh, and in the theatres, suggests that the writers were not members of the lowest class, who probably could not afford to go to the theatres or even the gardens.

This type of song was produced in large quantities by the Radical movement of the 1790's. The various Radical societies which were formed in the early 1790's, as a result of the tremendous effect of Tom Paine's book *The Rights of Man* were pledged to limited parliamentary reform and drew their support from members of various classes, e.g. the Society for Constitutional Information led by John Cartwright and John Horne Tooke was composed of Radical politicians and dissenters, with a high entrance fee and carrying on its meetings at dinners, whereas the London Corresponding Society led by Thomas Hardy was made up of skilled artisans and tradesmen who met in taverns and coffee houses and paid a penny a week. In both cases, however, singing seems to have been an integral part of their meetings as shown in the headings to some of the printed broadsheets which they issued:-

'Songs sung at the Anniversary of the Revolution of 1688, held at the London Tavern, Nov. 5 1792.'

'The Associators' sung by Sinecure Reeves at the Crown and Anchor.'

'The Berry Bush' written by J. Field and sung on Monday, July 8th 1793, at the Crown and Anchor Tavern, Strand, at the first general meeting of the London Corresponding Society.

Many leading figures in the movement wrote songs for it, e.g. the poet James Montgomery, Thomas Spence, and John Thelwall, but many other authors were anonymous. The subjects dealt with cover a wide field: the Rights of Man, Tom Paine, the London Corresponding Society, the Revolution of 1688, Benjamin Franklin, the French Revolution. There were many satirical songs about Pitt, Burke (the 'Swinish Multitude'), sinecures, informers, unjust taxes, and so on. The latter are clearly directed against a particular evil, whereas the former, which attempt to define the reformers' aims, although expressed in noble and lofty terms, give no clear indication of how these aims are to be achieved.

The music was that of the popular songs of the day, familar from their performance in the London and provincial pleasure gardens, and at the theatres. At that time vast numbers of 'English' or 'ballad' operas were staged, with music by composers such as Charles Dibdin, T. A. Arne, Michael Arne, Shield, and Samuel Arnold, and single songs from these became and remained for many years popular favourites.

From a sample of 33 songs, 15 use popular tunes such as Rule Britannia, Hearts of Oak, Vicar of Bray, and Lass of Richmond Hill, eight are set to folk tunes such as Derry Down and Chevy Chase, and ten to songs from the English Operas.

It is fitting that our first example should be a parody of 'God Save the King' (which first became known in 1745):-

> God save — 'The Rights of Man!'
> Give him a heart to scan
> Blessings so dear!
> Let them be spread around,
> Wherever Man is found,
> And with the welcome sound
> Ravish his ear!

> FAME! Let thy Trumpet Sound,
> Tell all the World around,
> Tell each degree:
> Tell Ribands, Crowns and Stars,
> Kings, Traitors, Troops and Wars,
> Plans, Councils, Plots and Jars,
> FRENCHMEN are FREE.

Here are three other typical examples:-

To the London Corresponding Society.

> Assembled in our Country's Cause,
> Hail the happy season;
> We fear no frowns — nor court applause,
> Pursuing truth and reason.
> Chorus: Boldly all with heart and hand
> Meet we here united,
> By each other firmly stand,
> To see our country righted.

> Brave the dangers that surround
> Bid them all defiance;
> Truth eternal is our ground,
> THE PEOPLE our alliance.

Song sung at the Anniversary of the Revolution of 1688: (held at the London Tavern, Nov 5, 1792).

See! bright Liberty descending,
O'er the verdant hills and plains:
And bold GALLIA, nobly sending,
FREEDOM to the slaves in chains.

See! fell tyranny defeated;
By each bold and patriot band,
May their triumphs be repeated,
O'er oppression's iron hand.

But as human institutions,
Are by nature prone to change;
Let succeeding revolutions,
Wise and equal laws arrange.

Thus secured shall future ages,
Who celebrate this day;
Say no more wild discord rages,
TRUTH and REASON bear the sway.

No title: (Tune — 'Heart of Oak').

Come, cheer up my countrymen ne'er be dismayed
For Freedom her banners once more has display'd
Be staunch for your Rights —Hark 'tis Liberty's call;
For Freedom, dear Freedom, stand up one and all!

Chorus: With heart and with hand,
Swear firmly to stand;
Till oppression is driven quite out of the land.

To redress all our wrongs, let 'Man's Rights' be apply'd
Truth and Justice they show, and by these we'll abide.
Luxurious Pomp, which brings Taxes and Woes,
No more we'll maintain with the sweat of our brows.

The following are examples of the satirical songs:-

The Associators.

Ye venal herd, in evil hours,
Come rally round your places;
Sinecures and pensions ours,
By grinding poor men's faces.

Bring the gold, the fees then bring,
And you shall loyal find us;
We care not whose hearts we wring,
We'll cast the poor behind us.

Why for the poor should we then care,
Since on them all we fatten:
Be they hungry, sick or bare,
We still on them will batten.

Though base and vile our principles,
And British laws we barter;
We dread not free Britons' wills
A fig for their great Charter.

Since the times must alter soon,
In spite of all our sorrow;
Let's enjoy the honeymoon,
We dare not trust to-morrow.

(Rather appropriate today!)

Burke's Address to the Swinish Multitude

Ye vile Swinish herd, in the sty of taxation,
What would you be after—disturbing the nation,
Give over your grunting—be off—to your sty!
Nor dare to look out, if a king passes by:
Get ye down! down! down! Keep ye down.

Now the church and the state to keep each other warm
Are married together. And where is the harm?
How healthy and wealthy are husband and wife!
But swine are excluded the conjugal life. . . .

Sweet Willy O!

The pride of the nation is Sweet Willy O!
The pride of the nation is Sweet Willy O!
The people around
His virtues resound
So great is the fame of the Sweet Willy O!

The king is delighted with Sweet Willy O!
His WISHES to Crown
He taxes us down,
G.R. is before us where-ever we go!

The poor are enraptured with DEAR Billy O!
If taxes are high,
And burthen'd they cry
They find their relief in the PIT —Billy O!

An end to our darkness and Pit, Billy O!
Our fun will arise when you set, Billy O!
The houses long BLIND
Their EYES would soon find,
And shed a SWEET tear on thy Pit, Billy O!

Citizen guillotine (a new shaving machine)
(tune, 'Bob shave a king')

To the just Guillotine
Who shaves off heads so clean
I tune my string!

Thy power is so great,
That ev'ry tool of State
Dreadeth thy mighty weight,
Wonderful thing!

Sweet Billy thee shall hail,
Johnny Reeves at his Tail,
Pride of our Days!

Placemen, Swan-like shall sing,
Guillotine, mighty King,
Echoes from crowds shall ring,
With thy just Praise.

No, Billy shall not swing,
An hour upon a String,
To stop his Breath!

Right Honourable Friend,
The Swine shall ne'er suspend,
Thy Neck from Halter's End,
In ling'ring Death.

No, no, the shining Blade,
Shall hail the FELON'S Head,
Fraternal wise.

One blest, but happy stroke,
One soft, tho' sudden shock,
Shall roll it from the Block,
'Midst joyful cries.

Long live great Guillotine,
Who shaves the Head so clean,
Of Queen or King.

Whose power is so great,
That ev'ry Tool of State,
Dreadeth his mighty weight,
Wonderful Thing!!!

Some of the Radical slogans (Toasts & Sentiments) too could well be used today:- 'Addition to our friends — Subtraction to our foes — multiplication to our rights — and division to the enemies of Freedom.' or 'Champagne to our friends and Thomas Paine to our foes.' There were similar Radical societies outside London in provincial towns and in Scotland, which in some cases produced their own songs such as those of John Freeth, a tavern keeper of Birmingham.

The various repressive Acts of Pitt's government and the impossibility of achieving their aims in the war atmosphere of the time led to the collapse of the Radical Societies by 1800, and the Reform agitation did not really revive until after 1815. The general impression given by the Radical songs is that they are literary productions of educated men, and it is not till the Luddite Risings (1811–12) that examples of the 'workers folk song' appear:-

Cropper Lads (The tune for this is a strong one in the Mixolydian mode).

Some cropper lads of great renown,
Who love to drink good ale that's brown
And strike each haughty tyrant down,
With hatchet pike and gun
O, the cropper lads for me,
And gallant lads they be.
With lusty stroke the shear-frames broke,
The cropper lads for me.

What though the specials still advance,
And soldiers nightly round us prance
The cropper lads still lead the dance,
With hatchet, pike and gun!

And night by night when all is still
And the moon is hid behind the hill.
We forward march to do our will
With hatchet, pike and gun!

Great Enoch still shall lead the van
Stop him who dare! stop him who can!
Press forward every gallant man
With hatchet, pike and gun!

　　　*　　*　　*　　*

Come all ye croppers stout and bold,
Let your faith grow stronger still,
Oh, the cropper lads in the county of York,
Broke the shears at Forster's mill
The wind it blew,
The sparks they flew,
Which alarmed the town full soon.

Around and around we all will stand,
and sternly swear we will,
We'll break the shears and windows too,
And set fire to the Tazzling mill.

Most of the 'industrial' or 'workers' folk songs at present known come from two of our oldest industries — mining and weaving. It has been suggested that this is because song creation in these industries had been going on for centuries before the Industrial Revolution and that this did not have such a shattering effect on them as it did on rural life and its folk songs. A.L. Lloyd in *Come all ye bold miners* gives examples of strike, eviction and trade union songs among miners and there are a few examples of weavers' songs.

II

THE REFORM AGITATION AFTER 1815

Peterloo *With Henry Hunt we'll go* (Tune: The Battle of Waterloo)
　　　　　'Twas on the 16th day of August, Eighteen hundred and
　　　　　nineteen
　　　　　A meeting held in Peter Street was glorious to be seen
　　　　　Joe Nadin and his bulldogs, which you might plainly see,
　　　　　And on the other side stood the bloody cavalry.

Chorus: With Henry Hunt we'll go my boys,
            With Henry Hunt we'll go,
            We'll mount the cap of Liberty,
            In spite of Nadin Joe.

Samuel Bamford *The Union Hymn.*

> O worthy is the glorious cause,
> Ye patriots of the Union;
> Our fathers' rights, our fathers' laws,
> Await a constant Union.
> A crouching dastard sure is he
> Who would not strike for liberty,
> And die to set old England free
> From all her load of tyranny:
> Up, brave men of the Union.

Street songs

(a)   The Reform Bill

> As William and BILL are the same,
> Our King if he weathers the storm,
> Shall be called in the annals of fame,
> The Glorious BILL of Reform.

(B)   A new political and Reform Alphabet with Fables on the Times.

> I for Injury. A performance that takes place every
> day and night by the rich against the poor man.
> K for King. A title of monarchy, an idol of immense
> weight
> P for Peelers. A body of great force. Brave and noble
> conquerors of an unarmed and peaceable people
> S for Stomach. 'Apartments Unfurnished' Inquire within.
> U for Union. A word despised by all oppressors.
> (Part only)

Corn Law Repeal.

> Now all you Corn Leaguers I won't keep you long,
> While I sing you a verse of a new hunting song.
> Now the season's upon us we'll take to the field
> And its time we were busy with Corn Law Repeal.

Chorus: Our cause it is springing and none can gainsay,
           The landlords and bakers are all knocked awry;
           And the poor man is up and he's dancing a reel
           And the song that he's singing is Corn Law Repeal.

           The Queen went a-hunting through Scotland and France
           She hunted Prince Albert to teach her to dance.
           Bobby Peel is a huntsman and not known to fail,
           He's hunting the rich with his old Corn Law Bill.

           Now bread so they tell us will soon get a fall;
           Monopolist grubber we'll hunt to the wall.
           So Ladies and Leaguers we'll all shout hooray!
           The League to the rescue and hasten the day!

III

CHARTIST SONGS

The Chartist movement produced a great body of literature, poems and songs, which is largely unknown today. It was modelled on the works of the great Reformers such as Godwin and Paine, on the poetry of the great romantics such as Byron and Shelley, and that of the radical poets of the 1830's, and on the popular Methodist hymns. This last characteristic, which is completely lacking in the earlier Radical songs, was introduced into political songs earlier in the nineteenth century when the Primitive Methodist movement spread like wildfire among the new class of factory workers. Throughout the century the Methodist movement provided many leaders for the labour movement and the tradition of the 'political hymn' or 'labour anthem' survived until quite recently. In the U.S.A. the basis was the Revivalist hymns which were used with such effect by Joe Hill and the I.W.W. Not all the Chartist songs are in this idiom, of course; many were based on the Romantic poets' work, and some are strongly satirical. The music used for this type of song was well known national airs, popular songs and folk songs. Ernest Jones' famous 'Song of the Low' is the first on record that had music specially written for it.

South Wales Chartist Song, 1839, to rally support for John Frost and other imprisoned leaders of the Newport Rising 1839.

           Uphold these bold Comrades who suffer for you,
           Who nobly stand foremost, demanding your due,
           Away with the timid, 'tis treason to fear—
           To surrender or falter when danger is near.
           For now that our leaders disdain to betray
           'Tis base to desert them, or succour delay.

                    *   *   *   *

A Hundred years, a thousand years we're marching on the road
The going isn't easy yet, we've got a heavy load
The way is blind with blood and sweat & death sings in our ears
But time is marching on our side, we will defeat the years.
We men of bone, of sunken shank, our only treasure death
Women who carry at the breast heirs to the hungry earth
Speak with one voice we march we rest and march again upon the years
Sons of our sons are listening to hear the Chartist cheers
Sons of our sons are listening to hear the Chartist cheers.

The Lion of Freedom (Northern Star 1841)—written to celebrate the release of
Feargus O'Connor from prison.

The lion of freedom comes from his den,
We'll rally around him again and again,
We'll crown him with laurels our champion to be,
O'Connor, the patriot of sweet liberty.

The pride of the nation, he's noble and brave
He's the terror of tyrants, the friend of the slave,
The bright star of freedom, the noblest of men,
We'll rally around him again and again.

Though proud daring tyrants his body confined,
They never could alter his generous mind;
We'll hail our caged lion, now free from his den,
And we'll rally around him again and again.

Who strove for the patriots? was up night and day?
And saved them from falling to tyrants a prey?
It was Feargus O'Connor was diligent then!
We'll rally around him again and again.

Presentation of the National Petition (Monday May 2nd 1842)

It was Nature's gay day,
Bright smiling May day,
Each heart was yearning our country to free;
Thy banners were bringing
The people were singing
Of the days of their fathers and sweet liberty.
Merrily bounding,

Banners surrounding
Each slave Clash'd his chains on that happy day;
To meet thus delighted
By all invited,
To join the brave throng 'neath freedom's bright ray
Thousands were marshalled,
The throng forward marched;
The burden of millions was borne onward too,
From the field to the Strand,
With banners and band,
The mighty assemblage of Chartists doth go,
Their foes fill with wonder,
As proudly they thunder
Their shouts for their Charter, their hearts with hope fill'd.
To St. Stephens they bear it,
By the table they rear it,—
A monument to testify their woes and their will.

Our Summons (Ernest Jones)

Men of the honest heart,
Men of the stalwart hand,
Men, willing to obey,
Thence able to command;

Men of the rights withheld,
Slaves of the power abused,
Machines cast to neglect,
When your freshness has been used.

Up! Labourers in the vineyard!
Prepare ye for your toil!
For the sun shines on the furrows,
And the seed is in the soil.

Hymn for Lammas-Day (Ernest Jones)

Sharpen the sickle, the fields are white;
'Tis time of the harvest at last.
Reapers, be up with the morning light,
Ere the blush of its youth be past.

Why stand on the highway and lounge at the gate,
With a summer day's work to perform?
If you wait for the hiring 'tis long you may wait-
Till the hour of the night and the storm.

Sharpen the sickle; how full the ears!
While our children are crying for bread;
And the field has been watered with orphans' tears,
And enriched with their fathers dead.
And hopes that are buried, and hearts that broke,
Lie deep in the treasuring sod:
Then sweep down the grain with a thunderstroke,
In the name of humanity's God!

The Song of the future (Ernest Jones)

The land it is the landlord's:
The trader's is the sea;
The ore the usurer's coffer fills,
But what remains for me?

The engine whirls for masters' craft
The steel shines to defend,
With labour's arms, what labour raised,
For labour's foe to spend.

The camp, the pulpit and the law
For rich men's sons are free;
Theirs, theirs is learning, art, and arms,
But what remains for me?

The coming hope, the future day,
When wrong to right shall bow,
And but a little courage, man!
To make that future—NOW.

Chartist hymns (from the Leicester Chartist newspaper *'The Extinguisher.'*)

Britannia's Sons

Britannia's sons, though slaves ye be,
God, your Creator, made you free;
He life and thought and being gave,
But never, never made a slave!

All men are equal in his sight,
The bond, the free, the black, the white:
He made them all—them freedom gave;
God made the man—Man made the slave!

Sons of poverty assembly by William Jones (tune Calcutta).

Sons of poverty assembly,
Ye whose hearts with woe are riven,
Let the guilty tyrants tremble,
Who your hearts such pain have given.
We will never
From the shrine of truth be driven.

Must ye faint—ah! how much longer?
Better by the sword to die
Than to die of want and hunger;
They heed not your feeble cry;
Lift your voices —
Lift your voices to the sky!

Rouse them from their silken slumbers,
Trouble them amidst their pride;
Swell your ranks, augment your numbers,
Spread the charter far and wide!
Truth is with us;
God Himself is on our side.

See the brave, ye spirit broken,
That uphold your righteous cause;
Who against them hath spoken?
They are, just as Jesus was,
Persecuted
By bad men and wicked laws.

Dire oppression, Heaven decrees it,
From our land shall soon be hurled;
Mark the coming time and seize it —
Every banner be unfurled!
Spread the Charter!
Spread the Charter through the world.

God of the earth and sea and sky by Thomas Cooper (tune Old Hundredth).

> God of the earth, and sea, and sky,
> To Thee Thy mournful children cry;
> Didst Thou the blue that bends o'er all
> Spread for a general funeral pall?
>
> Sadness and gloom pervade the land;
> Death—famine—glare on either hand;
> Didst Thou plant earth upon the wave
> Only to form one general grave?
>
> To us,—the wretched and the poor,
> Whom rich men drive from door to door, —
> To us, then, make Thy goodness known,
> And we Thy lofty name will own.
>
> Father, our frames are sinking fast;
> Hast Thou our names behind Thee cast?
> Our sinless babes with hunger die;
> Our hearts are hardening!—hear our cry!
>
> Appear, as in the ancient days!
> Deliver us from our foes, and praise
> Shall from our hearts to Thee ascend –
> To God our Father, and our Friend!

From Robert Owen's *Social Hymns* 1840
    Community—(tune Hillary).

> O happy time, when all mankind
> Shall competition's evil see:
> And seek with one united mind
> The blessings of community.
>
> When social love's benignant flow
> Shall peace on earth, goodwill restore;
> And charity, like ocean's flow
> Connect and compass every shore.
>
> Then will the claims of wealth and state,
> This goodly world no more deface;
> Then war and rapine, strife and hate,
> Among mankind will have no place.

Then will mankind, in common share
The gifts their industry supplies,
And prove, escaped from selfish care
The joys of heaven beneath the skies.

IV

EARLY TRADE UNION SONGS

Blackleg Miners

Oh, every evening after dark
The blackleg miners creep to work,
With corduroys and coaly shirt,
The dirty blackleg miners!

They take their picks and down they go
To dig the coal that lies below,
And there isn't a woman in this town now
Will look at a blackleg miner!

They'll take your tools and clothes as well
And throw them into the pit of hell.
It's down you go and fare you well,
You dirty blackleg miners!

So join the union while you may,
Don't wait until your dying day,
For that may not be far away,
You dirty blackleg miners!

Striking Times (a street ballad of 1853).

Cheer up, cheer up, you sons of toil, and listen to my song
While I try to amuse you, and I will not take you long.
The working men of England, at length begin to see,
They've made a bold strike for their rights in 1853.
(Chorus) It's high time that working men should have it their own way
And for a fair day's labour, receive a fair day's pay.

This is the time for striking, at least, it strikes me so,
Monopoly has had some knocks, but this must be the blow,
The working men, by thousands, complain their fate is hard,
May order mark their conduct, and success be their reward.

Some of our London Printers, this glorious work begun,
And surely they've done something, for they've upset the Sun,
Employers must be made to see they can't do what they like,
It is the master's greediness causes the men to strike.

(Ten verses in all).

Many more are printed in *Come all ye bold miners*

V

SONGS OF THE FARMWORKERS

These songs are the militant songs created during the extraordinary upsurge of trade unionism among the agricultural labourers in many rural districts of England in the 1870's. Sparked off by the labourers of Wellesbourne in Warwickshire led by a local Primitive Methodist preacher, Joseph Arch, the movement grew rapidly and resulted in the formation of the National Agricultural Labourers' Union in 1872.

Many of the local leaders of the Union were Primitive Methodists, and the early Union meetings were conducted on the lines of chapel services, beginning with a prayer, often without a chairman, men speaking as they felt impelled, in an atmosphere of great enthusiasm. This atmosphere was conducive to singing and the songs that were created must have had a tremendous effect on the workers who sang them.

Justice of the Peace.

My name it is Squire Puddinghead
A Justice of the Peace, sir;
And if you don't know what that means,
Just ask the rural police, sir!
When culprits nabbed for petty crimes
Within my court assemble,
If I am sitting on the bench,
Oh! don't the wretches tremble
At the Great Unpaid!
Ask any but justice
Of the Great Unpaid.

If Polly Brown but takes a stick
From Farmer Giles' fences,
I fine her twopence as its worth,
And fourteen bob expenses;
And if a tramp sleeps in a field,
Such is my lordly bounty,
I give him lodgings for a week,
Provided by the county.

The Union leaders I would hang,
'Twould be a task delightful:
But since I can't, I am content
To do the mean and spiteful;
And if my colleague, Captain Fair,
Would be the poor's protector,
The vilest things I dare to do
Are backed up by the rector.

My Master and I.

Says the master to me, 'Is it true? I am told
Your name on the books of the Union's enroll'd
I never can allow that a workman of mine,
With wicked disturbers of peace should combine.

I give you fair warning, mind what you're about,
I shall put my foot on it and trample it out;
On which side your bread's buttered, now sure you can see,
So decide now at once for the Union or me.'

Says I to the master, 'It's perfectly true
That I am in the Union and I'll stick to it too;
And if between Union and you I must choose
I have plenty to win, and little to lose.

For twenty years mostly my bread has been dry,
And to butter it now I shall certainly try;
And though I respect you, remember I'm free—
No master in England shall trample on me.'

(Nine verses in all).

Now We Have Got a Union, Boys (tune, Auld Lang Syne).

> Now, if you will pay attention, lads,
> And listen to my song,
> It is about the working men
> And how they have been wrong'd
> On us the farmers have been hard,
> For years they've kept us down,
> Five shillings worth of work they've had
> For less than half a crown

Chorus: Now we have got a Union, boys,
>   For tillers of the ground,
>   Soon for five shillings worth of work
>   We will be paid a crown.

> Half-starved we pass our lives away
> No better than poor slaves,
> And when our days are ended here
> We have but paupers' graves.
> Now if you will you may be free,
> Hear and obey the call,
> United we can raise ourselves,
> Divided we shall fall.

> But man hath robbed his fellow-man
> What heaven for him hath sent;
> While rich men glut, the starving poor
> Are told to be content.
> The rich men soon will have to learn
> Their slaves we'll be no more,
> We'll put our shoulder to the wheel
> To raise the starving poor.

(Five verses in all).

VI

SONGS OF THE SOCIALIST
MOVEMENT 1880-1914

The 1880's saw the beginnings of new Socialist bodies which were particularly strong in London. The Democratic Federation, which later became the Social Democratic Federation, the Socialist League, and the Fabian Society were all set up in this decade, followed by the Independent Labour Party in 1893 and the Labour Party in 1900. William Morris was associated with the movement from its early days, and from then on produced songs and poems of great power, influencing the many other songwriters of the movement. The 'romanticism' which was expressed in the literature and graphic arts of the time also had a significant effect on the character of the songs, though some were affected by other influences such as hymns and music-hall songs.

The first collection of Morris' songs was *Chants for Socialists* published by the Socialist League in 1885, which was followed by many songbooks published by the ILP, Fabian Society, Socialist and Labour Church Union, Socialist Sunday Schools, Co-operative Women's Guild and the Clarion. Already the gulf between what might be called 'Right' and 'Left' wings of the movement is reflected in the words and music of their songs.

Chants of Labour edited by Edward Carpenter, author and composer of 'England Arise'. was first published in 1888, and republished in 1892, 1897, 1905, 1912, and 1922, so that its contents must have been popular. It may therefore be considered a representative collection, of which the following from the contents are examples:-

Author	Title	Tune
William Morris	Come comrades come	Down among the dead men
,,	No master	The hardy Norseman
,,	Voice of toil	Ye banks and braes
,,	March of the workers	John Brown's body
,,	All for the cause	English air
Edward Carpenter	England Arise	Original
,,	The people to their land	Zu Mantua in Banden
J. B. Glasier	Ballade of Law and Order	Vicar of Bray
Jim Connell	Workers of England	Lilliburlero

There are also songs by Robert Burns, Shelley, Ebenezer Elliott, and Ernest Jones from the past, and others from other countries.
There follow two examples:—

There are Ninety and Nine (words from the Boston Globe) a parody of one of Sankey's hymns.

Original.

There were ninety and nine that safely lay
In the shelter of the fold
But one was out on the hills away,
Far off from the gates of gold—
Away on the mountains wild and bare,
Away from the tender Shepherd's care
Away from the tender Shepherd's care.

But all through the mountains, thunder-riven,
And up from the rocky steep,
There arose a cry to the gate of heaven,
'Rejoice I have found my sheep!'
And the angels echoed around the throne,
'Rejoice, for the Lord brings back his own!'

Parody

There are ninety and nine that work and die
In want and hunger and cold,
That one may live in luxury,
And be lapped in the silken fold!
And ninety and nine in their hovels bare,
And one in a palace of riches rare.

But the night so dreary and dark and long
At last shall the morning bring:
And over the land the victors' song,
Of the ninety and nine shall ring,
And echo afar, from zone to zone,
'Rejoice! for Labour shall have its own!'

The Police (tune-Lass of Richmond Hill)—a satirical song from Germany.
Where three men meet together,
There some detective dolt
Sees signs of evil weather,
And noses out revolt.
To run them in he is not slow,
Lest careless he be found,
For 'tis his duty still to show
He makes the world go round

Chorus: Long Live the good Police,
Long Live the good Police!
Our gentle friends, our good kind friends,
Our dear friends the Police!

If e'er a mortal sneezes,
Or looks too gay or grave,
Straight by the ears he seizes
So manifest a knave;
And if by chance he sneezes twice,
Arrest him on the spot,
Before the scamp can do it thrice—
Plain signal of a plot!

At every nose red-coloured
He stares with ill intent;
And then the merest dullard
Known mischief may be meant,
For why? For why? A ruby nose
May mark a RENDEZVOUS,
Then off to prison straight it goes,
Ere it the State undo.

Robert Blatchford's paper the *Clarion* became the centre from which many novel forms of propaganda stemmed, such as the Clarion vans, cycling clubs, and choirs. The famous composer Rutland Boughton worked with Clarion choirs in Birmingham in the first decade of this century, and some of his songs appear in the *Clarion Song Book* of 1904. Boughton, Ethel Smythe and Edgar Bainton were the first professional composers to place their art at the service of the Labour Movement.

VII

1918—39

The Great War and the October 1917 Revolution changed the world. It is not surprising, therefore, that the workers should no longer be satisfied with the old songs and should want to sing the revolutionary songs that came out of the young Soviet Union. The tremendous vitality of these songs was matched by that of the IWW songs, especially those of Joe Hill, that came from the USA, so that in George Lansbury's *16 songs for 6d,* in addition to the 'Red Flag', 'International', 'March of the Workers', 'England Arise', and 'A Rebel Song', one finds 'March Song of the Red Army', 'Whirlwinds of Danger', 'The Red Army March', 'Red Cavalry Song' from the USSR, and 'We will sing one song' (My old Kentucky Home), 'Casey Jones', and 'Alleluia I'm a bum', from the USA. These songs were also in the *Proletarian Song Book* published in Glasgow, 1919.

Later, during the great depression in the USA, American songs such as 'Buddy can you spare a dime' were taken up in this country. Both the Soviet and American influences were to remain in our workers' songs, but there was a third which was to have a great impact in the later 1930's—the work of the German composer Hanns Eisler and his colleagues, including the great dramatist Berthold Brecht, carried on in Germany from the 1920's until Hitler seized power in 1933. Many of Eisler's songs themselves, such as 'Soldarity Song', 'The Comintern', and 'The United Front Song' (Brecht), became internationally famous and were sung in this country, where they had a great effect on Alan Bush, as can be seen in his songs, 'Hunger Marchers'. (words by G.R.Atterbury), and 'Make your meaning clear' (words by Randall Swingler).

Eisler created new forms to convey his meaning such as the use of jazz elements, sarcasm and satire. He gave detailed directions on methods of performance; the music was dominated by the text; he required a staccato style, precise intonation and clear enunciation. In many cases speech was used in place of song. These methods were copied in other countries, including this. Songs such as Eisler's, with the exception of a few such as the 'Solidarity Song', were usually in parts and difficult for untrained singers, and whilst they were sung by Co-operative and similar choirs, it is doubtful if they had the popularity of either the American or Soviet songs, or such satirical songs as 'Harry was a Bolshie', 'The man that waters the workers' beer', and 'Red fly the banners O'.

The foregoing applies mainly to the Left wing of the movement. By contrast in 1933, the Labour Party published a song book containing fifty-six well known 'Community' songs similar to those in the News Chronicle and Daily Express books, with 20 'Hymns of Labour', most of which really are hymns, the only redeeming feature being the inclusion of the Internationale and Red Flag. There is not one Soviet or American workers' song in it. The same applies to Cooperative songbooks of this date.

With the outbreak of the Spanish Civil War and the formation of the International Brigades, many Spanish songs became famous throughout the international progressive movement, such as 'Hymno de Riego', 'Song of the 15th Brigade', and 'The Four Generals'. One of the most famous of the songs sung by the British Battalion of the International Brigade was 'Jarama'.

Both the Workers Music Association and Unity Theatre were formed in 1936 and their songs had a certain influence on the movement from then on, in particular some of those from Unity's Musical shows of 1939 and 1940.

The period does not seem to have been one of the production of many distinctive workers' songs in this country, perhaps because of the popularity of Soviet and American songs. So far as the latter are concerned, this popularity is also found in the field of popular music, dance music, jazz and music from the Hollywood films. There follows five examples:-

United Front Song (words by Brecht, music by Hanns Eisler)

> As man is only human,
> He must eat before he can think.
> Fine words are only empty air
> And not his meat and drink.

(Chorus) Then, Left! Right! Left!
> Then, Left! Right! Left!
> There's a place, Comrade, for you,
> March with us in the workers' united front;
> For you are a worker too.

As man is only human,
He'd rather not have boots in his face.
He wants no slaves at his beck and call,
Nor life by a master's grace.

And since a worker's a worker,
No class can free him but his own;
'The emancipation of the working-class
Is the task of the workers alone.'

Make your meaning clear (words by Randall Swingler, music by Alan Bush)

Rise now, you long exploited,
And let your voice be heard In answer with Dimitrov,
And this shall be your word:
We will not fight for profits, We will not die for pay,
Nor let our rulers drag us down
In ruin and decay.
(Chorus)   Rise, rise, rise, working people,
And make your meaning clear!
Our foes are the exploiters.
Our battleground is here.
And peace shall end what wars defend,
The rule of greed and fear.
And peace shall end what wars defend,
The rule of greed and fear.

They bid us fight for freedom;
But all they ever gave
To Britain's working people
Is freedom to starve or slave.

Democracy's their catchword
To send our sons to die.
We heard them use it once before
And know it for a lie.

Truth is a thing we'll fight for
To save the world we make
That we ourselves may own it
And rule it for our sake
We rise and give our answer
To the makers of all wars:
The peoples fight for the people's right,
Their just and only cause.

Jarama

> There's a valley in Spain called Jarama,
> It's a place that we all know so well;
> For 'twas there that we gave of our manhood
> And most of our brave comrades fell
>
> We are proud of our British Battalion
> And the stand for Madrid that they made,
> For they fought like true sons of the soil
> As part of the fifteenth Brigade.
>
> With the rest of the international column
> In the fight for the freedom of Spain,
> They swore in the valley of Jarama
> That fascism never should reign.
>
> We have left that dark valley for ever
> But its memory we ne'er shall forget,
> So, before we continue this meeting,
> Let us stand to our glorious dead.

Pity the downtrodden landlord (words by B. Woolf, music by Arnold Clayton)

> Please open your hearts and your purses
> To a man who is misunderstood
> He gets all the kicks and the curses
> Though he wishes you nothing but good.
>
> He wistfully begs you to show him
> You think he's a friend, not a louse
> So, remember the debt that you owe him
> The landlord who lends you his house.

(Chorus)
> So pity the downtrodden landlord
> And his back that is burdened and bent
> Respect his grey hairs,
> Don't ask for repairs,
> And don't be behind with the rent.

(Three verses in all)

The Unity March (words by Geoffrey Parsons, music by Berkeley Fase)

We who are heirs of the fighters for liberty
Men who put tyrants to flight,
We must be proud to inherit their struggle
And proud to continue their fight.

(Chorus)   Come comrades sing with us
Join in the people's chorus,
Come comrades, march with us,
Victory lies before us,
Let the fascists hear the people's tread
Show them we speak as one.
Stand united thro' the days ahead
And a new world will be won
Come comrades, fight with us,
Till hatred and injustice cease,
Join the ranks and fight the fight
For liberty and peace,
Peoples of the world unite
For liberty and peace.

Join in the song that we sing when we march along
Join in and swing to its beat,
Lift up your voices and sing with a rhythm
That goes to the tramp of your feet.

VIII

THE POST-WAR PERIOD

As after the first world war, the workers were no longer satisfied with the old songs, and wanted something to express the conditions of the time-the growing Socialist world, the post war Labour government, the cold war. This applied particularly to the new generation growing up, who showed a great interest in the songs created and discovered by Peoples Artists of the USA. Other influences were the International Youth Festivals and the work of A.L.Lloyd, Ewan MacColl and Alan Lomax in unearthing and making known our 'industrial' folk songs particularly in the mining industry.

New songs began to appear in the folk song idiom, sometimes with jazz elements, created by such authors as A.L.Lloyd, Ewan MacColl, John

Hasted, and later Fred Dallas, John Brunner, Alex Comfort, and Stan Kelly. These songs are very popular in the CND and peace movements, although the CND 'anthem', the 'H Bomb's Thunder', uses a tune called 'Miner's Lifeguard', which was an American Miners' Union song, and previous to that a Welsh Hymn, 'Calon Lan', or 'Life is like a mountain railway'. So the tradition of adapting hymns is still with us!

STANLEY BROADBRIDGE

The Lancashire Cotton 'Famine' 1861-65

'As long as the English cotton manufacturers depended on slave-grown cotton, it could truthfully be asserted that they rested on a twofold slavery, the indirect slavery of the white man in England and the direct slavery of the black men on the other side of the Atlantic.' (Karl Marx. NEW YORK DAILY TRIBUNE, October 14, 1861.)

Most accounts of the period 1861—5 in Lancashire draw a picture of a cotton industry dislocated by lack of supplies of raw cotton, as a result of the American Civil War and the blockade of Southern ports by the North. The workers, it is said, suffered with stoical resignation deprivations caused by events outside this country's control, a silence only broken to speak out in favour of the North which had caused their sufferings. The truth was more complex than this. There would have been depression in the cotton industry in 1861—2 in any case, as a consequence of the overproduction which had taken place during the boom years of 1859—60. When the blockade began to hinder the arrival of supplies of cotton, some of the larger manufacturers and merchants actually managed to profit from it for a while, since their large stocks now commanded a higher price than expected. And towards the end of the cotton famine, in 1864, there is evidence of employers refusing to buy stocks of cotton which were then available, because of the low price of the finished article. In addition, throughout the period unemployment was caused here and there by the installation of labour saving machinery.

However, though intermingled with the manifestations of normal cyclical crises, the effects of the cotton famine were undoubtedly to add greatly to the misery of the times in Lancashire. The famine extended and prolonged unemployment, reduced earnings and worsened conditions of work, for instance through the use of inferior substitutes for American cotton. The Lancashire workers were faced with normal economic struggle against their employers but they also recognised the political issues involved in the Civil

War. And in spite of their sufferings they gave hearty support to Lincoln in the fight to prevent the establishment of the Confederate States as an American republic grounded on slavery.

The Lancashire cotton industry was at the height of a boom in 1860, when profits were reaching 30% to 40% of capital invested, production was higher than ever before and labour sought after. Some cotton districts were advertising for and securing workers from Norfolk and other distant counties. The boom was continuing early in 1861, but then prices of raw materials began to rise as markets for manufactured goods contracted. Marx, in the article quoted from above, noted that up to August, 1861, the decrease in the American demand for cotton goods was offset by accumulation of stocks and speculative consignments to India and China. But these markets were soon glutted and prices forced down. As a result the increased price of raw materials could not be covered and the spinning, weaving and printing of cotton was ceasing to pay costs of production. He quotes the case of one of the largest Manchester mills engaged in coarse spinning which in September 1860 was making a profit of 1 d per lb. of warp sold but in September 1861 a loss of 1½d. Attempts were now being made to replace American cotton by fibres from eastern India, but here England was paying the price of past exploitation of the sub-continent in the shape of lack of transport and communications and the wretched subjection of the Indian peasant who was in no position to take advantage of the situation to force improvements.[1] In fact the Indian cotton was very inferior and one of the main means of worsening already bad conditions in the mills.

The Reports of the Inspectors of Factories agree that there was over-production in 1860 which it would in any case have taken several years to absorb and that stockpiling reduced the first impact of the crisis. That for October 1862 notes that 'the demand for labour was . . . already restricted many months before the effects of the blockade made themselves felt. Fortunately, many factories were thereby saved from ruin. The supplies rose in value so long as they were in stock and this prevented the appalling depreciation in value which is otherwise inevitable in such a crisis.' The report for October 1861 had earlier forecast: 'it is not at all improbable that many factories will materially reduce their working day during the winter months. However, this was to be anticipated; quite apart from the causes which have interrupted the ordinary supply of cotton from America and the English exports it would have been necessary to reduce the hours of labour during the coming winter on account of the strong increase in production in the preceding three years.'[2]

Many factories were not, however, saved from ruin in the coming years. In 1861 there were 2,109 cotton mills in Lancashire and Cheshire, 35% of which used only engines of 20 h.p. or less. These, for the most part small weaving sheds built by speculators or mills owned co-operatively by cotton workers who had not the capital to weather a depression, bore the brunt of the crisis. By October 1862 60% of the spindles and 58% of the looms were idle. Of the remaining firms few were working anything like full time, which was 60 hours. Imports of raw cotton fell from 1,261 million lbs. in 1861 to 583 million lbs. in 1862 and did not recover to their previous level until 1866.

I

Inevitably, the employers used every device to keep their mills open at the workers' expense. Even in the early months of 1861 several manufacturers attempted to reduce rates by 5% to 7½%. The workers struck, demanding short time rather than wage cuts, but after a month were defeated and suffered both a wage cut and short time. The factory inspectors' report for October 1863 quotes from a pamphlet by Blackburn cotton spinners: 'the adult operatives of this mill have been asked to work 12 to 13 hours per day while there are hundreds who are compelled to be idle who would willingly work partial time . . . There is in this district almost sufficient work to give all partial employment if fairly distributed. We are only asking what is right in requesting the masters to pursue a system of short hours rather than to work a portion of the hands overtime while others are compelled to exist upon charity.'[2] But, of course, a reserve army of labour, kept at the public expense, helped to keep wages down.

Wages also fell as a result of the use of inferior fibres, which broke more often in both spinning and weaving. In a few instances they were reduced by as much as 50%, even when working full time, by this means. The factory inspectors found minders of self-acting mules who earned only 8s.11d. after 14 days of full employment in 1863 and had their house rent deducted from this; in 1860 the wage had been 11s. for six days. Cotton waste was often mixed with inferior fibres from India with consequent reduction of output; yet weavers were expected to weave good cloth from poor yarn and were heavily fined if they failed to do so. Fines, which had been 3d to 6d on American cotton rose to 1s to 3s.6d. In one district weavers dropped from four looms to two, yet got only 3s.4d. per loom in 1863 as against 5s.7d. in 1800. One inspector, Mr. Redgrave, pointed out that in some cases wages were so low that it was better to be on relief than employed.

The weavers ascribed the spread of disease to the glue used in the woof of Indian cotton, which was not merely flour size as in the past. This glue was used because it increased the weight of fabrics by one third but it also reduced wages by making the yarn brittle, with a consequent tenfold increase in the number of breaks. The factory inspectors alleged that there was shirting made for export weighting 8 lbs a piece of which 2 lbs was accounted for by glue. 'Textiles of other kinds are often given as much as 50% of glue so that the manufacturer does not lie by any means who boasts of becoming a rich man by selling his fabrics at less money per pound than he paid for the yarn of which they are made.'

Redgrave gives a telling description of working with Indian cotton (Surat). 'On opening a bale of cotton there is an intolerable smell, which causes sickness . . . In the mixing, scribbling and carding rooms, the dust and dirt which are disengaged, irritate the air passages and give rise to coughs and difficulty in breathing. A disease of the skin, no doubt from the irritation of the dirt contained in Surat cotton, also prevails . . . Bronchitis is more prevalent owing to the dust. Inflammatory sore throat is common from the same source. Sickness and dyspepsia are produced by the frequent breaking of the weft, when the weaver sucks the weft through the eye of the shuttle.'[2]

No wonder Sam Laycock wrote, in the 'Surat Weavers' Song':

> Confeaund it! aw ne'ver were so woven afore,
> Mi back's welly brocken, mi fingers are sore;
> Aw've bin stanni' an' rootin' among this Shurat,
> Till aw'm very near getten as bloint as a bat.

And a Methodist parson, offering a prayer for cotton, qualified it with the words 'but not Shurat, O Lord, we pray thee, not Shurat'. 'At our mill things are getting worse', John Ward of Clitheroe recorded in his diary in the spring of 1864. 'I have given up my odd loom as I cannot keep two looms going, and last week I had only 5/1½ after a very hard week's work, but they have promised us better work as soon as the cotton is done that they have on hand. They have promised so often that we can hardly believe them.' But in the autumn he is recording: 'The weft we have had this last week is worse than ever, but we are forced to put up with it as we don't know how soon we will have to stop altogether.'[3]

Bad though conditions were for those employed, they were far worse for the mass of the workers who were thrown out of employment altogether, many for months at a time. The factory inspectors' report for October 1862 gives only 40,146 (11%) working full-time, 134,767 (38%) on short time and 197,721 (51%) wholly unemployed. Even these figures do not give the full picture since they include Manchester and Bolton, where the finer yarns were spun, a line little affected by the crisis. If these areas are excluded, only 8.5% were fully employed and 53.5% were unemployed. By December, 1862, there were close on half a million workers on relief, or 24% of the total population of the districts concerned. In Ashton, however, 42% of the population were on relief, in Preston 48%. Many operatives were reduced to singing on the streets of the larger towns:

> War's clamour and civil commotion
> Has stagnation brought in its train;
> And stoppage brings with it starvation,
> So help us some bread to obtain.

A visitor to Preston reported: 'In my rambles I was astonished at the dismal succession of destitute homes and the number of struggling owners of little shops, who were watching their stocks sink gradually down to nothing and looking despondingly at the cold approach of pauperism. I was astonished at the strings of dwellings, side by side, stript, more or less, of the commonest household utensils—sometimes crowded, three or four families of decent working people in a cottage of half-a-crown a week rental; sleeping anywhere, on benches or on straw, and afraid to doff their clothes at night because of the cold.'[4]

Similar stories came from all over Lancashire. 'A Lancashire Lad' (John Whittaker) wrote in *The Times* of April 22 1892: 'I cannot pass through a street but I see evidence of deep distress. I cannot sit at home half an hour without having one or more coming to ask for bread to eat. But what comes casually before me is as nothing when compared with that deeper distress which can only be seen by those who seek it . . . There have been families who have been so reduced that the only food they have had has been a porridge made of Indian meal. They could not afford oatmeal: and even of their Indian meal porridge they could only afford to have two meals a day.'

The Clitheroe weaver, John Ward, explaining why he had not kept his diary for two years wrote, in April 1864:

'It has been a very poor time for me all the time owing to the American war which seems as far off being settled as ever. The mill I work in was stopped all last winter, during which time I barely kept me alive. When we started working again it was with Surat cotton and a great number of weavers can only mind two looms. We can earn very little. I have not earned a shilling a day this last month and there are many like me. My clothes and bedding is wearing out very fast and I have no means of getting any more, as what wages I get does hardly keep me, after paying rent, rates and firing . . . I went thrice to Preston to see my brother Daniel, but him and his family were no better off than myself, having nothing better than Surat to work at, and it is the same all through Lancashire . . . The principal reason why I did not take any notes these last two years is because I was sad and weary. One half of the time I was out of work and the other I had to work as hard as ever I wrought in my life and can hardly keep myself living. If things do not mend this summer I will try somewhere else or something else, for I can't go much further with what I am at.'[3]

Yet at a time that distress was mounting most of the employers, in their other capacity as landlords, were attempting to exact the last farthing in rents from unemployed workers. Four pages of examples, from all the affected areas, are given in *Facts of the Cotton Famine*[4]. Only in one small area, Whitworth, near Rochdale, was it the rule 'for employers not to collect or ask for cottage rents during the distress'. Everywhere else only a small proportion of the arrears was remitted. Thus there were arrears amounting to £8,147 in the parish of Mossley in Ashton, of which £70 was remitted. In Preston one employer whose normal rents totalled £1,427, collected £962 in 1862, £1,047 in 1863, and £1,176 in 1864, remitting none of the arrears. In Wigan one employer stopped arrears out of pay when employment recommenced, at so high a rate that it left scarcely anything to live on.

Although the employers were thus exacting their pound of flesh the Central Relief Committee recommended (19.1.63): 'No portion of the relief afforded must, in any case, be granted for the payment of rent', thus solving a problem by refusing to admit its existence. But if landlords would not remit rents they could not prevent their tenants from 'flitting', nor prevent a decrease as a result of lessened demand. By October 1863 the factory inspectors' reports state that rents have fallen 25% to 50%; a cottage formerly rented at 3.6d. a week might be had for 2s.4d.

II

Relief committees were not set up until 1862 so that at first the workers could only turn to their own resources or the hated Poor Law. Their own funds were much depleted as a result of the wage struggles of the '50s; the long-drawn out strikes at Preston and Colne had proved particularly ruinous and involved workers from all over Lancashire and Cheshire. Deposits at Co-operative Societies were run down at the same time that their sales dropped drastically, and the Savings Banks found themselves faced with large-scale withdrawals. At Preston £17,000 was withdrawn between November 1861 and May 1862, and the Self-Acting Mule Spinners Society distributed £700 of its funds amongst its members. In Stockport Savings Bank deposits fell by £10,000 in the same period and sales at the Co-op stores from £600 to £300 a week. Such reserves were, however, far from adequate to meet the crisis. Many workers were reduced, however reluctantly, to begging.

Many others preferred distress and near starvation rather than applying to the hated Poor Law Guardians, who were forbidden in theory to offer relief outside the workhouse and would only give aid after the most searching enquiry into the applicants' means, private life and past record. Usually a 'labour test' was insisted upon; no relief was given except in exchange for labour and of the most harsh and degrading kind. H.B. Farrall, who was sent as a special Poor Law Commissioner to Lancashire, suggested that the test should be digging in the open fields, which was unsuitable enough for workers accustomed to work in heated factories. In Rochdale oakum picking was imposed for a time as a labour test, to be followed later by wool picking. One member of the local Board of Guardians, Mr. Livesay, is reported by the *Rochdale Observer* (14.6.63) as saying that 'he believed the principle to be unsound, tyrannical and unchristian and he most determinedly protested against the application of a felon's task to the honest industrious man who, through misfortune over which he had no control, was driven to his present state of pauperism'.

This was a grievance of the workers throughout the crisis, not only against the Poor Law Guardians but also members of the Relief committees who came from the same class background. Because of the rise in the value of the large stocks of cotton and cotton goods on hand at the beginning of the blockade, few cotton mills failed except the small ones, one third of whose owners had started life as operatives. It was therefore upon workers that the burden of distress fell yet they were expected to be grateful for what was parsimoniously given and to accept relief as if it were undeserved.

Needless to say this role was not accepted and protests were common. On June 26 1862 a mass meeting of operatives was held in Stevenson Square, Manchester, at which Mr. Thomas Evans moved a successful resolution: 'That it is unwise and unjust to compel honest working men to perform that kind of labour which common felons are required to perform.' He did not object to the 'labour test' itself but to that species of labour which degrades a man. He complained particularly of the method of grinding corn in workhouses. Men set to this work had to do a certain portion in a day but did not see the corn measured before it was put into the mill. Neither could they see it while grinding; they were put in a kind of box where they could see nothing but the ceiling and knew nothing of the progress of the work or any trick an unjust overseer might serve them. Another speaker Job Billcliffe of Manchester affirmed that as at present dispensed the poor law was a law to keep the poor, poor. He contended that every man should have pay commensurate with the labour performed; the system at present adopted was to get as much labour out of a man as possible at the cost of the smallest amount of relief, in the shape of money or victuals. The meeting passed a resolution 'that the relief at present given by the Manchester Board of Guardians is totally inadequate to meet the wants of the people in the present crisis'. Thomas Evans was deputed to visit the Guardians and was able to get them to agree to a plan, later adopted by some other boards and by many relief committees, whereby the unemployed might attend school in exchange for aid.

The Poor Law, however, depended upon rates levied on householders and businesses, many of them adversely affected by the crisis and all averse to paying more than they felt to be a 'fair share'. It therefore proved impossible to relieve distress through the Poor Law alone and other measures became necessary. In February 1862 local relief committees were set up in the worst hit areas—Ashton, Stockport and Preston, followed by others at Blackburn (April), Oldham and Prestwich (May). By August, seventeen committees were in being and the number eventually was 170. The Lord Mayor of London set up a central fund in April 1863 which in two years had raised over half a million pounds. In Manchester, a meeting called by the Lord Mayor in the Town Hall in April 1862 decided that no relief committee was necessary in the city, but within a month other views had prevailed and a central committee was set up consisting of 'men of wealth and influence in the various localities'. It is clear that, though many gave donations and served on committees from the highest motives, there were also many who were motivated more by the desire to avoid disturbances on the part of the distressed operatives. These used their influence on the committees to oppose any undue generosity and make the conditions of aid as onerous as possible.

John Bright, who himself came from a mill owning family, attended a meeting in Rochdale in January 1862 of a 'committee to help the poor'. Criticising the establishment of the committee, he said people should not get the idea they could spend all in periods of prosperity and then go on poor relief. He thought the Board of Guardians and the millowners might make loans to workers to be paid back later. He 'could not avoid coming to the conclusion', as the *Rochdale Observer* (18.1.62) recorded, 'that the calling of the meeting was premature.' According to the same source there were then 10 or 12 mills closed and the rest on half-time, and some families had little more than 1s. a head a week coming in.[5] Despite such opposition a fund was opened in Rochdale in February to provide a soup kitchen, though its funds were to be exhausted by May. The *Observer* printed a recipe for soup: '65 gallons of water, 65 lbs. of beef, 43 lbs. barley, 25 lbs. peas, 10 lbs. oatmeal'. This was to be sold at 1d. a quart except to the destitute who were to have it free. On February 8 the paper reported that 'the persons presenting themselves for soup had in many instances a very respectable look' and that there were so many applicants that the soup was sold out by 10 a.m.

The Rochdale experience was not untypical. In most areas there were to be found those who were not only unprepared to give themselves but prepared to oppose charity by others, and who used their position on committees to advance their own opinions at the expense of the un-employed. Thus several committees refused aid to members of Co-operative societies unless they drew their last shilling out of the store; others gave tickets for relief which could not be used at Co-op shops. This question was referred to the Central Relief Committee which replied with a lengthy opinion on January 19 1863. Its general tenor was that relief must be refused to anyone who had any resources at all of his own, but as for members of Co-operative societies: 'the utmost . . . which can fairly be required is that the holder should have mortgaged his share and that he is not at present drawing any pecuniary benefit from it. In such case the holder might fairly be entitled to relief.'

This was not the end of the matter. In October 1864 the Poor Law Board received a letter from the secretary of the Edgeside Holme Co-operative Store, a Mr. Lord, enclosing a relief ticket from Haslingden Board of Guardians marked 'this ticket is not available at Co-operative stores'. When pressed, the chairman of the Board said that the stores had higher prices than other shops: 'as long as the poor people had no more sense than to support the co-op stores they could not expect to be better off. He thought the poor people ought to spend their money in the most economical way; and he was certain that a man with 19/- to spend at the shopkeeper's would make it go as far as 20/- spent at the co-op store.' In fact, enquiry in the area showed that prices were not higher at the co-ops which paid a dividend of 2s to 3s in the pound.

In these ways the relief committees acted as 'watchdogs' for the bourgeoisie, as Marx pointed out, citing evidence from the factory inspectors' report of 1863 to the effect that if a man was offered work and refused it, however low the wages, he was struck from the committee's list.[1] Aid, when given, was carefully regulated in order not to harm the pool of labour. An average of 2s a week per head was arrived at which would provide a quarter to a third of ordinary wages, according to the size of family. 'It was assumed', wrote an observer, 'that such a scale . . . would not materially lessen the inclination for any kind of work for wages, whenever such work was to be had, especially as relief was coupled with what was called "disciplinary work" which consisted either of out-door labour or of elementary instruction in schools for men and boys, and instruction in sewing schools for women and girls.'[4]

This system was later extended by the Public Works Act of 1863 which made available £1,200,000 (ultimately increased to £1,850,000) to be loaned to local authorities for works of public utility and sanitary improvement within the cotton areas. In fact this money was often misused. Manchester borrowed £135,000 up to November 8 1863, which was paid to a contractor who only employed 204 distressed operatives. The continuance of this policy, whereby operatives were only employed if first registered as paupers, brought a meeting of protest on October 22nd 1864, when the operatives pointed out that public works were largely staffed by regular navvies and not the unemployed cotton workers.

In many areas, however, the money was used on public improvements, of benefit to the capitalist class in that they were carried out at considerably less than the normal cost. The money was borrowed from the Public Works Loans Commission at below the market rate of interest and the wages paid to the workers, based on size of family, ranged from 4s to 12s a week. In Blackburn, according to the factory inspector Mr. Redgrave, the men were tried at all kinds of labour in the open air. They dug deep into a heavy clay soil, they did drainage work, broke stones, built roads, made excavations for streets and for canals to a depth of up to twenty feet. They frequently stood in mud and water ten to twelve inches deep in pouring rain. Yet these people were used to working in an almost tropical temperature, by skill rather than strength and at wages double or treble those received.

By the middle of 1864, as the worst of the crisis passed, there were occasional complaints of the lack of labourers, especially in weaving, though low wages may have been the main cause rather than real scarcity as strikes began to be more frequent. Now the Public Works Act, so far from keeping the operatives under, was beginning to offer them a little security so that it came under attack from the employers. At Bacup it was alleged that the demand for labourers had so grown that many ex-factory hands were earning 4s to 5s a day in the quarries. Accordingly the local relief committee suspended its activities in April 1864. Other relief committees followed suit gradually in the succeeding months, bringing to an end what Marx called 'this new edition of the *Ateliers nationaux* of 1848, which had this time been opened in the interests of the bourgoisie'. As the Central Relief Committee put it, in a resolution of thanks to C.P. Villiers of the Poor Law Board (June 20, 1865) 'the advantages derived from the Public Works Act cannot be measured by the amount of employment provided but its indirect influence on the discipline of labour and as a stimulus to the profitable application of capital have exceeded the more direct, and therefore more apparent, benefits derived from it'.

The attempts to keep relief down to a minimum did not, however, always succeed as smoothly as was intended. Clear evidence comes from the Stalybridge area where relief tended to be above the 2s average and an attempt was made to cut it down in March 1863. At the same time the committee decided to give tickets, usable at the local shops, instead of money (allegedly to prevent drunkenness) and to keep one day's money in hand 'to help in accountancy'. These measures were denounced from the pulpit by the old Chartist leader, the Rev. J.R. Stephens, who displayed a ragged pair of trousers issued by the relief committee to illustrate its parsimony. The result was a large meeting called by the operatives in the 'plantations' on March 19, which adopted a resolution to refuse to attend school if the plan were not changed. This, of course, was the nearest to strike action that people on relief could take. The next day the workers refused to accept the new tickets and a demonstration followed. There was a march to the mill of the most unpopular member of the committee, a Mr. Bates, when all the windows and some of the machinery were smashed. A police charge resulted in the taking of several prisoners but these were speedily released and the police driven from the field. The clothing stores of the relief committee were then sacked, as was the shop of one of its members and eventually the central office. By now two companies of hussars had arrived, the Riot Act was read and more arrests made.

Of the 80 people arrested on March 20, 29 were committed for trial at Chester. The next day most of the shops were closed, placards announced that the Riot Act had been read and crowds in the streets were forbidden. Nevertheless the workers assembled outside the police station and when a discharged prisoner appeared he was greeted with cheers. When other prisoners were brought out to be taken in buses to the station the soldiers were showered with stones. Meanwhile a delegation was elected by a mass meeting to go to the mayor and demand relief in cash. During the evening a running battle developed with police and military, only ending with the bringing in of a company of foot soldiers with fixed bayonets and an additional troop of cavalry. On Monday March 23, as soon as the schools were open, resolutions to refuse tickets were adopted almost unanimously and, of 1,700 present, only 80 took them. The workers then went out to demand bread from the bakers but were sternly dealt with by the military.

There were similar events in Ashton, Dukinfield and Hyde, while in Stockport and Oldham the workers were only kept down by a large number of special constables who were rapidly sworn in. The sequel was an appeal to the Mansion House Committee in London by the Rev. Floyd. The committee sent £500 to Stalybridge and recommended payment in cash and not in tickets, thus justifying the workers' stand. The Manchester committee refused to give in, even when the Stalybridge committee tried to resign. After a threat to refuse relief entirely, a compromise was reached, mainly to the committee's benefit, whereby the total relief was reduced to 2s per head to be paid half in tickets and half in cash.[4]

After this pressure to reduce relief increased elsewhere. By February, though employment had become more difficult, 19,000 fewer persons were relieved than in the previous month. In March, there was a reduction of 9,000 in the number employed but there were still 12,000 less relieved. In Hulme, Salford and Chorlton, members of the local relief committee accused the Central Committee of starving the people. 'Whether wholesome or not, this discipline drove a large number of operatives to seek employment in other occupations', records an observer; 'the plea of the Central Committee for such severe pressure was—first, to oblige every possible source of independent employment to be tried, so as to prevent men from settling down into permanent pauperism; second, to get the able-bodied men into training for employment under the Public Works Act . . .'[4]

III

During all this time there were taking place those 'galloping improvements in machinery' which helped to change the structure of the cotton industry, facilitating concentration in larger factories, under fewer capitalists, and reduction in the number of operatives required. Marx gives examples from the reports of the inspectors of factories for 1863 to illustrate this general thesis:—

A Manchester manufacturer stated: 'We formerly had 75 carding engines, now we have 12, doing the same quantity of work . . . We are doing with fewer hands by 14, at a saving in wages of £10 a week. Our estimated saving in waste is about 10% in the quantity of cotton consumed.' In another fine-spinning mill in Manchester an inspector was told that increased speed and the introduction of some self-acting machinery has enabled a reduction of a quarter in the number of operatives in one department, over a half in another. A third spinning mill had made a saving of labour of 10%, a fourth considered its expenditure on new machinery as fully one-third less than in wages and hands while the yarn was much better so that more and cheaper cloth could be made from it. The reduction of labour on the one hand, increased production on the other, was remarked upon in this report as a general trend which had begun some time since and was continuing. It was also affecting employment of children. The master of a school near Rochdale told an inspector that there had been a great falling off in the girls' school 'not only caused by the distress, but by the changes in machinery in the woollen mills, in consequence of which a reduction of 70 short-timers had taken place'.[6]

In all, between 1861 and 1868, the number of spindles increased from 30 millions to 32 millions; the number of power looms decreased but production rose owing to improved machinery; at the same time the number of cotton factories was reduced from 2,887 to 2,549 and the number of operatives from 450,000 to 400,000. So, Marx noted, the 'rapid and persistent progress of machinery' heightened and made permanent 'the "temporary" misery inflicted on the workpeople by the cotton crisis'. In the event the productive capacity so increased and consolidated during the crisis was brought into action immediately after the end of the American civil war and in no time brought a renewed glut in the world market, so that a new cyclical crisis began in 1866–7. Again, notes Marx, the employers resorted to their usual way out of a difficulty, that of reducing wages by 5%. But 'the workpeople resisted, and said that the only remedy was to work short time, 4 days a week; and their theory was the correct one. After holding out for some time, the self-elected captains of industry had to make up their minds to short time, with reduced wages in some places, and in others without'.[6]

IV

Meanwhile the Confederate States had been counting upon the sufferings and losses consequent on the stoppage of raw cotton supplies to aid their cause. The strength of Radicalism in Britain was well-known and the Radicals, in particular the Chartists, had always pointed to America as the land of democracy, only marred by slave-owning. However it was thought that the Radicals would be disarmed by the imputation that the North was the author of the distress and that support could be expected from many classes of the population.

This assessment was not far wrong as concerns the ruling class. In 1863, J.M. Sturtevant, president of Illinois College and supporter of Lincoln, toured Britain for three months meeting a number of employers and members of the aristocracy, and took back a very gloomy picture of 'the present attitude of England towards the U.S.'. He found people vaguely sympathetic in general to the anti-slavery aims of the North but yet thinking that the South had the right to secede, as the American colonies had seceded from

Britain. At bottom, he felt, such people wanted a divided America because they feared the growth of its commercial power. This attitude was 'greatly aggravated by the periodical press, especially the London *Times* and the *Saturday Review*. The journals that are in sympathy with American liberty have not the ear of the people.' He was presumably thinking of the *Daily News* and *Spectator*, alone among London publications to stand up for the North. But the provincial press by no means echoed the war cries of the *Times*.[7]

Employers did not, however, speak altogether with one voice. Liverpool merchants were eager to retain their imports of slave-grown cotton and set on foot a vigorous agitation for armed intervention on behalf of the South. They also aimed to destroy the rival American merchant marine, built almost entirely in Northern ports. A privateer for the Confederates, the 'Alabama' was built at Birkenhead and allowed by the government to set sail. It caused renewed danger of war by inflicting great damage on Northern shipping for which the British people eventually had to pay a large sum in compensation. However, even in Liverpool merchants were aware of the implications of intervention to support the South, and one is quoted by Marx as saying: 'Nobody in England dares to recommend war for the sake of mere cotton. It would be cheaper for us to feed the whole of the cotton districts for three years at state expense than to wage war on the United States on their behalf for one year'.[8]

As for other industries, coal and iron were dependent on orders from the North for munitions and railway construction. So also were the small manufacturers of Birmingham who were largely engaged in arms manufacture, and whose representative in Parliament was John Bright, the most outspoken supporter of the North, both in Parliament and in rousing speeches to the workers. Cobden, influenced by millowners who wanted to eliminate competition from New England and by the fact that the South stood for Free Trade against the protectionist North, at first took up a wavering attitude but was won over by Bright. Among politicians the Liberal Gladstone regarded the Southern States as a nation 'rightly struggling to be free', and his zeal on their behalf went further than the Conservative support given by Lords Palmerston and Derby. But Bright put his finger on the fears underlying conservative attitudes when he hammered home the point that if democracy triumphed in America nothing could prevent its triumph in England too.

'Privilege thinks it has a great interest in the contest', he declared in a speech to London trade unionists in March 1863. It has seen the prosperity of a republic, without aristocracy or State priests. 'Privilege has shuddered at what might happen to old Europe if this grand experiment should succeed'. But you, the workers struggling for your rights, Bright continued, have no such cause for jealousy. In the North 'labour is honoured more than elsewhere in the world'; in the South 'labour is not only not honoured, but it is degraded. The labourer is made a chattel'. For those who wish the freedom of their own country the issue is clear. 'I have faith in you', he told his hearers. 'Impartial history will tell that, when your statesmen were hostile or coldly neutral, when many of your rich men were corrupt, when your press—which ought to have instructed and defended—was mainly written to betray, the fate of a Continent and of its vast population being in peril, you clung to freedom . . .'[5]

Pro-war agitation was angled by 'incidents' between Britain and the North, blown up by the London press. A first was the removal of two Southern envoys from a British ship, the 'Trent', by a Northern vessel in November 1861. This led to loud demands for intervention in defence of the rights of the British flag, which were strongly countered by the radicals. Congratulating Bright on a speech at Rochdale in December, calling for a policy to give hope to slaves and promote friendship between English-speaking peoples, a United States diplomat—Motley, historian of the Dutch republic—wrote: 'I honour you more than I can tell, for your courage in thus standing up, in the midst of the tempest of unreasoning wrath now sweeping over England, to defend not an unpopular but apparently a hated cause'. But on another occasion Motley pinpointed the hatred: it was 'not to America so much as to democracy in England'.[5]

But the point Marx is mainly concerned to bring home is the attitude and influence of the working class in preventing intervention. The misery in manufacturing districts '*motivated* by the blockade of the slave states' is, he notes, 'incredible and in daily process of growth . . . English interference in America has accordingly become a bread-and-butter question for the working class'. At the same time the ruling class is using every means to inflame the workers against the North: even *Reynolds's Weekly Newspaper*, the only workers' journal still in existence and widely circulating, 'has been purchased expressly in order that for six months it might reiterate weekly . . . English intervention'.

The working class, unrepresented in Parliament, nevertheless 'is not without political influence. No important innovation, no decisive measure, has ever been carried through in this country *without pressure from without*'. By this 'the Englishman understands great, extra-parliamentary popular demonstrations, which naturally cannot be staged without the lively co-operation of the working class'. Of this the working class is aware so that it is 'fully conscious that the government is only waiting for the intervention cry from below, *the pressure from without*, to put an end to the American blockade and English misery'. In these circumstances, Marx concludes, 'the obstinacy with which the working class keeps silent, or breaks its silence only to raise its voice against intervention and *for* the United States is admirable. This is a new, brilliant proof of the indestructible excellence of the English popular masses'.[8]

The early *ad hoc* demonstrations were succeeded at the close of 1862 by more formal organisation. In October of that year Lincoln, who had hitherto insisted that the North fought for the Union alone, proclaimed the freedom of slaves in the South and this brought a new response. One meeting was called on the last day of the year by two Manchester working men—J.E. Edwards and E. Hooran—at the Free Trade Hall. Edwards noted in his speech that a leading article in the *Manchester Guardian* had been directed to deterring working men from assembling in support of the emancipation of slaves. But the chair was taken by a well-known radical publisher, Abel Heywood, then mayor of Manchester, and the resolution adopted, moved by Edwards, ran: 'that this meeting, recognising the common brotherhood of mankind and the sacred and inalienable right of every human being to personal freedom and equal protection, records its detestation of negro slavery in America'.

Having adopted this standpoint the meeting set up a 'General Emancipation Society' which in turn adopted an address to be sent to Abraham Lincoln:

'As the citizens of Manchester assembled at the Free Trade Hall we beg to express our fraternal sentiments towards you and your country . . . We honour your Free States as a particularly happy abode for the working millions whose industry is honoured. One thing alone has in the past lessened our sympathy with our country and our confidence in it, we mean the ascendancy of politicians who not merely maintained negro slavery but desired to extend and root it more firmly. Since we have discerned however that the victory of the Free States in the war which has so severely distressed us as well as afflicted you will strike off the fetters of the slave, you have attracted our warm and earnest sympathy. We joyfully honour you . . . for many decisive steps towards practically exemplifying your belief in the words of your great founders "all men are created free and equal".' (*Manchester Guardian* 1.1.63.)

To this Lincoln himself replied on January 19:

'To the working men of Manchester. I have well understood that the duty of self preservation rests solely with the American people. But I have at the same time been aware that favour or disfavour of foreign nations might have a material influence in enlarging or prolonging the struggle . . . I know and deeply deplore the sufferings which the workingmen at Manchester and in all Europe are called to endure in this crisis. It has been often and studiously represented that the attempt to overthrow this government which was built on the foundation of human rights and to substitute for it one which should rest exclusively on the basis of slavery was likely to obtain the favour of Europe. Through the action of disloyal citizens the working men of Europe have been subjected to a severe trial for the purpose of forcing their sanction to that attempt. Under these circumstances I cannot but regard your decisive utterances upon the question as an instance of sublime Christian heroism which has not been surpassed in any age or country'.

Not long after the Lancashire workers received proof that the people of the North, in the midst of their own trials, had not forgotten those who were. suffering elsewhere. In February 1863, there docked at Liverpool the first ship carrying provisions, the 'George Growald' freighted by a New York merchant of this name. In all, provisions to the value of £27,000 were to be sent and donations in cash of £1,333. When the 'George Growald' tied up all the Liverpool men employed at the docks, from customs officials to porters and stevedores, refused payment for their services, while the railways offered free transport. The captain was presented with an address at a dinner organised by the Manchester Central Relief Committee but he was also welcomed with his officers by a packed meeting at the Free Trade Hall; so great were the crowds that an overflow meeting was held for the 2,000 who could not get in.

Once again a categoric resolution was carried:

'This public meeting desires to express its heartfelt gratitude to the noble donors in America who in the midst of a dire domestic struggle for freedom and nationality have so generously contributed to the succour of the operatives of Lancashire and the meeting declares its conviction that no amount of privation will induce the people of the cotton districts to sanction any recognition of a Confederacy based upon the doctrine that it is right for man to hold property in man'. (*Manchester Guardian* 25.2.63.)

There were 'Union and Emancipation Societies' throughout Lancashire by this time, organising enthusiastic meetings in support of the North. On the platforms, side by side with prominent radicals, were working class leaders, many of whom had been active in the Chartist movement. Ernest Jones addressed a meeting at Ashton on November 16 1863, when he showed up the hollowness of the claim for 'right of secession'. He went on: 'I fully endorse the "sacred right of insurrection". It is not to be lightly used—but on good and adequate grounds—insurrection is more than a right, it is a duty . . . Working men, I say the South is your enemy—the enemy of your trade, the foe of your freedom, a standing threat to your property . . . Slave labour is direct aggression on the free labour of the world . . . the key that shall reopen our closed factories is the sword of the victorious North'. (*The Slaveholder's War.*)

A report in the *Manchester Guardian* (4.5.1863) of a meeting held in June indicates that there was also some organised support for the South. This meeting at the Free Trade Hall was called by ministers of religion from all parts of Britain to support emancipation of the slaves, in response to a suggestion from Protestant clergy in France who had recently done likewise. For days before Manchester was placarded with appeals to the public not to support the meeting, signed by 'the executive committee of the Southern Club'. Members of the latter were evidently among those in the densely crowded hall for there was heckling, some fighting among the audience and the chanting of slogans and counter-slogans. Towards the close the *Guardian* reporter himself rose from the press table to make a speech in support of the South but was dragged from the platform and had to be rescued by police. Far from drawing the necessary conclusions the *Guardian*, in a pompous leading article (5.6.1863), admonished the clergymen for meddling with politics and told them to stick to the pulpit where they belonged.

In the spring of the following year Ernest Jones was at Rochdale addressing a crowded meeting presided over by the mayor. 'It is a long time since I last addressed you and those were stormier times than these (cheers and laughter). But I have not forgotten the men of Rochdale, their love of freedom and of truth, and I trust that those who are now struggling, honourably and constitutionally, for the freedom of the black will join in every effort for a fresh instalment towards the Charter of an Englishman's liberty. (applause) Those who pat the slave-owners of America on the backs would like to be slave-owners in England too (cheers and hear! hear!) . . . I trust that we shall find that in establishing liberty universally throughout the American continent we shall be placing the crowning pinnacle on the ediface of freedom here as well.' (*Rochdale Observer*, 13.3.64.)

This pressure from without forced the British government to forego recognition of the Confederate states while the United States army was completing their defeat. It was not the wisdom of the ruling class, said Marx, but the heroic resistance of the working class of England to their original folly 'that saved the West of Europe from plunging headlong into an infamous crusade for the perpetuation and prolongation of slavery on the other side of the Atlantic'. These views were echoed by none other than Cobden, in a letter to the United States minister in Copenhagen written shortly before his death:

'Democracy has discovered how very few friends it has in Europe among the ruling class. It has at the same time discovered its own strength and, what is more, this has been discovered by the autocracies and absolutisms of the Old World, so that I think you are more safe than ever against the risks of intervention from this side of the Atlantic. Besides, you must not forget that the working classes of England, who will not always be without direct political power, have always, in spite of their sufferings and the attempt made to mislead them, adhered nobly to the cause of civilisation and freedom.' (*Rochdale Observer*, 5.2.65.)

Ernest Jones judged rightly when he saw the mass agitation as a promise not only for American but also of British freedom. It led on directly to renewed demands for the suffrage, to a mass movement in conjunction with radicals which culminated in the Reform Act of 1867. More than this, the internationalist feeling fostered among the working class played a big part in ensuring the adherence of leading workers to the First International when it was formed in November 1864, and support for its subsequent work. From this sprang forces which ultimately brought about a revival of socialism in the British labour movement.

REFERENCES

(1) Marx, K. and   On Colonialism (F.L.P.H., 1960) pp. 221—3
     Engels, F.
(2) Reports of H.M. Inspectors of Factories
                     for October 31, 1861 (London, 1861) p. 19
                     for October 31, 1862 (London, 1863) pp. 18—20
                     for October 31, 1863 (London, 1864) pp. 63, 42—3
(3) Ward, John   'The Diary of John Ward of Clitheroe, Weaver, 1860—64' edited by
                     R. Sharpe France in Transactions of the Historic Society of
                     Lancashire and Cheshire, Vol. 105, 1953 (reprinted as pamphlet)
(4) Watts, J.   Facts of the Cotton Famine (1866). pp. 82—9, 137—8, 200,
                     218—20, 262—82, 303
(5) Trevelyan,   Life of John Bright (London, 1913). pp. 304—313
     G.M.
(6) Marx, K.   Capital, Vol. I (Ed. D. Torr, Allen & Unwin, 1946; or F.L.P.H.)
                     pp. 131, 133, 433—5
(7) Sturtevant, J.M. Three Months in Great Britain (1864) (pamphlet)
(8) Marx, K. and   The Civil War in the United States (Lawrence & Wishart, 1938)
     Engels, F.   pp. 130—141
(9) Sturtevant, J.M. Letter from Abraham Lincoln (Ashton, 1864) (pamphlet)

The following supply additional information:

Arnold, R.A.   History of the Cotton Famine (1864)
Greenleaf, J.   'British Labour against American Slavery' in Science & Society,
                 Vol. XVII, No. 1, 1953
Henderson, W.O.   The Lancashire Cotton Famine, 1861—5
Waugh. E.   Home Life of Lancashire Folk—the Cotton Famine (1868)

Close examination of contemporary sources, in particular the local newspapers of the cotton towns, is essential before the detailed history of this period can be written. Only a few could be consulted in compiling this account.

A. J. PEACOCK

"The Revolt of the Field"

in East Anglia

There has recently been a revival of interest in the agricultural trades unionism of the 1870's. Mr. John Dunbabin's general article on 'The "Revolt of the Field": the agricultural labourers' movement in the 1870's' and his paper on 'Labourers and Farmers in the late nineteenth century—some changes'[1] take most of their evidence from Dorset, Herefordshire, Oxfordshire and Kent. The following discussion of East Anglia, the scene of the great lock-out of 1874, tends to confirm their conclusions.[2] But it also brings out some further points, notably the importance, in determining the incidence of unionism, of such *local* factors as the setting up of School Boards and disputes over specific charities. Moreover, by concentrating on a limited area and by utilising local records, it is possible to establish the identity and backgrounds of many of the participants and to shed some interesting light on their motives and organisation.

I

Although the events in Wellesbourne (Warwickshire) were eventually to provide the greatest stimulus to agricultural unionism, the East Anglian labourers were stirring long before it became national news. The Tichborne case, as George Mitchell eventually pointed out, was no longer news, the press was anxious for a story and local newspapers began to report even tiny meetings in other parts of the country, and these undoubtedly had an effect in preparing the labourers for unionism. The *Cambridge Express,* for instance, gave great prominence to a remarkable meeting in Leicestershire on 10 February, 1872, which is interesting in itself as showing at work both the religious influences mentioned by Ernest Selley [3] and Dunbabin [1], and also one of the less obvious reasons for the labourers' unrest—namely education charges. A Mr. Tyler opened the proceedings with a prayer that 'those who labour and toil for their bread may be permitted to receive a supply according to their deserving', and the Chairman, a Mr. Tailby, delivered the main speech: He had been thinking of a union for years, he said, and the creation of a School Board had clinched his ideas.

'We shall have to sacrifice our children's money by letting them go to school,' he went on, 'or else we shall be pulled up before the Magistrates. Well, if we don't get more money from our employers we can't afford for our children to go to school until they are 13 years of age. I will leave it to the meeting whether we can or not. (Voices: No, we can't).'[4]

Meetings of this kind took place throughout East Anglia in the early months of 1872. Two hundred labourers at the Chequers Inn, Guyhirn, near Wisbech, for instance, met in March and signed a memorandum asking for 15s. a week or 3s. a day for day-labourers.[5] A similar meeting was held in the same week at Chatteris.

An advance in wages was the prime objective of the labourers, and there was no mention of creating unions at the very early meetings, many of which were followed by almost immediate increases. There was a scarcity of labour in some parts of East Anglia[6] and this undoubtedly prompted many farmers to make the awards, but another motive was certainly to nip the development of combinations in the bud. At Ely, where the Nine Hours Movement had been attracting a lot of attention, rates went up very quickly from 12s. to 13s. a week[7], at Chatteris the farmers gave an extra 1s. the week after the Rev. M. A. Gathercole had presided over a meeting that set up a committee to form a union[8], and the farmers at Longstowe decided to increase wages from 11s. to 12s. in early April for the same reason.[9] In March there were innumerable meetings, however, that *did* lead to the creation of unions. On the 7th, the Brampton (Hunts.) Agricultural Labourers' Society came into being, with a weekly subscription of 2d. and an entrance fee of 6d.[10] Three weeks later a meeting was held at Alconbury Weston, addressed by the Brampton leader, where 100 enrolled themselves 'as a Society'[11], and in South Cambridgeshire a remarkable movement began at Duxford. George Smoothy, a labourer, posted notices throughout the village at midnight, announcing a meeting on Good Friday to consider the creation of a union, which 400 attended.[12] It was decided to set up an organisation and at a later meeting at Sawston 2,000 people turned up, and 94 became members of the South Cambridgeshire Agricultural Labourers Society.[13] In Wisbech a decision to form a 'Labour Protection Society' for agricultural and riverside workers was taken early in March.[14]

The Unions made rapid progress, at first it seems, in the villages where there was a labour shortage and later everywhere in the area. These were undoubtedly aided by the tremendous publicity now being given them. The Wellesbourne strike was fully covered in all three Cambridge newspapers from about 30 March. The South Cambridgeshire was the most widely noticed union. By the beginning of May branches had been formed in places like Sawston, Linton, Whittlesford, Babraham, Brinkley and Abington, and the leaders of the union had been invited into Essex, where branches were created, for example at Great Chesterford. The Brampton Union, later called the Huntingdonshire Labourers' Union, was reported to have had between 14,000 and 15,000 members in the county by the first week of May,[15] while new movements were reported from places like Botesdale (Suffolk), where a union was formed (this was an area where labour was scarce) from amongst the labourers of Rickinghall, Wortham, Burgate, Wattisfield, Hinderclay, and Walsham-le-Willows.[16] By the end of June 1872 over 1,000 were said to be 'in the Union' in Wisbech and the neighbouring villages.[17] In the same month there were reports of the beginnings of what was to become the Peterborough District Agricultural Labourers' Union[18], and by July there was in existence a Haverhill (Suffolk) Agricultural Labourers' Union with 200 members.

Events moved fast. The creation and growth of the unions brought rapid wage increases in many places. They also produced aggressive attitudes which led to strikes and some violence. The first strike (it is not clear if those involved were union members or not) seems to have taken place at Newton, near Sudbury, in April.[19] In May labourers at Bottisham struck for an increase of 1/- a week (they were receiving 11/-)[20], and many at Southoe ceased working for 'one of the most indulgent and liberal masters in the kingdom', after having been refused an extra pint of beer at noon; they also wanted a wage increase of from 12/- to 15/- a week.[21] In Yaxley a pitched battle took place between farmers and labourers after a union meeting[22] and at St. Ives a meeting organised by the Huntingdonshire Union ended in violence[23], as did another held on the same day at Alconbury.[24] These are but a few of the many strikes and fights reported in the local press.

As the unions spread the movement achieved some cohesion and help was obtained from outside East Anglia. In April several of the organisations sent representatives to the famous Willis Rooms meeting in London which was called to discuss questions relating to agricultural unions, and presided over by George Howell. Among these representatives were Lane and Cooper, President of the Huntingdon Union, Coles from Wisbech and John Savage of the South Cambridgeshire.[25] The meeting created the London Central Aid Committee which publicised the labourers' movements and may have been responsible for sending the first 'outsiders' into East Anglia. Early in May unionists at Whittlesey had the assistance of John Bedford Leno of London, once a prominent Chartist, who delighted his audience, or so it was reported, by telling the local vicar, Dr. Burgess, to 'hold his noise and go home to dinner', and urged the labourers to organise and trade only with 'tradesmen who sympathised with the present movement'.[26] Three months later the Huntingdonshire Union held a huge meeting at Brampton at which messages of encouragement were read from people like George Dixon, Benjamin Lucraft, Auberon Herbert, A.J. Mundella, and Lord Edmund Fitzmaurice, and at which the guest speakers were George Odger and George Brooke of Leadenhall Market, London, a Guardian and a member of the Common Council.[27]

Representatives of the East Anglian Unions were also present at the Leamington Spa Conference of May 1872 that led to the creation of Joseph Arch's National Agricultural Labourer's Union. Among these were H. Jarrold of Thetford, where a 'local association' had been formed in April, J. Wright of Norfolk, Oldham from Feckenham, Norfolk, and A. J. Challis, a representative of the South Cambridgeshire.[28] The 'National' appeared in the East in the summer of that year[29] and made rapid progress, particularly in villages near Cambridge itself, where a violent builders' strike had been going on for many weeks.[30] Arch and Henry Taylor, Chairman and Secretary of the N.A.L.U., spoke at large meetings and strong branches were formed at places like Willingham, Cottenham, Landbeach and Waterbeach. In July 1873 the South Cambridgeshire, by then the South Cambridgeshire and North Essex Agricultural Labourers Union, amalgamated with the National[31], while earlier in the year the Huntingdon[32] and Wisbech organisations[33] had also joined Arch. The Peterborough District Union, however, refused the approaches of National officials. At a meeting in Manea (an Owenite centre earlier in the century)[34], for instance, Edward Richardson, a unionist from Parson Drove, was administered a severe rebuke for trying to get labourers to desert Benjamin Taylor, the leader of the Peterborough, who 'had done more for the labouring cause for nothing than Mr. Richardson would do if his pay continued, and if he lived to be as old as Methusela'.[35] The Peterborough Union, which was a breakaway from the Huntingdon, stayed outside the N.A.L.U. and eventually became, along with William Banks Lincolnshire Labour League and James Flaxman's Eastern Counties Union[36], a part of the Federal Union of Labourers which was established in November 1873[37], an organisation often at loggerheads with the National.

From this time onwards the history of agricultural unionism in East Anglia became a part of Arch's, or the Federal's, story. Membership, and wages, continued to increase, and the number of strikes grew to embarrassing proportions. At Exning, near Newmarket, for instance, there was a strike for 16/- a week[38], and the Peterborough got involved in a prolonged dispute at Haddenham.[39] Migration was another remedy the Eastern labourers very soon turned to, and within a few weeks of their bestirring themselves in 1872 manufacturers began offering to move them to other areas. William Cafferata, for example, the owner of the Great Northern Plaster Works, wrote in April to the Mayor of Cambridge promising work at Newark in 'the mines, quarries, and mills'.[40] The following month fifty agricultural labourers left East Anglia for Liverpool, where they earned 27/- a week in the docks—as strike breakers![41]

The labourers had other means of conducting their struggle than the sophisticated ones of strikes and migration, and some harked back to the methods of a century earlier. Poaching and egg stealing to eke out a living went on so openly as to shock the rather prim Clifford.[42] Fences were destroyed, blacklegs were beaten up, sheep were let into corn fields, corn was trampled down[43] and rick burning was by no means uncommon. There were said to be fears, after fires at Kirtling, 'that the old scenes of rick burning . . . might be repeated'.[44] In Duxford someone 'warmed up' stacks belonging to Swann Ellis who had shut his coprolite pits to send his 400-500 non-union men out as blacklegs 'in search of a harvest'.[45] In September 1874 John Smith's stacks were fired in Littleport, after the men there had been forced back to work[46], and a week later there was an outbreak of incendiarism at Great Wilbraham, and more at Chatteris.[47] Less dramatically, the labourers in some places made attempts at exclusive dealing by setting up co-operative stores[48], and a rather bizarre, if un-original, suggestion for keeping the men strong for the union came from a prominent leader of the agricultural labourers, George Mitchell, who urged 'the damsels not to marry swains who were not members of the union, and suggested to the married women that they should forsake their beds if their husbands forsook the Union'.[49] It has not been possible to discover whether Mitchell's advice was heeded or not.

All this provoked retaliation, once it was realised by the farmers that the concessions they had made had failed in their intention of stopping the appearance of unionism. They were not above raising mobs to break up union meetings and frequently appeared at open-air gatherings to provoke violence. Other weapons in the farmers' armoury were, of course, dismissals and evictions, and G.M. Ball contended during the lock-out that evictions explained much of the emigration from the area that took place.[50] Thurgood, a labourer who was prominent in the South Cambridgeshire, and who had been employed on 'crank work at 8/6d. a week at Littlebury', was sacked for union activities during the harvest month of August 1872, an action which led to a strike[51], and he may have been the first unionist victimised in East Anglia. At Six Mile Bottom men were locked out in the following May[52]; Benjamin Taylor's men on strike at Haddenham were confronted with the rural equivalent of 'the document' in the same month[53]; and there was a full scale lock-out over a restricted area of Essex at the same time.[54] At Horningsea two coprolite diggers who had joined the N.A.L.U. were prosecuted by their employer, Thomas Banyard, who assaulted the unfortunate Edward Richardson, and were later refused their jobs back until they renounced the union.[55]

The farmers had other means of combating the labourers. Some reduced wages at the slack time of the year—at Exning, for example, where cuts of 2/- a week were implemented in November 1872, only a month after a strike that had won a four shillings rise.[56] Some replaced striking workers by machinery. At Littleport the fear of the growing use of threshing and reaping machines was certainly a cause of the labourers creating a union, and there were cases of violence against people who drove the new implements.[57]

Other employers used 'blackleg' labour, usually coprolite diggers, Irish or soldiers, during the harvest.[58] This, too, often led to violence and prosecutions. Charles John How of Lavenham, Suffolk, for instance, was given six months for inciting a crowd to put nails in suger-beet to break the rasps in Duncan's sugar-beet factory after the firm had taken on twelve Belgian blacklegs.[59] At the Saffron Walden Petty Sessions George March, a local union secretary, and three others were imprisoned for 14 days for assaulting a strike-breaker at Ashton, whom they 'coerced . . . to quit his employment'.[60] In the same week Stephen Cracknell and Thomas Newman received 21 days for similar offences at Swaffham Prior.[61]

The farmers found prosecution an invaluable weapon. Most of these, like Banyard's prosecution of the erring coprolite diggers, were under the Master and Servant Act of 1867 and the Criminal Law Amendment Act of 1871, which rendered *criminal* a breach of contract on the part of the employee; whereas a similar dereliction by the employer only constituted a civil wrong. The unions shared the urban workers' hostility to these laws, and, in May 1872, a meeting of the Peterborough at Ellington decided to give every branch member a copy of the Master and Servant Act. The following year repeal of both Acts figured among the major aims of the newly inaugurated Federal Union[62], not surprisingly since proceedings under them were extremely frequent. The Cambridge Division Petty Sessions Register records that between March 1872 and August 1874, 30 people were prosecuted under the Master and Servant Act, with fines and compensation varying from 12/- to £2/-/-.[63] Some of the proceedings were against groups of workers. At Cottenham, for example, where there was a strong N.A.L.U. branch, six people were collectively charged and fined a total of £8/16/6d.[64]

In addition to prosecutions under the Master and Servant and Criminal Law Amendment Acts, farmers prosecuted scores of men for trivial offences. At Great Chesterford labourers were fined (the prosecutors waited until after the harvest was in) for lighting a bonfire and burning Jonas Webb in effigy within fifty feet of the highway[65], and in the Huntingdon County Court, Lane of the Huntingdon Union was charged with the non-payment of a trifling sum for food consumed at a rally.[66] A particularly vindictive prosecution was reported from Linton when 'George Preston, of West Wickham, labourer', was charged with 'feloniously stealing one faggot of wood, of the value of 2d. the goods and chattels of Mr. John Allen, his master, on the 22nd instant [and] committed for a month'.[67] Three months later George Taylor of Cottenham prosecuted Sevill and Sarah Maskell for stealing wood valued at 6d. The wife was discharged, the husband found guilty, fined 2/6d with damages 2d. and costs—a total of £1/2/8d.[68] Dismissals, the eviction of union labourers, increased use of machinery and prosecutions, did not exhaust the ways of attacking the unionists. A crowd of 1,500 on Parker's Piece, Cambridge, heard of an old woman at Cherry Hinton who had had her parish relief withdrawn when her son joined a union. 'When she applied to the Chesterton Board, she was told by a Guardian that she could not have relief out of two unions—the Chesterton Union and the Labourers Union.'[69] Private benefactions were also withheld, as at Ramsay where it was reported that Mrs. Fellowes, the wife of a county M.P., had 'curtailed her gifts of clothing this year through the labourers joining the unions . . .'[70]; and selective wage increases were often given to non-union labourers.[71]

Faced with the tremendous union activity of 1872 and 1873 the farmers, and particularly the large owner-occupiers, began to combine. At first the local Chambers of Agriculture were the places where anti-union sentiments were aired and means of combating the evil discussed.[72] Later, specific organisations to break the unions came into being, based, or so it seems, on an Oxfordshire model.[73] The first of these was the Newmarket Farmers' Association, a body said to have been originally intended to protect farmers and labourers alike from the 'itinerate agitators' who were reckoned to be responsible for the unrest. Membership subscriptions were based on a payment of 6d. an acre which was 'to form a fund to reimburse any farmer who may be unjustly treated by his men'.[74] In March 1873 the West Walsham Farmers' Defence Association was created in Norfolk[75], and two months later the Huntingdonshire Farmers' Defence Association came into being.[76] Within a month the latter was said to have had over 100 members representing a total of 50,000 acres.[77] The Isle of Ely Farmers' Defence Association, 'under the able presidency of Joseph Martin Esq., of Littleport'[78], came into being specifically to fight Taylor's Peterborough Union in the Haddenham district of Cambridgeshire and within a week had locked 200 men out.[79] The *Return of the Owners of Land,* the 'New Domesday Book' of the 'seventies, shows all the leading opponents of the union, as very substantial owner-occupiers, Hunter Rodwell, for example, and John Dobede of Exning, the squire of the village where the lock-out began. [128 and 130]

The purport of the Defence Associations was clear from the outset. Meetings of the Huntingdon were held monthly and great power was vested in an elected management committee. If there was an incident the committee was to investigate, give advice and had the power to order a lock-out in either one or a group of parishes. Where a farmer could not do without union labour he could be given permission to retain men 'not exceeding one man for every hundred acres of land in his occupation'. Members pledged themselves 'to obey all orders and directions of the committee of management'.[80] The Isle of Ely Association was far more militant, its members agreeing to employ no unionists, and pay no more than 13/- a week.[81] The Norfolk F.D.A., on its creation, requested the Board of Guardians of each district 'to form a committee to help and advise the general committee of the Association'[82], but without success it should be added.

The labourers at Exning, near Newmarket, where there had been an increase in the use of drills at seed time, made wage demands early in 1874 and were locked out by the local Defence Association. Frederick Clifford has made the story familiar, but many details of the struggle still need to be filled in. The unions were exhausted by the drain on their resources when thousands of labourers went on strike pay. They obtained a tremendous amount of help from sympathisers outside their movement, particularly when they went on their celebrated fund-raising pilgrimage from Newmarket to Halifax, but it was not enough. The farmers created more and more effective defence organisations[83], used more and more machinery[84], more and more girls and boys, and others, as strike breakers.[85] Gradually the labourers were forced back to work and the lock-out finally ended when the union decided, in June, that it 'no longer felt justified in supporting the labourer in enforced idleness'.[86]

So much for the nature of the conflict in East Anglia between 1872 and 1874. In the remainder of this essay I would like to discuss the backgrounds of the labourers' enemies and sympathisers, to bring out the local origins of some of the disputes, and finally, briefly to mention the sequel to the great lock-out.

II

The importance of religious disputes in determining men's attitudes to the union struggles of the 1870s has often been noted[87] and the significance of Dissent in East Anglia is evident from the reports of scores of meetings and speeches. Cole Ambrose, a farmer from Stuntney Hall, Ely, who was often allowed to speak, hostilely, at union gatherings, declared at Newmarket during the lock-out that the labourers were 'being led by a lot of meeting parsons'.[88] W.H. Hall, a landowner and a union sympathiser, told a farmers' meeting that 'A large number of the agitators were Dissenters and had got the gift of the gab and he knew some of the most religious of the labourers were Dissenters.'[89] A Baptist from Newmarket said early in the dispute that the 'spouting demagogues' who were leading the labourers were 'chiefly Methodist local preachers of the labouring class, which accounts for their freedom of speech, and for the religious element observable in the meetings they hold', and two years later wrote to the *Cambridge Chronicle* saying that he and his fellow ministers dare not 'utter a word opposed to the union sentiment [or the labourers] . . . will leave the chapel in a mass' and went on to deplore the fact that this was happening when so much was expected from 'the coming revival wave'.[90] Moody and Sankey were touring the country. During the lock-out unionists preached pro-labour sermons from the pulpits of various dissenting chapels. In Waterbeach, for example, where C.H. Spurgeon had once been minister, Edward Richardson preached in the local Baptist chapel and collected £5 from the congregation for strike funds.[91] G.M. Ball was a Methodist and so too was George Mitchell. On a national level, of course, the labourers received tremendous support from leading nonconformists, notably Spurgeon, who came to the

East at the height of the dispute.[92] Bendigo, the ex-pugilist, 'now a Revivalist preacher, complete in black frock-coat, hat and gloves'[93], preached on their behalf on one occasion and raised over £15.[94]

The labourers' literature expressed nonconformist dislike of the established church, and the labourers' hostility to the clergyman—the farmers' friend, the landowners' lackey and the upholder on the bench of laws that were oppressive, harsh and cruel.[95] 'Thou shalt not take my name in vain, nor speak disrespectfully of my ways' went a travesty of the Commandments circularised by unionists, 'for I am on the Bench of Magistrates. If thy children have not sufficient food . . . thou shalt not call this murder.'[96] A part of a union parody of the church catechism went as follows:—

'What is your name?   Clodhopper.

Who gave you your name?   My masters, the landowners and
                             farmers, when I was a tiller of the soil
                             a scarer of birds, a keeper of cows
                             and sheep, follower of the plough,
                             a producer of wealth, that my masters
                             might live in idleness and luxuriousness
                             all the days of their lives.'[97]

The Church of England was overwhelmingly hostile to the unions, and clergymen were prominent in the Defence Associations. The Bishop of Peterborough publicly attacked the unions in his area.[98]* The Rev. John Martin, of St. Andrew the Great, Cambridge, used his pulpit to preach anti-union sermons[99], and the Rev. Conway was an early opponent of the union at Alconbury.[100] The Rev. W.J. Josling of Moulton, however, was perhaps the most vehement of Arch's clerical critics. In a stupid and arrogant speech to the Newmarket F.D.A.[101] he described himself as 'an out and out Tory', and went on to say that the Bishop of Manchester's *Times* letters on the lock-out[102] were 'bosh' and 'Oxford rhetoric.' He would tell the Bishop, he said.

'that walking between Newmarket and his parish church, he could see more sense under the bodies of horses there training, than he could find in the parish school or around his labourers' hearths . . . '

Although members of the Church of England were prominent among the labourers' opponents there were exceptions, and in a few places clergymen

*   It is revealing of later changes, but also of the rosy effect of memory, that a later Bishop of Peterborough wrote to R.H. Tawney on 22.6.1921 supporting the agricultural minimum wage and ended his letter: 'I am indeed anxious that the Church should not display the same apathy as she did in the days of Joseph Arch.'

were among the strongest union sympathisers. At Wisbech the Rev. W.E. Winks spoke at the inaugural meeting of the local union[103], and the Rev. R. Hoskin acted as chairman of some of the meetings held by Taylor's Peterborough union.[104] The Rev. Joshua Cautley, Vicar of Thorney, was another union sympathiser[105], and the Rev. C.E.T. Roberts, curate of Holy Trinity, Ely, contributed a very powerful letter to the press at the beginning of the lockout warmly supporting the labourers and complaining of a cathedral dignitary's attempts to prevent him 'speaking the truth in a minister's proper place'. [106] The following month the Littleport labourers invited Roberts to arbitrate on their behalf. Later in the lock-out a Diocesan conference was held at Ely to discuss 'the duty of the church, clergy, and laity, in relation to the dispute between labour and capital', and by no means all of the clerics present were guilty of airing anti-union sentiments.[107] Many of the early sympathisers withdrew their support as the movement grew, but there were a number of Church of England clergymen who sacrificed a tremendous amount to help the labourers, and remained loyal to them throughout the struggle of 1872-1874. The most notable of these was a remarkable man, the Rev. Dr. Burgess of Whittlesey.

Whittlesey was a strong union centre with many members, in the Peterborough organisation. Burgess[108], who had long been a noted opponent of the 'gang' system[109], appeared, along with his colleague the Rev. William Waller, amongst the early subscribers to union funds and as a speaker on union platforms. He was a blind temperance advocate who used his pulpit to preach pro-union sermons that were widely noticed in the press. The labourers were referred to by him as 'journeymen farmers', and he chose texts like 'Be content with your wages' (Luke, iii, 15,) to prove that 'the present rate of wages must be increased if the work of children in the fields is to be superseded by their effective attendance at school'.[110] Burgess also appeared in the press as an opponent of the Isle of Ely Farmers' Defence Association[111] and, shortly after a serious operation, stood up for the labourers during the lock-out.

As on previous occasions, when the agricultural labourers bestirred themselves, practically all of their leaders were drawn from other than their own ranks, from people independent of the farmers. Arthur James Challis, the first secretary of the South Cambridgeshire union, was 'a very respectable tradesman, and valuer of Sawston'[112], and his colleague Philpott was a publican [sic]. Day Wiles, an originator of the union in the Wisbech area, was a toll bar keeper, and among those prominent in the early days of the Peterborough were Harding, a shoemaker, Tigerdine, a coal porter, while Benjamin Taylor, the leader, was High Bailiff of Peterborough. Anthony Fisher, who was active among the labourers at Exning, was a carpenter. Lane of the Huntingdon union (the 'Garibaldi of Peterborough')[113] was a plasterer and among his colleagues were John Cooper, a tailor from Huntingdon, Pestell, a publican from Brampton, and Watson, a baker from Ellington.

The motives of people like these must have been mixed. Some undoubtedly acted purely out of a sense of justice. Others, Dissenters like Cooper and John Savage, may have seen the labourers' movement as a means of advancing their religious and educational ideas.[114] Yet others may have had less creditable motives. The hostile press never tired of 'exposing' people, like Edward Richardson, who became full-time officials of one or other of the unions, at far greater wages than they had been earning. Rather more damagingly it was possible to point to the benefits secured by people like Challis who was forced to admit in court that he was paid a commission of 10/- for each labourer who emigrated to Queensland from his district.[115]

The labourers were not without some support from farmers. One of Lord Rendlesham's tenants was reported to have 'sported union colours' in Saxmundham.[116] Jex Blake spoke up for the workers before the Norfolk Farmers' Defence Association[117] and farmers J.P. Denson and James Toller actively helped the N.A.L.U. in Waterbeach. Toller was a Baptist who had, as will be shown later, been involved in disputes over charity lands, and religious motives may have been of prime importance in determining his, and many of the other sympathetic farmers', attitudes. Certainly in his village religious feelings ran very high, so high as to have given rise to 'several religious battles' that caused great concern.[118] Other reasons for supporting the unions were concern with tenants' rights, as evinced by John Todd of Cottenham[119], and hostility to the preservation of game, which was vigorously attacked from union platforms in South Cambridgeshire by a farmer named Bennett.[120]

During the lock-out some attempts were made to exploit the farmers' grievances and drive a wedge between them and the landlords. The Anti-Game Law League represented by George Odger and Randall Cremer put in an appearance in the East[121]; and when Arch visited Sawston he attacked the Game Laws and taunted the farmers with having to 'vote as your landlord tells you',[122] The Liberal *Cambridge Independent* jeered at the farmers for allowing the movement 'that was begun during the cattle plague of 1865-1866, and speedily resolved itself into a union of tenant farmers, known as Chambers of Agriculture' to collapse and become 'another landowners' forum'.[123] G.M. Ball told the farmers they were suffering from the same evils as the labourers—'landlordism . . . . they had sent people to represent them', he said,

> 'who were diametrically opposed to their interests. They had sent men who had done all they could to place burdens on the farmers and take them off their own shoulders . . . If the farmers had acted like men, and said they would form political clubs, and planned . . . for their own protection, they would have taken a step in the right direction. But instead of that they had been lickspitting to the landlords and were themselves the slaves of that class of people . . .'[124]

All this was to no avail, and Ball must have realised that there was no hope of splitting the bulk of the farmers from the landlords, and he ended his speech with an attack on the farmers on Cobbettite lines, charging them with extravagance, with drinking and having hordes of servants and governesses; he told the labourers that they 'must remember that they are only entitled to what remains after all the servants and expenses are supplied . . . The labourers [were] stepping stones to other people's prosperity.'

There was not, however, a solid front of landlords allying themselves with the farmers in the struggles of 1872-1874. Despite attempts by the farmers to persuade the landowners to join actively with them, the vast majority remained outside the dispute. A few, however, did join the Farmers Defence Associations and became objects of tremendous hatred. Lord Walsingham, for example, presided over the Norfolk F.D.A. and said the union was 'a nuisance disseminating false principles and theories producing discontent and setting class against class'.[125] Later he became a patron of the National Farmers Union, set up in Leamington 'to prevent and repress strikes, to counteract the dangerous influence of union delegates' and 'to liberate labourers from union control'.[126] The Marquis of Bristol was prominent in the fight against the Lincolnshire union[127] and so was Hunter Rodwell, chairman of the West Suffolk F.D.A. who turned all his unionist labourers out and gave non-unionists a shilling rise.[128] Lord Stradbroke, Lord Lieutenant of Suffolk, who had talked of 'vagabonds who went about the country making speeches'[129], supported the farmers, as did John Dobede of Exning[130] and Duleep Singh.[131] Not all landowners remained out of the dispute or helped the farmers. Some made genuine attempts to bring the struggle to a close. Speaker Brand was one[132] and Lord Waveney urged arbitration on people like Stradbroke[133] and those who supported the 'blood and no surrender policy of the farmers'.[134] Sir Edward Kerrison, of Oakley Park, Suffolk, asked that there be an attempt at reconciliation[135] and J. Tollemache, M.P. from Helmingham Hall, met his tenants and stated his disapproval of locking-out and left them in no doubt about his desire that they should not behave as the Newmarket farmers had.[136] Sir Harry Verney was another landowner who tried to act as an arbitrator, and one landowner, an M.P., as early as April 1872 ordered his tenants to pay their labourers an extra 3/- a week and reduced rents by 2/-.[137] The occasional landowner, moreover, positively sympathised with the unionists. The most famous of all, on a national scale, was undoubtedly Lord Edmund Fitz-Maurice, but the most notable in East Anglia was W.H. 'Bullock' Hall, a friend of Baldwin Leighton, and a landowner at Six Mile Bottom, who returned from France to find his employees locked out, even although they had not asked for a rise. Hall appeared on union platforms, and spoke up for the labourers at meetings of the Newmarket F.D.A. where he urged arbitration and attacked the intolerance of the Church, farmers and landlords with great gusto. He provided the labourers in his village with a reading room, helped some others form a co-operative store, and gave financial assistance to the National Union. During the dispute of 1874 he employed workers who had been locked out elsewhere on his 'pleasure ground'.[138]

The few people like Bullock Hall from among the ranks of the land-owners, who supported the labourers, were Liberals who were using the labourers' movement locally, in the way Chamberlain, Morley, Mundella and others did nationally, to embarrass the Conservatives and build up support for their party among the labouring classes. This was sound policy, their opponents realised it, and this probably explains the actual timing of the great lock-out. Wage demands, strikes, letters to farmers, even lock-outs on a small scale, as the above will have shown, were common in East Anglia in 1872 and 1873, but were not subject to the vicious counter attacks they met later. This may have had something to do with the fact that a General Election was in the offing. Gladstone dissolved Parliament in January 1874. The election, with the Conservatives winning handsomely for the first time since 1841, took place in February, and the lock-out began in the immediate aftermath of victory. Hitherto the farmers may have hesitated to attack head-on a popular movement for fear of the political consequences; now the restraints had gone. It is true that when the lock-out began prices had also started to fall[139], but A.J. Whellams, an emigration agent of the Government of Ontario, went on record as saying that the election had 'more than a little' to do with the timing of the lock-out.[140]

The labourers of East Anglia had powerful Liberal support from another quarter, the University of Cambridge. Sedley Taylor, a Fellow of Trinity College, appeared on union platforms, in Cambridge, and so did W.H.H. Hudson and Alfred Marshall, both of St. John's. Their role in the labourers agitation was to explain Liberal objections to the laws of supply and demand, which opponents had used in their propaganda from the very beginning. As Mr. Dunbabin points out, deductions from these varied, but the prevalent conclusion was that unions were useless. The Rev. John Martin in a harvest thanksgiving service, for example, warned labourers that farm profits were not high enough to permit wage increases, and elaborated on the theme that wages depended on supply and demand.[141] Robert Stephenson of Burwell, a member of the Newmarket F.D.A., wrote many letters to the press in the same vein. 'Whether that value (wages) be high or low', he said, 'that the labourers must take, and we must pay. The labourers may possibly say—Perhaps the rate won't be sufficient for our family wants. I reply to that it must be so in the nature of things . . .'[142] The *Cambridge Chronicle* published a series of articles in the same vein entitled 'Notes of Alarm' and signed 'C.S.M.', number thirteen of which particularly agitated the friends of the unions.[143] The labourers, the author contended, had become 'the tools and dupes of unscrupulous democrats', and he urged the landowners and farmers to stop employing union members. Farmers could not meet higher costs by increasing prices, he went on, as these were regulated by foreign price levels. If the unions succeeded, profits would be reduced to bare interest and investment would cease. Rents could not be lowered because they paid the proprietor a bare three per cent. If the unions were victorious, land would be forced on to the market in smaller and smaller lots, as the Radicals and Liberals wanted.

Sedley Taylor and Marshall attacked C.S.M. vehemently from public platforms. The former said his arguments were 'fallacious', but that he welcomed anything that would make land cheaper. Furthermore, it was not feasible to talk of the laws of supply and demand in the abstract. 'To apply abstract conclusions of political economy unmodified in their [the labourers] case would be like expecting a mass of treacle to obey the laws laid down in treatises on mechanics regulating the motion of water', he said. 'The Union, however, by supplying information on the price of labour elsewhere, and exhorting and encouraging the labourer to go where it is more highly remunerated, tends to bring about a state of things more nearly corresponding to the assumptions of political economists.'[144] Marshall spoke in a similar fashion. The laws, he said, 'when applied to Newmarket labourers . . . make some false assumptions'. First it was assumed that the farmers competed for labour and second that wage increases would not make labour more efficient. The farmers, Marshall went on, were not attacking the evils but the principles of unionism. 'The farmers have forced us to sympathise with the labourers, let us sympathise with our hearts and our purses.'[145] 'The farmers cling to a system that is happily passing away. That system keeps the labourers bound and therefore ignorant; ignorant and therefore bound . . . if the farmers triumph, the old bad state of things must continue.'[146]

The unions in East Anglia, as elsewhere and as Sedley Taylor's remarks indicate, relied on migration and emigration as a means of improving conditions. Tacitly they acknowledged the fact that many farms were overstocked with labour, and it was the policy of the N.A.L.U. to set up a string of emigration agencies throughout the country to move the surplus labour; and very early on in the struggle emigration agents of various colonial governments were appearing at practically every union meeting, A Mr. A.B. Daveney, a Canadian agent who set up a special office in Norwich, appears to have been the first in the area. Later there were many more people from Canada, as well as representatives from the Dominion Shipping Line, and the governments of Queensland and New Zealand. Mr. Spencer A. Jones from Queensland had an agency in the Rev. Burgess's village of Whittlesey.

The emigration agents were regarded as allies by the unionists, but their actual role in the events of 1872-1874 ought to be examined in more detail. They may or may not have been invited to take part in union activity in the first place, but their constant references to idyllic conditions abroad, and their comparisons of the labourers' lot in England with that in the colonies undoubtedly added to the discontent prevailing at the time. They may also have helped prolong the dispute once it had started. It has already been mentioned that some union officials, like Arthur J. Challis, had a direct interest in persuading labourers to emigrate—and prolonging the lock-out would certainly have produced more emigrants! Cole Ambrose, a farmer of

Stuntney Hall, Ely, and an emigration agent, appeared at union meetings urging emigration *and* in a Defence Association urging a lock-out.[147] Charles Jay, of Braintree, Essex, was another farmer/emigration agent who urged the labourers to *increase* their demands. Jay and Ambrose, who G.M. Ball said he would take on at anything except drinking, actually argued about each other's motives at union meetings.[148] The press always held the agents responsible for much of the trouble in the East, and in August 1874 the *Cambridge Chronicle* reported that 'In some of [the] agricultural districts the labourers have threatened that if any of these deceivers come amongst them again they will drive them out of the neighbourhood.'[149] Smythe, a Canadian agent, publicly apologised for the misleading things he and others had placarded about the countryside[150], and Joseph Arch told a Royal Commission on Agriculture, many years later, that 'the emigration agents and the shipping companies . . . made our union a means to get into the various counties'.[151] Edward Jenkins was actually Agent General for Canadian emigration.

III

Why, Mr. Dunbabin asks, did discontent become articulate at precisely this time in the seventies? Conditions had been deplorable for years and, as he stated, town unionists were worried about competition from farm workers and were able and willing to help organise them, or give considerable financial assistance to them. Advanced Liberals were also prepared to help, and wages were appalling and declining in real terms[152], partly because of education charges. These are all general reasons applicable everywhere; that is with the exception of education charges. There must have been other more detailed reasons why unions appeared in some places and not in others, however, for instance the size and type of farms.

It was a commonplace in the seventies that arable farming, being more labour intensive, was more prone to labour troubles than pastoral farming and it would seem that the strikes and disputes in East Anglia conformed to this rule, and also the rule that the employers involved in the disputes were the very large farmers. Martin Slater, chairman of the Newmarket F.D.A., farmed 'about 800 acres under the Duke of Rutland'[153] and Mr. Henry Stanley of Bury, the secretary of the West Suffolk Defence Association farmed 'close on 700 acres . . . at West Thorpe'.[154] In that area, a trouble spot, 'holdings [did] not average less than 500 or 600 acres',[155] Exning was dominated by large holdings, and Edward Staples, the most hated of the labourers' enemies, farmed 1,000 acres there and Sabin, another of the labourers' enemies, held 1,200 acres.[156] The majority of the members of the various Defence Associations were also large farmers. The first hundred entrants into the Huntingdonshire F.D.A. had an average of 500 acres each[157], for example. The twelve employers in the Wilford Hundred, of which Woodbridge is the centre, who were presented with wage demands from the National Union in March 1874, employed between them 'about 170 men'.[158]

Clifford, throughout his book, repeatedly suggests that the dispute was not only a farmers' dispute, but especially an owner-occupier contest. These were people employing large numbers of labourers, on whom the (sometimes) sobering effect of the landowners could not apply. 'The great landowner', he quotes a Newmarket farmer as saying,

> 'did not answer our appeal. The backbone of our Association consisted of men who farm their own land, along with land belonging to others— owning, say, from 100 to 1,000 acres. As owners and occupiers . . . we had to measure the strength of our opponents; and we did so without fearing the action of labourers, or the lukewarmness of landlords. We found many tenant-farmers afraid to join us for fear of giving offence to their landlords, though they were glad enough to see the cudgels taken up by us.'[159]

The existence of large arable farms is one possible reason explaining the appearance of unionism in certain villages. Another may have been the existence of a radical tradition dating back to the early post-Napoleonic war years. Until a detailed study of discontent throughout the century is made for East Anglia as a whole it is impossible to be definite about so nebulous a thing as this, yet it is a fact that some of the trouble centres of the seventies were also the trouble centres of an earlier time. Littleport, for example, where feeling against the introduction of machinery led to unionism in Arch's time, was the very centre of the Fenland troubles in 1816. Exning had a reputation of being one of the greatest trouble spots in the East in the early part of the century[160], and Cottenham appears to have had a tradition of incendiarism and violence.[161] The town of Ely, if contributions to the Chartist land company are an indication, was a fairly strong Chartist centre, for that part of the world, and Whittlesey was prominent in the events of 1816 and the 'Swing riots'.[162]

In many of the villages where unions appeared in the seventies there had also been continuous trouble over the local charities—trouble often, perhaps usually, exploited by the Nonconformists. The labourers had long resented the way charities were manipulated, and at a time of declining real wages these had become of more and more importance. Only three years after the Fenland had been 'pacified' after the labourers' rising at Ely, and in the year of Peterloo, 'a daring spirit of insubordination' broke out at Coveney, in the Isle of Ely, 'which' the *Cambridge Chronicle* reported,

> 'had it not been timely checked might have led to serious consequences.

After four days' previous deliberation the poor (all receiving alms from the parish) made a regular *Oyes Oyes* proclamation though the streets, notifying that the poor would meet at the church-yard gate on Easter Monday in order to take possession (out of the hands of the feofees) of the charity lands annually let for the general benefit of the poor, and divide them severally among themselves. Notice of such illegal intention having reached the magistrates at Ely, Sir Henry Bate Dudley issued his warrant for apprehending nine of the ringleaders, who were committed for further examination.'[163]

There are many reports of trouble over charities in the years between the incident at Coveney and the appearance of the unions associated with Arch, and during the struggle of 1872-1874 the local press contained scores of stories of disputes at village level. At Whittlesey a rumour had it that the sums of money collected by the unionists were to 'be used for the purpose of remedying the abuse of charitable trusts left for the poor . . . [the maladministration of which had] supplied fuel to the sparks around us. The subject now excites intense interest here' the report went on, 'and no one can see where the controversy will end.'[164] In Over there was trouble[165], in Ely[166], in Babraham, where the South Cambridgeshire union was strongly entrenched, and in Waterbeach. At this place the union 'publicly acknowledged the liberality and kindness of Mr. James Toller', a deacon of the Baptist Church and a popular farmer and trustee who had tried to get the charity lands rented higher.[167] G.M. Ball continually dwelt upon the running of charities during his speeches and told the labourers that they had been robbed of £75 millions[168], and during the lock-out J.E. Matthew Vincent, the editor of the *Labourers Union Chronicle*, was prosecuted for a libel on the Rev. John Spurgin, the Vicar of Hockham, who had levied a tithe on twenty tons of coal annually distributed to the poor.[169] At Clopton, in Suffolk, the Rev. R.F. Palmer gave notice to quit to all unionists who held parish allotments, and announced that their names were to be struck off the list of coal and bread charities.[170] The place where most trouble took place in these years, however, was Cottenham, a village some six miles from Cambridge.

A dispute over the Cottenham charities had been raging for six or seven years before the unions appeared, and the leading figure in the dispute was John Todd. Politics in the village were sharply divided along the lines of Church versus Dissent, and Todd was the leader of the Nonconformists who were strongly organised to contest School Board and other elections. The dispute over the charities became a part of the religious struggle. The Rev. Anson admitted that 'For many years the distribution took place with a partiality as unblushing as it was shameful, and with a view to advance political and denominational purposes.'[171] Todd, after many years of struggle, had, with the help of a local M.P., obtained a public enquiry with the result, first of all that the poor were given eighteen more acres of land,

and secondly that the vicar was forced to publish accounts, which showed that the charity lands were all 'held by a rich farmer and butcher, at a low rent'.[172]

When the labourers began forming unions in Cottenham their agitation was treated as an extension of the Church versus Dissent squabble. George Sanderson, who worked for Todd, was the moving spirit in calling the first meetings in the village[173], and later on Todd himself became very active on behalf of the unions using the campaign *inter alia* to air his views on tenants' rights. Eventually he was presented with a testimonial 'by the working men of Cottenham, in grateful recognition of [his] self-denying labours towards improving the administration of the Cottenham charities'. The inscription on it was from Psalms xii, 1, 'Blessed is he that considereth the poor'.[174]

In Cottenham, then, were present all the elements needed for discontent to become articulate, plus a possible labour shortage.[175] Low wage rates prevailed,[176] there were obvious injustices over the charities, there was Church versus Dissent feeling made worse by the coming of a School Board[177], and there was a ready-made leader in John Todd.

In other villages these elements were also present, in Exning for example. There, although there was no labour shortage, large holdings predominated, and, as early as June 1872, the village was referred to as 'a depot of malcontents'.[178] Wage rates were low[179], and housing there, according to Clifford, was a 'crying evil'.[180] There had also been trouble over the school. John Dobede, the squire and a J.P., before whom appeared a number of unionists on assault charges[181], had contributed one-third of the money necessary to maintain a school under the voluntary system but 'the institution had languished'[182], and at the time the unions appeared the School Board were trying to obtain land opposite Dobede's house which he maintained he wanted to add to his park.

In Sawston and Waterbeach, the N.A.L.U. stronghold, these factors were also present, a School Board, strong Church versus Dissent feeling, trouble over the charities and leaders like James Toller able and willing to take part in the labourers' struggles. In some villages, however, there is no mention of any attempts at organisation among the labourers, and it is interesting to speculate why. In Histon and Impington, for example, twin villages only three miles from Cottenham, there were no stirrings, and neither were there, for that matter, in 1816, during the 'Swing riots', or in the nineties, when the next wave of unionism took place in East Anglia. The two villages have a history in which labour movements have played no part whatsoever.

In 1871 Histon and Impington had a population of around 1,400, as against almost 2,500 in Cottenham.[183] Wage rates do not seem to have been particularly high, according to farm record books preserved in the Cambridgeshire Archives, but some of the old paternalistic practices, like the 'Horkey' (an end of harvest feast) remained[184], and these may have had an inhibiting effect on the labourers. The paying of differential rates to workers went on and, although nonconformity was present (the Chivers, who were to become the chief employers, were Baptists[185]), the Primitive Methodists were not established there as they were in union centres like Waterbeach and Sawston.[186] Clifford seems to suggest that he considered the absence of village allotments, as at Exning, largely accounted for union-ism's appearance in many places[187], but it has not been possible to find any details about the situation in Histon and Impington. There was no history of trouble over the charities, which in Impington anyway were very small[188], no School Board existed to heighten Church versus Dissent feeling[189], and the industry that the villages have become famous for was only twelve months old at the time of the lock-out, and so unlikely to have had much effect.[190]

IV

The causes of the labourers' defeat in 1874 are manifest. They were not absolutely essential to the harvest, and the farmers were helped by the extraordinary good weather, and able to cripple the unions financially by the lock-out.[191] The results of the defeat, however, are not so clear at this remove of time, but certainly many of the wage increases the unions had obtained were soon lost. In January 1875 it was reported from Sawston that 'farmers have reduced . . . wages by 1/- or 2/- a week'[192], and at the end of the year Grimwood Cooke, of Horseheath Park, Linton, (Cambs.) said that at the harvest 'men [had] been more plentiful, willing, obliging, and satisfied with less harvest wages than they were willing to *let* themselves at last year'.[193] Reports of this kind abound in the local press.

Machinery, as has been shown, was used increasingly during the lockout and this continued after it was over. More drills were used at seed time, more steam cultivators[194] and more harvest machinery. Large numbers of labourers were not re-employed after the dispute was over[195], and piece-work it seems became more prevalent, at least for a time: a Royal Commission in the 1890s found that trends towards piece-work were purely local, but that the practice had diminished in recent years more often than it had increased. Many of the perquisites the farmers made so much of in their propaganda may have been lost, and the paternalism that was equally lauded by the opponents of unionism received a severe blow. East Anglian landlords in the aftermath of defeat often transferred cottages to their tenants, enabling them to increase their control over their employees, as Edward Staples of Exning wanted at the height of the struggle.[196]

The labourers' lot was considerably worsened, as they expected, by the effect of the Agricultural Children's Act when it came into force in January 1875. This was strictly carried out in some areas. The Newmarket correspon-dent of the *Cambridge Chronicle* reported in February that the 'Act [was] being strictly carried out by the Boards of Guardians' in that area.[197]

Prosecutions under the Act were common from then onwards.[198] The strict carrying out of the legislation regulating children's employment in agriculture, the refusal to re-employ many workers, and a considerable outbreak of rick burning, are indicative of a hardening of class attitude from which the labourers suffered. This can also be shown or so it was maintained by contemporaries by the events connected with a by-election that took place in Cambridgeshire within a very short time of the ending of the lock-out.

Immediately this by-election became necessary a squabble broke out in the Cambridgeshire Conservative party. The landowners' nominee for the seat was Francis Sharp Powell, once member for the county, who received a majority of votes at the selection conference over Benjamin Bridges Hunter Rodwell, the farmers' candidate. Rodwell, as leader of the West Suffolk Farmers' Defence Association, and the East Anglian Farmers' Consultative Board, had taken a leading part in the lock-out and was hated by the labourers.[199] Powell was eventually forced to withdraw and the Liberals decided that beating Rodwell was impossible and ran no candidate against him. The *Cambridge Independent* represented Rodwell's success as a victory for the farmers in the Conservative party 'manifesting their independence and upsetting the nominee of a caucus of landlords'.[200] Powell, in his valedictory address, said that 'It is now manifest that the tenant farmers who have votes will, in larger numbers, support a candidate who, in their judgement, has won their battle in a controversy with a class not in possession of the franchise'.[201] The following year in a by-election in West Suffolk, which resulted in a Conservative victory for Lt. Col. Wilson over Easton, the Liberal, similar circumstances were said to have been at work.[202]

Unionism, like the labourers, suffered severely from the defeat of 1874. Many labourers were said to have retained their cards when they returned to work, but many more, angered at the harsh and abrupt way the strike had been terminated, gave up their membership and were lost to the movement for ever. Contributions to the union from Exning, for example, which had been £19/-/- in the three months April to July, 1874, were down to £4/6/- for the period October 1874 to January 1875.[203] Furthermore, emigration had taken away many of the best labourers and erstwhile leaders, so weakening what organisation remained. In Waterbeach, for instance, Berry Robinson, the president[204] and Elias Clay, the treasurer of the local branch of the N.A.L.U., both emigrated to America.[205] The movement was also discredited by internecine squabbles, when even Burgess and the Peterborough disputed in public over charity lands.[206] Nationally it suffered from the adverse publicity following disputes between Howard Evans and Gibson Ward[207] and Arch and J.E.M. Vincent. Later a rival union to the National was created and one-time colleagues fell to calling each other names. Arch, according to Ward, was 'a charlatan' and the cause of the N.A.L.U. 'one of brigands'.[208]

All this did insurmountable harm on a local level. The labourers felt themselves betrayed and did not respond to the newly orientated policies of the unions—the appeal for political reform, law reform and land reform, including a scheme, produced by Alfred Simmons, of balloting for land that harked back to Chartist times.[209] Throughout most of 1875 many branches remained in existence, but by the end of the summer there were reports, like that from Wisbech, that branches were refusing to send money to Leamington until there was 'a great reform' there.[210] A year later correspondents wrote that branches as strong as that at Waterbeach were dead.[211] The 'deadly sweeping away of members' that got worse and worse as 'the serious economic slump in the farm industry came about'[212] was under way and it was another fifteen years before any more really significant movements took place among the labourers of East Anglia. Prospects in the mid-seventies were grim, as a labourer's lament complained.

> Each day growing older
> We get the cold shoulder
> By farmers thrust out in the cold
> Who jeeringly say 'get out of the way'.
> That's how you get served when you're old. (213)

REFERENCES

(1)   *Past and Present,* No. 26 (1963) pp. 68-97: *Bulletin of the Society for the Study of Labour History,* xi (1965) pp. 6-8

(2)   A new study of this is long overdue. The best work on it is F.E. Clifford, *The Agricultural Lock-out of 1874* (1875). For the events involving the Federal Union see Rex C. Russell, *The 'Revolt of the Field' in Lincolnshire* (Lincolnshire no date). Also Reg Groves, *Sharpen the Sickle!* (1949). There is a fairly long report of the lock-out in *The Annual Register* pp 115-121 which quotes extensively from an article in *Blackwoods Magazine*

(3)   E. Selley, *Village Trade Unions in Two Centuries* (1919) p.47

(4)   *Cambridge Express* (C.E.) 17.2.72. The complaint about school fees is heard repeatedly, and in Cambridgeshire Boards were established in many villages where unions became active. See later, and also a report of the speech by Joseph Arch in A. Clayden, *The Revolt of the Field.* (1874) pp. 17-18. See too the reference to the Rev. Burgess's sermon on the subject, p.170. The Education Act of 1870 'allowed for the charging of fees (up to a maximum of 9d a week) while it was left to the local School Boards to decide whether or not they made attendance compulsory'. They had limited powers of remitting fees. Brian Simon, *Education and the Labour Movement.* (1965) p. 126. The labourers were probably equally worried about the provisions of the Agricultural Children's Act which was made law the following year (although it did not come into force until January 1875). This forbade the employment of children unless they had attended school a certain number of times. For the way the Act was used see reference to Newmarket p.179

(5)   *Cambridge Independent Press* (C.I.P.), 16.3.72

(6) *C.I.P.* 30.3.72. on the Ely area
(7) *Ibid.*
(8) *C.E.* 16,23.3.72
(9) *C.E.* 13.4.72
(10) *C.I.P.* 16.3.72
(11) *C.I.P.* 30.3.72
(12) *C.E.* 6.4.72
(13) *Cambridge Chronicle* (C.C.) 6.4.72
(14) *C.I.P.* 30.3, 13.4.72
(15) *C.I.P.* 4.5.72. A report in the *C.C.* 22.6.72 says that at that date there were 15 branches in existence
(16) *C.I.P.* 25.5.72
(17) *C.I.P.* 29.6.72
(18) *C.C.* 15.6.72
(19) The *Beehive*, 20 April 1872
(20) *Ibid.*, 25 May 1872
(21) *C.I.P.* 18,25.5.72. *C.C.* 18.5.72
(22) There are conflicting reports on the Taxley incident. See *C.I.P.* 25.5, 1.6.72, *C.E.* 25.5.72, The *Beehive*, 25 May 1872
(23) *C.C.* 15.6.72
(24) *C.I.P.* 15.6.72
(25) The *Beehive*, 27 April 1872
(26) *C.C.* 4.5.72. This is an odd report as Burgess became an ardent supporter of the unions. See later
(27) *C.C.* 3.8.72. S. Hutchinson Norris, *Auberon Herbert: Crusader for Liberty,* (1943) pp. 132-3
(28) The *Beehive*, 31 May 1872
(29) G.M. Ball seems to have been the first 'delegate' in the area, helping around Wisbech. *C.I.P.* 13.7.72. The East Anglian Unions, however, had been in touch with Arch's Warwickshire organisation, the precursor of the N.A.L.U., several months before. See e.g. the *C.C.* 6.4.72 for a report of the South Cambridgeshire Union deciding to ask the Warwickshire Union for copies of its rules (quote from the *Daily Telegraph,* 3 April 1872)
(30) See e.g. *C.C.* 25.5.72
(31) *C.E.* 5.6.72. Speeches by Challis announcing the decision to amalgamate (there had been objections) in the *Labourers' Union Chronicle,* 7 and 21 June 1873
(32) *C.I.P.* 30.11., 7.12.72., 4.1.73
(33) *C.I.P.* 11.1.73
(34) W.H.G. Armytage, *Heavens Below: Utopian Experiments in England, 1560-1960.* (1961). pp. 145 f.f.
(35) *C.I.P.* 29.3.73
(36) For the Norfolk Unions see Marion Springall, *Labouring Life in Norfolk Villages 1834-1914.* (1936). Chap. 7
(37) *C.I.P.* 8.11.73. Reg Groves, *op. cit.* pp. 65-66. Russell, *op.cit.* for details of the Federals' activity in Lincolnshire. Also George Edwards, *From Crow-Scaring to Westminster* (1957 edit.) p. 40 f.f.
(38) *C.C.* 5.10.72
(39) *C.C.* 3.5.73 (for details of the formation of the unions in Haddenham and of the lock-out)
(40) *C.E.* 20.4.72

(41) *C.I.P.* 4.5.72

(42) Clifford, *op.cit.* pp.113-4. *C.C.* 5.9.74

(43) *Capital and Labour,* 19 August 1874, reporting incidents from the Bury St. Edmunds district

(44) *C.C.* 27.6.74. See the threatening letter from Woodbridge sent to Lord Rendlesham, *Ibid.,* 15 August 1874

(45) *Capital and Labour,* 19 August 1874, *C.E.* 15.8.74

(46) *C.C.* 5.9.74

(47) *C.C.* 12.9.74. *C.E.* 12.9.74

(48) See the second annual report of the Wisbech District of the N.A.L.U. in *C.C.* 23.1.75, which states that cooperative stores had been started by three branches. The Waterbeach branch of the National considered setting up a store in March 1873 (*C.C.* 29.3.73) and W.H. 'Bullock' Hall helped establish the Westley Waterless Industrial and Provident Society in January 1874 (*C.C.* 17, 24.4, 1.5.75)

(49) *C.C.* 25.4.74. The antiquity of this suggestion is well known: it was seriously put forward again as recently as 1962 by a Petersfield supporter of the Campaign for Nuclear Disarmament. *Sunday Telegraph,* 11 February 1962

(50) On evictions see e.g. *C.E.* 11.4.74, report from Newmarket. In the Exning area Edward Staples, a farmer regarded as the labourers' greatest enemy, tried to obtain the cottages from the local squires so as to be able to evict unionists. *C.I.P.* 4.4.74, report on the origins of the lock-out 'from careful and impartial enquiries'. Also Clifford, *op.cit.* p. 35

(51) *C.E.* 17.8.72

(52) *C.E.* 17.5.73, and letters on 24.5.73

(53) *C.C.* 3.5.73

(54) Clifford, *op.cit.* pp. 9-12. The Essex lock-out is fully reported in the *Labourers' Union Chronicle,* e.g. issue of 21 June 1873. The end of the struggle is reported on 28 June 1873

(55) *C.C.* 26.4, 10,24.5.73. "Cambridgeshire enjoyed 'a boom' from about 1850 onwards through the setting up of a coprolite industry. The sale of these minerals not only raised the value of the land by some £150 per acre, but created such a demand for labour that ordinary wages went up to twenty four shillings per week, whilst a good 'fossil digger', working in the piece, could almost double that sum. Population increased accordingly, and for nearly a generation our county was the most prosperous in England, the rent running from £2 to £3 an acre." Edward Coneybeare, *History of Cambridgeshire* (1897), p. 259. Also on the coprolite industry see *Victoria County History of Cambridgeshire and the Isle of Ely,* Vol 2., pp.119-20, 367-8. Coneybeare's estimate of wages seems very high. The work was incredibly hard and many of the labourers who had been enticed away from the farms to work 'on the fossils' returned to ordinary agricultural work. *C.E.* 1.3.73. Letter from F. Barlow on the dangerous nature of work in the coprolite pits, *Ibid.,* 4 September 1875

(56) *C.C.* 5.10, 30.11.72

(57) *C.C.* 13.6, 10.8.72. See also the editorial of 6.4.72, and the report from Huntingdon on the increased use of machines at harvest in *C.I.P.* 1.8.74

(58) Report of the Irish 'invading' the harvest fields for the 'first time for twenty years' in *Capital and Labour,* 15 July 1874. See the letter from the Peterborough Union to Gladstone complaining about the use of soldiers. *C.I.P.* 5.10.72. Despite the shortages of labour in some parts of East Anglia many of the farms

were over-stocked and so the removal of labour by their workers had less effect than it might have done, and of course the farmers themselves, as Clifford continually points out, were often able to do much of the essential work themselves. *C.I.P.* 16.5.74 quotes an amusing story from the *Norwich Mercury* about a farmer who locked his men out, started to work himself, and fell into a well from which he had to be rescued by a locked-out labourer, but not until after his employer had agreed to re-instate them at 2s. more a week 'with nothing said about the Union'

(59)   *C.C.* 29.3.73

(60)   *C.I.P.* 16.8.73

(61)   *C.I.P.* 16.8, 18.10.73. The sentences were later modified. Details of the case also in the *Minute Book of the Cambridgeshire Quarter Sessions* in the Cambridgeshire Record Office

(62)   *C.I.P.* 18.5.72, 8.11.73

(63)   Cambridgeshire Record Office, reference PS/C/R4

(64)   *Ibid.*

(65)   *C.I.P.* 14.9.72. *Brighton Daily News,* 11 September 1872. The case was dismissed. The prosecution was brought by the Parish Authorities

(66)   *C.C.* 11.1.73

(67)   *C.C.* 1.2.73

(68)   *Cambridge Division Petty Sessions Register, op.cit.* 17 May 1873 Bates Tolliday, 76, a pauper, of Histon was prosecuted by a farmer of Girton for stealing a piece of wood valued 1 d. which had blown off a tree. *C.E.* 3.7.75

(69)   *C.E.* 5.7.73 See also Clayden, *op.cit.* pp. 91-95 and Howard Evans, *Radical Fights of Forty Years,* (no date) pp. 54-55

(70)   *C.I.P.* 11.10.73. See the report of the speech by Mrs. Fellowes at the annual meeting of the Eynesford Agricultural Association, where she advised the girls to 'avoid unbecoming dress' and talked of the 'two evils drink and dress'. *C.E.* 2.11.72

(71)   See e.g. *C.C.* 9.5.74 for the Ely F.D.A.'s decision to advance non-union wages by 1s. a week, and *Ibid.,* 23.5.74 for a report of one West Suffolk landlord making a condition in his leases that non-unionists be paid 1s. more than unionists

(72)   See the report of the Cambridge Chamber of Agriculture meeting as early as April 1872, a part of which read, 'This meeting views with extreme regret the agitation that has been attempted by persons unconnected and unacquainted with agricultural subjects, with the object of implanting discontent in the mind of the agricultural labourer; and that in the opinion of this meeting such agitation is not calculated to promote the interests either of the employer or employed, whose welfare must depend on the law of supply and demand.' *C.C.* 10.4.72. *Beehive,* 20 April 1872

(73)   An 'Oxfordshire Association of Agriculturalists' was formed and resolved not to employ union members in future. *Oxford Journal,* 27 July 1872, *C.C.* 31.8, 19.10.72

(74)   *C.C.* 5.10.72

(75)   *C.C.* 15.3.73

(76)   *C.C.* 31.5, 7.6.73. *C.I.P.* 24.5, 7, 21.6.73

(77)   *C.C.* 21.6.73 Statement of Honnybun, Secretary of the Hunts. F.D.A.

(78)   *C.E.* 7.6.73, *C.C.* 7.6.73. Eventually the Defence Associations joined together in the 'East Anglian Farmers' Consultative Board'. *Ibid.,* 18.7.74

(79)   *C.I.P.* 3, 31.5, 14.6.73

(80) *C.E.* 7.6.73. The Huntingdonshire organisation did not engage in a lock-out, however

(81) *C.I.P.* 3.5.73

(82) *C.I.P.* 21.3.74

(83) A West Suffolk Farmers Defence Association was created at Bury St. Edmunds. There were others. Clifford *op.cit. passim*

(84) *C.I.P.* 18.4.74. L. Kent's speech at the weekly meeting of the Newmarket F.D.A. 'They could do very well without these Union men, especially if they used steam machines, to work which they could get mechanics for £2 a week '

(85) e.g. *C.C.* 11.4.74. Speech by G.M. Ball

(86) Groves *op.cit.* p. 78. *C.I.P.* 1.8.74

(87) e.g. 'I do not believe that the mass of peasants could have been moved at all, had it not been for the organization of the Primitive Methodists . . .'. J. Thorold Rogers, *Six Centuries of Work and Wages* (1909) p. 515. The Primitive Methodists, however, were not entirely happy about the part many of their members played in the events of 1872-4. See the report of their 55th Annual Conference in *C.I.P.* 4.7.74. On the other hand see the extracts from The *Methodist Recorder* in The *Beehive* 20 April 1872, earlier in the dispute, which give a different impression

(88) *C.C.* 4.4.74

(89) *C.C.* 25.4.74

(90) *C.C.* 6.7.72, 2.5.74, letters from James Smith. See, also, Smith's letter replying to G.M. Ball denying that the labourers' movement was one of dissent, and pointing out that the Liberation Society was divided over whether or not to ask Arch to address it. *C.C.* 9,16.5.74. Ball said that Smith in a pamphlet had said the labourers' condition was due to 'beer, tobacco and bastardy'. *C.E.* 16.5.74

(91) *C.C.* 3.5.74

(92) *C.E.* 18.7.74. See also Spurgeon's speech to the Liberation Society, *C.I.P.* 16.5.74

(93) Denzil Batchelor, *Big Fight, The Story of World Championship Boxing* (Pan Edit. 1956) p.55

(94) *C.C.* 13.6.74

(95) The most publicized incident of magisterial harshness took place in Oxfordshire when two clergy magistrates committed sixteen women at Chipping Norton for intimidating two blacklegs. Clayden, *op.cit.* p. 131 *f.f.* Groves, *op.cit.* pp. 59-61. *Labourers' Union Chronicle*, 7 June 1873. Arch and company made repeated demands for the clergy to be prohibited from the magistrates' bench

(96) *Capital and Labour*, 10 June 1874

(97) *Ibid.* See also the card circulated at a meeting in Newmarket 'From the farm labourers of Christian England to their arch enemies . . .' *C.I.P.* 18.7.74

(98) The *Beehive*, 13 and 27 July 1872

(99) *C.I.P.* 12.10.72. Report from Pampisford

(100) *C.I.P.* 4.5.72

(101) *C.I.P.* 2.5.74

(102) The Bishop had asked, 'Are the farmers of England going mad?', and had said that they were driving the labourers to 'a peasants war'

(103) *C.I.P.* 13.4.72

(104) *C.I.P.* 1.3.73

(105) *C.C.* 21.6.73

(106) *C.I.P.* 21.3.74. 'Imagine poverty so distressing', Roberts wrote, 'Imagine men, too, who have no change of clothes for Sunday: imagine the straits they have to endure, and can we be surprised that they combine to get something more in the shape of wages, than the miserable pittance they.are now receiving, but which their wealthy neighbours deem a sufficiency.'

(107) *C.I.P.* 25.7.74. See e.g. the speeches of the Rev. Lott and the Archdeacon of Sudbury

(108) Review and notes on his book *Essays Biblical and Ecclesiastical* in *C.C.* 2, 9.8.73. Brief biographical sketch in Boase, *Modern English Biography* Vol. 4. Burgess's living in Whittlesey was crown patronage and worth £500 a year. He had gained considerable popularity among the labourers by making St. Mary's 'free'. *C.C.* 24.5.73

(109) *C.C.* 11.4.74. Letter from Burgess

(110) *C.C.* 17, 24.5.73. Burgess did not go far along the road to any left wing ideas. See, for instance, the report of his sermon from Matthew xx.13. ('Friend I do thee no wrong: didst thou not agree with me for a penny.'), from which he made two deductions. First, 'that the keeping of compacts and promises is God's method of the world being rightly governed', but that government could and should alter laws to prevent the accumulation of land into a few hands. Second 'that the variety of social problems is a Divine ordinance' and therefore 'labourers unions, must, as a very condition of prosperous working, dismiss all communistic or socialistic doctrines'. *C.E.* 21.6.73

(111) *C.C.* 28.6.73

(112) *C.I.P.* 27.4.72. Jonas Webb in the *C.C.* 11.5.72, called Challis 'a shopkeeper charging notoriously for his cottages'. See Challis's reply, however, in *C.I.P.* 25.5.72. *Harrod's Directory of Suffolk and Cambridgeshire 1873* described him as 'grocer, draper, upholsterer, ironmonger, and valuer of general stock, fixtures, etc.'

(113) *C.I.P.* 8.2.73. Brief biographical details on Taylor in a letter from Savage in the *Beehive,* 27 July 1872

(114) Savage, in particular, was violently anti-clerical, and repeatedly made remarks about the clergy 'grinding down the faces of the poor'. See e.g. the report of a meeting in Whittlesey, where he said 'God was with them', and the letter attacking him. *C.C.* 11, 25.5.72

(115) Challis was giving evidence in a case in which a unionist was being prosecuted for assaulting someone who would not join. The prosecutor elicited the information that Challis was an agent of the Queensland Emigration Company. *C.C.* 14.3.74. Details of the case are also in *Quarter Sessions Roll, Easter 1874, Quarter Sessions Roll, Michaelmas 1873,* and a transcript of evidence is in the *Minutes of the Cambridgeshire Quarter Sessions.* All in the Cambridgeshire Record Office

(116) *C.I.P.* 25.4.74

(117) *C.C.* 27.6.74

(118) *C.E.* 3.7.73, report of attempts to close the village feast. See also issues of 5 and 19 June. For a description of the village by C.H. Spurgeon when he was there see J.C. Carlile, *C.H. Spurgeon* (1933) p. 79

(119) *Speeches on the Agricultural Holdings Bill delivered at the Cambridgeshire and Isle of Ely Chamber of Agriculture, 1873 and 1875, by John Todd.* Also C.E. 5.7.73. Report of a meeting at Cottenham

(120) *C.E.* 5.7.73

(121) *C.E.* 6.6.73, *C.I.P.* 18.7.74. The Anti-Game Law League was created late in 1872 and its journal was *The Circular, Brighton Daily News,* 11 September 1872
(122) *C.E.* 10.7.75
(123) *C.I.P.* 30.5.74
(124) *C.I.P.* 4.4.74
(125) *C.C.* 27.6.74
(126) *C.E.* 27.6.74
(127) *C.I.P.* 25.4.74, *C.C.* 25.4.74
(128) *C.C.* 9.5.74. *The Return of the Owners of Land 1873* shows Rodwell of Ampton owning 824 acres, worth a rental of £805
(129) *C.E.* 18.4.74. Lady Stradbroke became a noted opponent of the unions. See her letters on the struggle in J. Thirsk and J. Imray, *Suffolk Farming in the Nineteenth Century.* (Suffolk Record Society, Vol. 1. 1958)
(130) *C.E.* 18.4.74. Dobede owned 2,700 acres worth a rental of £4,917. *Return of the Owners of Land 1873. op. cit.*
(131) *C.E.* 25.4.74. George Mitchell wanted Duleep Singh to act as an arbitrator in the dispute. *Ibid.*
(132) Clifford, *op.cit.,* p. 78 f.f.
(133) *C.E.* 2.5.74
(134) *C.I.P.* 2.5.74
(135) *C.C.* 25.4.74
(136) *C.E.* 16.5.74
(137) The *Beehive,* 13 April 1872
(138) *C.E.* 25.4.74
(139) Between Christmas 1873 and April 1874 the price of wheat went down by 6s. a quarter, beef and mutton by 2s. a stone. See e.g. *C.C.* 11.4.74, *Capital and Labour* 15 July 1874
(140) *C.C.* 4.4.74
(141) *C.I.P.* 12.10.72
(142) *C.I.P.* 11.4.74
(143) 25 April 1874. C.S.M. was said to be a member of the University, and could possibly have been C.S. Maine of Trinity
(144) *C.I.P.* 16.5.74
(145) *C.E.* 16.5.74
(146) *C.I.P.* 16.5.74
(147) *C.I.P.* 4.4.74
(148) *Ibid.,* Ambrose said that Jay, when he farmed, 'was the worst farmer and paymaster in the district'. Jay in return questioned whether Ambrose was in fact an accredited emigration agent; Ambrose's real role will perhaps never be known—one report said he had locked his men out!. At the meeting at which the dispute between Jay and Ambrose took place there were no less than three other agents among the speakers, Daveney, Whelland and Child, a railway agent
(149) *C.C.* 22.8.74
(150) *C.C.* 29.8.74
(151) *Royal Commission on Agriculture.* (Parlty. Papers 1882 xiv)
(152) 'Mid-Victorian prosperity brought little visible gain to the agrarian worker throughout this period (1850-1870) . . . Indeed in many ways the agricultural labourer was little if any better off in the 1870s than half a century before . . .' Derek H. Adcroft 'Communications on The Revolt of the Field': *Past and Present,* No. 27, April 1964, p. 109 and references cited there. Also Henri Taine,

Notes on England (3rd edit. 1872) Chap XI, and Richard Heath, *The English Peasant* (1893)

(153) Clifford *op.cit.* p. 30. *C.C.* 30.5.74 reported that in Cambridgeshire only the large farmers were locking the labourers out

(154) Clifford, *op.cit.* p. 58

(155) *Ibid.*, p. 65

(156) *Ibid.*, pp. 47 and 97. *C.I.P.* 4.4.74

(157) *C.C.* 21.6.73. See also *C.C.* 8.5.75, report of the annual general meeting of the H.F.D.A. where Hunnybun says that if all members paid up at 2s.6d. per 100 acres the Association would have had £74.10.0., which makes a total acreage of 59,600

(158) Clifford, *op.cit.*, p.90

(159) *Ibid.*, p. 10 f.n.1

(160) e.g. *C.C.* 23.6.20, 10.8, 14.9.21 (in the last issue there is a list of incidents in the village between 1808 and 1818)

(161) The *Northern Star,* 18 September 1847. See also the issue of the *Northern Star* for 25 September 1847 on incendiaries in Cambridgeshire at that time

(162) A.J. Peacock, 'Captain Swing in East Anglia', *Bulletin of the Society for the Study of Labour History,* No. 8. Spring 1964. H.J. Hanham, *Elections and Party Management,* (1959) p. 16. f.n.1

(163) *C.C.* 7.5.19

(164) *C.C.* 17.8.72

(165) *C.C.* 24.1.74. Letter from ON—LOOKER.

(166) *C.C.* 10, 17.7.75

(167) *C.E.* 28.9, 12.10.72, 12.7.73. According to *Kelly's Post Office Directory of Cambridgeshire 1875* the Waterbeach charities were worth £270 a year. Toller owned 516 acres of land. *Return of the Owners of Land 1873. op.cit.*

(168) *C.C.* 28.3.74

(169) *C.C.* 4.4.74, *C.I.P.* 4.4.74. The libel is in the *Labourers' Union Chronicle,* 3 July 1873

(170) *C.C.* 11.4.74, *C.I.P.* 11.4.74

(171) *C.E.* 28.6.73. *C.I.P.* 21,28.6.73. The Cottenham charities were said to produce 'about £450, for education and apprenticeships, Charity Houses, gifts for the poor, of money, bibles and prayer-books'. *Kelly's Post Office Directory of Cambridgeshire 1875, op.cit.* Todd owned only 26 acres of land. *Return of the Owners of Land 1873, op.cit.*

(172) *C.E.* 29.3.73

(173) *C.C.* 20.4.72, where Sanderson is described as 'night soil man'. The *Brighton Daily News.* 19 April 1872 has him simply as 'a single man'

(174) *C.E.* 28.6.73

(175) Cottenham had been famous for its cheese products a few years earlier, but just before the events described in this article took place the pastures had been taken over as arable land, and this may have led to a demand for labour. On cheese making in the village see Val Cheke, *Story of Cheese Making in Britain* (1959), pp. 15 and 154

(176) Details of wage rates, harvest rates, cottage rents etc. at Cottenham in *C.C.* 20.4.72

(177) Todd and his colleagues won the first Board elections overwhelmingly, with Todd at the head of the poll. James Toller similarly won in the election of 1875 at Waterbeach. *C.E.* 23.1.75

(178) *C.E.* 8.6.72

(179) *C.I.P.* a statement 'from careful and impartial enquiries' on the origins of the lock-out 4 April 1874

(180) *op.cit.* p. 35. The *Daily Telegraph* called Dobede's cottages in Exning 'pigsties'. Quoted in a letter from Benjamin Brown, Burwell, in *C.C.* 2.5.74. For the way tied cottages were used against the labourers in Exning see f.n. 50. See also a union song on housing in Josiah Sage *The Memoirs of Josiah Sage* (1951) p. 29

(181) e.g. *C.E.* 6.6.74, report of case wherein John Gault of Dullingham is charged with assaulting Robert Sanderson. The case appears to have been brought by the Farmers Defence Association

(182) *C.C.* 25.4.74. As in many other almost revolutionary situations, for instance in Bradford in 1840, at the very critical point there occurred an epidemic to heighten feelings. This happened in the Newmarket area in 1874 when smallpox appeared in a serious form, the result of bad housing it was claimed. *C.E.* 8, 15, 22.8.74

(183) The strong union centres, it seems too obvious to stress, were nearly always the larger villages. Sawston had a population of 1,729, Whittlesey was very large indeed, Waterbeach had 1,619 and Littleport 3,869. *Census of England and Wales 1871.* 33 and 34 Vict. C. 107. Richard Jeffries, *Hodge and His Masters* (1949 ed.) made the same point, that densely populated corn villages were those where 'agitation takes its most extreme form'. pp. 289-292

(184) *Smith H. Rowley Farm Account Books.* Reference 300/A/2 to 300/A/12. On the 'horkey' in Suffolk see J. Thirsk and J. Imray, *op.cit.* It is also described by Richard Cobbold in *Margaret Catchpole* (1845)

(185) J. Stanley Chivers, *Histon Baptist Church 1858-1958* (n.d.) gives some details of village life in the fifties, and of the Chivers family

(186) *Harrods Directory of Suffolk and Cambridgeshire 1875, op.cit. Kelly's Post Office Directory of Cambridgeshire 1875. op.cit.* Also T.F. Teversham, *History of Sawston,* (Sawston 1942) Vol. 2

(187) Clifford, *op.cit.* pp. 37-38

(188) *Harrods Directory of Suffolk and Cambridgeshire 1873. op.cit.*

(189) *C.C.* 8.5.75 for a report of trouble at Sawston over the School Board. Letters on the business from E.S. Daniel and J.M. Uffon in *Ibid.,* and issue of 15 May 1875 End of the trouble reported in *Ibid.,* 6 November 1875.

(190) Jam making commenced in Histon in 1873, and Chivers' factory was set up two years later. H. Rider Haggard, *Rural England,* (1902) Vol. 2. p. 51. Article on Stephen Chivers in Ernest Gaskell, *Cambridgeshire and Huntingdonshire Leaders,* (no date, probably 1908-10). Short history of the Chivers family and the factory in the firms' publications, *From Orchard to Home* (n.d.) and *Another Chapter* (n.d.)

(191) For an analysis of the union's finances in the Exning district of the N.A.L.U. from 4th April to 6th July 1874 see *Capital and Labour,* 19 August 1874.

(192) *C.C.* 20.1.75, report signed 'Little Abington'

(193) *C.C.* 9.10.75

(194) *C.C.* 26.12.74, report on the Wisbech Steam Cultivating Company

(195) *East Anglian Handbook for 1875,* pp. 8-9

(196) See f.n. 50

(197) *C.C.* 27.2.75

(198) e.g. *C.C.* 6.3.75. Also G.E. and K.R. Fussell, *The English Countrywoman* (1953), pp. 76-80

(199) See Arch's comments at a meeting at Sawston. *C.E.* 10.7.75

(200) 10 October 1874 quoting the *Ipswich Express*

(201) *C.C.* 3.10.74. On the Cambridgeshire by-election see also H.J. Hanham, *op.cit.* pp. 20-21, 29-30

(202) *C.C.* 19.6.75, obituary note on Wilson in *Ibid.*, 11 September 1875

(203) *Capital and Labour,* 19 August 1874. *C.C.* 23.1.75

(204) *C.E.* 12.4.73

(205) *C.E.* 26.4.73

(206) *C.C.* 27.2.75. It was reported in August 1874 that the county court was to be applied to 'to test the right of the Union to stop the lock-out pay after taking subscriptions'. *Ibid.*, 1 August 1874

(207) *Capital and Labour,* 26 August 1875

(208) *C.C.* 8.1.76

(209) Simmons was leader of the Kent and Sussex Agricultural and General Labourers Union. Details of his scheme in *C.C.* 11.9.75

(210) *C.C.* 7.8.75

(211) *C.E.* 4.11.76

(212) E. Moore Darling, 'A Fair Deal for Hodge', *The Listener,* 14 June 1956 and correspondence in the subsequent issue from Rex Russell, E.D. Jaques, and Neville Masterman

(213) *Bulletin No. 10 of the Cambridgeshire Local History Council,* Autumn 1956

DONA TORR

Tom Mann and his Times 1890-92

A first volume of Dona Torr's life of Tom Mann, *Tom Mann and his Times,* (1856-1890) was published in 1956. It was then expected that a second volume covering 1890-1910 would shortly appear, the original plan having been for a three volume work, but the author's death took place later the same year. Among her papers there was a plan of the second volume, many notes, and a draft of the first chapter and parts of a second. These were subsequently worked on and annotated by E.P. Thompson who had discussed the book with the author during her last illness. Printed here is the almost complete draft chapter, and some of the material for the next, including an unpublished correspondence between Tom Mann and John Burns, transcribed by Edward Thompson. We are indebted to Edward Thompson for going through this version and allowing the use of his own work, including some notes to the first section and arrangement of and additions to the second, not least his transcript of the Mann-Burns correspondence. We have to thank Lawrence & Wishart for their assistance. And we are grateful to Walter Holmes for permission to publish this addition to the major work of a distinguished Marxist historian.

I

The Port of London was at work again; the Lord Mayor, the Cardinal, and the Bishop had retired; the Mansion House Committee was dissolved; the press looked elsewhere for stories; the dockers remained. So did their employers the competing dock companies, wharfingers and shipowners. The strength of the great uprising which had kept the port still for five weeks had lain in the order and discipline achieved by leaders versed in trade union traditions; the engineers, Burns and Mann, working closely with the stevedores. But the Strike Committee's functions had ceased. The great bulk of the strikers had never belonged to a union—there had been none to receive them. Everything had to be started from the beginning. This was true of other new unions formed in that period, but their difficulties were small in comparison with those at the docks.

191

For Tom Mann and Ben Tillett, president and secretary of the new Dock, Wharf, Riverside and General Labourer's Union, and their greathearted fellow officials, Tom McCarthy, Clem Edwards, and Harry Orbell, the job had only just begun. First, of course, there were the imported blacklegs; the dock officials at once broke the pledges given and discriminated against union men; however, the blacklegs had not enjoyed themselves much and there was still some money to spare, so they were asked to join the union and those who refused were given a week's wages out of the surplus funds and told to get out. More than 1,000 men were thus disposed of. But the struggle to get the Mansion House Agreement honoured in face of diverse interpretations speedily invented by the various dock companies and wharfingers, whose methods of employment had never been uniform, the battle for union discipline when union organisation was in its infancy, the struggle for unity between 'preferred' and 'non-preferred' men, where disparities might be great—these were a task barely imaginable.

Of the immediate gains, symbolised by the 'docker's tanner', the chief were fixed time and overtime rates, guaranteed 2s. (four-hour) calls, and fixed time and place for call-ons; far the greatest was the recognition of the union, the right of collective bargaining, the undermining of the sub-contractor's autocracy and powers of dividing the workers. But whether the terms were to be carried out, and all or any of the new rights sustained, depended solely upon collective strength and persistence, upon union organisation and attention to complex details, settling innumerable piece rates and allowances, checking call places and times, the make-up of gangs, etc. 'Of all the work of the strike', writes Tillett,

> 'nothing was more exacting than the work afterwards of adjusting and administering. Tom Mann, Clem Edwards, Tom McCarthy and myself spent nights and days at the work, the adjustment work gave us more than we had thought possible . . . . Tom Mann did that work while we scoured and added to our ranks port after port.' (*Short History of the Docker's Union*, 1910, p.32)

The last sentence reminds us that the union was becoming, overnight, a national union. Sixty-three new branches were formed in the first three months of 1890 and at the first congress in September the union claimed a membership of over 60,000 of whom 24,000 were in London. Other districts represented by delegates were: Brentford, Bridgewater, Bristol, Cardiff, Dundee, Gloucester, Hull, Kings Lynn, the Medway, Newport, Northfleet, Plymouth, Portsmouth, Southampton, Swansea. In the north-west—covering Liverpool, Belfast, Glasgow—a separate union, the National Dock Labourer's Union, had been formed in 1889 by Richard McGhee and Edward McHugh which was still struggling for recognition. Ben's story of the early work outside London should be read in his own words. In the big ports it was the same as in London: on the one side, brutal rapacious sub-contractors, free play for thieves and bullies, wholesale robbery of the men; on the other, the great meetings, the new union organisation, the struggles for recognition, the first achievements as to regulation of wages, hours and call-ons, the blows struck against blackguardism, the beginnings of self-respect. What Ben learnt on his travels completed the conversion to socialism begun by his fellow strike leaders:

> 'It manifested the class war so vividly to myself that I have no other reason to urge for being a revolutionary socialist than the bitter class hatred and sordidness of the capitalists as a body.' (*Short History . . . p.36*)

One or two illustrations must serve to indicate some of Tom's problems in the first year: these were largely bound up with the employers' treatment of the agreement and with trade union discipline and unity. The Mansion House Agreement was the first of its kind and a maze of conditions resting only on custom had to be adapted to it. A constant source of trouble was the attempt of employers to drop the customary threepence paid to pieceworkers for a half-hour's mealbreak; this was often done by reclassifying pieceworkers as dayworkers. The agreement had only been signed a couple of months when the directors of Hay's Wharf, Southwark, then the great tea wharf, abolished all mealtime payments, thereby provoking a strike unsanctioned by the union (January, 1890). Tom and his colleagues, far from wanting a strike just then, were anxious to continue negotiations already begun; but the union rules were still in the hands of the Registrar and the executive did not have full powers. 'We could not compel them then to return to their work . . . not like now when we are in fair thoroughgoing order', related F. Brien the following year. (*Royal Commission on Labour*, 1892, xxxv B65). The negotiations broke down and this strike could not be neglected by the young union which eventually decided to grant strike pay. From that moment Tom did his utmost by speech and action to turn the strike into a new experience of solidarity. But after three months of strenuous effort the men were defeated, many were victimised; and the cost to the union was £5,266, with almost £1,200 more for the other four wharfs which became involved. Some late Australian contributions helped to meet this cost.

'Dear Jack', wrote Mann to Burns from the dockers' first headquarters at the Great Assembly Hall, Mile End Road, on March 5, 1890:

> 'Enclosed please find receipt for Australian cheque for £500 with sincere thanks from the Union, who are glad to get it, we are spending £300 a week more than we get in, with no immediate sign of reducing the expenditure. Hay's, Brookes, Hedger, Sharpes and Hersoks are still on . . . We had a cheque for £50 from Australia sent through Shipton (secretary of the London Trades Council). The Trades Council is completely revolutionised during the past six months . . . Ben is working effectively.'

The same letter refers to the Liverpool strike of the National Dock Labourer's Union ('the Glasgow Union') and the attempts to transport blacklegs from London:

'The Liverpool job is a big one; 198 were taken from London, including a number of our men who were instructed to take the money, and three reliable men accompanied them who succeeded in bringing back 151 out of the 198 and got them their fare and 5/- per man. The Liverpool men belong to the Glasgow Union which is making headway but they are paying no strike pay. P.O. for 5/- enclosed to cover postage to thank the Australians . . .'

Later news to Burns (April 30, 1890) shows that the Hay's Wharf strike had ended in considerable demoralisation, with plenty of blame, besides threats of personal violence, for Tom:

'We have decided to stop strike pay so as to choke off those who would gladly hang on for months, so we reduced strike pay to 8/- this week and 6/- for two following weeks, giving the £1 in a lump to those who cared to take it; about 400 have done so but we have had a hell of a time. I am obliged to carry a revolver, they threaten all kinds of nice things, going to make soup of me and so on, but I reckon I'll come out all right in the End . . .'[1]

An echo of the Hay's Wharf strike, heard eighteen months later, recalls another problem—the position of the old-type 'preferred men' in the new union. When in November 1891 the Labour Commission was listening to evidence on the union, Tom being one of the commissioners, two tea-coopers of long standing at Hay's Wharf thought it worth while to walk along from Southwark to Westminister Hall, where Mr. Tom Mann was sitting in his glory, in order to explain at length why they had torn up their cards. George Lloyd said he had been forced into the strike by Mr. Tom Mann, although they had no real grievances; and were afterwards 'kept out by being continually talked to'. He now got less money than before the strike had been 'for the benefit of another class of labour', though he admitted that his own class was represented on the executive. (See *Royal Commission* xxxv B 7772-7828). His companion, J. Bowall, had been forced into the union by his own gang but had done his best to get the men back from the moment the strike began. He had interviewed Tom Mann:

Lord Derby (chairman): 'What did he say to you?'—'What don't speak don't lie'. Witness, who could not read, handed in a cutting from an unidentified newspaper, reporting a speech in which Mann, referring to someone who had returned to work, was alleged to have said: 'the wharfowners could brew him and bake him because if they did not the union would . . . They should know him that day week, that day fortnight, and that day year . . .'

Lord Derby: 'Did Mr. Mann tell you that the union had made a great mistake and that they would support you now you were out?'—'Yes'. Witness had worked as a blackleg under the constant protection of the police but if he went for an evening walk his life was in danger. 'I was quite aware that Tom Mann did not understand the business because when I spoke to him at the meeting in the Green Man . . . he said, "I thought you were all one". I said: "You do not understand this business any more than if you had never entered it!" '

Mr. Tom Mann: 'What is your object in coming here today?'—'To give evidence against the chairman of the society, Mr. Tom Mann . . .' 'You have come to complain of the threats you received from Tom Mann in Bull Court? . . . Did you receive some personal threat from me?'—'According to the paper, that piece of the newspaper which I cut out . . . and I think it is a shameful thing that I am to be roasted and boiled, I never heard of such a thing . . . to be roasted and boiled in a week or a month or twelve months. If he did not boil me the union would . . .' etc.

Mr. Tait: 'How many men do you represent here today?'—'Myself' 'Alone?'—'Alone'. 'Who asked you to come?'—'No one . . . I offered to come.' (ibid, 8442-8500)

The accusation that meal-break troubles were 'the result of Messrs. Mann, Burns, and the rest signing away the men's meal-time' was repeated more than once by those who did not want the union or union agreements. 'It is only since the great dock strike that these disputes have cropped up about meal-times . . . and there will be more and that will be the result of Messrs. Mann, Burns and Tillet interfering in what they know nothing at all about.' (ibid. 8587). But this was only one aspect of the employers' attempts to level down, against which the union must at all costs enlarge the fight for unity and levelling up. The provision for regular call-ons was another clause, ignored unless the union was strong on the spot; in November, 1891 the India docks were 'taking on men at all hours of the day'. (ibid, 953).

It was fortunate that Tom, through his work in the Surrey docks, was already familiar with the better-paid men. For the success of the union would depend on its ability not only to maintain the right of the lowest paid to one penny more per hour and twopence overtime, but to draw solidly together 'preferred' men and others. This depended on understanding of detail. The union official must find ways of replacing the customary personal or group relations, coupled with bribery and sweating, by union relations; he must master every detail of every job, protect customary rates and allowances, negotiate new ones for all special types of work, and, above all, resist the undermanning of gangs. As Ben recalled:

'Tom Mann worked like a giant possessed; his negotiating capacity taxed to the utmost, as well as his time and his great reserve of strength . . . Two generations of wrong had to be redressed . . . We were up against an army of managerial autocrats. That we did so much is still a wonder to me.' (Tillett, *Memories and Reflections*, 1931, p. 158).

At the same time, abused as he was by the S.D.F. for becoming a trade union official—'Mann, the Champion Compromiser', drawing £3 a week for helping to sweat the dockers (*Justice*, November 30 1889)—Tom kept up his socialist propaganda and inspired the union's 'educational work'. 'For educational purposes', he tells us, 'i.e. to get beyond the immediate concerns of the hour and to deal with the Labour movement nationally and internationally', the union organised large Sunday morning meetings. Tom's Sunday socialist speeches were heard by union members who judged them in the light of his daily work. The grain porters down in Victoria Dock, for example, had some remarks to make. Their jobs filling grain sacks by hand in ships' holds, carrying them to the quay for weighing and then overside into barges, are particularly heavy and variable, involving claims for a number of extras on piece-rates—'hot' money, 'dirty' money, 'awkward' money etc.[2] for which, after a special conference with the company, attended by Mann, the employers had agreed to substitute a higher overall rate, with provision for exceptional extras to be decided by an umpire. After some time of smooth working disagreement arose with the umpire and Tom was sent for; he found the men who had left the ship sitting quietly awaiting him in the Club Room near Tidal Basin:

'I at once took the chair and opened out: "Good day lads . . . Who'll state the case?" After a few seconds one of the biggest fellows, well over six foot, came up to me at the table and said: "Look here, Mr. Tom Mann, the other Sunday morning there was a meeting on the waste ground, wasn't there?"
"Yes, and I was there."
"Yes, and you told us then the workers didn't get more than one half of the wealth they produced, didn't you?"
"Yes, that's so."
"Well, we bloody well want some of the other half."
and he returned to his seat.'
(*Tom Mann's Memoirs*, 1923, p.110)

Immediately after the dock strike and during the continuing trade improvement there followed rapid development in the organisation of the unskilled workers, a great increase in the membership of the old craft unions and the beginnings of organisation among the blackcoated workers. The example of the dockers and gas labourers was imitated by printers' labourers, many of whom worked 12 to 14 hours a day in filthy cellars, and the Printers'

Labourers Union formed was the parent of NATSOPA. General Labourers were included in the General Railway Workers' Union (1889) but the Amalgamated Society of Railway Servants (1872), an old model trade benefit society which had survived the great crisis, also increased its membership in the three years from 1888 to 1891 from 12,000 to 30,000. Among the agricultural workers Joseph Arch's National Agricultural Labourers' Union (1872), which had shrunk into a friendly society of a few thousand, had gained over 14,000 members by 1890, while the Eastern Counties Labour Federation had 17,000 by 1892. Among unions catering for builders' labourers, carmen, carters, navvies, the best known was the Navvies, Bricklayers' Labourers and General Labourers' Union (1890) of which John Ward of the S.D.F. was general secretary.

Of the craft unions the A.S.E., Tom Mann's own union, enrolled 9,000 new members in the nine months after the dock strike. Between 1888 and 1891 membership of the eleven principal engineering and shipbuilding unions increased from 115,000 to 155,000, and that of the ten largest building trade unions from 57,000 to 94,000. The Boot and Shoe Operatives increased from 11,000 to 30,000, the Miners' Federation, founded in 1888, from 36,000 to 96,000.

The huge inchoate armies of slave driven respectability, the blackcoated workers, at last began to organise; crushed youth and anaemic middle age awakened; the National Union of Clerks (1890) and the Shop Assistants' Union (1891) opened their battles against the 60 to 90 hour week and shameful conditions of work hitherto impotently endured. Postmen initiated the struggle of Civil Servants for the elementary rights of trade unionism and for a weekly minimum of 24s. On the eve of May Day 1890, after demonstrating with bands and banner in Holborn, 2,000 of them crowded the Memorial Hall, Farringdon Street, when, among letters read from supporters was one from Tom Mann, (*Star*, May 1, 1890).

'Within a year after the dockers' victory', the Webbs record, 'probably over 200,000 workers had been added to the trade union ranks, recruited from sections of the labour world formerly abandoned as incapable of organisation . . . Even the oldest and most aristocratic unions were affected by the revivalist fervour of the new leaders.' (*History of Trade Unionism*, 1894. 392, 393).

In this time of new life and new possibilities contact with the London Trades Council kindled Tom's quick imagination. Shortly after the strike, when he became a delegate to the council from the Battersea branch of the A.S.E., he had found a 'wretchedly flat state of affairs' (Mann and Tillett, *The New Trades Unionism*, June, 1890). With a group of lefts within and Tillett and others outside he worked for new affiliations; the tide was setting that way too; in nine months time, by June, 1890, the membership had increased from 18,824 to 45,000.[3] Tom's vision was of the Trades Council as a real 'Labour Parliament', representing not only London's 150,000 trade unionists but the 700,000 London workers still outside to whom special help should be given by forming unions, drawing up rules, coaching new officials etc. (*Labour Elector,* January 11, 1890). He was quickly elected to the executive, on November 7, 1889, and was a very active delegate until July 1891, when his duties on the Labour Commission took him away.

During this period he helped in the rules revision and gave the report on the new rules adopted in 1890, which included the provision that delegates must have worked or be working at the trades they represented. In particular, when the Silvertown rubber workers struck at the close of 1889 he worked hard on behalf of the strikers as a representative of the Trades Council executive. He failed to get a special delegate meeting of all trades called in their support (*Trades Council Minutes,* December 19,1889); the engineers employed at the works refused to join the strike. Tom also tried to get 'representation from all the different sections of workmen employed in the Silvertown works' to meet the Trades Council deputation but this too failed and the strike was defeated. Tom took part in the settlement negotiations. (ibid. November 7 to December 19, 1889).

Engels, who was unaware of these efforts, referred to the main problem of this twelve-weeks' strike in a letter written on January 11, 1890: 'the strike was broken by the engineers, who did not join in and even did labourers' work against their own union rules!' (*Selected Correspondence, Marx and Engels,* 1936, p.463). Within a few months Engels and Tom Mann, working in different sections of the movement, and many others were turning their attention to a great labour demonstration, carried through despite the apathy and doubts of the old guard in the trade union world.

'Goaded by the attacks of the Socialists and New Trade Unionists', records George Howell, the London Trades Council found itself obliged to participate in 'May day celebrations in favour of the "solidarity of labour", Eight Hours and other idealistic proposals.' (*Trade Unionism Old and New,* 1891, pp. 191-7).

May day demonstrations for the legal 8-hour day, resolved upon by the foundation congress of the Second International (July, 1889), took place in 1890 in the U.S.A. and in all the chief European countries, to the dismay of the ruling classes. Amid the general excitement provoked by press accounts of preparations on the continent and arrests in Paris, *Punch,* whose cartoons had already depicted haggard men about to destroy the Goose that Lays the Golden Eggs, or to sew tares from a basket labelled Socialism, or to step into an abyss labelled Anarchy, now portrayed 'The New Queen of the May' with a bomb in one hand, a lily in the other, a sash labelled 'International', and garlands labelled 'Eight Hours', 'Strikes', 'Agitations', 'Solidarity', 'Dynamite'; but, perhaps as an antidote to continentalism, also printed some lolloping sympathetic lines (April 30, 1890):

> They've kept us scattered till now, comrade; but that no more may be;
> Our shout goes up in unison by Thames, Seine, Rhine and Spree.
> We are not the crushed down crowd, chummy, we were but yesterday;
> We're full of the Promise o'May, brother; mad with the promise of May.

Eleanor Marx and Edward Aveling had initiated in the London east end an agitation which had first introduced English workers to the new Socialist International whose foundation congress John Burns had attended. To carry out the eight hour day resolution they had organised the Central Committee for the Eight Hours Legal Working Day Demonstration, first parent of London's later May day Committee. To them we owe our first London May day, its international tradition then begun, and the grandeur of the demonstration. The participation of the thirty-year-old London Trades Council, representing mainly the old crafts but now including in its procession the dockers, we owe chiefly to Tom Mann. By proposing a separate demonstration organised by the council he made it possible to overcome the difficulties arising from the invitation of the Central Committee and the dread word 'legal'. At the delegate meeting on April 10 he moved: 'that this council of delegates recommend the trade societies of the metropolis to demonstrate in favour of an eight hours working day'. This having been carried, he seconded Drummond's motion that a demonstration should be organised by the Trades Council on May 4. (*L.T.C. Minutes*, see also *London Trades Council*, p. 76).

To Burns, who was supporting the Central Committee, Tom wrote on April 30 with some anxiety:

'Respecting the Trades Council position, *re 8 hours.* They have decided on a resolution drawn up by myself, and afterwards slightly modified, to the effect that we strive to bring about the 8 hours "by every legitimate means" and call upon Government to at once start the same in Government Department. I shall be Chairman of the Central Platform provided by the T.C. and I shall urge the importance of Trade Union Action as a means of education up to the demanding of better conditions; I sincerely hope that your speech and mine will be on the same lines; I shall not of course insist on any sweeping measures as that I am sure is impossible. More and more I am convinced of the impudence of men like Graham, there has been no talk about pledging ourselves to individual effort such as Graham talks about. I suppose you have definitely promised to speak on the platform of the Aveling section. If so, it would be policy to emphasise the importance of Trade Unionism. Large numbers would like to find you and I advocating different methods. If you have any special recommendation let me have it, please, and I will comply. I have endeavoured to state the case in May number of *Nineteenth Century* and should like your opinion upon it; I don't know what I shall get for it but I shall hand over the cheque towards the £35 *Elector* account . . .

'There is no serious difference between the Legalists and L.T.C., we are providing seven platforms and giving one of them to S.D.F. to appoint their own speaker etc.: they have now asked that we provide a second and they will pay for it, so we shall do so; I am on the Sub-Committee *making arrangements*. It has so upset Ben he has gone to Bournemouth for a day or two. I was at Hull last week and had good meetings . . . '

Harmonious joint arrangements having been achieved (not without some trouble from George Shipton, secretary of the Trades Council, who made a prior booking of Hyde Park which nearly excluded the Avelings' section) the council had its separate procession, platforms and resolution. Both processions assembled at the same time on the embankment, the Trades Council on the river side, the Central Committee on the north side of the roadway; they then marched by separate routes to the park where each had seven platforms, the Trades Council north and south of the Reformers' Tree and the Central Committee parallel with these by Broad Walk. (*Reynolds's Newspaper*, May 4, 1890).

Thus in the eyes of the deeply impressed public, the demonstration of Sunday, May 4, 1890—the processions which took over two hours to file into the park, the crowd which finally totalled half a million (*Star*, May 5, 1890)—was a single demonstration for the eight-hour-day, a revelation of the new 'idealistic' independence and solidarity of the working class. Fred Henderson wrote in next day's *Star:*

> We toilers of the field and town
> By long oppression trodden down
> In every clime beneath the sun
> Have seen the new life to be won;
> Seen that all the strife we waged
> Was but fool with fool engaged:
> Where we erst as foemen stood
> Lo, to-day reigns brotherhood.

George Shipton was chief marshal of the Trades Council procession, in which the dockers, despised outcasts eight months before, now marched 'in their rough working clothes' together with the ancient aristocracy; 'sandwiched' between them, as the *Star* recorded, were 'hundreds of gentlemen comps, kid-gloved and top-hatted'. No such demonstration in Hyde Park had been seen since 1866; 'In point of numbers the most remarkable ever held in London' (*Reynolds's* May 11, 1890). Every feature excited comment: the novel 'small shield-shaped banners' with white letters on crimson backgrounds marking the sections of the Central Committee's procession, and the 'acres of splendidly painted silk' carried by the unions. 'Along both routes the classes came out to see the masses', reported the *Star* next day. 'The balconies of the great houses . . . were crowded with ladies and gentlemen of the upper ten thousand. From the upper windows the servants looked on.'

Tom Mann had been given the task of marshalling east end workers, not attached to any particular organisation, who were joining the demonstration.

(*Star*, May 1). After marshalling some thousands of 'unattached men' on the embankment with the help of two 'mounted farriers' Tom, wearing his president's blue sash of the Dockers' Union, was chairman of the main Trades Council platform, from which the resolution was moved by Ben Tillett. Tom's support for the full socialist demand of a legal eight-hour-day was well enough known, his second pamphlet on the subject, *The Eight Hours Movement* (1889) was just then selling widely, but he spoke loyally to the Trades Council resolution which only recommended getting an eight-hour-day 'by every legitimate means in their power'. The resolution, *Reynold's* noted (May 11) 'went quite as far as was judicious for the Council'; the fact that they were met under the auspices of the Council showed that this body 'which some thought lethargic, was now making progress'.

Tom's platform, well surrounded by dockers, railwaymen, barge builders and ropemakers, was the only Trades Council platform which drew a crowd. By far the greatest masses were gathered round the platforms of the Central Committee, where the speakers included John Burns, Will Thorne, John Ward, Cunninghame Graham, Bernard Shaw, Stepniak, Paul Lafargue and the Avelings. Burns, amid cheers, flung out his challenge to Bradlaugh: if they both spoke to an audience of 200,000 he could still win 90 per cent of it for the legal eight-hour-day. Four branches of the S.D.F. marched with the Central Committee and the S.D.F. had its two platforms near the Trades Council; their resolution added the demand for socialist ownership to that of the legal eight-hour-day.

'What would I give if Marx had lived to see this awakening!' was Engels' first thought as he watched the great scene from the roof of a vehicle. 'I held my head two inches higher when I climbed down from the old goods van.' (Gustav Mayer, *Friedrich Engels*, 1936, p. 253). Great though the success had been in other countries, he wrote later in an article in the *Vienna Arbeiterzeitung* (May 23, 1890), the grandest and most important part of the whole May Day festival was that

'on 4 May 1890, the *English proletariat*, newly awakened from its 40 year winter sleep, *again entered the movement of its class* . . . The grand-children of the old Chartists are entering the line of battle.'

Soon after May day the New Unionists on the Trades Council attempted to end the reign of George Shipton, founder and secretary of the Amalgamated Society of Housepainters and Decorators, who had been secretary of the council since 1872. W. Parnell of the Cabinet Makers was the hope of the militants. A number of curious incidents, such as the withholding of affiliation from dockers' branches which had paid their fees, culminated on the day of the election, June 5, when Parnell, whose name was already printed on the ballot paper, was informed that his union had just held a meeting and elected new Trades Council delegates. The Woolwich engineers' delegate, Fred Hammill, soon to become a leader of New Unionism, hurriedly took up the challenge, but Shipton triumphed by 61 votes to 46.[4]

That same month, the Trades Union Congress being due in September, Shipton opened a public attack on the New Unionism, immediately answered by Tom Mann and Ben Tillett. The Old Unionists' case was well presented by Shipton in an article 'Trades Unionism: The Old and the New' (*Murray's Magazine*, June, 1890). New Unionism, he said:

(1) Discarded friendly society benefits; Mr. Tom Mann had expounded this policy 'with great unction at the first half—yearly meeting of the Dockers' Union', in March 1890. Similar principles had been declared in the first half-yearly report of the Gasworkers in 1889—'We have only one benefit attached, and that is strike pay . . . The whole aim and intention of this Union is to reduce the hours of labour and reduce Sunday work'; and by the General Railway Workers' Union at the 1890 Congress—'The Union shall remain a fighting one, and shall not be encumbered with any sick and accident fund.' (See Webbs, *Trade Unionism*, p. 392);

(2) Believed in loose associations or federations linking together ('more or less') men not only of different grades but different trades;

(3) Relied upon 'demonstrations by bands of music, banners, Phyrgian caps of liberty, and other symbols of aggregate force, as a method in industrial warfare';

(4) Was 'selfish in its character' meaning 'less work for more wages and nothing more';

(5) Relied upon stimulating discontent and decrying existing unions;

(6) Disparaged old union leaders;

(7) Sometimes disavowed conciliation and arbitration;

(8) Relied upon 'legislation rather than upon combination'; the State 'to do for the individual what the "old trade unionists" contend the men should do by themselves, for themselves . . . The one party seeks to operate politically through legislation, the other by means of liberty and association.' The old leaders had won perfect freedom of association and the repeal of all the vicious acts relating to labour; they 'sought to develop manhood, self-reliance and mutual help by association'. The new unionists 'seek to go back to the old state of things'; they rely upon State aid and upon Acts of Parliament.

This final fundamental point rested of course on the claim that 'freedom of contract' in selling labour power, now represented by craft privileges and high overtime rates, had already been won by the unions for themselves. Let others do likewise! 'To quote the words of the late John Bright', said Howell, 'the demand for a legal 8 hours day was "the offspring and spawn of feeble minds" transplanted from the continent of Europe . . . by men who have misappropriated to themselves the name of Socialists'. (*Trade Unionism Old and New*, p.186). Middle class liberals were already bewailing the 'cowardice and apathy' of workers who, as the future Lord Haldane complained, asked help from the State instead of 'insisting . . . on combination in their dealings with their employers'. But Haldane's lament over 'the decay of trades unionism in certain districts where this kind of socialism has taken hold' was not a well-timed prophesy. ('The Liberal Creed', *Contemporary Review*, October 1888).

Tom Mann and Ben Tillett replied to Shipton the same month.[5] It is a spirited reply, marked by some of Tom's most characteristic expressions, which gets to the heart of the matter in one sentence: 'The real difference between the "new" and the "old" is that they who belong to the latter . . . do not recognise, as we do, that it is the work of the trade unionists to stamp out poverty from the land.' But Shipton's case was answered in detail in what is one of the great documents of English working class history:

New unionism must be judged by its fruits. Many identified with it had long been members of their own societies and had grieved bitterly over the workers' poverty, particularly that of the unskilled and unorganised, and at the callous disregard shown by the old societies, even for the labourers in their own trade. The old school had proved unable to organise the unskilled and even to further their own interests. But 'new' unionist activity was overcoming the 'frightful apathy' and had added 9,000 members to the A.S.E. that year. The 'deadly stupor' affecting other old societies was also yielding to 'new' unionist efforts.

'Branch meetings became more lively, special meetings more frequent, the interests of the labourers were discussed with a new vigour and sympathy . . . new unions were formed and the old ones became less stone-like . . . Steps were taken to mix with the labourers at every opportunity. Sundays and week evenings were entirely devoted to the purpose of spreading the principles of progressive trade unionism.'

As to 'manhood' and 'self-reliance' (Shipton's phrases) their 'methods of determining a change in our present industrial system' were 'on a strictly trade union basis'. 'All our public utterances, all our talks to our members, have been directed towards cultivating a sturdy spirit of independence and instilling a deep sense of responsibility.' They had discouraged appeals to Parliament because 'we are convinced that not until Parliament is an integral part of the workers, representing and responsible to industrial toilers, shall we be able to effect any reform by its means'.

'The statement that the "new" trade unionists look to government and legislation is bunkum; the key note is to *organise* first, and take action in the most effective way so soon as organisation warrants action, instead of specially looking to Government. The lesson is being thoroughly well taught and learned that we must look to ourselves alone, though this of course does not preclude us from exercising our rights of citizenship.'

Mr. Shipton insisted that 'the voluntary principle' must be the basis of trade unionism, that infringements of it 'were contrary to law and morals'. If this meant that unionists must not refuse to work with non-union men 'we frankly tell Mr. Shipton that there is nothing we are more proud of than the fact that it is now known . . . that in hundreds of places no non-unionist need apply. The voluntary principle, forsooth!' Did Mr. Shipton disapprove of those London shops which engineers and compositors had made union shops? If so, 'the sooner he becomes a paid servant of the capitalists the better'. 'A very startling statement is the charge that we, the "new" school, "want to do less work and get more money" . . . we really had not expected censure for this . . . except from the capitalists.'

'Schemes of federation' had failed, according to Mr. Shipton; the Dockers' Union, however, was an *amalgamation* now including 55,000 members representing 26 different trades.

If they kept contributions mainly for trade purposes and left sick and funeral benefits to the Insurance Companies that was because the work of trade unions was to get higher wages and shorter hours; 'our experience has taught us that many of the older unions are very reluctant to engage in a Labour struggle no matter how great the necessity, because they are hemmed in by sick and funeral claims, so that to a large extent they have lost their true characteristic of being fighting organisations.'

The 'new' unions might be 'a loose form of organisation' but they insisted on regular attendance at branch meetings, compliance with rules and leadership by democratically elected committees and urged regular affiliation to Trades Councils.

If 'new' unionists 'rely upon demonstrations, bands and banners' then the habit must be growing for an old union, the London Society of Compositors, was also going in for bands, banners and rosettes. Mr. Shipton himself had been 'the gorgeously attired Chief Marshal of the 4th of May 1890 Demonstration'.

The 'new' unions were said to be led by an 'academic middle-class'. What about Tillett and Thorne? Middle-class persons had however given valuable help in the early stages of some of the unions 'while old Trade Unionists like Mr. Shipton stood idly by'.

The London Trades Council itself had lost the confidence of the workers. 'The Council generally, and its secretary particularly, had shown a decided inclination to associate with those who were "superior" to workmen, whilst to take part in Labour struggles or to assist in the organisation of the unskilled, that was against their principles and practice'. The secretary preferred 'picnics to the Channel Tunnel, Sandringham,[6] and deputations in connection with various semi-political and patriotic and semi-demi-trade unionist and pseudo-philanthropic movements'.

The pamphlet concludes with a re-affirmation of the new unionist outlook and aim and a call to action:

'Poverty in our opinion can be abolished, and we consider that it is the work of the Trade Unionist to do this. We want to see the necessary economic knowledge imparted in our Labour organisations, so that Labour in the future shall not be made the shuttlecock of political parties. Our Trade Unions shall be centres of enlightenment and not merely the meeting place for paying contributions and receiving donations . . . '

'A new enthusiasm is required, a fervent zeal, that will result in the sending forth of trade union organisers as missionaries through the length and breadth of the country . . . brotherhood must not only be talked of but practised . . . what we desire to see is a unification of all, a dropping of all bickerings and an earnest devotion to duty taking the place of the old indifference. The cause we have at heart is too sacred to admit of time being spent quarrelling amongst ourselves . . . we are prepared to work unceasingly for the economic emancipation of the workers.'

'Our ideal is a co-operative commonwealth . . . Whilst striving for the ideal . . . we can be continually gaining some advantage for one or other section of the workers. The abolition of systematic overtime, reductions of working hours, elimination of sweaters, an ever-increasing demand for a more righteous share of the wealth created by Labour—all these are points in our programme, not one of which can be delayed.'

'We will above all things endeavour to be true to ourselves and we call upon all who will to respond to the call of duty as a religious work.'

When the Trades Union Congress met at Liverpool in September the two sides in this controversy could be clearly distinguished, not only by their views but by their dress. According to John Burns, the 'old' unionists 'looked like respectable city gentlemen; wore very good coats, large watch-chains and high hats', presenting 'an aldermanic . . . form and dignity'. No tall hats were to be seen among the 'new' delegates. 'They looked workmen. They were workers. They were not such sticklers for formality or Court procedure, but were guided more by common sense'. (J. Burns, *The Liverpool Congress*, 1890, p. 6).

Burns and Mann were delegates from the engineers, Tillett was one of the delegates of the 56,000 dockers, and the 60,000 gasworkers were well represented by Will Thorne and others. Harry Quelch, delegate of the South Side Labour Protection League with a membership of 5,000, moved a preliminary resolution that congress should not adjourn for a river trip with the Lord Mayor. This was lost but it soon became evident to at least one observer that 'more than half of the 500 delegates . . . are socialists and more than 90 per cent of the young men.' Joseph Burgess, soon to become editor of the *Workman's Times*, added: 'It is with them and their views that the future lies.'[7] The resolution in favour of a legal 8 hours day, on which Burns made the chief speech was carried by 193 votes to 155. George Shipton now publicly declared his conversion to the legal regulation of the hours of labour. (Webbs, *Trade Unionism*, pp. 394-5). One of the most securely entrenched of the old school, Henry Broadhurst, whose own union, the Stonemasons, now supported the New Unionists, finally gave up the battle and, after expressing a hope that the new unions 'will not prove broken reeds in the day of their trial', resigned the secretaryship of the Parliamentary Committee and committed the T.U.C. to the guidance of God.

With the eight hours' resolution so well supported Tom Mann had only to second a vote of censure on the Parliamentary Committee for failing to carry out instructions on the Miners Eight Hours Bill (which was lost, 258 to 92); he also seconded Tillett's motion that the Parliamentary Committee should extend labour organisation by supplying organisers, which was opposed and on which Burns remarked that neglect of the unskilled by the T.U.C. had often led them to 'journalistic blacklegs, dead stumped parsons and self-seeking lawyers'. (*Autobiography*, 1901, p.31). Tom's motion in favour of municipal workshops for the unemployed was agreed to despite the complaint of D. Holmes (Burnley Weavers) that 'Congress might as well ask municipalities to take possession of the sun and moon.' (*T.U.C. Report*, 1890 p. 59). Finally, in seconding Burns' vote of sympathy for the giant struggle of the Australian waterside workers, a battle for the rights of trade union organisation, Tom was able to announce that the Dockers' Union, barely a year old, had already voted £1,000 and telegraphed £500 of it to Australia.

The tide of new life, which had touched all sections of the workers skilled and unskilled alike, was running high at the 1890 T.U.C. John Burns became a member of the Parliamentary Committee and was to become its chairman in 1893; Tillett was elected to the committee in 1892. Victory in the trade union movement was by no means complete: but the influence of the Dock Strike and the New Unionism was making itself felt in many fields.

'In a most curious way', remarks J.L. Garvin,[8] the dock strike 'gave birth to a new social conscience and to new political emotions.' In a most curious way, Chamberlain began to study Bismarck and State Socialism and to consider old age pensions; in a most curious way, Mr. Gladstone's 'high wall' was broken down and the Liberals adopted Asquith's Newcastle Programme, including universal male suffrage, payment of M.P.'s, compulsory land purchase etc. etc.: in a most curious way, elementary education was made free by the Tories in 1891: in a most curious way, a number of attacks, culminating in the Taff Vale case of 1900, were once more opened on the rights of trade unionism.

On the eve of the dock strike Chamberlain had been boasting at Highbury that the Unionist alliance had 'secured the country against the dangers of disintegration' and made possible 'legislation which, I confess, Radical as I have been during the whole of my life, I had hardly dared to hope for during the next generation'. (*Reynolds'*, August 18, 1889). By November 1891, in Birmingham, once Liberal as the sea is salt, the town hall—where Tom Mann used to listen to the Tribune of the People and Republican Joe Chamberlain—was 'as densely crowded for Lord Salisbury as ever it had been for John Bright or Gladstone'; on November 25, Chamberlain, seated beside the Tory Prime Minister, finally 'declared the Unionist alliance indissoluble'. 'By this time his own ascendancy over Tory democracy in the great towns everywhere was undisputed.' (Garvin, p.443)

Interrupting the triumphant complacency arises the voice of the dockers' president: 'I see no grounds whatever for believing that Parliament is about to lead the way in solving the social problem. . .' This above all was the great achievement of the strike for the dockers' tanner. We have spoken of the inception of Tory democracy at the moment when working class leaders had allowed the weapon of democratic struggle to fall from their hands. The dock strike and the extension of the elementary rights of trade unionism to men hitherto declassed were a challenge to Tory democracy and feudal socialism. The rapid growth of organisation thus stimulated, the breaking down of craft barriers exemplified in the new constitution of the A.S.E. of 1891 which admitted labourers, the new militancy on the industrial field, the demand for political independence, the beginnings of Socialist influence—these were soon to bring into being a political party of the working class for which a mass basis had at length been created. The Bradford Labour Union, nucleus of the I.L.P., was founded in the spring of 1891 following the great Manningham strike in Yorkshire; for the next three years the new *Workman's Times* played an important part in organising the new forces.

The legal 8 hours day, however, was not won, nor even seriously fought for; largely because of internal divisions it was 18 years before the Miners' Eight Hour Bill was passed. When, from 1891, the last phase of the great crisis set in the new unions found it necessary, in the absence of State insurance, to introduce some friendly benefits; before very long some of the new leaders had fitted pretty comfortably into the established bourgeois democratic machine, and the general labourers' unions were not more militant than others.

Tom Mann had correctly foreseen that many of the successes won would be lost when trade depression returned but in forecasting this he insisted again that trade unions must be clear as to their goal which was nothing less than the abolition of poverty; to work for this goal required organisation. Those who set up a 'Chinese wall' between democratic and Socialist demands failed to appreciate this position. 'Better we shall never see the fruit of our labour than. . .reap it at the cost of principle. Again we proclaim the Class War, raise the Red Flag on high and shout for the Social Revolution', was the barren comment of *Justice* upon the dock strike (September 21, 1889). Its abuse in the following months completed the estrangement of Burns and deterred Tom Mann from further work with the S.D.F.: he did not formally resign but never resumed active membership.[9]

'The English Social Democratic Federation is, and acts like, a small sect', said Engels in a newspaper interview a few years later (*Daily Chronicle*, July 1, 1893). 'It is an exclusive body. It has not understood how to take the lead of the working class movement generally and to direct it towards Socialism. It has turned into an orthodoxy. Thus it insisted upon John Burns unfurling the red flag at the dock strike, where such an act would have ruined the whole movement, and, instead of gaining over the dockers, would have driven them back into the arms of the capitalists. We (i.e. the revolutionary Marxists) don't do this. Yet our programme is a purely socialist one. Our first plank is the socialisation of all the means and instruments of production.'

Tom Mann made his position clear in two striking articles in the *Labour Elector* (January 4. 11. 1890) which sum up the efforts of the foregoing years to make socialism the inspiration of new life in trade unionism. It is here that he insists that the goal must be 'the complete abolition of poverty' and that the chief weapon must be, not Parliament, but the trade unions. He is no anti-parliamentarian, Tom writes, but many thought 'that if we insist upon good men going to Parliament social evils will rapidly disappear'. 'I can see no ground whatever for believing that Parliament is about to lead the way in solving the social problem.'

The immediate task must be to organise all sections of workers into trade unions, in order 'to enlighten them as to the fundamental causes that create degradation in the midst of nineteenth century wealth'. The trade union is far the best place for discussing labour questions effectively—and evidently Tom was thinking here of socialist groups: 'Many of us have seen that time spent in theoretic speculations is almost wasted amongst men who are not willing to submit themselves to the discipline of a trades organisation. It is not talk about the future so much as practice in the present that is wanted.' The union can best educate workers 'in the benefits of organised action and in a real understanding of their industrial position'. Brought into direct contact with one another they can thrash out labour questions 'with the advantage of having the theory illustrated by the everyday incidents which they must discuss at their meetings' and so 'be weaned of the indifference and selfishness which so often characterise those who refuse to undergo the salutary discipline of a trade union'.

The next step must be to combine in Trades Councils. Why was the London Trades Council so weak? Its influence would be immeasurably greater if there were only a few thousand London trade unionists who looked upon trades unionism 'not merely as a means of maintaining their present rates of wages at a minimum of cost and trouble to themselves, but as the germ of an organisation capable by a full exercise of its industrial, educational and political powers of completely freeing labour and making the worker master of his fate'.

The underlying aim here is akin to that which Lenin set before Russian Social-Democrats twelve years later.[10]

'The only weapon of the proletariat in its struggle for power is organisation.'—this is what Tom Mann was feeling towards. But, turning away from the theorising and individualism of Socialist cliques, Tom turned directly to organisations in which he had already experienced the potentialities of disciplined collective action. His aim—to bring to the mass organisations of the working class both socialist ideas and the necessary leadership and strength to fight for them—remained constant in the coming years though various avenues opened possibilities for action.

II

When addressing the first annual congress of the Dockers' Union in September, 1890, Tom Mann had noted that 'the attitude of the employers of today is decidedly different to that of a year and a half ago. . . In every port in the Kingdom steps of some kind are being taken to enable the employers, as a class, to act concertedly.' But at this time he welcomed organisation among the dock directors and wharfingers, in the hope that it would reduce the chaos of competing small capitalist interests, make possible uniform conditions of wages and employment and be a first step towards 'industrial order'.[11]

The Shipping Federation, however, officially formed in August, 1890, to enable shipowners 'to combine for protection against the tyranny of the "new" unionism', soon showed a face as ugly as any employers' association in British history. From the first it acted in close alliance with the dock companies. So also Tom Mann and the Dockers' Union worked closely with the seamen's union and its founder and secretary Havelock Wilson. Seamen and dockers were closely related and the National Seamen's and Firemen's Union, founded on the north-east coast in 1887, had increased its membership during 1889 to 65,000. Havelock Wilson had imbibed his trade unionism from boyhood attendance at the Durham miners' gala, from Australian seamen, and from small seamen's friendly societies in the north-east; erratic and egocentric he had no time for Socialism and regarded the union he had founded as his private property. No doubt he did something to draw persecution upon himself, but the injustices he fought were real enough — both for himself and the seamen. 'In the whole history of the trade-union movement of Britain', wrote Tom later, 'there is no case of such persistent, systematic, and venomous persecution of a union official as that to which Havelock Wilson was subjected by the shipowners of this country'.[12]

According to Ben Tillett, the Shipping Federation 'while whining about the brutality of trade unionists . . . have yet armed men with bludgeons, revolvers and supply of intoxicants . . . gangs of half-drunken men who have resisted with violence men fighting for dear life the principle of fair remuneration. In every dispute the same demoralising work has continued, aided very often by the police.' (*Minutes of 2nd Annual Congress of Dockers' Union,* 1891, p.5.). Agents of the Federation established 'Free Labour Associations' aimed principally at the shore workers in London, Cardiff, Hull, Gloucester and elsewhere.[13] Ugly incidents of violence occurred in more than one port and in the years following the great dock strike many plots were hatched in the public houses against the union organisers. 'Blackguards have set about me', writes Ben, 'I have been sandbagged, brutally hustled, beaten insensible. Knuckledusters, life preservers . . . have been used upon me. Even my meetings were disturbed by the drunken fools inflamed by the incitement of those who exploited them'. (*Memories* . . . pp.173-4).

Though the Federation and its agents were active in London, the Bristol Channel was chosen for its first full-scale onslaught, in the spring of 1891. Cardiff was the storm centre and the employers' leader, Sir William Thomas Lewis (later Lord Merthyr), was able to bring dock companies, coalowners, shipowners and railway interests into a common attack. The seamen were the first to be attacked, but the dockers came out in sympathy and also in dispute upon a host of grievances which had been the subject of protracted negotiation, in particular the vicious system of sub-contracting which was as bad as that formerly obtaining in London.

Henry Orbell, Ben Tillett, and when he became ill Tom Mann, joined Havelock Wilson at the scene of the conflict. Numerous police reinforcements were drafted in from Birmingham and London. At the height of the struggle, in April, sixty north-east coast seamen were brought, by deception and under heavy police guard, to Cardiff. They were good union men and, finding that they had been brought as blacklegs, joined the strikers as a body, leaving their baggage with the authorities who sent it to various Cardiff boarding-houses to be held as a form of hostage. Next day Havelock Wilson headed a great demonstration which called at every boarding-house to demand return of the baggage and went on to a grand mass meeting of seamen and dockers addressed by himself, Tom and Ben. Charged with 'unlawful assembly and riot' Wilson was sentenced on perjured evidence to six weeks' imprisonment. The seamen's strike was broken; the Shipping Federation enforced its 'ticket'—all seamen to engage through Federation offices where preference was given to non-union men. The Cardiff dockers went back with nothing gained.

The Bristol Channel struggle marked the end of the first phase of union building and the onset of new and bitter struggles which culminated at Hull and in Bristol in 1893. Gone were the days of middle-class sympathy and philanthropic interest which had marked the London Dock Strike. The press was becoming more hostile and the middle-class public lent a readier ear to the employers' propaganda about 'firebrands' and 'excesses'. The law was now being freely called upon by the employers and authorities, in particular charges were brought alleging 'intimidation'. When, after a favourable judgment in the High Court, such cases abated charges were brought for 'obstruction' and picketing. In January, 1893, Ben was charged with 'incitement to riot' at Bristol.

Meanwhile the unions had a hard struggle to bend the law to the service of justice in cases relating to employers' liability and compensation. 'Every dock was a shambles . . .', Ben records. 'Compensation for life or limb or health was stubbornly refused by the dock and shipping authorities . . . No inspection of gear, inefficient machinery, dangerous appliances, rotten slings and ropes, sacks loosely loaded . . . all bore their consequences . . . Only too often the poor bloody tatters of a man were gathered up and thrown in the wings of the ship'. It was not until 1895, after Tillett and James Sexton had presented the dockers' case at the Labour Commission, that the docks were included within the scope of the Factory Acts — but employers' liability was withheld until 1908.[14]

There were also difficulties within the movement, particularly as concerns joint action. Tom and Ben took a very conciliatory line towards troubles with the South Side Labour Protection League, of which their fellow Socialist Quelch was secretary, and this small general union continued its separate existence. Later attempts at amalgamation with the National Dock Labourers' Union in the northern ports were also unsuccessful. The proposal of Will Thorne and the gasworkers that the two new brother unions should make their tickets interchangeable (as the same men were often gas stokers in winter and dockers in summer) was not considered practicable at this difficult early stage. The smaller weekly contribution paid by the gas-workers, and the dockers' claim to preference in employment on account of length of service led to some friction which was overcome by the mutual goodwill of the leaders.

It remained an urgent task to bring all port and associated workers into closer unity to meet the employers' counter-attack. Eventually, after a year's negotiations, there came into being in the autumn of 1891 the Federation of Trades and Labour Unions connected with the Shipping, Carrying and Other Industries, of which Tom became President and Clem Edwards (assistant secretary of the Dockers' Union) general secretary.[15] The Federation's rules, covering objects, financial contributions, powers of the executive council, took more than fifty meetings to draw up.[16]

At a mass meeting in January 1891, to witness the unfurling of the new banner of the Millwall branch of the Dockers' Union, Tom had referred confidently to the forthcoming federation; when it was achieved 'they would put their foot down and say they did not intend to work with non-union men' (*Daily Chronicle*, January 14, 1891). In the event by the close of the year a new phase in the economic crisis had opened and the union, far from continuing the offensive, was conducting a stubborn de-fensive fight to maintain its position. In September Ben reported to the second annual congress setbacks in several London districts: the Medway, owing to depression in the cement industry, Tilbury, Northfleet, and at King's Lynn and other centres. In a letter to John Burns in October Tom wrote that the union's paying membership had fallen from 55,000 to 40,000.

It was at this point, early in September, 1891, that 300 dockers employed at the Hermitage and Carron wharves, Wapping, went on strike. The oc-casion, as at Hay's Wharf in January, 1890, was the meal hour issue, the employers imposing a cut which amounted to about 3s. a week. With the new trade depression beginning to settle, this strike was the first full-scale display of strength in London by the joint forces of the dock employers and the Shipping Federation. It was also the first test of the new Federation of Trades and Labour Unions — and it was to bring a crisis in Tom's relations with his old comrade, John Burns.

The strike was fought with much bitterness. A regular service of blacklegs was shipped to Wapping by the river steamer 'Bismarck' owned by the Victoria Steam Boat Association; the Shipping Federation also kept the steamship 'Scotland' in Albert Dock as a 'floating boardhouse' for 'free labourers', 'where the union men could not get them', and armed the blacklegs with revolvers. 'At least in ten or twelve cases men have appeared at loopholes at the Carron and Hermitage Wharves, have presented revolvers at the pickets outside and have threatened to shoot them'; the police, active in protecting the blacklegs, refused to interfere with their arms. (*Royal Commission on Labour*, B 8640-45, 8708, 8196). Lightermen who refused to take goods to the wharves in dispute were sacked and blacklisted. Despite heavy support from the London Trades Council, which sent official speakers to the big Sunday demonstrations in Victoria Park and advised a boycott of the company's steamers, the continuing supply of blacklegs spelt defeat for the strikers. (*L.T.C. Minutes*, September 17, October 1, 7. 1891; *Annual Report*, 1891, p.6).

John Burns' only official connection with the Dockers' Union was as one of the Trustees[17] but his great prestige entitled him to give an opinion on its affairs. Since the great strike there had been signs of a slackening of his close friendship with Tom. Burns had been busy with work on the L.C.C. and in Battersea, where he had established a reputation by working for improved housing and sanitation and by ready attention to local grievances; to be M.P. for Battersea, his birthplace, was an ambition steadfastly followed and the previous June the Battersea Labour League had started a special election fund for the next election (*Workman's Times*, June 12, 1891). Still in demand for all dockers' meetings and demonstrations, Burns had of necessity taken little share in the difficult organisational work following the London strike. The mutual dislike between himself and Tillett made matters no easier and in July 1891 he had complained in a letter to Tom of extravagance and bad accounting by Ben in claiming minor expenses from union funds; he also objected to the way in which the Dockers' executive had loaned £570 to the *Trade Unionist*.

The following correspondence tells the story of his intervention in the Hermitage and Carron strike, his reaction to Tom's candidature for general secretary of the A.S.E. at this time, and the outcome. On October 5, 1891, when the strike had been on for about three weeks, Burns wrote to Mann, on the headed notepaper of the L.C.C.[18]

Dear Tom,

It seems to me that the price of winning Carron and Hermitage wharf dispute is too high if it is intended to be a general strike. After the Cardiff and Southampton incidents and also Hays Wharf where the men were beaten is it worth while courting disaster when such may be averted.

I think it will be suicidal to extend the area of dispute farther than is necessary and if the meal hour dispute can be settled say by a hourly wage of 7d. that would be better than asking for, and striking for, a privilege — that is payment for meal hours; which no-one can defend as a right.

Considering the state of Trade and the time of year and also the condition of the men themselves towards this dispute who are in the Federation do try in the interests of the preservation of the Unions to bring about a settlement, even at the cost of giving up the interests of the 300 men to defend which may, I believe will, jeopardise the Riverside Unions and through them the whole Labour movement.

Your willingness to give up the dinner hour if breakfast is paid (here the draft breaks off)

Tom's reply, dated October 9, was friendly:

Dear Jack,

Thanks for your letter I agree with every suggestion you make with regard to limiting the area of dispute, and in negotiation to get the question if possible on a more satisfactory basis.

I have purposely refrained from any prominency in this case because I did not consider the terms we obtained from the firm as the result of the negotiations were bad ones. They first determined upon 28/- a week for the right to control the men 7½ hours including meals we got this up by stages until they promised definitely 33/- and would have paid it, and I was favourable to closing with this. The Wapping men however (and they are good sober steady fellows) could only look upon this as meaning an all round reduction and one that ought to be resisted for a time if only for purposes of protestation, ultimately this prevailed and I of course kept quiet hoping to see them score but expecting defeat which is now pretty near . . .

Dr Jack,

re Engineers Sec'ship May I make use of your name on Committee etc.? I think I shall have good support in London but Manchester and Newcastle are doubtful.

Faithfully yours,
Tom Mann

P.S. I shall probably be at London West Branch tomorrow night.

The West London branch of the A.S.E. was Burns' own branch and Tom evidently thought of going there from Bow in hopes of talking with his friends. Burns, however, did not attend the branch but immediately replied with another letter on the strike situation, ignoring Tom's request about the A.S.E.

Dear Tom,
    The policy of the drift will not suit.
    If you believe as you say there is but one step to take and that is to face your men and stop them from going to their defeat. Even if better terms could be got and all the men reinstated the price to pay for it by a general strike is out of all proportion to the gain. The men's places are filled as at Cardiff and you have nothing to gain by extending the dispute except to punish yourselves. Stop it at once or it is a bad job for you and the Union.

Yours truly,
John Burns

He also wrote on October 10 to Clem Edwards:

Dear Edwards,
    Don't wreck the Federation just formed you are beaten stop the strike at once. It never ought to have been started under the conditions it was.
    Face your men and make them accept the defeat of 300 rather than secure the defeat of 30,000.

Yours truly,
John Burns

Tom, having failed to see Burns, wrote again on October 11:

Dear Jack,
    It is not quite so simple a job as yr letter w'd imply. I have had three hours with the Strike Committee, I urged the necessity for closing after getting every fact in connection with the business, they are not willing to close believing they can yet score if they get the support of other Unions. Now I have been one to encourage the formation of the Federation and now that it exists it must at least be recognised or we shall not be able to federate after, perhaps you know it has taken a year to bring so much about. Well, last night the Executive of this Federation met, a decent set of fellows too. And I was *unable to bring them to my views* they believing it possible to do great good, and of course there is this chance at any rate that determined action will prevent a general *reduction* w'h is contemplated if this goes down. I mean the wiping out of meal time payment. Tomorrow evening I c'd make a stand and close it, but to do so at the present hour w'd be to sectionalise and antagonise, not so much myself as

an individual but it w'd suit certain representatives to have Dockers officials declaring it must and shall be closed with a most mischievous weapon, I have used plain English to them and shall not hesitate to do so as fully as you w'd wish immediately it reaches a state when more good will be done than harm by such a course. I hear from Woolwich you have decided to stand for Gen Sec A.S.E. is that so? as if it is its a pity you didn't give me a hint and I *certainly* w'd not have stood?

I was at West London last night there was a good attendance but there were more drunken interruptions during the one hour and a half I was there than I have ever observed in any other branch in a similar time.

Yours truly,
Tom

The strike continued. A fortnight after Tom's request for support in his A.S.E. campaign Burns replied to it, on October 24:

Dear Tom,

I have carefully considered your request for my name on your committee for Engineers and after the anxious thought and deliberate conviction have decided not to take any part in the election whatever.

Yours truly,
John Burns

Two undated drafts among the Burns' papers refer to this episode. The first to an unknown correspondent:

Dear Sir,

The rumour attributing to me opposition to Mann's candidature, and that I am doing my best to keep him out is absolutely untrue.

I have for reasons that commend themselves to me decided to take no part in the election at all.

If I see reason to alter that decision I will let you know what I intend to do.

(This last sentence replaced a previous draft: 'When that attitude is altered then I will freely let it be known whom I will support'.)

The other letter was to Tom addressed for the first time by his surname:

Dear Mann,

To avoid all misunderstanding I write to you to say that it was ridiculous you and I not speaking yesterday.

I nodded to you and presuming you did not notice it I intended speaking to you after the meeting but missed you.

There is no desire on my part to quarrel with you if there was it would be childish indeed.

We will have to work together for Labour, easier and better it will be, for that, and both that no trivial pique or disagreement should prevent it.

I write this note so as to make my position clear.

Yours truly,
John Burns

There is no evidence that Burns had replied to Tom's previous letter in which he had detailed the difficulties, both with the Strike Committee and with the Executive of the new Federation, in the way of ending the strike. Instead he had written an outspoken letter to Ben Tillett on October 17:

Dear Tillett,

I have seen for some weeks that the dispute at the Wharves would end in the defeat of the men have told Mann and Edwards so. I see now that the dispute is being needlessly prolonged and what is worse neither Mann nor you guiding it either to a speedy end either through admitting defeat or vigorously trying to secure success.

This I regard as positive cowardice and whether it offend or not I tell you frankly that this conduct on your part is almost criminal when at the same time you are spending your time and energy and the Dockers' money in going to religious conferences and addressing meetings in different parts of the country, where dockers interests cannot be served. As a Trustee of the Union I protest against it and as a man I am compelled to say that the conduct of this dispute is the saddest blow that your union has received. If it is a case of rats leaving the sinking ship and also candidly if the Dockers Union has simply become a platform from which you can speak whilst they suffer let me tell you I won't stand it, and ere other action is taken by me I give you my opinion of your action and say, stop this strike at once, ere disaster sets in on you and the men in your union.

Yours truly,
John Burns

Here was no 'trivial pique or disagreement' but an outright accusation, that two men who had been constantly engaged for the dockers' interests were guilty of cowardice, and of criminal negligence dictated by self-interest, in handling a dispute. Tom would certainly have seen this letter, and would not have missed the bitter jibe ('rats leaving the sinking ship') aimed at him for entering the A.S.E. contest and at Tillett who was now prospective parliamentary candidate for Bradford West, with the full permission of the Dockers' Annual Delegate Congress.[19]

On the Friday of the seventh week of the strike Burns came down and addressed the union, telling them 'they were beaten and must go back'. On the Sunday, when the strike was finally abandoned, an orderly procession ended in a meeting outside West India Dock Gates addressed by Orbell and by Mann who handled the situation in a way best calculated to promote solidarity, set out the circumstances of the case, and in part replied to Burns.

'Admittedly.', he is reported as saying, 'good friends of theirs' had held the strike should have been over weeks ago, but the 'Dockers' Union was essentially democratic and would not yield its guidance to any autocracy. Other trades unions might be led by a dictatorial and autocratic policy to success but they held in the Dockers' Union that such a policy was a bad one'. 'They were pledged to other unions and something of a substantial federation was likely to be brought about, but they held to their own policy and he himself, while he had full right to try and persuade men to his side felt it had been his duty to sink his opinion when he found himself in the minority . . .' (*Morning Advertiser*, November 2, 1891).

Tom went on to show that the union had sustained the men and increased its membership, and that with the support from organised collections it was no poorer. The men were not scuttling back as best they could — and they had not done yet with the gentlemen at Carron Wharf. He was going to give evidence that week at the Royal Commission and submit to cross examination on the dock question. He had a scheme for replacing the present owners by a corporation directly responsible to the people. The constant disputes in connection with the docks, wharves, and granaries of the Port of London were forced on them by the conditions, which he vividly exposed. The strikers passed a resolution to allow no victimisation, not to return to work in small groups, and that ship hands and wharf hands should return together.

Seven weeks later a further query from Burns about the debt on the now defunct *Trade Unionist* was passed to Tom whose reply, dated December 21, shows that relations between the two had become ones of formality:

Mr. John Burns

Dear Sir,

Your letter of enquiry respecting the indebtedness of Trade Unionist to Dockers Union has been placed before me and in reply I beg to say that the position is exactly as it was at the time yourself & colleagues last went over the Finances of the Union i.e. the sum used by authority of the Executive Council & endorsed by Quarterly Delegate Meeting.

No money is being advanced now nor has any been since you were last communicated with upon this matter the actual sum is £570.

Anything further you require shall be glad to acquaint you of.

Yours truly,
Tom Mann

Despite the heavy claims of his work for the dockers, few months went by in 1891-2 when Tom did not spend at least a weekend, often many days, in the provinces lending assistance to one or another section of the labour movement — helping striking builders' labourers in Derby, addressing a trades council demonstration in Yorkshire, doing some propaganda work for his own union the A.S.E. The incidents of a weekend visit to Bradford, in August 1891, reveal something of the variety of his propaganda work at this time. This was, moreover, Tom's first close contact with the Yorkshire labour movement with which he was to remain closely associated during the next few years.

On the evening of Friday August 21, he was addressing a meeting in Colne Valley, at Slaithwaite. He had sent a telegram only that morning informing the newly-formed Colne Valley Labour Union that he would call *en route* for Bradford, but the news had quickly passed round the industrial village and about 300 crowded the room to hear Tom Mann. After the meeting he had a quiet chat with the committee members. The union had been formed exactly a month before, on July 21, 1891, when a small group of textile workers and others had met in the Slaithwaite Social Democratic Club. The first entry in the minutes is a resolution to form a Labour Union in the Colne Valley 'on the lines of the Bradford Labour Union', the second concerns election of officers and committee, the third runs: 'resolved that the Secretary write Mr. Tom Mann of London inviting him to be candidate on behalf of the Labour Union for a Parliamentary seat at the next election' (*Minutes Book: History of the Colne Valley Labour Party*, 1941).

Since 1884 Socialist propaganda in Leeds, Bradford and the West Riding had been mainly undertaken by a small group of gifted young working class propagandists in the Socialist League. Making little impression at first, they had come to prominence by giving active leadership in the struggle of the 'new' unionism — to builders' labourers and tailoring workers, in the great Leeds gas strike of 1890, above all among the woollen and worsted workers through the influence of such younger union leaders as Ben Turner. The textile workers, who had their own paper championing the cause of independent labour and trade unionism, the *Yorkshire Factory Times*, were now involved in hard-fought struggles — often against employers prominent in local Liberal politics — to defend conditions already so poor that they roused Tom to indignation when evidence was given on the Royal Commission.

The long strike at Manningham worsted mills in Bradford had led to conflict between the Liberal municipal authorities and the workers in April 1891. In May the Bradford Labour Union was formed with the aim of securing independent labour representation 'irrespective of the convenience of any political party' in municipal affairs and in Parliament. Formed with active Socialist support this, and other new Labour unions in the Colne Valley, at Halifax etc., arose directly out of industrial struggle, or from conflict between the workers and their Liberal employers which demanded expression in the political as well as the industrial field. In a climate of sharpening class struggle the need for 'independent labour' representation seemed self-evident: the Colne Valley Labour Union did not even bother to adopt any programme or statement of objects. Tom Mann and Ben Tillett, nationally famous champions of militant trade unionism, embodied the aspirations of the Labour Unions in a practical sense; hence the invitations to these two to contest the East Bradford and Colne Valley constituencies. Ben had been invited to contest by the Bradford Labour Union as soon as this was inaugurated.[20]

Tom did not accept the Colne Valley invitation on this occasion; on the other hand he did not give a final refusal. He told the committee members that the economic issues should be fought out in the trade unionists' clubrooms: and pointed out the need for a much stronger and more active trade union movement in the Colne Valley. But he also promised to consider the invitation further (*Yorkshire Factory Times*, August 28, 1891: *History of Colne Valley Labour Party*, p.7). An interview he gave to the *Bradford Observer* at the weekend, which attracted a good deal of attention, clarifies his attitude to this question. Great progress had been made in the last six years by the new movement of labour, he said, there was a splendid outlook with many dangers passed. But a danger remained, that 'the leaders were sometimes too superficial; agitating for Labour representation before arriving at a clear idea of a labour policy, and skipping, so to speak, the real work of trade unionism which is to organise the workers into solid bodies of men systematically meeting and maintaining their contributions'.

On the Saturday afternoon a mass demonstration of the Bradford Trades Council passed its first resolution in favour of putting forward Labour candidates at the coming municipal elections — a result of the Manningham strike. On the Sunday afternoon Tom was at the annual demonstration of the Bradford branch of the General Railway Workers' Union, attended by over 4,000 including deputations from neighbouring branches. The procession was headed by the borough brass band and the splendid silk banner of the Manchester and Salford branch. Supporting the resolution on the eight hour day for all railway workers, Tom hammered home his constant theme of *organisation*. The hours and conditions of railway workers, shameful as they were, were largely due to imperfect organisation; sympathetic meetings in London and Bradford multiplied a thousand times would never alter that fact unless they resulted in more perfect organisation. If the railwaymen could not do better in the future than they had done in the past they were not worth talking to. 'Out of their own ranks must come their own deliverers, and . . . meetings ought to result in a great alteration in the proportion of organised and unorganised workers.' If unity was maintained they could, with the help of other workers, revolutionise the conditions under which they lived.

This is one instance among many at this period of Tom's persistent habit of urging the workers to do things for themselves — never in the old-fashioned 'self-help' way but in a 'scientific' way, as he said, based on the facts of society, the economic basis of capitalism and socialism. He never commiserated with workers suffering under conditions they were in a position to improve by their own actions. Rather, he told them in straight terms to get on with the job for themselves, offering as the key to achieving their goal, organisation. When he was asked by the *Bradford Observer* whether he thought that the strong trade union bodies he advocated would have the effect of raising wages, Tom replied:

'I do; but it is not merely a question of raising wages. The aim of trade unions is the perfection of human nature, and insistence on the right of culture for all instead of for the few, and teaching men to appreciate the refinements of life.'

Questioned further about the agitation in the Bradford district for labour representation on local bodies and in Parliament, Tom developed his views. The tendency of the times was towards indifference to Liberalism and Toryism.

'I do my best to encourage contempt for politicians. We ask them for nothing; we intend to do our own business. When they approach us, it is only with a view to controlling us for their own purposes, and I do not conceal the delight I feel when I see consternation in the camp of either party.'

He did not himself give much priority to representation of labour in Parliament:

'I do not concern myself much about Parliamentary parties. My aim is to spread among workmen a knowledge of industrial economics, and the channels for the diffusion of this knowledge are the trades unions and the Co-Operative Movement, especially the productive branch of Co-Operation. This knowledge . . . will soon assert itself in municipal life, and then the workers will take care to put upon local bodies men in sympathy with their aims. We want all our energy for these things; by them we shall prove our capability and until then it is a waste to attempt Parliamentary work. I am therefore not anxious to run Labour candidates for Parliament.'

Finally, however, while stressing yet again the fundamental importance of the mass movement, he qualified this statement:

'The real worker for the people is the man who is changing his habits and thought, and he must work amongst the rank and file. Always remember that Parliament will not change the people, but as the people are changed, they will very soon change Parliament. At the same time I do not deny that there is an advantage in having a few working men in Parliament. They would be specially useful to pilot Labour measures in Committee rooms.'[21]

Yet another engagement was fulfilled this weekend. On the Saturday evening Tom spoke at the Bradford branch of the A.S.E. on the position of the union. Numerically the strongest, financially the richest, society it had led the van of the whole trade union movement, he said, but the position in the localities was not what it should be. Of the 70,000 members who turned up at lodge rooms and paid contributions, few took that interest in the social question required 'of all true men'. There were still 250,000 unorganised machine-men and labourers. There were a number of small unions in the industry which should be brought into amalgamation. The need for sectional unions would cease if the executive of the A.S.E. could be persuaded 'to produce a more elastic constitution . . . to broaden the basis of entrance'. He hoped to see 'good men from each locality' at the forthcoming delegate meeting 'who would advocate a policy of "more go" in the General Office'. Loud and continued applause followed his invitation to the audience to say whether the union had an efficient staff of organisers, 'men who could hold their own in debate with the educated sophisticated employers of today', or whether he was advocating a hot-headed policy.[22]

Ben Tillett, also present at this meeting, spoke on the theme of the aristocracy of labour. He asked his audience 'to be democratic of labour rather than aristocratic upon twenty-nine bob a week'. The *Yorkshire Factory Times* (August 28, 1891) included in its report his tribute to Tom in this connection:

'Now Tom Mann was an aristocrat, but when he (Tillett) had been working some time and some of the would-be, or should-be reformers did not help him, and he said, "Tom, come and help us", Tom had replied "Alright, Old Man", and he did—that fine aristocrat of labour—help him all through to that day'.

The events of this one busy weekend illustrate the new interests in the labour movement. Tom's attitude to and involvement in these; his confidence in the power of leadership, his old vigour in no way weakened but matured by recent responsibilities; and his stature in a movement within which, little more than three years before during his propaganda days at Bolton, he had been little known.

Tom's cool attitude to Parliament was the outcome not only of his dedication to the fundamental task of organising and educating the workers but also to the attraction of the doctrine of municipal socialism. In 1889 he, with John Burns, had joined the Fabian Society, several S.D.F.-ers being members of both organisations. At first this society seemed to him simply a group of well-educated people who were active socialists, fertile in practical, well-devised schemes for putting to good use the new weapon of municipal government. They were trying to convert the middle and upper classes to ideas of municipal socialism — if they succeeded, all the better. But some of the ideas took hold.

In August, 1890, a year before his interview with the *Bradford Observer*, Tom told a Newcastle audience that 'the fighting out of the Labour question would take place in the municipalities, not in Parliament. Parliamentary power would become decentralised and greater powers would be granted to local bodies,' (*Workman's Times*, August 29, 1890). He pointed out that there was not a single representative workman on the council of that great industrial city, and urged more attention to municipal elections. By the autumn of 1891 he was being reproached by the *Workman's Times* (October 2, 1891) for 'becoming enamoured with the idea of evolving the New Socialism by means of municipal and co-operative action'. Though the same article itself shows some infection with the new conception by noting: 'We have in all our town and cities the germs of socialism already existing. In the Corporations and Local Boards we have the framework of what the future Commune will be built of.'

This was a period when the Fabians were actively popularising the gas and water socialism they had derived from Chamberlain: 'Rates and housing; gas and water, trams and docks, markets, libraries, public houses, schools and workhouses all began to take on a new aspect when their transfer from private companies to municipal monopolies was seen as a step towards socialism.' (*History of the Fabian Society*, ed. Pease). Something of the spell laid upon John Burns by work for the newly formed L.C.C. can be caught from his reminiscences fifty years later. (*Star*, March 21, 1939):

'We fought for unification so that we could ameliorate the poor by taxing the rich, with Battersea, a parish of the poor, assisted by Belgravia, a parish of the rich ... Unused to municipal life, and, in the opinion of many, unsuited to the details of civic administration, I left the workshop to take my part in the management of the city.

'With the ardent spirits who ushered in the dawn of a new municipal life, and upon whom developed the duty of recasting and carrying out London's work, I cheerfully and energetically worked ... In those early years I always kept before me a high ideal of a dignified, unified, beautified London, free from poverty and uncontrolled by selfish interests. My programme was:

'Extension of the powers of the Council so that the City with all its funds and endowments be included in and used by a real Municipality for London.

That all monopolies such as Gas, Water, Tramways, Omnibuses, Markets, Docks, River Steamboats, and Electric Lighting should be municipalised and the profits devoted to public purposes.

Establishment of Municipal Hospitals in every District and control by

the Council of those which already exist.
Artisans' dwellings to be constructed and owned by the Council.
The Police of the City and Greater London to be controlled by the
L.C.C.
Cumulative rating, the taxation of ground landlords and the provision
of new sources of revenue.
Efficient sanitary and structural inspection of dwellings and workshops.
Direct employment of all labour by the Council at 8 hours a day and
trade union rates.'

In directing attention to the importance of municipal work, Tom was well
in touch with the tendency of the times. Between 1882 and 1892 Labour
representatives on local bodies, including school boards and boards of
guardians, grew from twelve to two hundred; by 1895 they numbered six
hundred. The County Councils Act of 1888 provided new opportunities for
working class participation in local government but it was the new unionism,
wrote Ben Turner, that 'brought the new agencies of labour representation.
There were not 50 labour men on public bodies in all England before 1888
and not one independent labour man' (*About Myself*, p.102). This was the
road by which Tom Mann approached the question of representation on
local councils, linking this closely with trade union work. One of the main
functions he had hoped the *Trade Unionist* newspaper would serve was to
bring together the growing trades council movement throughout the country
and to encourage it in the sponsorship of municipal candidates.

Tom, however, did not leave union work to take part in managing a city,
nor did he long remain involved with the Fabians. Whatever his critics may
have thought, he himself still inclined to think it would be through organised
strength in trade unions and trades councils that the working class would find
political as well as industrial expression. 'It is not absolutely certain that it
will be through the agency of the Trades' Union Movement that the worker
will come right side up', he said at the Dockers' Second Annual Congress in
the autumn of 1891. 'It may not be, but I rather think it will, noting the
forces that are in action now.' (*Tom Mann's Presidential Address* &c, p.16).
Meanwhile he was also surveying another field of working class
activity — Co-operation.

During the years 1891-3 Tom paid a number of rousing visits to Co-
operative Societies up and down the country and local papers often filled
columns with his addresses. In particular he addressed the 24th Co-operative
Congress, held at Rochdale in June 1892, to honour the pioneers of 1844, at
which another prominent visitor was Beatrice Potter shortly to become Mrs.
Sidney Webb. The Fabians in their first conceptions of the paternal state and
municipal socialism (*Manifesto: Fabian Essays,* 1888) attributed no importance whatever to the existing organisations of the working class. The other
two socialist societies, the S.D.F. and the Socialist League, only saw one side
of the truth, namely that the Co-ops had not superseded capitalist

production and were steeped in liberalism and class collaboration.[23] But after the Dock Strike, under the influence of the 'to the People' movement in general and Beatrice Potter in particular, the Fabians widened their conception of 'permeation'.

The new tone was set by the address given to a conference of trade union officials and Co-operators at Tynemouth in August, 1892, later published as *The Relation between Co-operation and Trade Unionism* by Beatrice Potter (Mrs. Sydney Webb). Its theme, which deeply interested Tom Mann, was that the day of the small self-governing workshop or unit of Co-operative production was past, whilst trade unionism alone could not 'secure for the workers the rent and profit now made out of their labour'. 'Something more than mere trade combination is . . . required if we are to realise the ideal of a community of workers obtaining the full fruits of their labour. The good trade unionist must supplement his trade unionism by co-operation, local and national, and seek to substitute the community in one or other of its organisations for the private . . . rent receivers.'

It was, however, two months before this that Tom Mann had urged his view, that co-operation should be supplemented by loyalty to trade unionism so bringing together two wings of the mass movement.[24] He spoke to representatives of a movement which, the gentle J.N. Ludlow had told the Royal Commission that same year, 'is becoming very much more of a middle-class movement than it used to be and perhaps less advantageous to the working classes than I hoped at one time it would be' (Q. 1804). Old Holyoake, Chartist, secularist and first historian of the movement, conducted some of the Congress delegates to the graves of James Smithies, William Cooper and others of the 'Twenty-eight', but they paused first at the grave of John Bright where Holyoake's praises were as heartfelt as his tributes to the Rochdale pioneers. In 1890 the inaugural address to the Co-operative Congress had been delivered by Lord Rosebery; Manchester and Salford had celebrated their thirtieth anniversary with an address from the Catholic bishop of Salford, while the north-western section had listened at Huddersfield to the Anglican bishop of Ripon.

Tom Mann, in his address to the Rochdale Congress in 1892, strikes a new revolutionary note. As he speaks, pleading for socialist activity in every sphere of working class existence, co-operative society, trade union and municipal council, his never-failing consciousness of struggle transforms the Fabian analysis into passionate life. He calls for closer unity between co-ops and trade unions (let him go and preach to the T.U.C., grumbled a leading co-operator)[25], attacks the long hours worked by co-operative employees and the 'high divi' policy, calls for a new crusade in co-operative and municipal affairs, and audaciously summons co-operators to march in the great London May Day processions (again he is a pioneer):

'What an object lesson might have been given to statesmen, capitalists and workers on May Day last if when the tens of thousands marched to Hyde

Park there had been included . . . a properly representative contingent of the London branch of the Wholesale, which might have included, in addition to banners, well arranged speciments of Co-operative produce, all trade union made.'

'Material progress is made, the standard of living raised, but *not for all.* Who will embrace those whom *an imperfect organisation* now casts aside?' 'Is it consistent for a member of a co-operative store to declaim against the evils of competition and quietly to acquiesce in the working of overtime?' 'Very few members are prepared at present to encourage shorter hours for employees at the expense of less dividend . . . As yet there is no really healthy appreciation of trade union principles on the part of co-operators as a body nor of co-operative principles on the part of trade unionists. Even yet it is dividend, dividend, that is demanded, thereby exhibiting the pure capitalistic qualities.'

'How feeble have been the efforts of co-operators as such on municipal bodies.' They should be coming to the front 'openly and if need be combatively' and 'to prove to themselves and to all concerned the many-sidedness of the industrial movement', Co-operative candidates should be put 'in the field of municipal and political activity'. Control of state and municipal trading monopolies was a task for co-operators. There should be unity between Fabians, Co-operators and trade unionists: 'the three forces working harmoniously together ought ere long to lead us out of the present industrial wilderness'.

In London, with 200,000 trade unionists, the co-operative societies were miserably weak. Could not the movement

'send forth its missionaries not merely to arouse those who sleep but to counsel those who are grasping the principle . . . Propagandist activity, earnest passionate advocacy of the principles, persistent rappings at the doors of the respective trades organisations'.

A 'wider interpretation' of a co-operator's duties was wanted. 'Is not a co-operator a citizen?' Collective control of production, whether by State, municipality or co-operative society, involved divergence of interests between the representative body of consumers and the wage workers employed by them. This had been shown in the Leeds (municipal) gas strike and could be seen in every co-op store. Hence the need both for fully organised trade unions and for collaboration between town councils and trades councils.

All this led up to the conclusion that the co-operative and trade union movements are necessary complements of one another. Today there is too much friction and jealousy between them, Tom told the congress that their proper relation would be that of the ideal marriage. His speech met with an enthusiastic reception, the more so since he had recently been championing co-operation within the trade union movement.

The following September he was again urging the importance of co-operation on trade unionists. 'Trade unions enable us as wage earners to secure fair conditions for the time being, but we require to organise also as wage spenders', he said in his presidential address to the third annual congress of the Dockers' Union (*Third Annual Report*, p.84). He had given the matter great prominence at the previous congress, urging union members, and also their wives, to take a much greater part in the detailed voluntary work of the Co-operative movement (*Minutes of 2nd Annual Congress*, pp. 15-16). He also pressed the question of municipal factories or workshops and (at the 1892 Congress) linked the question of co-operative manufacturing establishments and municipal activity: 'The same principle that permeates the co-operative movement ought to permeate our municipal councillors.'

Later he presented the full case for replacement of the capitalist system by co-operative and municipal enterprise, through the joint power of the trade union and co-operative movements, at a meeting organised jointly by the Kettering Co-operative Society and Trades Council in December, 1893, in a lecture 'The Faults of our Present Industrial System — and How to Remedy Them'. The present industrial system, he is reported as saying (*Kettering Guardian,* December 8, 1893) 'was controlled for the profit making of a section instead of for the use of the general community'.

'But the time was coming when the reward for labour would be the total value created by the labourer . . . Co-operation, rightly understood, demanded all that. They would establish a condition of things which was spoken of of old: "If a man will not work neither shall he eat" . . . If they felt that trade ought to be conducted for use and not for profit and that the full profit should go to labour let them endorse Co-operation and Trades Unionism in all its forms. Let them do all they could through the Municipalities and Parliament so that trade ere long would be controlled in the public and not in the private interest . . .'

By contrast with the sectarianism of Hyndman and his fellows Tom in these years was alone in his restless visions of the '*many-sidedness of the industrial movement*' as he put it at the Rochdale Congress. His sense of the *power* of the organisations of the people—of the fruits within the people's grasp if only these organisations were rightly used—his broad, constructive approach to existing organisation—these were things which many a 'strict Socialist', proud of his superior knowledge, did not yet begin to understand.

REFERENCES

(1)   This passage occurs in a letter chiefly concerned with London's first May Day, quoted from further below

(2)   'Hot' money when the grain carried on the men's backs 'sweated'; 'dirty' money when it was so dusty that the men were half choked in the hold and needed drink; 'awkward' when the corn bunkers were so awkwardly placed that the wages earned collectively by each gang of seven were reduced

(3)   The London Trades Council annual report for 1890 records an increase of 25,354 members from 38 societies in 31 distinct industries, income risen from £156 to £385. (See also, *London Trades Council 1860—1950,* 1950, pp.70—1)

(4)   *London Trades Council Minutes,* June 5, 1890
Tom Mann's part in this is referred to in *London Trades Council* (pp. 71—2). The attack on Shipton was opened 'by the compositors' delegates, Matthews and Marks, who suggested that the Council should not re-elect him as he had lost the confidence of his own society, which for the first time since 1880, had not re-elected him its Secretary. After an interval of utter confusion, in which Mann carried on a discussion with the chairman (C.J. Drummond of the London Society of Compositors) from the floor, agreement was reached on procedure. The only speakers were Mann "as opposed to the present secretary" and James Macdonald, who had proposed F. Hammill (A.S.E.) for the secretaryship, and then Shipton replied. Shipton was re-elected by sixty-one votes to forty-six, and the meeting terminated on a note of amiable compromise. Mann said he was satisfied with the decision and wished to work for the general good of the Council; Shipton declared his willingness to do all in his power to discharge his duties in harmony with the feeling of the minority. The old dominant group had not been ousted, but had been compelled to move with the new powerful current in the trade union world. It was this basis of compromise which characterised the Council in ensuing years, though that is not to say that there was no friction'

(5)   *The 'New' Trades Unionism. A reply to Mr. George Shipton* by Tom Mann and Ben Tillett, June, 1890 (a penny pamphlet). Shipton published *A reply to Messrs. Tom Mann and Ben Tillett's Pamphlet etc.* 1890

(6)   'The Heir Apparent to the Throne, His Royal Highness the Prince of Wales, has entertained the representatives of Labour, delegates to the London Trades Council and others, though some of them were roundly abused for their acceptance of the invitation to visit Sandringham'. G. Howell, *Conflicts of Capital and Labour,* 2nd. ed. 1890, p.489

(7)   Burgess was made editor of the *Workman's Times* by its proprietor after recommending that it 'should deal with Labour politics from the independent point of view and it should not be afraid of socialism.' (J. Burgess, *John Burns,* 1911, p. 148)

(8)   *Life of Joseph Chamberlain* (1932) II, p.508

(9)   His relations with Hyndman were, however, later friendly and after his return from Australia in 1910 he joined the Social Democratic Party, as it had then become, for a short time. He later joined the British Socialist Party on its formation in 1916, thus becoming a foundation member of the Communist Party in 1920

(10)   'The task of Social-Democracy is . . . to divert the labour movement, with its spontaneous trade unionist striving from under the wing of the bourgeoisie and to

bring it under the wing of revolutionary Social-Democracy . . . Social-Democrats lead the struggle of the working class not only for better terms for the sale of labour power, but also for the abolition of the social system which compels the propertyless to sell themselves to the rich'.(*What is to be Done?* (1902), *Selected Works,* ii,pp. 62–3, 78)

(11)   *(Dockers' Record,* October, 1890.) Later he was to press a scheme for munici-palisation of the docks as a truer solution to the problem

(12)   *(Memoirs,* pp. 256-7.) Tom, recalling the early days when he worked with Wilson at a time when the latter's name was synonymous in the trade union movement with conceit and dictatorial reaction, emphasised that, however much their views differed, he had then 'always found him a straight-forward, honourable and loyal comrade. Moreover he was always at his post early in the day, tackling the most difficult tasks with the utmost readiness '

(13)   See Ben Tillett, 'What is Free Labour?', *Dockers' Record,* October, 1890; J. Havelock Wilson, *My Stormy Voyage Through Life,* 1925, I, pp. 209-11

(14)   Tillett, *Memories,* pp. 172-3; *Sir James Sexton, Agitator,* 1935 chapter 15; *Report of Commission of Enquiry into Conditions of Labour on the Docks,* 1895

(15)   Unions federated included the Gasworkers, Dockers, Sailors and Firemen, General Railway Workers; and the South Side Labour Protection League with some twenty smaller unions covering watermen, lightermen, crane-drivers, ship repair workers, bargemen and coal porters

(16)   *Royal Commission on Labour* B 8614-8847: Appendices 25, 55, 57. *Third Annual Report of Dockers' Union,* 1892, p.7. Even so they proved unsatis-factory and, often failing to secure much-needed amendments, the Dockers Union had to withdraw at the close of 1892 and the Federation came to an end

(17)   The union also contributed £1 a week to his income (the John Burns Wages Fund) until September, 1894

(18)   This and the following letters are preserved in the British Museum; additional MSS 46286, Burns' letters in draft or as copies

(19)   A deputation from the Bradford Labour Union had waited upon the congress and asked for its authority to nominate Tillett as candidate. After Ben had declared that 'should he be successfully returned to Parliament, and he found his secre-tarial duties (for the union) seriously interfered with he would unhesitatingly retire from Parliament', a resolution approving his candidature was passed by 22 votes to 3. *Minutes of 2nd Annual Congress,* September 1891, pp. 25-6

(20)   *(Workman's Times,* May 8, 1891.) He then refused: 'My work *outside* the House of Commons is the most important, more valuable than any could be *inside*' but some months later agreed to stand for West Bradford. Tom confessed long after that in refusing Ben had acted under his advice. (*Clarion,* September 24, 1909)

(21)   The interview was republished in the *Yorkshire Factory Times,* August 28, 1891, under the heading: 'Mr. Tom Mann and Direct Labour Representation. "Not anxious to run Labour Candidates". Strange Attitude '

(22)   This was one of Tom's efforts to shake up the A.S.E. by an energetic propaganda campaign—which intensified when he put up for the general secretaryship in 1892. He narrowly missed election, polling 17,152 votes as against John Anderson's 18,102

(23)   After Chartism 'so called Co-operation began to flourish: it was really an improved form of joint stockery, which could be engaged in by workmen but was

and is fondly thought by some to be, if not a shoeing horn of Socialism at least a substitute for it'. (W. Morris and Belfort Bax, *Socialism, its Growth and Outcome*, 1893, p. 181)

(24)   *The Duties of Co-operators in regard to the Hours and Conditions of Labour*, by Mr. Tom Mann, President of the Dockers' Union, Manchester. (Paper read at the 24th Annual Congress of Co-operative Societies, Rochdale, June 1892)

(25)   *Workman's Times*, June 18, 1891

ERIC HOBSBAWM

The Lesser Fabians

Probably no part of the modern British socialist movement has attracted so much research since the war as the early Fabian Society. There are a number of doctorate theses about it in print and in typescript. Mrs. Margaret Cole has published what amounts to its new official history. The numerous historians, who have studied the origins and early years of the Labour Party, have also had their say about it. Consequently the general nature of the Fabians and their contribution to the labour movement before the first world war—after 1914 it ceases to be of any importance for some decades—is by now quite well understood.

We know that there is no truth in several myths propagated by the first official Fabian history, Edward Pease's. The Fabians did not start as a gradualist movement, but only developed into one towards the end of the 1880s, largely under the influence of Sidney Webb and his 'old gang', which dominated the society thereafter. They were in no sense the pioneers of the Labour Party. On the contrary, they put their money on the 'permeation' of the Liberal Party and at certain moments sections of the imperialists and higher civil servants. They opposed the formation of the ILP, missed the opportunity of leading the movement for an independent labour party, and though they joined the Labour Representation Committee, they almost resigned from it in the early years, and paid no attention to the young Labour Party until the permeation policy had become evidently bankrupt just before 1914. Moreover though their gift for public relations has led many people to believe in their and the Webbs' remarkable success in influencing the development of local government, education and social legislation, in fact most research shows that their influence has been very much exaggerated.

Time rather than research has also led us to another revision of Fabian history. Like Edward Pease, most marxists have claimed that the Fabians' major achievement was to turn the British labour movement away from Marx and towards a gradualist social democracy. This is undoubtedly correct. More than this: they actually provided much of the ideological foundation

231

for continental revisionism, as Eduard Bernstein, its founder who knew them well in London, admitted. Of course, here again it is easy to exaggerate the Fabians' independent contribution: there were enough powerful reformist elements in the British labour movement even without Sidney Webb. However, what is more obvious now than it was in the past is that by the standards of the Labour Party today, Sidney Webb and the early Fabians were not extreme reformists but dangerous radicals. They, or rather the Webbs and Shaw, took socialism seriously, as is shown by their subsequent political evolution. They never doubted that it meant the socialisation of the means of production, distribution and exchange, and they eventually recognised in the Soviet Union the pioneer of a new civilisation. This does not offset the fact that, for most of their political lifetime, their powerful influence was thrown onto the side of the right wing of the labour movement; but it should not be forgotten. They were, marxists will think, for most of their life mistaken about the tactics of achieving socialism, but in the end the Webbs and Shaw frankly admitted their mistake.

In general, therefore, the picture of early Fabianism is reasonably clear. In detail, however, there are many aspects of it which are still unknown, or known only to a handful of research workers. One of these is the nature of the ideas of the lesser contributors to the famous *Fabian Essays* of 1889, a book which, like so many important books in the history of the socialist movement, is more often referred to than read. The following pages deal with these men: Hubert Bland, William Clarke, Graham Wallas and Sydney Olivier. Mrs. Besant has been omitted, since she can hardly be classified as a Fabian and her connexion with the society was shortlived anyway. They illustrate the complexity of the intellectual and social elements which went to form the early British socialist movement of the 1880s and the original Fabian Society. They also illustrate the absorption of Fabianism by Sidney Webb, which gradually eliminated the other elements or allowed them to drop out of sight.

No biography of Bland exists, but that of his wife (*Doris Langley Moore*, E. Nesbitt, 1933) contains much material. For his ideas *Essays by Hubert* (1914) is important. A biographical memoir and selection of articles by Clarke is available in J.A. Hobson and H. Burrows, *William Clarke* (1908). There is no biography of Wallas, but cf. *Economica* XII (1935) 395 ff and *Political Quarterly*, 1932, pp 461 ff. For Olivier, see M. Olivier, *Sydney Olivier, Letters and Selected Writings* (with a memoir, 1948). But most of the following discussion is based on the writings of these men in *Fabian Essays*, in socialist and other publications of the 1880s and 1890s, on letters and other material in the Fabian Society archives, the Wallas papers, and on references in the works of other contemporaries.

I

Hubert Bland (1855-1914) was in many ways the most anomalous of the
leading Fabians. A Tory and imperialist by origin, where others came from,
or via Liberalism, he came to socialism via aestheticism and William Morris.
An open distruster of the theory that all collectivism was socialist, one is not
surprised to find him at daggers drawn with Webb, and a permanent opposition within the Fabian Executive. Most readers of *Fabian Essays* will have
been struck by the fact that Bland's dissents completely from Webb's whose
ideas it describes as 'sham socialism', (pp. 212-213). R.C.K. Ensor was to
make this contrast into the basis of an extremely acute analysis of Fabian
policy later. For Bland, as for other socialists, the impracticability of violent
revolution had been demonstrated in the middle 80s; though not its undesir-
ability. He concluded somewhat in the manner of Hyndman and German
Social-Democrats, that it was impossible until 'the capitalist system has
worked itself out to its last logical expression'—'the well-defined confron-
tation of rich and poor' (pp. 202-3); a point of view with which even Shaw on
occasions showed sympathy. Like most others he envisaged the struggle as a
political one, fought between a party of the masses and a party of privilege, a
split forecast by the Home Rule crisis of 1886; like many others he did not
exclude a gradual transition to socialism. But 'the ballot box (is) merely a
war-engine with which to attack capitalism' (pp. 202-3). In the long run the
interests of capitalists and workers were incompatible, though the fact that
Radicals and Socialists shared a desire to extend democratic rights blinded
many Fabians to this. The 'conversion' of the Liberals was an illusion, based
on the inadmissible identification of 'state control' and 'socialism', and the
belief of the imperceptible passing of capitalism into its opposite. To rely on
changing the character of the Liberal Party by pressure from within was to
make a ridiculous underestimation of the adaptability, patience and delaying
power of capitalist politicians, and might well lead merely to harnessing the
socialist horse to the capitalist cart.

   Essentially this was a slightly more sophisticated version of the social-
democratic and marxist case against Fabian permeation; and Bland was, of
course, an active member of the Social Democratic Federation. Beyond a
conviction that something more was wanted than doctrinaire street-corner
propaganda he had little in common with his colleagues. His criticisms of
Webb's views were particularly acute, being clearly based on close
acquaintance. Thus he was the first to notice the dual nature of
'permeation'—the belief that Liberals could be *converted* to socialism, held
simultaneously with the belief that they may have to be coerced by mass
pressure. Thus again there was effective venom in the description—clearly
aimed at Webb—of the

   'not yet wholly socialised Radicals or Socialists who have recently broken
   away from mere political Radicalism and are still largely under its influ-

ence of party ties and traditions. They are in many cases on terms of intimate private friendship with some of the lesser lights of Radicalism and occasionally bask in the patronising radiance shed by the larger luminaries. A certain portion of the "advanced" press is open to them . . . Of course none of these considerations . . . reflect in the very least on their motives or their sincerity; but they do colour their judgment . . .' (p. 215)

And Bland was the first Fabian clearly to describe Bismarck's policy as one of 'erecting timely legislative breakwaters' against the 'swelling tide of socialism'. (p. 210) Why did he then remain in the Fabian leadership? One can't escape the impression that it was largely to assert his right to do so, as an original member, against the reformist interlopers of later years; but it is difficult to see why he did not transfer his activity to the Independent Labour Party as well, as so many others did. However, as the years went on, his uncompromising radicalism mellowed a little. Palliatives (the word is still redolent of Hyndman) 'came into the way of our direct march'—but they were necessary, and in any case they were 'symptoms of a disease we could not cure, but only alleviate'.[1] The fault lay not in adopting reformism, but in allowing socialism to be 'lost sight of altogether'—as for example, in the Webbs' Minority Report. But as Bland aged, and Socialism came no nearer, one can understand such concessions.

Yet if his objection to Webb and Liberals made Bland an acute critic of 'permeation', his natural conservatism blinded him to very similar weaknesses on the other side. 'The usefulness of the Society' he wrote to Pease at the time of the Boer War 'will be entirely crippled if we throw ourselves dead athwart the Imperialist or any other strong streams of tendency . . . We may possibly be able to do for 'sane' Imperialism what we have already done for 'sane' Socialism'.[2] If Webb's views on Liberals had been illusions, then so were Bland's on Conservatives; and one sympathises with Olivier who jeered about 'sane imperialism—the corned beef as distinct from the roast beef party'.[3] So Bland continued, 'holding a watching brief for the Carlton and Army and Navy',[4] sporting his bourgeois morning dress and monocle, with as much care as Shaw his Jaeger suit, maintaining his Catholicism and his suburban mistresses with holy pride, running a sprawling bohemian menage, writing his articles in the *Sunday Chronicle* for northern artisans, and prevented from spiting Webb only when his inborn toryism drove him together with the remainder of the old gang against younger rebels. He was, by all accounts, an unpleasant personality, but a great debater, and one whose writing occasionally compels a reluctant respect. If he frittered away his talents, they must have been considerable, for in the company of Shaw, Webb and Wallas he somehow held his own.

II

William Clarke's case (1852-1901) is far more instructive. He represented a trend whose importance in British life has rarely been recognised because it has never, as on the continent, been organised in independent parties, leftwing, anticlerical and radical: the Mazzinian or Camille Pelletan type. Clarke, like H.W. Massingham, was a pure specimen of the radical intellectual, whose genuine enthusiasm for democracy did not stop short with the achievement of political reform but pressed on logically towards the economic reform which alone could give reality to the political. He was an admirer of Mazzini and Whitman and his able political theory was a logical attempt to put the absolutely desirable concept of 'democracy' in a definite historical setting, with the help of the marxist analysis, though Clarke appears, personally, to have been opposed to political Marxism.

The democratic movement, of which Radicalism and Socialism were parts, the theory ran, was not the result of accident, but of specific nineteenth century conditions, for

'the massing of men together changes the conditions of production and distribution, creates vast and striking inequalities of human condition, and so produces the social forces from which democratic progress springs'.[5]

The development of capitalism, tending inevitably towards the victory of trusts and monopolies (Clarke travelled and lectured much in the U.S.A.) merely intensified this trend. Two things followed from this analysis. One was that the attempt to turn the clock back by trust-busting or 'three-acres and a cow' was doomed and useless: unless there was to be socialism, there would be monopoly capitalism and not a hypothetical free enterprise economy. Clarke made this point more strongly than most; and it may explain why his *Fabian Essay* was the most universally popular of all, for both Marxists and Webbians united in their firm conviction, as against cooperators, Owenites and others, that the past was irrevocably dead. Only later did some, like the Webbs, absorb the doubts of orthodox economists and query the inevitable progress of monopoly capitalism. The second conclusion was, that capitalism became progressively less compatible with democracy.

'Liberty to trade, liberty to exchange products, liberty to buy where one pleases . . . subjection to no imperium in imperio; these surely are all fundamental democratic principles. Yet by monopolies every one of them is either limited or denied. Thus capitalism is apparently inconsistent with democracy as hitherto understood . . . Collision between the opposing forces is inevitable' (p.98).

Clarke was at considerable pains to divorce democracy from capitalism, the democratic movement from laissez faire and Cobdenism, which 'intrudes into the legitimate succession' of radicalism. Democracy was in the interests of all; though social developments made the town workers into its chief carriers. The intrusion of the middle class and the British party system had obscured this; but fortunately with the breakdown of the party system largely through the 'entering wedge of the socialist movement', it was once again becoming clear. Presumably because a democratic movement now existed free from the disturbing influence of also having to stand for certain vested interests. Fortunately English economic development, and hence English social legislation, was more advanced than that of other countries. Democracy in its social and industrial aspects, i.e. socialism, was therefore likely to grow without those 'wider developments of revolutionary socialism'[6] of the continent 'identical though its doctrines may be at bottom with those of Marx'.[7] Thus for instance, English socialism was likely to be decentralised, not centralised as in the marxian pattern. But while Clarke desired nothing more than the end of the class war the existence of which he assumed, he had no illusions about socialism by consent. Liberals must be pushed to the left by the pressure of the organised working class vote, and perhaps by such pressure as that exercised in the early '80's by the Irish and their satellite Scots and Welsh movements; for 'Ireland is the nemesis of the English ruling class' and aimed at economic and social revolution, as the Land Act of 1881 showed.[8]

Democracy (I can find no clear definition of the term in Clarke) was an end in itself. But was it also an effective, practical system of government? Clarke took some trouble to defend it against the traditional criticisms of sluggishness, timidity and conservatism. Democracy *could* exercise volition. The very fact that it was now turning to the solution of administrative problems, the question of poverty and industrial organisation, proved that it was progressive, certainly more so than the orthodox parties which refused to face these problems. But this suppleness and awareness of democracy was not accidental. It was in tune with science, not only because it depended on social and technical conditions which also made possible the advance of science, but even more so because it relied on a scientific analysis of social development and thus 'carries science to a higher point'. Here lay the importance of Marx. 'Ricardo merely states what is, Marx shows why it is. As soon as people grasp the main points of Marx they will change what is into what ought to be'—for, of course, the recognition of historical trends did not mean that democrats waited for their spontaneous working out. 'The time will come when the general drift of Marx's explanation of the economic evolution will be as much an article of faith of the social creed as is Darwin's explanation of biological evolution'.[9] Scientific socialism thus 'affords the groundwork of an art of social life—i.e., for the application in the State of the results of economic knowledge.' On this basis democracy rested secure.

This analysis had, it is clear, numerous points of contact with the

Fabianism of 1888; and its practical conclusions were the same, though Clarke was not a regular member of the discussion circles which hammered out Fabian theory. Yet, even if we did not know of his frictions with Shaw, his furious detestation of 'permeation' and his belief that the Fabians had no 'ultimate aims' or if they had, they differed from his own,[10] it is equally clear that the points of contact were limited. Webb derived from orthodox intellectuals, administrators and businessmen anxious to develop a theory more in accordance with the facts of post-laissez-faire than that current in 1850-70; Beatrice from the social conscience; Shaw, for personal reasons, sank his private rebelliousness in Webb's reformism. But Clarke derived from generations of radical cobblers, pamphleteers and artisans, halfway between manufacturers and factory-workers, fighting a life-long struggle for 'freedom' against 'privilege'—the always active, always submerged tradition of British Jacobinism. Between Chartism and the 1880's it had hoped to achieve its millenial ends through an alliance with business; now it was once again prepared to strike out independently. Sooner or later the current would carry most British Jacobins towards a sort of socialism, and into the Labour Party. But what distinguished Clarke's knot of petty-bourgeois intellectuals from Fabians and other socialist pioneers was their unshakable, religious, belief in Liberalism as the cause of Progress and their reluctance to break with it until it collapsed into the arms of the 1916 Coalition. While the Fabians moved in the orbit of the liberal radicalism, the Jacobins gravitated towards them; Clarke, Massingham and others. When they moved away from it, they shrank back. Gradually a knot of such left-wing liberals, often, as individuals, much more radical than many Fabians or I.L.P.ers formed outside socialist groups and clustered round various newspapers and reviews, such as the *Progressive Review* (Clarke, J.A. Hobson, Massingham) and later the *Echo* and *Daily News*. They had their brief day after the Boer War, when they appear, with the help of other radical groups in the Party, to have persuaded the Liberal Party into collectivism, as the Fabians had vainly attempted to do in 1888-93. They were undoubtedly the intellectual begetters of Lloyd Georgeism, not merely, like the Webbs, the drafters of some of its reform measures. But by that time William Clarke was dead. He had resigned from the Fabian Society in 1897, after some years of inactivity.

Clarke's peculiar contribution to this left-liberal group lay in his attempt to base the future of democracy squarely on the Marxist historical analysis; but like so many left-wingers in the '80's, he vastly overrated the speed of the approaching capitalist crisis. The end of the Great Depression, the victory of Imperialism and jingoism among the broad masses thus left him peculiarly defenceless. Mazzinian democracy rested on the assumption that men desired it as an absolute end. This was not so. There was not, Clarke concluded in 1899, a general trend towards democracy, as he had previously supposed. The ideal of the English people 'does not include what they understand as liberty, it does not include the faintest aspiration towards equality'.[11] But the iron laws of capitalist development could not be broken, and Britain was falling behind in industrial development. Imperialism could not permanently help it. It thus faced the choice either of becoming an agrarian peasant country, or, more likely, a parasitic playground for the U.S.A. and the dominions. But this would not be compatible with democracy. Elsewhere in Europe democracy might go on evolving, though probably not along parliamentary lines. Clarke's 'Social Future of England' said little which was not also said by Shaw's plays, by Hobson's *Imperialism*, in forgotten articles which recorded the disillusionment of the radical left between 1895 and 1900, the horror at the discovery that the stream of progress had apparently suddenly reversed itself; the despair, often unacknowledged, of ever achieving socialism. Clarke's despair, however, is more poignant and more terrible even than Shaw's, for the dispassionate logic in which it was expressed. He had long felt it. As the 1890s drew on, he had gradually withdrawn from active politics, from propaganda and from much political journalism and concentrated on writing essays and middles, chiefly in the Spectator. He had made a career as a leading political journalist, not merely through the 'self-help' of the young East Anglian noncollegiate student at Cambridge, but as part of a campaign for the 'cause'. He had succeeded because the provincial lecturing, the voluminous journalism happened, after 1870, to have become a fairly lucrative profession rather than because he had set out to earn money. He had succeeded in making a living, but failed in fighting for democracy.

The photographs show a clumsy, sad-looking man with thin hair and light eyes; one cannot help feeling that there was something roman about this awkward, underrated figure. Certainly he was a writer of clarity and power.

III

Graham Wallas (1858-1932) shared some things with Clarke: a fervent belief in Liberalism, the instincts and automatic gestures of liberal democracy, and a relatively brief stay in the Fabian Society, which he left because of his objection to its anti-liberal trend. It is no accident that he was, and Clarke was not, a member of the original quadrumvirate which formulated Fabian ideas. Perhaps because he came not from struggling East Anglians and a non-collegiate career at Cambridge, but from Shrewsbury and Corpus Christi, Oxford, he was far more of a moralist, and certainly a more ingrained gradualist. In fact, with Webb, he was the most 'instinctive' gradualist among the Fabian leaders. However, we have less direct information about his Fabian views than we would like; for, with the exception of his Fabian Essay, he wrote little on political subjects but scattered articles until after his resignation. The *Life of Place* may be regarded as an example of Fabianism in action, but its political theory is implied, if not allegorical. Nor does the Fabian Essay on 'Property' fill the gap, being little but a series of extremely able footnotes to now forgotten controversies of the '80s, interspersed with moving moral reflections. Wallas was undoubtedly the best academic brain among the brilliant Fabian group; though, as he was to discover, the right outlet for his fervent moral passion for social service was to prove not politics but educational administration, and above all, teaching. By all accounts he was a teacher of the very highest gifts. Certainly the best of him went into the long series of lectures and classes, first in adult education, later at the London School of Economics, which have been largely lost. Much of our picture of his Fabianism must therefore be pieced together from fragments.

Wallas' earliest socialist article—he joined the Fabians in 1886, though he had known Webb since 1882, through Olivier, a fellow Oxonian—was concerned, typically enough, with 'Personal Duty under the Present System'. Wallas indeed approached socialism primarily, one might say exclusively, as one concerned with standards of personal behaviour: driven by the social conscience, impelled by a revolt against 'faith'; his first overt act of rebellion was to resign from his position as a master at Highgate school 'on a question of religious conformity'. The social conscience led him to socialism, doubt and rationalism to the belief in gradualness. Clearly individualism had to be rejected, or interpreted in the elastic manner of Mill's utilitarianism, to allow for selfless service to the community. But once it had been so reinterpreted, as Sidgwick pointed out, the case against socialism was one of pure expediency. Wallas, younger than Sidgwick, had fewer inhibitions about associating the term with the specific programme of the collectivisation of the means of production, and declaring it as a nobler ideal of life than individualism.

Yet in one respect Wallas' conception of socialism was similar to the vaguer ones of his predecessors: the only vested interests it recognised as standing in its way were ignorance and sluggishness, the only obstacles technical ones inherent in the nature of so great a social transformation and (this is where Wallas made his peculiar contribution to the social sciences), in the nature of political man and political operations in the modern world. 'Socialism hangs above them . . . ready for them if they will but lift their eyes'; (pp. 148-9) 'if once we can get the working man to understand how easy it is to get national education paid for out of that surplus product of their labour which is at present absorbed by the monopolist classes, it is difficult to say what may not follow'.[12] Hence Wallas' impatience with the controversies between Jevons and Marx, purely verbal arguments as he thought, to be solved on a pragmatic basis in favour of Jevons.

But this attitude was saved from utopianism by Wallas' brand of rationalism, and transformed into a far subtler theory of gradualism than that of any other Fabian. There were two possible ways of approaching political problems, the religious and the scientific. The religious propaganda for a pure faith neglected opportunities for compromise in the hope of a more complete success in the future. But history had shown that such tactics must either succeed completely or fail completely, for if they failed to achieve their object, they would have made no impression at all on the institutions they set out to overthrow. This Wallas believed to have been the case with Chartism. But if they succeeded, would they not then, like the original Christian Church, sweep away in their triumph all achievements of the past, including the unquestionably good ones like Greek thought and Roman law? The scientific method, on the other hand, meant constant doubt. True, in 'watch(ing) the way each principle works . . . and ascertaining its limit of validity'[13] there was the danger that analysis would impede action, but the results would be better and more lasting. Moreover, history showed that social changes proceeded slowly. The change from one society to another was the gradual rearrangement of a pattern of life, in accordance with the 'slow and often unconscious progress of the time-spirit', (p. 131) though the rearrangement could be speeded up by determined bodies of men with clear ideas. A cautious, compromising, realistic policy of slow changes, of small increments either way, small but cumulative reforms would therefore be the best. To speak of the achievement of socialism as though it were the storming of a fortress was wrong. There was no fortress, because there was no 'enemy': capitalism and exploitation were not 'single fact(s) to be destroyed by the shock tactics of class war and forcible revolution.'[14] Moreover as a matter of fact, the most powerful engine of social change was one which least lent itself to the military metaphor: it was the growth of social passion. Wallas was the one Fabian who said, loudly and unambiguously:

'We rejoice that the common social feeling which we like all other men are conscious of, is yearly increasing now, and is likely to increase still faster in the future. We rely on that as the motive power that will drive the engine of reform.'[15]

Like Clarke, Wallas too had made his politics depend on one assumption, which seemed axiomatic in 1890, but less convincing subsequently.

Wallas' Fabianism was thus so 'natural' and so much in tune with the trend of the Fabian discussions, that it is not surprising to find, in practice, that it was indistinct from the more precise versions of Shaw and Webb. Where it reinforced them, it found no independent expression; where it differed, it was as yet in so subtle and intangible a form that it hardly seemed important. It was only after his breach with the Society that the personal Wallas emerged; and this is not therefore the place to outline or to assess the work of the author of *Human Nature in Politics* and the *Great Society* which no longer fit into the Fabian framework into which the earlier Wallas had still fitted. Why did he cut loose? Ostensibly because of disagreements on policy and political attitude. But behind these there was perhaps another disagreement: on personal duty, on the essentials of socialism. Increasingly Wallas had become dissatisfied with the belief, upon which the Fabians acted, that the transition to socialism must be envisaged in terms of economic and administrative reforms alone, that the Fabians had 'no distinctive opinions' outside their specific sphere of 'practical democracy and socialism'; though they had never claimed that this would solve all problems. He had protested, more strongly than the others, against the marxist 'economic interpretation of history'—'the narrow and mechanical reference of all human actions to economic motives'.[16] He had stated in print, even earlier than Shaw, the power of human personality to overcome—or at any rate to short-circuit—historical development. Where Shaw and Webb retained the traditional socialist assumptions that the economic solution of the problems of capitalism must be the condition of the solution of the moral ones, if they did not automatically lead to it, Wallas, acutely conscious that socialism was not the 'only condition of human happiness' (p. 148) slipped easily into dealing chiefly with its other conditions. The historian of reforming tactics became the analyst of social and political psychology. Perhaps the disappointment of the '90s played its part in this too, perhaps the experience of the political committee of the Eleusis Radical Club and the experience of school-board and London County Council would have, in any case, led him to query orthodox liberal-democratic theory in his way, as the Webbs queried it in theirs, and as dozens of scholars and investigators all over Europe were querying it at the same time. However, the Wallas of *Human Nature* and the *Great Society* was no longer a Fabian, except in the sense that all progressive Englishmen interested in social reform were Fabians; and social reform was an increasingly subordinate interest with him. He was, as he had always been, a liberal, in the broadest sense; emphasising 'toleration' perhaps a shade more than 'equality'; 'peace', for which he fought hard and actively with men like Lowes Dickinson, rather more than the abolition of exploitation; an occasional ally of the Webbs, but chiefly and increasingly, a teacher. He was even doubtful whether he could any longer call himself a socialist.

IV

Like Wallas, *Sydney Olivier* (1859-1943) came to socialism as a member of the upper class burning to save his soul through service. It is this, indeed, which linked him with Fabianism, with which otherwise he had little emotional sympathy. There is no doubt of his fervour. 'The activity (of socialists)', he wrote in his Fabian Essay, typically enough on the Moral Basis of socialism, 'is followed because it is seen to be reasonable, because it is the path indicated by common sense towards the satisfaction of the individual passion for the extension of freedom and love', (p. 120) and throughout his early years we find many echoes of his original Positivism. He had earlier rejected Marx precisely because he appeared to him to underrate the importance of disinterested social dedication, and indeed, by the insistence on the class basis of socialism, to discourage it. Clearly it was this, as well as the usual dissatisfaction with the inadequacies of early socialist tactics, which made Olivier anxious to discover a theory of socialism which would suit people like himself; and, together with his three friends, to formulate it. Yet once the Oxford man had been granted his specific place in the fight for Socialism, Olivier was prepared to make him a strong radical. He was an active member of the revolutionary Social Democratic Federation and a contributor to its paper *Justice*, even while writing his Fabian Essay (which, incidentally, continues to speak of 'social revolution'). Within the Society he was a consistent supporter of the left; every group of rebels against the 'old gang' from the early '90s to H.G. Wells could normally rely on his active help; especially on imperial questions, for the eminent colonial civil servant was a fire-eating anti-imperialist. For of course if socialism was too big a matter for the proletariat alone, it was also too big to be cramped into Webb's framework of administrative and economic reform. Why did not the Society take a stand against the Boer War? The official Fabian attitude that 'we are not well enough informed about the problem, and will arrange a winter course of lectures on it' petrified him.[17]

> 'Imperialism is . . . a living power because it represents a sort of primitive avatar of real elementary force; certain very successful methods and discoveries of the low-grade will-to-live . . . you can't get ahead of a real elementary force except by going better in elementary force yourself. That is what the Liberal Party did once aspire to do and succeeded in doing: that is what Socialism came to the front with and formed, inter alia, the Fabian Society. And if the Society . . . or the Executive should suppose that the question of this war in South Africa does not concern it, or should fail, after facing it, to come to one particular and definite line of conclusion, it will mean that the dry-rot that has collared the Liberal Party . . . has also got hold of the Fabian Society, and really there is no further reason for its separate existence.'

The outburst is typical of Olivier; the criticism curiously parallel to Wallas'; nor was Olivier answered by being fobbed off as 'always the enfant terrible of the Society, subject to sudden and feverish outbursts, the results doubtless of compulsory restraint in another place'.[18] Few Fabians could genuinely share Webb's reaction to the 'slump in socialism', to draw in his horns, and in the interests of 'practical success' to limit his proposals and plans to a progressively narrow field, until their connexion with socialism seem, to the outside world, remote. Moreover, of course, Olivier's interests had always been peripheral to Webb's Fabianism. The subjects which he burned to discuss—morality and ethics, 'Socialist Individualism', socialism and the family, foreign trade, art and literature, and above all, colonial problems were mostly those on which the Fabian Society had then no special opinion. He was even heard to cast doubts on the traditional Fabian economic analysis, the 'rent' theory which was the cornerstone of the Society's Basis. Fortunately, however, Olivier's career as a distinguished public servant kept him frequently abroad, and very much out of the active socialist movement after 1890. He therefore did not suffer so violent a depression as other socialists, and retained his connexion with the Society, though resigning from its Executive over South Africa. Certainly he maintained enough buoyancy to welcome H.G. Wells as an ally in the attempt to reform it.

Olivier's smaller articles and lectures, so far as I am aware, contain merely a series of supplements to standard socialist discussion; some of them not peculiar to him; speculations about the disintegration of great towns and the growth of the simple life under socialism, predictions of the supersession of the family, tempered by reminders of the strength of the family instinct and so on. But in the Fabian Essay we do detect something of the specifically Olivierian approach, embedded in much that was common ground to all the Essayists except Bland. Socialism, whatever else it may be, is 'primarily a property form . . . an industrial system for the supply of the material requisites of human social existence.' (pp. 103-12)

The moral justification of socialism is utilitarian: as a system better able than the existing one to supply the material needs, and to create the conditions for 'the realisation in individuals and in the State of the highest morality as yet imagined by us'. But morality itself is at bottom social—outside society moral standards cannot exist, inside it, 'those actions and habits are approved as moral which tend to preserve the existence of society and the cohesion and convenance of its members' and the other way round. The progress of moral ideas is 'the progress of discovery of the most reasonable manner of ordering the life of the individual and the form of social institutions under the contemporary environment'. The ideal morality would be one in which the moral would be regarded merely as rational, the immoral as irrational, diseased or insane. Of course among the social forces shaping morality we must count not merely the material desires, but the 'social instincts' without which no society could in any case exist. In fact, therefore, the 'intricate tissue of moral consciousness' from which moral decision and action arises is 'the recognition by each individual of his dependence on society or sensitiveness to its interest'. (p. 127)

But as society changes (and here Olivier echoes the marxian theme) moralities which were previously socially useful become so merely to a minority which rules the society, no longer to the majority of its members. But precisely at the point where the parallel marxian argument announces: here begins an epoch of revolutions, Olivier, Comtist and Fabian, argues: here begins the re-education of the rulers. This, however, can only be done by and through a change of social institutions. But the social institutions are being changed every day. The factory system, machine industry, etc., have abolished individualist production. Ethics must follow suit. Indeed they do. 'The expectation is already justified by the phenomena of contemporary opinion. The moral ideas appropriate to Socialism are permeating the whole of modern society. They are clearly recognisable, not only in the proletariat, but also in the increasing philanthropic activity of the members of the propertied class who, while denouncing Socialism as a dangerous exaggeration of what is necessary for social health, work honestly enough for the alleviatory reforms which converge irresistibly towards it'. (p. 127)

Olivier had arrived where he began in his protest against the 'perverse socialism' of the Marxists. The argument, with its semi-posivitist background, is very Oliverian; yet it fits easily into the general Fabianism of his colleagues. Perhaps a shade too easily. For, at bottom, the element which kept Wallas and Olivier together with Shaw and Webb was a common faith in the growth of social love as a practical alternative to social revolution, not merely a desirable one; just as the heterogeneous crowd of mid-eighties' socialists had been kept together by a common belief in the imminent end of capitalism. Both were illusions. When one disappeared, the movement of the 80's broke up. When the other disappeared, or was seriously weakened for several years, the Fabians too tended to break up. What remained for the decade of 1895-1905 was the Webbs, and a small and unimportant group carrying out their personal policy. After 1905 even that came under attack.

REFERENCES

(1)   To E. Pearse, 5.11.1911 (Fabian Archives)
(2)   To E. Pearse, 17.10.1899 (ibid)
(3)   Olivier to Pearse, 20.10.1899 (ibid)
(4)   S.G. Hobson to Olivier, 24.10.1899 (ibid)
(5)   *To-Day*, December 1888
(6)   *Political Science Quarterly*, December 1888, 564
(7)   ibid 564
(8)   ibid 560-5
(9)   *To-Day*, loc. cit.
(10)   Shaw to Wallas, 16.12.1890 (Wallas Papers)
(11)   *Contemporary Review*, January, 1899
(12)   MS. Address on Education (Wallas Papers)
(13)   'The Issues of the L.C.C. Election' in *Fabian News*, March, 1895
(14)   *Men and Ideas* (1940), 104
(15)   *Sunday Chronicle*, 1890, 'The Motive Power of Socialism', Fabian Cuttings Book
(16)   *Men and Ideas*, 104
(17)   Olivier to Pearse, 20.10.1899 (Fabian Archives)
(18)   Bland to Pearse, 17.10.1899 (Fabian Archives)

BILL MOORE

Sheffield Shop Stewards in the First World War

The Sheffield Shop Stewards[1] led the fight in Britain against the war and against the attempts by employers and Government to break down the Trade Union rights won over a long period—but not until the latter end of 1916. Up to 1916 this struggle was led by the Clydeside workers, under the Clyde Workers' Committee, the history of which is well enough known, especially from the writings of Willie Gallacher who was its president. The organisational basis of the Clydeside workers' strength was the shop stewards' movement. Shop Stewards had been appointed in the engineering industry, at least in the A.S.E.—Amalgamated Society of Engineers, for some years before 1914; but only as dues collectors. It was the collaboration of the national trade union leadership with the Government, for the prosecution of the war, leaving the workers virtually compelled to fight their own battles at workshop level, that brought about a transformation of the shop steward from a dues collector into a leader of the workers against employer and Government alike.

As G.D.H. Cole has written: 'The new movement developed earliest upon the Clyde. Official shop-stewards were appointed at an increasing pace . . . But side by side with these official developments came an unofficial development. The workers themselves in many shops chose spokesmen without reference to any District Committee' and 'the next step was not long in coming'. 'Both official and unofficial shop stewards in many cases formed themselves into Works Committees and elected chairmen, secretaries, conveners, etc. These conveners and the other shop-stewards soon felt the need for a wider form of combination, and for contact between one shop and another, and the Clyde strike of February 1915 provided the nucleus of an unofficial organisation which could be used for this purpose. The Strike Committee developed into the Clyde Workers' Committee and as the shop stewards' movement on the Clyde grew and extended, the Clyde Workers' Committee developed itself into a central organisation representing unofficially all the various shops in the district.'[2]

It was in the latter months of 1916 when the Clyde Workers' Committee, after a glorious career of struggle, had been broken and its leading members deported from the Clydeside, that the Sheffield workers came to the forefront. They were, for the most part, still a long way behind the Scottish engineers in understanding what the war was about. Due in great measure to the work of the indefatigable John Maclean there was, on the Clyde, right from the start a widespread understanding that side by side with its fight against the 'official' enemy, the ruling class would use the war situation to cut back the hard won Trade Union rights of its own working class; in these circumstances the fight for the living standards of the people and the fight against war must become merged into one fight against capitalism.

The history of the Sheffield shop stewards in the first world war is a history of the development of this understanding. Beginning with a purely economic struggle on standard Trade Union lines, with the workers by and large supporting the war, the movement grew into a workshop struggle, against conscription and dilution, led by the shop stewards due to the virtual defection of the national Trade Union leadership; it ended with the shop stewards leading a mass rank and file political struggle against the continuation of the war itself. What is outstanding about the Sheffield struggles is not just that they took over from the Clydeside but that once they got into their stride they were never defeated on any major issue, and their organisation was never broken. Their shop stewards' organisation was not just a copy of the Clydeside organisation but an advance on it. It was systematised, democratised to include *every* worker (skilled, semi-skilled, unskilled, men and women, Trade Unionists and non-unionist) and was rigorously fought for in every factory.[3] It was undoubtedly the tightness of this organisation that made the Sheffield engineering workers invincible. There was no conflict on major issues with the Sheffield District Committee as a whole, only with a few individual members. The ranks were not divided. As much as possible of this story is told in the actual words of the old-timers who were there on the job.

The 'Treasury Agreement' of March 1915 had laid down that the Unions should give up the right to strike, should relax all customs that restricted the production of munitions, and should permit dilution on war work. In return they were promised that dilution should be strictly confined to war work, that the restrictions should continue only for the duration of the war, that dilutees should get the rate for the job, and that there should be limitation of profits. All these promises by the Government were eventually broken, but even before this happened trouble started.

The first movement was made by the day-workers in the A.S.E. Brother Jack Parsons describes it as follows:

'As a result of the demand for munitions and the agreement on dilution, men came in and were put on repetition jobs. They smashed the machinery. Nothing mattered only their huge wage at the weekend. The skilled men had to keep the machinery going and all for the weekly daywork rate. This was the trouble. We said that we were entitled to something apart from the ordinary daywork rate.'

A Dayworkers' Committee was soon set up. This, continues Brother Parsons,

'was an unofficial body, but it had an interview with the Rates and Wages Committee for Munitions in London, and with the Minister of Munitions, Dr. Addison, still as an unofficial body. While in London they visited the E.C. of the Union and although unofficial they were more or less smiled upon and told to go ahead.'

They went in for a daywork rise and got it in the early part of 1915. The problem remained, however, throughout the war, and we find it still causing trouble at the end of 1917.

In the middle of 1915 a step was taken by the Government which earned it the hatred of the mass of the workers. The Munitions of War Act was passed which not only gave legal force to the 'Treasury Agreement' but also included an extra clause forbidding workers leaving their munitions jobs without a leaving certificate from their employers. This Act became known as the 'Slavery Act'. The response was immediate.

'The question of workmen denied the right to change their employment, even on advantageous terms, by firms, was considered by the Committee and the following resolution was carried: "That our members be instructed that if they desire to change their employment, they must first leave their present employment, and then secure employment elsewhere, and ignore notices in the works to the contrary, and same to be inserted in the Monthly Journal".'

Thus runs a resolution of the District Committee of the A.S.E., on June 1 1915. This refusal to be intimidated by the Authorities was a foretaste of the future.

Arising partly out of the experience of the unofficial Dayworkers' Committee, partly from the need for immediate shop action around these constantly recurring Government attacks, the new shop stewards' movement was born, destined not just to collect dues but to lead and organise the struggle. An A.S.E. District Committee resolution late in 1915 called on all members to elect shop stewards. This was not quite so straightforward as it sounds. A resolution of No. 12 Branch, A.S.E., on February 25 1916, reads thus:

'That this Branch draws attention to the need for shop stewards, also the difficulty of getting members to stand for that position by reason of the fact that District Committee has not local autonomy to grant victimisation pay to our members, which must be granted before our members will take on this duty.'

Nevertheless in spite of the danger of victimisation the factories in a few months were covered by a network of shop stewards inside the A.S.E. It was not long before their strength was tested over the case of Leonard Hargreaves, who was called into the army in October 1916, despite the fact that he was a skilled fitter. The Government had given a pledge that men who volunteered for munitions work and received badges to show that they had done so would not be called up. This pledge began to be broken with increasing frequency.

Two incidents had already served to put the workers on their guard and also indicate a changing attitude on the war. The first is recorded in the District Committee minutes of August 6, 1915:

'Standing Orders were suspended and Brother (?) introduced the question of Mr. Samms, Labour member of the Board of Guardians, who under the Defence of the Realm Act had been sentenced to two months, arising out of conversations with wounded soldiers at the Firvale Workhouse (which was used as a military hospital), and the following resolution was moved: "That this D.C. of the A.S.E. appeals to the Home Secretary with a view to the squashing of a sentence on Mr. Samms as being both impolitic and unjust. Also with A. Henderson and W.C. Anderson".'

Arthur Henderson, a signatory of the Treasury Agreement for the unions, had been a member of the privy council and of Asquith's coalition cabinet since 1915, with the endorsement of the T.U.C. and Labour Party. Will Anderson was M.P. for the Attercliffe Division, Sheffield. Samms was a pacifist, opposed to war, who had been doing a bit of anti-war propaganda on his own initiative.

The second incident is recorded in the minutes of the District Committee on September 14 and September 16 1916. It concerned a turner called Bingham working at Hadfield's who was suspended for a month for leaving work without permission; 'when the foreman, Mr. Crowther, suspended him', runs the D.C. minute, 'he was reported to have said that if he could he would send him to the trenches . . . ' Crowther and Bingham were both brought before the District Committee on September 28, and although the matter was afterwards allowed to drop, it is clear that the District Committee was on its toes regarding any attempt to put skilled men in the army. Sympathy with pacifist propaganda, the significant use of the word 'impoli-tic' to indicate that there was general resentment against the sentence on Samms, and the very real fear of the army—these are all signs that in fact the whole attitude of the people to the war was rapidly changing.

A year or so earlier, a resolution in No. 12 Branch (September 10 1915) calling for the rules about the leaving certificate to be withdrawn, could speak of these as a direct insult to the workmen 'who are working loyally and consistently in truly patriotic manner towards a successful termination of the war now in progress'. Now however, on October 20 1916, three days before the Hargreaves case broke into the news, the following resolution was passed by the same Branch:

'That this meeting of the Sheffield A.S.E. No. 12 Branch urges His Majesty's Government to seek the earliest opportunity of promoting negotiations with the object of securing a just and lasting peace.'

Interminable trench warfare, the submarine blockade, queues for food and everything else, the daily casualty lists—all these plus the constant attacks in the shops was leading to more than war weariness. It was in this changing atmosphere that the Hargreaves case broke.

On October 23 1916, Leonard Hargreaves wrote the following letter to his Branch of the A.S.E., No. 14:

19 Bankfield View, Halifax.

'Dear Bro.
I left Vickers Ltd., employ on Thursday last, as I had been called up for the Army, and as I had only a badge without certificate, I was bound to go into the Army, as Vickers held my papers until it was too late to either appeal or anything else. I hope you will send all particulars to the above address, my number in the branch was one hundred and fourteen. Hoping you will make enquiries at Vickers, and see that there are no more of our members who get served like myself for I know quite well there are scores who have badges without certificates, I have joined the A.S.C. (mechanical transport).

Yours truly,
Leonard Hargreaves

P.S. I enclose Insurance Card. Will you kindly let me know how I stand now I have joined His Majesty's forces.'

This letter was immediately reported to the District Committee and to the Shop Committees throughout the city. The normal Trade Union channels of negotiation were tried, without result. The feeling soon grew among the workers that they could not afford to let the matter go past.

On November 8 the District Committee and the shop stewards called a mass meeting, to which they also invited skilled workers of all other trades. This was a significant step forward: up to this time the shop stewards movement had been confined to the A.S.E., but now it began to spread. At the mass meeting the District Committee as such retired, since it was bound by the official Trade Union line. But since most of the District Committee members were shop stewards, there was no noticeable change in the leadership when the shop stewards took over. The meeting decided they would give the Government one week in which to return Hargreaves. If he was not returned then work would stop. Zero hour was fixed at 4 p.m. on November 15. Letters to this effect were sent to the Prime Minister, the Minister of Munitions, the War Office and the various Trade Union executives. The Government did not reply, and the Unions only sent formal acknowledgements of receipt, except the Patternmakers' secretary who said: 'Your six-days' ultimatum to the Government is the most foolish and short-sighted action I have ever heard of.'

The day after the mass meeting delegates were sent to all the main engineering centres of the country to win support from the workers there and to get them standing by for solidarity action. This was a regular feature of all strikes in order to establish reliable channels of information free from 'security' snooping and provocative agents. On November 14, at the last minute, Brother Harbinson, District Secretary, received the following telegram from A.S.E. headquarters:

'Wire full particulars of Leonard Hargreaves case, number of years at trade, length of membership and full military address immediately.

Edifying Peck London'

A telegram and following letter were sent, the letter receiving the following reply:

'Dear Sir and Brother,
I have to acknowledge with thanks the receipt of your letter of the 14th November re the member Bro. Leonard Hargreaves. We are taking the matter up with the Manpower Board.

Yours faithfully,
Robert Young Gen. Sec.'

On the afternoon of November 15, 200 shop stewards were waiting at the A.S.E. Institute, Stanley Street, ready to take whatever instructions were necessary to the factories. With them were delegates on cycles and motorcycles ready to travel the length and breadth of the country, to Glasgow and London, Barrow and Derby, Manchester, Coventry and Birmingham, to bring out the workers everywhere in support. In addition delegates were ready to go by train to stay in the other centres in order to maintain reliable communications. Four o'clock came and no message from the Government. The delegates departed to their various destinations. The shop stewards went off to the factories and work stopped throughout the city. The battle was joined. Late on November 15, Brother Harbinson received the following telegram from A.S.E. headquarters:

'On representation of executives and in view of proposals submitted by Ministry for dealing with enlistment of skilled men War Office have given orders for Hargreaves to be returned to civil life and therefore stoppage of work cannot be justified or permitted.

Edifying'

This was taken to the mass meeting the next morning. But meantime another telegram had been received, from Hargreaves himself, to say that he had heard nothing of release. This confirmed warnings which the shop stewards had been giving the men about the sort of promises to be expected from the Government. The reaction from the mass meeting was very precise: no Hargreaves, no work! The men demanded to see Hargreaves in the flesh before they would go back. Meanwhile throughout the country mass meetings were being called in support. The workers of Barrow-in-Furness, who had already established a shop stewards organisation, pledged themselves to come out inside twenty-four hours if the Government refused to give in. Late in the evening of November 16, Brother Harbinson received a further telegram:

'O.H.M.S. Parliament Street.

You are instructed by executive council to post telegram sent to you with reference to Hargreaves and also this message at the institute stop council are interviewing Prime Minister at earliest possible moment on behalf of today's conference on the whole question stop if members are out these must return to work immediately.

Armitage   Gavigan   Edifying'

Brother Gavigan, the District President, and Armitage had slipped off to London without telling anybody. It was at this moment that Sir Robert Hadfield personally took a hand in the matter. The following day, Friday November 17, he rang up the Institute and spoke to Brother Harbinson, who tells the story thus:

' "Now, Harbinson", said Sir Robert, "I want you to pick up Hargreaves tonight. I am bringing him to the station across London; you pick him up in Sheffield at a certain time (it would be around 9 o'clock Friday night) and on no account let him go to Halifax." (He was intending to go home to his wife). I picked him up at Sheffield. Hargreaves was adamant that he did not want to come, but I said he must. I said I would send a telegram to his wife. We went to the back entrance of the Post Office in Pond Street, and immediately I asked for a telegram to send to Mrs. Hargreaves the girl was thunderstruck. Telegrams were supposed to stop at a certain time, but they let me send one to Mrs. Hargreaves! Hargreaves stayed with me at my home. Nobody saw him, and I took him along to the Bramhall Lane meeting and presented him to the workers on the platform. That was the end of the strike . . . they returned to work.'

The effect of the strike was tremendous. In the first place it showed the men what strength came from solidarity. 'It was the first time', says Brother Parsons, 'we could say that in Sheffield solidarity showed itself. It was fought on principle, the principle that a skilled man should not be taken into the army. For the first time we forced the employers of Sheffield to such an extent that it was either Hargreaves coming back or no munitions from Sheffield. It was the first real victory we were able to pull off.' Brother Sweeting points out that it was so speedy that there was really no time for incidents. Brother Bill Ward recollects a popular poem that came out of it, beginning:

'You can't take me,
I'm in the A.S.E. . . . '

In the second place it brought tremendous prestige to the shop stewards. The value of their organisation was clear to everybody. 'Immediately Hargreaves' case was settled', says Brother Ibbotson, 'the shop stewards movement was built up. It broadened out and before long embraced all craft organisations.' Thirdly, there was an immediate response by the Government. The A.S.E. Executive was able to sign an agreement with the Government whereby every skilled man who volunteered for munitions work was to be issued with a Trade Card by his Trade Union, which was to serve as a certificate of exemption from call-up.

The final result was the most fundamental: it was the first mass expression of feeling against the war itself, and as such marked a considerable step forward in political consciousness. There was a dread of the army behind the whole affair, a feeling that was general throughout the city. At the various meetings the attack on the engineers was described as part of the universal attempt of capitalism to hold workers in subjection. The war was denounced as an imperialist war for robbing the workers, not a war of liberation.

The Hargreaves affair was rapidly followed by the consolidation of the shop stewards' movement. In January 1917, another great mass meeting was called by the shop stewards to consider the next steps to be taken, and to this meeting were invited all skilled and some semi-skilled workers, a further step forward. A unanimous decision was taken to extend the organisation to include *all* workers in the factories: skilled, semi-skilled, and unskilled, men and women. There were to be four levels of organisation:

1.   In every department there was to be a *Workshop Committee* comprising delegates elected by *all* the workers in the shop. Shop Stewards were to have, if possible, the endorsement of their Union, but even non-Unionists were not disallowed if they had the confidence of the workers. In fact, this led to widespread recruiting to the Union.

2.   There was to be a *Works or Plant Committee*, made up of representatives from each Workshop Committee.

3.   *A Sheffield Engineering Workers Committee* was created, to comprise representatives from all the factories in the city.

4.   The Sheffield Workers' Committee was visualised as part of a national movement, and in fact very shortly there was formed the National Shop Stewards and Workers' Committee Movement.

These organisational principles were fought for in every factory. They were also embodied in a pamphlet written by J.T. Murphy, *The Workers' Committee: an outline of its principles and structure.* This pamphlet had what an article in No. 14 of the *Firth Worker* described as an 'unprecedented sale' (at that time, March 1918, some 25,000 had been sold):

'Copies have been ordered for all parts of the United Kingdom, and even from France, South Africa and New Zealand. That it has aroused the widespread interest of all classes is shown in the enquiries from Government Officials, Trade Union Officials, Employers' Federations and social students of all classes. Dr. Addison, the Minister of Reconstruction, in his first speech on the subject at Huddersfield referred to it, as showing that the workers were preparing and erecting machinery which would be powerful enough to secure for them a voice in any proposals put forward. It has already become a classic of industrial unionism literature . . . '

That it was necessary to fight, not just for this organisation but also for the political and economic understanding that were its basis, was shown by an interesting incident in March 1917. On March 21 the engineers in Barrow came out on strike over the premium bonus. Brother Ibbotson tells the story:

'We had a mass meeting of shop stewards and decided to support Barrow on the premium bonus strike, but the rank and file kicked up and it came unstuck. There was a big mass meeting at Bold Street (near Staniforth Road) which decided not to support Barrow. Ten days later another mass meeting, at the Coliseum, decided to support it. By this time, however, the matter had been settled.'

The trouble was that the premium bonus system was not operating in Sheffield and as a result the rank and file of the workers were not interested. It took ten days' hard work on the part of the stewards to change the minds of the workers. In a matter of weeks, however, a new issue arose that provided a very considerable education for them: the great dilution strike of May 1917.

The 'Treasury Agreement' of 1915 had specified that dilution was to be strictly confined to war work. In March 1917, Tweedale and Smalley's of Rochdale tried to extend it to private work: the grinding of cotton spindles. The men detailed to instruct the dilutees refused and were sacked: 400 Union men walked out in protest. A month was spent in fruitless Trade Union negotiation. In the meantime the Government had introduced a Dilution Bill into Parliament which asked for the extension of dilution to private work and at the same time would have abolished the Trade Card, only brought in after the Hargreaves strike, and, final insult, would have left workers' exemption entirely in the hands of the military tribunals in consultation with the employers. This was the last straw. Two resolutions from No. 12 Branch show the general feeling:

'This meeting of Sheffield No. 12 Branch A.S.E. regards with the utmost concern the proposals made by the Prime Minister to break the clear and emphatic pledges given to the Trade Union Movement by responsible Ministers of State against Industrial Conscription and his expressed intention to introduce a measure of industrial conscription and thus complete the militarisation of the nation.' (March 9, 1917)

'That our secretary write the Lord Mayor stating that we are strongly opposed to industrial conscription and we think we have done enough without anything further.' (March 23, 1917)

If the Government was to be defeated, it had to be on the issue that had arisen in Rochdale. On May 3 all Rochdale came out. By May 5 there were 60,000 out in Lancashire, and on the same day the Sheffield District Committee passed a resolution calling for a strike in support. On May 6 there were mass meetings throughout the country, including Sheffield. At 4.30 p.m. on May 7 the following telegram was received at the A.S.E. Institute, addressed to Gavigan, District President:

'Informed men threaten to stop work tonight. Their attention is called to delegate meeting recommendation that no stoppage take place of our skilled men and apprentices are fully protected. Full report will be issued by delegate meeting in a day or two   Young   Edifying'

Less than two hours later Brother Gavigan received the following telegram at his private address:

'Resolutions passed at District Committee meeting held on fifth disapproved by executive council. District Committee instructed to notify members that society can in no way be associated with any down tools policy. Instruct members to remain at work.   Edifying'

The District Committee refused to be intimidated and the strike was on. Let the old-timers give the picture of the tremendous solidarity and confidence of the workers:

Bro. Sweeting: 'I was left at the Institute to answer any telephone calls. The telephone rang and I answered. It was a member at Jonas and Colver's who asked if it was definite that the District Committee had decided all must cease work at 5 o'clock. I said it was. He said he had only enquired because they had a heat in, which would not be out until after then. I knew there was a possibility of the matter being settled speedily, so I told him to carry on until the heat was done, but they would have finished at 5 o'clock otherwise. I knew that if they finished at 5 o'clock, not only would the heat have been ruined but the furnace would have had to be rebuilt, which would have meant them being out of work much longer.'

Bro. Ibbotson: 'About 20,000 attended a meeting at the Skating Rink (Olympia). 5,000 copies of *Solidarity* were sold that day. I've never seen such a meeting.'

Bro. Sweeting: 'We engaged the Albert Hall and asked how much the rent would be. We were told that it depended on 'how this meeting goes'. Needless to say, the rent had to be paid!'

Bro. Sweeting: 'During the dilution strike we took the members out on picket. One day I advised them all to bring a big, thick stick with them because some of the cossacks (mounted police) had rushed us in Earl Marshall Road. I went in from that day and then went to report these cossacks to the Chief Constable, Major Hall-Dallwood. He said: "Will you tell me, Mr. Sweeting, how it is that your men went out armed yesterday?" "Is it really necessary to have to tell you?", I asked. "Yes". "Well, don't you know that the best line of defence is to be prepared to attack?". They never attacked us again after that!'

Another side of police activity was related by Bro. Harbinson—the attempt to seduce the leaders and get them to take the men back:

'The Chief Constable came along to Barnes, Burgess and myself and said we could go along to Arthur Neale's (leading Sheffield solicitor) if we wanted. We went and had a talk with them. They brought out the cigarettes and later invited us to supper. The talk finished and he (the Chief Constable) said he was sorry for the way we had been treated! I tried for a taxi, but I had to walk from Manchester Road to Firth Park at two o'clock in the morning'. A further instance of what the men had to put up with was the case of the Government spy, told by Bro. Bill Ward:

'He posed as a conscientious objector on the run and was received as such by the lads. He was working his way up to Glasgow and asked for help. There was the signature of Arthur McManus on the note but it couldn't be checked of course. There was a shop stewards' meeting at the time and Walt Hill asked him if he'd care to be present. The man heard the full story of what we were doing that evening. Walt Hill even took him home and later gave him money before he finally went to Glasgow. I was later able to give Dr. Chandler[4] a copy of *John Bull* which came out two years afterwards carrying the headline: "How I Tricked the Sheffield Reds". The man was out of the country when the story was written.'

There were compensations, however, as related in the story by Brother Sweeting:

'We took the police on many a ramble those days. Once we had three contingents at Stanley Street. A police sergeant asked where we were going. "What's that to you?" "Come along if you want to know." They did. We went down Attercliffe Road and another contingent met us at Staniforth Road. We went to Vickers' gates and held a meeting there. Then to Sheffield Rolling Mills. Then we marched them back through the recreation ground, ran them down the hill and all the way back to the Institute. Following that we thanked them very much for coming with us as we had enjoyed their company very much!'

The local paper, the *Sheffield Telegraph* had an article on the strike that, in spite of the sarcastic tone, gives a picture of the enthusiasm, confidence and increased political awareness among the workers. It speaks of the motor-cyclist couriers:

'We had these motor cyclists round our own district last week, conveying information about the progress of the strike in other places. Some of the "young bloods" of the movement really imagined the great day of the revolution had begun, and now the hated capitalists, and the even more intensely hated Lloyd George Government were going to be swept away by the oncoming revolution. The Russian Revolution has for the moment upset the mental balance of some of these youthful social and industrial reconstructors. . .'

Certainly there was a marked increase in anti-militarist propaganda. The strike could only increase the disillusionment of the workers with the aims and results of the war. Especially so when the authorities, including the Trade Union leadership, now proceeded to the most high-handed action. On May 12 there was a national meeting of shop stewards at Derby, preparatory to trying to meet the Government on the 15th. Dr. Addison, Minister of Munitions, refused to meet the stewards, and the E.C. of the Union refused to intercede with him. The E.C. went further. A telegram was despatched to Bro. Harbinson on May 12 which read:

'Council has suspended Sheffield District Committee and can only recognise Bro. Gavigan as District Secretary, and Executive Council instruct you to at once cease acting as alleged District Secretary.

Edifying'

The *Sheffield Telegraph* printed the telegram with the comment:

'According to a document handed to us on the authority of Mr. Robert Young, General Secretary, and Mr. William Gavigan, District Secretary, the E.C. of the A.S.E. entirely disapproves of a "down tools" policy and notify the members of the Society that, the delegate meeting having arrived at an agreement with the Government with regard to its members and military service, the E.C. trust the members of the A.S.E. will loyally accept the same.'

The response was hardly what the E.C. expected. No. 12 Branch, meeting the following Friday, May 18, proceeded to pass the following resolution:

'That this meeting of Sheffield No. 12 Branch regards with displeasure the suspension of the Sheffield District Committee and demands the reinstatement of the above, and also desires to censure the E.C. for using the capitalist press to defeat the aspirations of the men in the shops.'

Two other resolutions were passed, for on that same day the Government tried the strong-arm tactic of arresting eight leading shop stewards at the Derby Conference, including Burgess and Hill of Sheffield:

'That Sheffield No. 12 Branch of the A.S.E. pledges itself not to return to work until Bro. Burgess and Hill are released, and any other of our brothers in other districts.'
'That this Branch of the A.S.E. No. 12 regrets that the E.C. has not seen fit to come to Sheffield to give us their views on the critical position, through the withdrawal of exemption cards and the question of dilution of labour in private and commercial work, and also to see that the Sheffield members should hear our delegate Bro. Lee's report, seeing that Sheffield is the centre of disaffection. Also that the E.C. shall meet the National Conference Committee with a view to meeting the Minister of Munitions, with a view to bringing this dispute to a close.'

The pressure from all over the country was so strong that that in fact was what the E.C. was compelled to do. A meeting was arranged with Dr. Addison. As a result the Government promised that there would be no victimisation and that the arrested men would be released, providing the shop stewards would urge the men to return to work at once. On May 23, the charges against the eight leaders were dropped and the Dilution Bill was withdrawn. On May 24, the Sheffield engineers went back to work.

The further discussions between the A.S.E. and the Government, however, resulted in the Government insisting that the clause extending dilution to private work should still stand, and, though the engineers rejected these terms in a subsequent ballot by 46,851 to 8,945, the men were back at work with nothing apparently settled. It looked as if the strike had failed. In fact, events showed that it had achieved a great deal. The position is summarised in the history of the engineers.

'The news of the rejection (in the ballot) coincided with Addison's appointment to the Ministry of Reconstruction and his replacement by Winston Churchill at the Ministry of Munitions. Churchill, seriously disturbed by the industrial unrest, was not prepared to take the same risks as his predecessor, and when he introduced the Munitions Bill 1917, in August, the extension of dilution to private work had been quietly dropped. Nor was this the only concession won. The leaving certificate—perhaps the most hated section of the 1915 Act—was withdrawn in October, leaving the men free to change their employment at will. In addition national wage advances were to apply to non-federated as well as federated firms. Employers were required to give 21 days notice of dilution and to produce a certificate from the Ministry of Munitions to prove that it was necessary. It became an offence to victimise trade unionists following a strike and more stringent provisions were made for enforcing the restoration of pre-war trade union rights and customs. In short, the Government which had started 1917 with the aim of gaining further concessions from the engineers found that as a result of the mass movement it had itself been forced to give ground.'[5]

Wage advances in July of 3s. and in October of a further 5s., together with a 12½% bonus, the result of the long struggle that began with the Day-workers' Committee, also showed the effect on the Government and the employers of the mass movement; though naturally they were referred to in a resolution in No. 12 Branch as 'this miserable award'. Incidentally, Bro. Gavigan was not allowed to get away with it. We find a resolution by No. 12 Branch on June 1, 1917.

'That we ask the E.C. to ask Bro. Gavigan to resign as we refuse to move a resolution for a new District Committee until he does so.'

There were two further resolutions on June 15:

'That this Branch pass a vote of no confidence in Bro. Gavigan and call upon the E.C. to ask him to resign, or to come and explain their reasons to a mass meeting.'

'That the Secretary write Capt. Barnsley if a man named '. . . . .',
working at Messrs. Burnand of Chippinghouse Road, electricians, was
granted an exemption card owing to the influence of Mr. Gavigan.'

In the event, Mr. Gavigan spent more and more time at the seaside where his
wife had taken a boarding house, and indeed soon disappeared from the
scene.

The Russian Revolution of March 1917, the Convention in Leeds, in June
1917, to set up Workers' and Soldiers' Councils (No. 12 Branch sent two
delegates), and the Russian Revolution of November, 1917—these events
stiffened the tremendous anti-war feeling that was openly growing. This can
be seen in the consciousness of strength shown in an example given by Bro.
Bill Ward:

'The owners of the Jungle and Olympia, the biggest places for a meeting,
refused bookings. We saw the Chief Constable, Major Hall-Dallwood and
asked him to intercede. We told him that there would be thousands out on
the streets if we didn't get the meeting. The Chief Constable said: 'You'll
get your meeting' and we did!'

The growing anti-war feeling can be seen in the worker's papers, in
Solidarity, the Scottish *Worker* and particularly the *Firth Worker* which
was started in June 1917. Here is a typical poem published in No. 14 of the
Firth Worker:

A Suggestion

(to our artists)

Paint two vast heaps of mildewed human skulls
In pyramidal shape, with top depressed,
Two islands in a blood-red lake where hulls
Of stately ships rust-anchored rest;
Beyond in middle distance withered trees,
And blasted cloisters of some abbey proud
Through which trails ghost-like, in the hidden breeze,
Black sulphurous smoke in semblance of a shroud.

Upon each pyramid a monarch stand,
Garbed in imperial robes of purple hue,
Each gripping firm the other by the hand
And whispering, Cousin, we have seen it through.
In distant background let fat vultures tear
Dead flesh from bones that seem from earth to spring,
And let your masterpiece this title bear
In letters deathly black-God save the King!

It was such open expressions of contempt and disgust with the war, with the Government, with society itself, and the strong current of revolutionary feeling that was fed by them that compelled the Government to take measures against the workers' press. On November 30, 1917, we find No. 12 Branch protesting:

'That this Branch send a resolution strongly protesting against the new regulations under the Defence of the Realm Act relating to censorship of opinions dealing with the issues of peace and war before publication.'

In July, 1918, the *Firth Worker* was suppressed, calling forth a further resolution from No. 12 Branch (July 12, 1918):

'That this Branch protests against the suppression of the *Firth Worker* and the coercive policy adopted by the Government re freedom of speech and the press.'

A few months later, still another resolution (October 18, 1918):

'That the following resolution be forwarded to the Home Office: "The Sheffield 12th Branch A.S.E. protests against the suppression of *The Socialist Labour Press* and other Labour publications and calls on the Government to rectify this matter immediately".'

Not, of course, that such suppression damped the initiative of the workers. On the contrary it only served to rouse them more. The story of the secret press is told by Bro. Ibbotson:

'In the latter part of 1917 there was a fund of £20 to £30 from the Coliseum meetings. We decided to go in for a printing press. We were licked for type at first, but Alf Barton helped us and we got it going. We issued a few leaflets (mainly anti-war). In 1918 when I was at Hadfield's, two fellows came to my house (I was on nights at the time). The wife called me up, and they told me we must dismantle the press as the police were after it. We fetched the press away on a horse and dray, up Frederick Street, past the police station, up High Street, and finished up in a back room past the Royal Hospital and installed it there. The police were on our track for printing a leaflet and for printing the *Red Flag.*'

The demands for an immediate peace and for friendship and support to Russia were growing. At the National Shop Stewards meeting in Manchester, in December 1917, 'an immediate negotiated peace' was discussed. At the Joint Conference of Shop Stewards and Amalgamation Committees early in January 1918, solidarity with the Russion Revolution was expressed and a demand was registered for the acceptance of the Russian peace proposals. In

March 1918, at a Conference held in Sheffield, the National Council of Shop Stewards discussed 'Peace without annexation or indemnity', the Russian peace proposals.

The war in fact ended with the shop stewards in Sheffield on top of their form. Their spirit is admirably expressed in two resolutions passed by No. 12 Branch, four days after the Armistice was signed, resolutions which express the dual struggle of the working people during these years: against war and against exploitation.

> 'That we request the D.C. and the E.C. to get in communication with all societies engaged in the engineering trade, with a view to an immediate demand for 6-hour day, with no reduction in wages and the total abolition of payment by result.'

> 'That we instruct our Secretary to write the Prime Minister and Mr. Anderson demanding that we immediately withdraw all troops from Russian territory.'

REFERENCES

(1)   The original version of this essay was dedicated 'To Brothers Harbinson, Ibbotson, Parsons, Sweeting, Ward, and the other workers in the engineering industry who wrote such a glorious page in the history of our working class.'
       We are indebted to the Labour Research Department and Messrs. Allen & Unwin for permission to quote from G.D.H. Cole, *An Introduction to Trade Unionism.* We wish to thank the Sheffield A.E.U. for permission given in 1952 to use the minute books of No. 12 branch. We also thank the above-named brothers for the time they gave in relating their personal memories of these historic events—struggles in which they were among the leadership

(2)   G.D.H. Cole, *An Introduction to Trade Unionism* (1918), p.55

(3)   As witness the discussion in No. 16 of the *Firth Worker* (April 1918) on the deviation of the Hadfield's Plant Committee

(4)   A well-known Sheffield socialist. His brother was an engineer

(5)   J.B. Jefferys, *The Story of the Engineers* (London, 1946), pp.184—5

R. PAGE ARNOT

The General Strike

In The North-East

Some contemporary documents with a commentary

There has survived what has been described as a document of 'unique interest'—*An Account of the Proceedings of the Northumberland and Durham General Council Joint Strike Committee.* [1] Drawn up immediately after the strike and presented to the council on May 20 it is in the form of a duplicated foolscap pamphlet reporting on the committee's work and in one place giving a detailed extract from the minutes of the meeting. [2] This account opens with proposals for the setting up of a regional council to co-ordinate the conduct of the strike in the area, proposals advanced at an informal meeting held on the eve of the strike, Monday May 3. Present at this meeting were: James White, area secretary, Transport & General Workers' Union; Ebby Edwards, financial secretary, Northumberland Miners' Association; Charles Flyn, northern divisional officer, National Union of Distributive and Allied Workers; Ferguson Foster, organiser of N.U.D.A.W.; and R. Page Arnot, director of the Labour Research Department.

But this was, in fact, the third local meeting which had taken place. A note by R. Page Arnot, written in 1961, fills in the background and his information can be supplemented by a contemporary report of a gathering on Sunday evening, May 2, at Chopwell. [3] There has also survived a copy of a four page bulletin published on the eve of the strike by the Spen and District Trades and Labour Council. [4] The following account draws on these documents, with a concluding note by R. Page Arnot. Page Arnot, then thirty-five years old, was one of twelve leading Communists brought to trial in October, 1925; sentenced to six months, he was released in April, 1926. By May 1 he was at Chopwell, Co. Durham, taking part in the events leading up to the strike. He writes:

'On Saturday morning, May 1 1926, the miners were locked out. That midday by a majority of over 3½ millions to 49,911 the conference of Trade Union Executives in London voted the resolution for the General Strike to begin on Monday midnight May 3/4. On the Saturday afternoon

I was the speaker at a First of May demonstration at Chopwell, one of the numerous mining villages that made up the Urban District Council of Blaydon-on-Tyne. After the open air demonstration I jotted down headings for a plan of campaign in the Durham-Northumberland area where under the Emergency Powers Act Kingsley Wood had been made Commissioner assisted by a general and an admiral.

'That evening, before a gathering in the Miners' Club, Steve Lawther and three officials of Lodges in adjacent pits discussed and agreed on a plan of action. A further proposal was advanced that a meeting be called at twenty-four hours' notice for Sunday evening, May 2, of all trade union secretaries and chairmen, all members of boards of the three or four local co-operative societies and all local Labour councillors of the county and urban district. This meeting took place with nearly fifty present, with checkweigher Will Lawther in the chair, and at it the plan of campaign was discussed and unanimously adopted. It included sending a call for Councils of Action to be set up all over that huge coalfield. Dozens of mining lads who never attended a lodge meeting and were therefore thought to be of little account turned up the next day ready to speed throughout the two counties on bicyles and motorbikes.

'Meanwhile on Sunday a call had been drafted and that afternoon Will Lawther and I went over to Sunderland where the printer Thomas Summerbell agreed to do a rush job with a printed bulletin giving a call for a General Strike and Councils of Action. His father had been one of the early Labour M.P.'s and he himself had met me some ten years earlier in the Wakefield House of Correction.

'Then we hastened to Newcastle where we found Ebby Edwards, financial secretary of the Northumberland Miners, in Burt Hall. We put before him the proposition of the Chopwell meeting that all leading officials of trade unions responsible in the Durham-Northumberland area should be called together to constitute a regional body. This meant in some cases district officials, of such unions as N.U.D.A.W. and T. & G.W.U., but in the case of most unions, such as the A.E.U., there was more than one district. J.E. Little, afterwards president of the A.E.U., was official for one of these; Charles Flynn, a friend of Ellen Wilkinson, was the N.U.D.A.W. man, a live wire. Ebby Edwards, himself a live wire, quiet, shrewd and energetic, agreed to do what he could and suggested seeing Charles Flynn.

'While the others were engaged elsewhere I went, as far as my recollection goes, to fix up activities with Alec Geddes, then a Communist Party organiser attached to this district, and four years previously Communist candidate at Greenock where he had a vote of over 8,000. Then we hied back to the already mentioned meeting on the Sunday night of representatives of the whole movement in Blaydon-on-Tyne.

'On the Monday, while Ebby Edwards was with some difficulty getting members of the projected regional committee, the Lawthers and I went over to Sunderland in the later afternoon to collect the printed bulletin, only to be informed that while it had been printed off it had not yet been guillotined or folded and that they had received the General Strike call from the Typographical Association which meant that they would have to stop work at once at the end of the shift. Eventually, however, after much arguing that it would be ridiculous to refuse to complete work on the strike bulletin on the ground that the strike had already begun we got our four-page paper and the despatch riders got busy.

'In the North-east area there was no difficulty about gathering pickets. On Tuesday May 4, Will Lawther and I got in touch with the local organiser of the National Union of Seamen, James Rogers, who had agreed to join in, though the union under the domination of Havelock Wilson had voted against the strike.[5] In the evening Rogers drove us up in his car towards the village of Chopwell. We decided to go in "by the back road" to make sure that that also was properly picketed. At a narrow part of the moorland road we came up with the picket; the numbers were, we ascertained, about 125, mainly young miners. Most of them were carrying pick shafts. This considerably reassured us that there need be no trouble about picketing. Very soon there was no traffic on the Great North Road except by permission of the Strike Committees.[6] Those in that area, local grocers or others, who relied on the official O.M.S., were disappointed and after a short time came to ask for Strike Committee permits instead'.

To return to Sunday May 2, the report of the second meeting in Chopwell, held that evening, shows that it was a businesslike one. It was attended by some fifty representatives of trade unions, co-operative societies, miners' lodges, and by Labour councillors.[7] It first laid down, in a brief preamble, that no time be spent on discussion of the purpose of the strike, its national or international implications, but that attention be concentrated on the immediate objective. This was to defeat the civil commissioner appointed for the region by the government and 'armed with the Emergency Powers Act in order to break the strike'. The apparatus of the regional commission was outlined. It comprised the various arrangements and the organisation built up during the past nine months by the Ministry of Health, the Home Office, the War Office, Admiralty and Air Force, and other agencies. In short, there would be 'concentrated against the strikers ... the whole of the civil and military institutions that are under central control; and also the civil institutions usually classed as Local Government'. So far as the latter were concerned it remained to be seen whether the civil commissioner 'would be able to make the full use of them that he would wish'. The bodies of men at his disposal were the various government officials, the Organisation for the Maintenance of Supplies[8], other strike breaking bodies 'composed mainly of middle class persons', the Fascists one of whose organisations had an arrangement with O.M.S., the special constabulary, regular police forces and armed forces equipped with various weapons.

'To meet all this we must improvise', the document continues. 'The improvised machinery must be simple, easy to throw up, all inclusive. All activities in each locality should be centralised in a single body to be called Council of Action, Strike Committee, Trades Council or what you will: all such bodies should be linked up and centralised in the county capital town under a body responsible for the whole region.' The first task was to set up a district Council of Action 'and plan out all the machinery and all the tasks for the locality'. Then replicas of this would be needed throughout the two counties 'so as to make a network of Councils of Action linked up with a central directing body whose authority and scope on our side would exactly answer to the Civil Commissioner'. Finally district officers of trade unions must be assembled to form the core of a regional authority to undertake the central direction. These last two tasks could be undertaken 'mainly by the printing and scattering broadcast of a special strike newspaper'. This was in fact issued on May 4.

The tasks of councils of action were then outlined, tasks which would call for the constitution of various sub-committees concerned with communications, food and transport, picketing, publicity and so on. There follows an important paragraph on food and transport:

'The T.U.C. instructions for the general strike, if and when it should come off, include the provision of Food, Transport and Health Services. Whatever the intention of the General Council in laying down these instructions, it is clear that on this point depends the success of the general strike. Whoever handles and transports food, that same person controls food: whoever controls food will find the "neutral" part of the population rallying to their side. Who feeds the people wins the strike! The problem of the general strike can be focused down to one thing—the struggle for food control.'

Just how accurate this forecast proved will appear in the report of the regional strike committee. In the event the government refused the T.U.C. General Council's offer to adminster essential services and there necessarily developed a form of dual control with the government attempting to gain mastery through O.M.S., the police and other agencies, while the strikers picketed and bent all efforts to keeping off the roads any transport which did not carry a permit from a strike committee or union.[9]

Meanwhile the Chopwell document ends with a section on morale. While all the machinery proposed is to defeat any attempt to break the strike, it is noted, such activities have also another object 'that is the building up of our own morale both locally and nationally, and the breaking down of the enemy's morale both locally and nationally. Every officer who reports that picketing has stopped his transport, every military officer who reports that he cannot trust his men to act against the strikers because of effective fraternisation, is a means by which, when the report has filtered through to

Whitehall, the morale of the Chief Civil Commissioner, and thence of the Cabinet, is impaired and weakened.'

The call to strike taken to Sunderland by Will Lawther and Page Arnot on May 2, which was printed by Thomes Summerbell and published by the Spen and District Trades and Labour Council, appeared on Tuesday, May 4, at a price of 1d., as 'North-East Strike Bulletin No. 1'. Distributed throughout the area in the first days of the stoppage, it announced in heavy black letter on the front page—General Strike! Below came sub-headings.

ALL Railwaymen to cease work TO-NIGHT

Transport Workers, Printers and
Metal Workers to Follow

General Council's Arrangements
for General Stoppage

The front page gives news of readiness for action in the area, of local councils of action going ahead, and of union executive committees following the lead of the General Council. On the first inside page the General Council's instructions for the strike are printed in full under the headings:

EXTREMELY IMPORTANT Read This! Official T.U.C. Programme

The remaining column describes the formation of the council of action in the Blaydon urban district under the heading:

Chopwell and District Council of Action's Fine Lead

It is understood, this item concludes, that arrangements are being made for similar councils in each locality, drawing in all sections of the labour movement. An appeal is added for workers to take the initiative where necessary: in any locality where a council of action has not been formed they should take immediate steps to have the necessary meetings held and committees appointed.

The facing inside page carries for the most part speeches of the miners' leaders—of Herbert Smith, president of the M.F.G.B., Arthur Cook, its secretary, who had spoken to the theme 'the whole movement is behind us', and Bob Smillie saying 'No Surrender'. There is half a column on international support for the miners and another with the latest instructions regarding the conduct of the strike, which includes a reminder that 'under the Trades Disputes Act of 1906 peaceful picketing is completely legal'.

On the back page, spaced out in heavy black letter, is the call.

WORKERS OF DURHAM AND NORTHUMBERLAND

The General Strike is ALREADY A SUCCESS.

Don't believe the lies put out by the Capitalist press.

The newspapers are trying to dope and deceive you into the belief that the General Strike will fail, and that the Government forces are bound to get the better of the workers. Nothing could be further from the truth.

From centre after centre of industry comes the news of the magnificent response to the call sent out by the General Council of the Trades Union Congress.

On Saturday a million miners were wantonly locked out, and the Government—which is supposed to represent the whole of the nation—put all its forces at the service of a small minority of profiteers and exploiters.

The organised trade unionists of Great Britain cannot suffer the miners to be beaten and starved into submission.

What happens to the miners will happen to you next.

Your own wages, your livelihood, the welfare of your wife and children, are at stake.

That is why there is a General Strike. That is why you are called out.

That is why, fighting in such a cause, you are bound to win.

The strike-breaking organisations of Sir Kingsley Wood have proved feeble weapons against the united will and determination of hundreds of thousands of the working-class.

Be of good courage, and victory is ours.

The finishing touches were being put to this publication late on Monday afternoon, May 3, and this brings us back to the original starting point, the small informal meeting held in the offices of N.U.D.A.W. in Newcastle on that same evening a few hours before the strike was due to begin. The five men there assembled, representing the miners, transport workers, distributive workers and including also Page Arnot, agreed to summon a meeting of representatives of other unions for the next day. Attempts had already been made to get more to this meeting, but nearly all trade union officials approached were completely occupied with other meetings, so now arrangements were made to see or telephone to as many as possible.

Page Arnot was deputed to call on James Robson, secretary of the Durham County Mining Federation Board, which he accordingly did on Tuesday morning, only to find Robson presiding at a council meeting. This particular story may as well be followed up here. Another call on Wednesday morning, to ask for representation from the Durham miners as soon as possible, brought the reply from Robson that he would bring the matter before his colleagues but it would require a board meeting to make the necessary appointment.[10] In fact the Durham miners' organisation only succeeded in forming a strike committee two hours before the strike was over.[11] Meanwhile Will Lawther, member of the executive committe of the Labour Party and also of the County federation's board, acted unofficially as the latter's representative on the regional strike committee.

The regional organisation was in fact formed at the meeting called on Tuesday, May 4, which took place at 2.30 p.m. again at the offices of the N.U.D.A.W., 47 Leazes Terrace, Newcastle. This time there was a wide representation of unions: Northumberland Miners' Association (Ebby Edwards); N.U.D.A.W. (Charles Flynn and Ferguson Foster); T. & G.W.U. (James White, area secretary); Durham Miners' Association (Will Lawther— unofficially); and representatives of the Shop Assistants Union, Northumberland Colliery Mechanics Association, N.U.G.M.W., Boilermakers' Union, Federation of Engineering and Shipbuilding Trades, Railway Clerks Association, National Union of Railwaymen, Builders's Federation; National Union of Sailors & Firemen (James Rogers—unofficially). Also present were representatives of the Gateshead Labour Party and Trade Council, Newcastle Trades Council, and the Labour Research Department.

James White of the T. & G.W.U. was elected to the chair and Charles Flynn of N.U.D.A.W. secretary. After the chairman had outlined the purpose of the meeting, and a statement had been given of the position of each union in relation to the general strike, it was moved by Flynn, seconded by Ebby Edwards, to form a general council to cover the Northumberland and Durham Area with two representatives from each union. It was agreed in addition to appoint a strike committee composed of one representative from each union, or group of unions, on strike or locked out. Proposals for sub-committees, on the lines originally suggested at Chopwell, were approved and Page Arnot was co-opted on to both the General Council and the Joint Strike Committee. It was settled that the former meet daily at 3 p.m. at Burnt Hall, Northumberland Road, Newcastle—offices of the Northumberland miners. The Strike Committee's first meeting was fixed for 7 p.m. that same evening. 'The meeting terminated with the first hint of the difficulties of a general strike in the shape of a complaint that the Miners' Clubs faced with a drink shortage were sending in motors for beer whilst Transport Workers were out on strike.'

As finally constituted the General Council included, besides the bodies already listed, representatives of the A.S.L.E.F., the E.T.U., the A.E.U., the Typographical Association (all directly involved and represented also on the strike committee), and the Plumbers' Union, the National Union of Clerks, the Lithographic Printers, the National Union of Printing, Bookbinding etc. Workers, the Newcastle Borough Labour Party, the I.L.P., the Tyne Watermen's Association and the Gateshead Strike Committee.

The T.U.C. General Council's instructions were 'that the actual calling out of workers should be left to the Unions, and instructions should only be issued by the accredited representatives of the Unions participating in the dispute'. It recommended that there should be no interference with health and food services 'and that the Trade Unions concerned should do everything in their power to organise the distribution of milk and food to the whole of the population'. And it defined the responsibility of the trades councils, in conjunction with local officers of unions, as 'organising the Trade Unionists in dispute in the most effective manner for the preservation of peace and order'. (12)

Accordingly, when members of the joint strike committee assembled again the same evening at 7 p.m., nearly all had a set of telegraphic instructions from their own union head office. All these had to be co-ordinated. 'So far was it from being a question of putting previously prepared plans into action', says the report 'that the committee were forced to spend the evening in problems of simple co-ordination' and the organisation envisaged could not be brought into being. For instance, no sub-committees were formed on the lines approved since it was not known whether the various unions might have 'conflicting regulations or policies.' So the strike committee decided to handle all questions which 'meant of course an enormous accumulation of work. It meant that, within a few days, the committee began to sit in the morning and to continue from morning to afternoon, evening and midnight.' On the other hand, this concentration of activity (e.g. all permits were granted only by the committee) meant that it rapidly became a working body, all members came to know each other well, and 'to get the measure of what was important and what was relatively unimportant.'

An example of the need to co-ordinate instructions follows. One transport union had called out all men concerned with transport of food but given permits for transport of building materials; another had stopped all the latter but was giving some permits for transport of food. Some problems 'necessarily took a good deal of time to clear away'.(13) The committee listed a number of points relating to food permits to be raised with the General Council and requested that the acting secretary (Walter Citrine) be asked to remain in direct touch with the strike committee as well as with union headquarters. At this meeting the committee also considered the Strike Bulletin issued that same morning and considered that it 'was very effectively printed and its tone was very calm and moderate'. Since many blackleg sheets were appearing the committee decided to take over this bulletin and issue its own publication as soon as a permit could be obtained from the Typographical Association. (14)

On the second day of the strike the question of permits for food and transport came to the fore, as also the fact foreseen from the outset, that it was on this question that the success of the strike turned. Not only was there confusion as between the instructions of different unions, but also applications for permits were flowing in to each separate union district office, to local transport sub-committees co-ordinating the transport unions, to trades councils, as well as to the strike committee itself. More serious, 'the abuse of permits . . . was beginning to reach gigantic proportions in the course of Wednesday afternoon'. Anything and everything was being transported under the pretence of 'food only' or 'housing materials only'. The committee therefore decided, after receiving reports from the transport unions, to withdraw all permits for transporting building materials and to issue no new ones; it had already taken over the powers of the local transport committee which was itself incorporated in the strike committee. It was also agreed to represent to the General Council that any exception in favour of housing now be withdrawn. This initiative was confirmed by a wire from Ernest Bevin urging the closest supervision over the issue of permits in view of abuses. [15]

Over and above this a major development was reported. Members of O.M.S. had been brought on to the quayside at Newcastle to discharge foodships, and two destroyers and a submarine had been moored alongside one foodship in the river. This was reported to the committee by James Tarbit, organiser of the N.U.G.M.W., together with the information that trade unionists employed at the docks under permit to unload food had forthwith ceased work. Later in the evening a message came through from the civil commissioner that he wished to see Tarbit and members of the strike committee, and shortly Sir Kingsley Wood appeared in person at Burt Hall where the committee was in session. There he had a long interview with three members of the committee—Tarbit, the chairman and the secretary—which was in the end adjourned until 12.30 the following day in order to allow the commissioner to consult his colleagues.

To this second meeting the civil commissioner came accompanied by General Sir Kerr Montgomery, head of O.M.S. for the region, and Mr. Moon, official food controller. The minutes of both discussions have been reprinted in full. [16] Briefly they indicate the civil commissioner making concessions to negotiate a return of trade unionists to unload food at the docks, under permit and so under strike Committee control, while refusing to withdraw O.M.S. men altogether: in effect a form of dual control was proposed, with the O.M.S. working under official direction and not interfering in any jobs for which the normal labour was authorised by the strike committee. Flynn agreed to report this proposal fairly to his committee but added that 'he would not be able personally to recommend the form of dual control proposed', a view with which the strike committee wholly concurred. [17] The committee further agreed to recommend to the General Council that they be empowered 'to withdraw all permits for transport of food and everything else for which permits have been issued', and decided 'that we now use the discretionary powers vested in us by the T.U.C. and withdraw *all* permits today'. This decision was endorsed the following day. [18]

In their report, which was of course drawn up after the strike had ended, the committee comment on this decision, pointing out that it was forced upon them by the local situation and reinforced by telegrams from head-quarters. 'It was a momentous decision in that it immediately raised a number of other problems, but no other policy was possible in view of the abuse of permits that had taken place. Had there been previously carefully worked out plans on the Trade Union side as there had been on the employers and governmental side, it would have been possible to start the general strike on Friday with a complete and immediate withdrawal of labour and therefore to issue permits under a system of strict controls.' This had not been the position and by their decision of Thursday 'the Strike Committee gained for the first time the complete control over transport which was vital to the success of any centralised conduct of a general strike'. Their decision was loyally accepted and operated, with miners aiding transport workers in peaceful picketing. These facts lie behind the assertion, when matters were discussed on Friday evening with Sir Charles Trevelyan, M.P. for Central Newcastle who came as emissary from the T.U.C., that there had been 'complete mastery of the difficulties' hitherto experienced and that 'the situation as a whole was now well in hand'.

It was the very success of the policy adopted that brought new problems. In particular the staffs of retail co-operative societies ceased work to a man and this meant that private traders in a position to convey essential foods had a handle on the co-operative movement. This was most notably the case in Gateshead and Newcastle where picketing was the least effective. Accordingly on Friday May 7 the strike committee released bread and milk through the Newcastle Co-operative Society over the weekend, giving permits to 15 bread vans and 'a larger proportionate number of milk carriers' for two days only. A similar arrangement was made at Gateshead.

On Saturday May 8 evening the whole question was discussed at great length. There was no food shortage in the outlying villages but the very effectivenes of the picketing might arouse some alarmist fears which would be 'only less serious than an actual food shortage'. The obvious course, it is noted, would have been to provision the strikers through the co-operative movement from the very outset of the strike. But such a policy could not be adopted because there had been no arrangement between the T.U.C. and the co-operative movement, indeed no understanding, insofar as the directors of the C.W.S. had before the strike issued a statement refusing credits. So there had been hand to mouth arrangements weaving a way through the various instructions coming to district offices from union head offices and the General Council. Then with the abuse of permits and the entry of O.M.S. at the docks had come cancellation of all facilities with the approval of headquarters. Now the committee had to contend with T.U.C. instructions on the one hand and local feeling on the other and between the two 'to find a correct line of policy, and that line once found, to pursue it steadily but carefully'. [19]

The decision eventually adopted was to send out telegrams releasing all food supplies in the possession of the retail co-ops, and on Sunday milk supplies were similarly released after discussion with the bodies concerned. But by now the C.W.S. directors were also demanding a lifting of the embargo as it affected them. Though the strike committee sympathised with the difficulties, and expressed readiness to seek a partial solution, it was clear that 'any general yielding on the question of removing the embargo on food supplies was at the moment completely out of the question'. Then came a blow in the form of instructions from the National Transport Committee to the effect that all transport men should be out with the exception of those delivering bread and milk for Co-operative Societies to their members [20] — instructions which effectively removed the discretionary powers formerly held by the joint strike committee and left it no room for negotiation. When, therefore, the C.W.S. directors (Northern Board) met the strike committee in Burt Hall again on Tuesday May 11, the secretary had to make clear to them that the committee 'was impotent to afford them any further relief or to take any further steps towards the progressive realisation of that strategy which alone could guarantee nothing (anything) more than a favourable draw for the strikers'.

Meanwhile it had become clear that, when the strike committee refused co-operation and withdrew all permits the civil commissioner would be faced with an acute situation. The O.M.S. organisation in the area, and other official bodies, had proved incapable of maintaining supplies. Sir Kingsley Wood's approach to the strike committee had become common property, having been mentioned in the House of Commons on May 6 by a Labour member with the implication that the civil commissioner had been forced to approach the local strike committee for assistance in maintaining supplies. This was altogether too near the bone and a government spokesman flatly denied that any discussions had taken place; a denial repeated more explicitly on May 10.[21] It was therefore clear that there would be no more negotiations from the commissioner's side. Since it was also obvious that there would be no outright capitulation to the strike committee which was pursuing the aim of bringing all transport of supplies under its sole control, there remained only one course open. In fact the strike committee informed the intelligence department of the T.U.C. by telephone on Friday night, May 7, that it was believed there had been a central governmental decision to break down picketing by force or to institute provocation on a scale which would, in the long run, provide an excuse for calling in military forces. [22]

There was not long to wait for confirmation of this view. Already on Saturday night the police conducted baton charges in various localities, where there had not previously been any friction. In Newcastle, where there were such charges on both Saturday and Sunday evenings, eye witnesses reported that there was no apparent reason: 'inoffensive citizens peacefully passing through the main thoroughfare of the town were severely clubbed and mauled by the police'. In a despatch to the General Council on Monday, May 10, the strike committee reported that it was sending a deputation to meet the chief constable because 'we must not have our people ridden down', and pointing out that its own efforts to avoid provocation and maintain order had to be pursued without any sanctions 'against disorder and overt violence on the part of the legally constituted authorities'.

On Monday reports of arrests and police intimidation were coming in from all parts of the region. 'The most sensational arrest was that of Will

Lawther and Harry Bolton, chairman of the Blaydon U.D.C. who were charged under Regulation 21 of the E.P.A.', a regulation also used for 'laying by the police more than 200 miners in . . . Durham and Northumberland'.(23)

This same day, Monday May 10, the committee reorganised its work to the extent of setting up a Transport Office and a centralised system of despatch riders, to be used in part to distribute the *British Worker*, the official T.U.C. paper whose Newcastle edition was finally issued for the first time on May 11, the day before the strike was called off. The report records that the strike committee put its resources behind this initiative, but in fact 'a stage had now been reached when the committee could no longer hope for the effectiveness of its own strike policy. The ground which might have been covered in the seven days from the commencement of the strike was by this time irretrievably lost'. But there was no cessation of activity and, though it was rumoured that police action was bringing defections, in fact all that happened was that some brewers' draymen returned to work on Tuesday. Then on Wednesday the second line of defence was called out and the engineers came out on strike: at the most important single centre on the Tyne, Elswick, every man responded. This was a great success of strength and 'the situation on Wednesday, May 12, 1926, was one which showed an advantage as compared with the previous three days of the week'. With this sentence the report of the strike committee ends, with much left unsaid.

It has been recorded that when the T.U.C.'s retreat became known in the north-east on May 12 and 13 it was received 'with incredulity which changed to fury'. *The Northern Light* said: 'There is only one explanation for this treachery—our leaders do not believe in Socialism'; the *Newcastle Workers' Chronicle* wrote, 'Never in the history of workers' struggle—with one exception of the treachery of our leaders in 1914—has there been such a calculated betrayal of working class interests'; the Council itself said: 'To hell with the Constitution . . . next time we must not be unprepared'. (24)

Meanwhile the struggle had not ended. On Thursday, May 13, Will Lawther and Harry Bolton, a J.P. as well as chairman of Blaydon U.D.C., were tried at Gateshead County Police Court and fined £50 for imposing a reign of terror in the district, with the alternative of two months' imprisonment; they chose the latter. There was a demonstration in support of the accused of several thousands who sang The Red Flag outside the police court. Among these was a contingent from the neighbourhood of Chopwell, Blaydon, Ryton and Spen—so that the story ends as it began with Chopwell and district. On Saturday, May 15, the *Northern Light*, a bulletin published by the local council of action, reported on the demonstrations of Thursday and their sequel:

'A band of 300 to 500 men and women (and not 90 or 100 as stated by the lying capitalist press) marched to Gateshead from Spen and Highfield behind the Victoria Garesfield Miners' Lodge banner. They marched orderly into the town and settled themselves round about the police court to patiently await the result of the trial. This quiet gathering did not suit the police and one officer in particular did his best to cause trouble.'

the account continues:

'Seeing what was brewing, and actually hearing some policemen say they wished to be given orders to charge the crowd, some of us did our best to keep order and succeeded after the decision of the Court had been given in persuading the demonstrators to leave for home. They had proceeded some distance along Askew Road, on their way home, when a body of policemen, led by a well-known inspector and sergeant at their head, bearing the outward resemblance of gentlemen, went behind the peaceable and innocent procession with their brutally trained and uniformed bullies and belaboured unarmed people unmercifully.'

Blackleg newsheets printed the lie 'that the demonstrators had attacked the police, but the hollowness of this frail excuse is exposed by the fact that not one policeman was injured, but a dozen or so of our men with wounds bore testimony to the brutality of the police. The powers that be are mistaken if they think tactics of this kind will crush our movement. We must get on with the fight and make our organisation better for the next time'. There are also specific charges of violence by the police after arrests and again it is affirmed that such brutality only helps 'to strengthen our determination to carry the workers' cause to victory'. An interview with those imprisoned after sentence is described: 'The message was, "Go on with the fight, let not the prisons daunt you." That is their spirit. Let it be yours.'

On Thursday, May 20, Edward Wilson, aged 40, a miner, appeared at Gateshead police court accused of contravening Regulation 21 [25] of the Emergency Regulations by doing a certain act likely to cause dissatisfaction among the civil population by distributing a document known as the *Northern Light*—in fact the number in which the extracts above occur. [26] Counsel for the prosecution, Mr. Frank J. Lambert, quoting these extracts, rested his case on the argument that the crowd at the trial of Lawther and Bolton was so hostile that: 'the police had to send for reinforcements and to form their men up for a baton charge. There was this baton charge and it was a serious baton charge. Men were knocked out and so forth and others were locked up. These men used serious threats to the police, while his (Mr. Lambert's) position, because he happened to be prosecuting in the case, was such that he had to close his office—which was a cowardly thing to force anyone to do—because he was simply carrying out his duties as a lawyer.'

Quoting further extracts, including expressions of determination not to be intimidated, Counsel for the prosecution stated that these men must understand 'that no one would be allowed to over-ride the laws of this land; and if these men insisted in this course of action, so would the authorities persist in their course of action, and they intended to meet force with force'. It was clear the men were still determined 'to show that the Council of Action was the ruling authority of Chopwell'. There was only one true statement in the paper—that every edition was eagerly awaited by the police. He would quote what the paper thought about the police force: 'The lowest aim in life is to be a policeman. When a policeman dies he goes so low he has to climb up a ladder to get into hell, and even then he is not a welcome guest'.

Edward Wilson had been found carrying copies of the *Northern Light* on the evening of Saturday, May 15, which he said he was selling for a penny. This might not be violence but clearly the council of action was 'resorting to this method of creating dissatisfaction amongst the civil population'. Cast your minds back to the strike, Counsel for the prosecution exhorted, 'the Council of Action was still carrying on in their terrifying way' and the police could not find where the paper was printed so that they could 'raid the place and blot it out altogether in the same way as they hoped to be able to blot out this so-called Council of Action'. He appealed to the Court for the safety of the people in the neighbourhood of Chopwell, Blaydon, Ryton and Spen, 'as there was no doubt about it that they were terrified to death' by members of this Council of Action. He asked the Court 'now that they had got them in their hands' to 'stamp them out'. They were making the lives of people in the district 'a perfect hell on earth'.

At the outset Counsel for the prosecution had stated that the defendant was a member of the 'Communist League' and now a police sergeant was called to make the same point, which Counsel for the defence promptly refuted. The presiding magistrate inquired whether he was 'a Liberal, like myself?' His client was a member of the Labour Party, answered Counsel, and thought he was acting in a lawful way; he had never been in a police court before and bore an unblemished character. The Bench then retired and returned to record a unanimous verdict of guilty and a sentence of three months with hard labour, a sentence appreciably harsher than that meted out the previous week, the chairman adding that if he had had his own way there would have been an additional fine of £100.

How are we to judge the assessment of the strike implied in *An Account*? The reference to it in Symons *The General Strike* remarks that there is apparent 'the kind of unjustified optimism that is a vital element in militant movements, and yet is also a dangerous and heady tonic'.[27] It is hard indeed to find evidence supporting this judgment in the report just summarised. It is true that it states at one point: 'On Friday (May 7) the success of the general strike appeared completely assured. It was clear to everyone that the O.M.S. organisation was unable to cope with the task imposed upon it. The attitude of the population was favourable to the strikers and unfavourable to the government. There were no disturbances: the Trade Unionists maintained an almost perfect discipline.' But this is a sober assessment of the response to the strike call, and of all-important public reactions, made moreover just after the negotiations of the committee with Sir Kingsley Wood and its firm steps to gain control of food distribution.

The later sections of the report, however, indicate that the committee, though acutely aware from the outset that the ultimate success of the strike turned on control of food supplies, were unable to pursue the tactics which could have brought success in a trial of strength. They were unable to do this firstly, as they point out, because of the total lack of preparation for the strike on the part of the General Council, in particular the absence of any kind of agreement or arrangements with the co-operative societies. Secondly, because, having taken resolute action in response to Sir Kingsley Wood's attempt to gain a degree of control in the docks and to abuse of permits, and created the possibility of building up effective strike committee control over food supplies, they were hampered by directions from headquarters which eliminated freedom of manoeuvre on this absolutely key front. Thereafter if the committee abided by the T.U.C.'s whole approach to the strike situa-tion—and it was their watchword that, where they had no discretionary power they must 'carry out the Trade Union Congress decisions to the letter no matter how many misgivings they might have'—there was no course but to enjoin passive defence against a calculated use of provocation and force on the part of the government.

It would be nearer the mark to suggest that, because of the very scope of the regional general council—which was planned from the start as a direct response to the government's regional commission from the workers' side—there was a high degree of awareness of the real nature and course of the struggle and so, too, of the total inadequacy of the General Council's conduct of it. Such a recognition necessarily precluded easy optimism and the matter of the joint strike committee's report, far from bearing witness to lightheadedness, provides evidence of thoughtful and serious attempts to introduce measures relevant to the concrete situation within the limits imposed.

If anything there is an overtone of pessimism at times. But it must be recalled that this report emphasised weaknesses and drew the lessons after the strike had been called off by the T.U.C. General Council in face of the government threats of repressive legislation and reprisals. In fact the official resort to direct action can itself be interpreted as an admission of defeat, or at the very least of acute anxiety as to the outcome of the struggle. Naturally, it was not a question of waiting until supplies actually broke down. Symons' argument that the Strike Committee overestimated its achievements rests almost solely on quotations from the blackleg press indicating that Newcastle presented an almost normal appearance, except for total absence of transport, and that there was no appreciable shortage of foodstuffs. 'There does not seem to be any evidence . . . that the Government . . . organisation broke down in any serious sense' (p. 132). The real point was what was likely to happen to the balance of power during a second week of the strike, with the workers' organisations just getting into their stride all over the country and fresh forces coming into action. These were clearly not to be easily broken, the strike was solid. Nor indeed were they ever broken. The govern-ment's salvation was that its threats broke the back-bone of the T.U.C.

leadership in Eccleston Square which, caught between this fire and fear of the organised mass movement, succumbed to terms of peace without honour or safeguards.

R. Page Arnot comments:

'These summaries, with ample quotation, from the scarce documents that are now available, cannot, of their nature, give all the background or the accompanying incidents of that first fortnight of May '26 on Tyneside. Nevertheless they seem to me to conjure up a vivid picture of the General Strike in an area where trade unions though long established had earlier been regarded as clinging to Liberal traditions. Nor had its towns ever been a stronghold of any of the socialist societies, such as the I.L.P. or the B.S.P. The Communist Party was very weak in numbers and had few members outside Newcastle City. But in parts of the coalfields north and south of the Tyne there had been strong radical sentiments and one or two left-wing groups in sundry villages. Of these Chopwell, where Karl Marx was being studied in educational circles, was outstanding. But the only Communist there on May 1, 1926, was a young lad who had joined the Communist Party in his teens.[28]

'The huge Lawther family and their checkweighmen friends from neighbouring pits exercised the main influence. Chopwell, part of Blaydon-on-Tyne, became the focus from which it was hoped to stimulate other villages, especially if the regional plan did not succeed. That it did succeed was due largely to Ebby Edwards and to Charles Flynn, in whose office each day there gathered the special staff of volunteers including the mountaineer-poet Michael Roberts. Of course none of the detailed plans for sub-committees suggested on Tuesday, May 4 worked out exactly, and that was where the volunteers came in handy.

'But Blaydon-on-Tyne as far as Durham County was concerned remained the storm centre throughout. There, the outstanding figure was Harry Bolton, J.P. This veteran miner went back from the meeting on Sunday night, May 2, to Blaydon, where early next morning as Chairman of the U.D.C. he assumed complete authority. He went to the U.D.C. offices, went round the numerous staff, including architects, medical officials, etc., instructed those whom he did not fully trust to take their holidays that first fortnight of May—immediately—and turned the remaining staff, offices and machinery, including the duplicator into an organ of the General Strike. [29] They did it with a will. And when things got too hot, the duplicator was transferred under cover of night in a maternity van to the first of the various hide outs for the continued production of the *Northern Light.* Responsible for its contents was Steve Lawther, with a clear militant outlook and at that time a constant supporter and seller of *Labour Monthly.*

'The whole episode showed the immense resources latent within the working class, given a clear line: and the fact that everything had to be improvised demonstrated this all the more'.

REFERENCES

(1)   J. Symons, *The General Strike* (Cresset Press, 1957) p. 125

(2)   There are copies at the Labour Research Department, 78 Blackfriars Road London, S.E.1. The document was printed in abbreviated form without schedules of members of committees in *Labour Monthly* Vol. 8, No. 6 (June 1926), pp. 359–74

(3)   Printed in *Labour Monthly* (June 1926) without mention of the place concerned; it is reprinted in R. Page Arnot, *The Miners: Years of Struggle* (Allen & Unwin, 1953), pp. 436-9

(4)   Library of the Communist Party, 16 King Street, London W.C.2

(5)   James Rogers eventually figures on the regional strike committee as representing the Seamen's Union 'unofficially'. He was afterwards dismissed by Havelock Wilson

(6)   'Traffic circulation on the great north-south arteries running through Durham and Northumberland was completely stopped by the implacable tourniquet of the miners' mass picketing'; A. Hutt, *Post-War History of the British Working Class* (Gollancz, 1937), pp. 150-1

(7)   See (3) above

(8)   Set up in September 1925 ostensibly as a voluntary and non-governmental agency but handed over to the government from the outset of the strike

(9)   Councils of action which issued permits for transport were clearly 'organisations of the working class facing the existing State machinery . . . It was clear that the issuing of these documents rested on the assumption that the unions and/or Councils of Action had powers to do, or to allow to be done, certain public things that would ordinarily be regarded as exclusively within the province of the constituted authorities, national and local.' In the great majority of cases the powers tacitly assumed were effective powers insofar as mass picketing prevented other forms of transport. (Hutt, op. cit., p. 149)

(10)   This is recorded in *An Account of the Proceedings* . . pp. 1, 5. All later quotations are from this document

(11)   R. Postgate, Ellen Wilkinson, J.F. Horrabin. *A Workers' History of the Great Strike* (Plebs League, 1927), p. 66

(12)   R. Page Arnot, *The General Strike 1926* (L.R.D., 1926). Detailed instructions were equally vague; e.g. all building workers were called out except those 'employed definitely on housing and hospital work'

(13)   Similar problems arose everywhere. In Nottingham, according to a note received from D. Mahoney who represented the railwaymen on the central strike committee, two days were taken up with a dispute between the T. & G.W.U. and the N.U.G.M.W. because the former had called out its brewery men, the latter not, so the discussion turned on the question—'is beer food?' Despite all efforts both local and national no settlement had been reached by the end of the strike

(14)   No permit was, in fact, obtained. The TUC was opposed to local publications and endeavoured, ineffectively, to get its own paper, the *British Worker*, published at certain regional centres, including Newcastle. The strike committee recognised as it greatest weakness the lack of a publication to counteract the misrepresentations of the B.B.C., the government organ and such local sheets as appeared in attenuated form. This and other matters figure in later sections of the report but in the present account attention is concentrated on food and transport

(15) 'From reports received food permits are being abused instruct Local Transport Committee to exercise close supervision and not issue permits for outside their own district and act in full agreement with the three Railwaymen's Unions' signed 'Bevin'. Dated May 5, 1926. Bevin was secretary of the T.U.C. General Council's 'Strike Organisation Committee', a body of six which conducted the central direction of the strike

(16) Arnot, *The Miners*, pp. 440-2

(17) 'Having heard this report and recognising that our men cannot, and will not work in conjunction with O.M.S. we instruct that a reply be sent to the gentlemen named, that we cannot agree to our men working under any form of dual control'

(18) 'We agree your action cancellation of permits endorsed. Signed . . . National Transport Committee'. Dated May 7, 1926

(19) The committee had become aware of local feeling at a conference held on the Saturday morning attended by 167 delegates representing 28 councils of action, 52 strike committees, 4 Labour Parties and 3 Trades Councils in the region. Here the main discussion centred on the embargo and its effect on the co-ops. There was no excitement nor alarmist feeling but rather a quiet determination to go on with the strike coupled with recognition that this was the most pressing problem on the agenda

(20) 'National Transport Committee now instruct that all men engaged in Transport should now be on strike excepting men employed by Co-operative Societies solely for delivering Bread and Milk to their members. Our Union members must act accordingly other Unions are instructed likewise. Local Transport Committees have been informed of this instruction . . . Signed Bevin' Dated May 10 1926

(21) *The Miners*, p. 440n. It was these official falsehoods which prompted publication of the strike committee's detailed minutes of the discussion

(22) Two days later the T.U.C. General Council itself received information that the cabinet had decided (a) to arrest all the members of the council, (b) to call up the Army Reserve, (c) to rush through a bill repealing the Trades Disputes Act, thus making union funds liable to seizure; this if the strike was not settled within two days. So it was reported in *'The Secret History of the General Strike'* published in *Lansbury's Labour Weekly,* Volume II, No. 63, Saturday, May 22, p. 5

(23) So the Strike Committee's report records. 'The circumstances of this arrest certainly bear the marks of deliberate planning. On Sunday the police, who were accompanying a food lorry, saw Lawther and Bolton outside a pub, and asked them to help in food distribution. Lawther, by the police story, asked if they had a permit from the Chopwell, Blaydon and Ryton Council of Action, and suggested that the food should be handed over to him for distribution. After some further argument, both men were arrested. When the case was heard Lawther and Bolton were accused of establishing a "reign of terror" in the district.' Symons, op. cit., p. 131

(24) Postage, Wilkinson and Horrabin, op. cit., pp. 68-9. The last two were in the north-east just after the strike ended, where they attended 11 'huge mass meetings' and met strike committees. E. Wilkinson *'Ten Days that Shook the Cabinet'*, *Lansbury's Labour Weekly*, Volume II, No. 63, p. 9

(25) For the text of Regulation 21 of the Emergency Powers Act, see Arnot, *The General Strike*, p. 157. It was only necessary for the authorities to claim that an action or publication was likely 'to cause dissatisfaction' to get a conviction. 'The superintendent of the local police assures us', recounted Special strike Bulletin

No. 6 of the Sheffield District Committee of the Communist Party (May 11) 'that any statement published, whether it be a statement of fact or otherwise if in their opinion it gives cause for dissatisfaction amongst the civil population then the E.P.A. gives them the power to suppress such publication'. The same line of approach was adopted towards sellers of papers, particularly those which escaped suppression (as did the *Northern Light* amongst many others) by changing the place of production each night

(26)   These extracts are given in a very full report of Wilson's trial which appeared in the *Blaydon Courier* of Saturday, May 22, 1926, and was reprinted in *Labour Monthly* (June, 1926). Subsequent quotations come from this newspaper report of the trial

(27)   Symons, op. cit., p. 132

(28)   Three months later, in August 1926, I addressed the Chopwell Communists on a hillside as no hall would hold the 200 members present

(29)   These facts came out in the local press at the time and were referred to at the trial of Edward Wilson; it was known, said Counsel for the prosecution, as 'The Blaydon Scandal'